OPEN SECRETS

A few marks

OA

MERIDIAN

Crossing Aesthetics

Werner Hamacher

Editor

Stanford
University
Press

Stanford
California
2008

OPEN SECRETS

The Literature of Uncounted Experience

Anne-Lise François

Stanford University Press
Stanford, California

Printed in the United States of America
on acid-free, archival-quality paper

Library of Congress Cataloging-in-Publication Data

François, Anne-Lise, 1967–
Open secrets : the literature of uncounted experience /
Anne-Lise François.
p. cm.—(Meridian : crossing aesthetics)
Includes bibliographical references and index.
ISBN 978-0-8047-5253-4 (acid-free paper)
ISBN 978-0-8047-5289-3 (pbk. : acid-free paper)
1. Silence in literature. 2. English literature—
19th century—History and criticism. 3. American
literature—19th century—History and criticism.
4. Passivity (Psychology) in literature. 5. Sublime, The, in
literature. 6. La Fayette, Madame de (Marie-Madeleine
Pioche de La Vergne), 1634–1693. Princesse de Clèves.
I. Title.
PR468.S52F73 2007
809'.9353—dc22
2007011283

Publication assistance for this book was provided by
the Hellman Faculty Fund of the University
of California at Berkeley.

For Nancy and Jean-Charles

Contents

Acknowledgments

The writing of this book has taken a course similar to the temporal sequences that are its subject matter: an initial iteration, followed by a certain lapse of time, followed by a second iteration in the end not all that different from the first. One absolute gain, however, lies in the debts I have incurred in the process to readers, colleagues, teachers, students, and friends, and it is by these that I would measure the book's improvement. I am thankful for my dissertation advisers Claudia Brodsky, David Bromwich, and Esther Schor, whose wisdom and critical guidance were a blessing from this project's earliest stages onward. Geoffrey Hartman, my first teacher of Romanticism, was long a presiding spirit until, true to the workings of a genie, he appeared in person at the eleventh hour to offer kind and timely advice. I am grateful to Marc Redfield and Ian Balfour, readers at Stanford University Press, for the care with which they read the manuscript and the insight of their suggestions, as well as for their own examples as critical readers of Romanticism. My thanks, too, to Mary Jacobus, Alan Liu, Deidre Lynch, and Susan Stewart who read earlier drafts of the manuscript and whose comments made finishing the book feel like a conversation to be continued.

I wish to thank the editors at Stanford University Press, especially Norris Pope and Tim Roberts, always kind and always professional, for the care with which they ensured the transition from manuscript to book. Joe Abbott's vigilant eye at the copyediting stages "prevented me from missing minor things" if not "the missing all." My research assistant Amanda Goldstein deserves special mention for her extraordinary work—creative, interpretive, and critical—in preparing the index as well as for her marvelous help in tying up many a loose end. I wish to thank Judith Marin for the tangible gift of her "La Promenade," which appears on the cover of the book, and for the less tangible gift of a lifelong friendship dating back to Torrey Pines State Beach, 1973.

Funding for my research and writing was generously provided by the Townsend Humanities Center, the Hellman Faculty Research Fund, the UC Berkeley Career Development Grant and Humanities Research Fellowship Program, and the Society for the Humanities at Cornell University.

Colleagues and students at Berkeley and Cornell have repeatedly if unwittingly challenged this book's hermetic sympathies by showing me how much the life of the mind gains in being shared. I wish to thank the extraordinary graduate students in my Critical Passions seminars at Berkeley and Cornell for the opportunity to try out some of the thoughts developed in the book. At Berkeley the manuscript has benefited, in part or whole, from engaged and thoughtful readings by numerous colleagues, including Robert Alter, Mitch Breitwieser, Dori Hale, Michael Lucey, Sharon Marcus, Kent Puckett, Nancy Ruttenburg, and Ann Smock. As successive chairs, Janet Adelman and Catherine Gallagher (in English), and Tony Cascardi, Francine Masiello, and Eric Naiman (in Comparative Literature) provided luminous critical feedback while also helping me navigate my first years as an assistant professor. Stephen Best, Leslie Kurke, Colleen Lye, Kathy McCarthy, and Chris Nealon supplied lessons in keeping critical thought alive, in the classroom and without. I am glad not to have escaped the notice of David Miller's discerning critical eye and still wish I could have written the book he would have preferred to read. Ann Banfield led me to a more precise appreciation of the European novel, while honoring me with the epicurean riches of her friendship—intellectual, culinary, and conversational. Charlie Altieri and Rei Terada, each in their inimitable way, sent me back gnomic echoes that I could almost imagine were my own thoughts. Rei and Chris deserve special thanks for their advice and encouragement regarding drafts of the book's first chapter. Judith Butler has been a remarkable friend and colleague whose support always came when it was most needed. Steve Goldsmith, Kevis Goodman, and Celeste Langan know better than I can say the role they played from start to finish—as mentors, interlocutors, and friends—in helping me define the scope of this argument and bring the book to completion. They and Joanna Picciotto, whose last-minute counsel soon proved indispensable, have moved me by their unpredictably sympathetic response to an ethos and aesthetic not especially solicitous of sympathy.

At Cornell, Anne Berger, Laura Brown, Cynthia Chase, Jonathan Culler, Brett de Bary, Debra Fried, Dominick LaCapra, Natalie Melas, Reeve Parker, Masha Raskolnikov, and Neil Saccamano contributed to the book's final form by their careful readings, while also providing an intellectual companionship so warm and rich as to make me believe the cold of Ithaca's winters a fiction. I am grateful to Neil and Louise Hertz for the opportunity as their tenant to ken a different kind of open book—the waters of Lake Cayuga. Eric Santner and participants in his seminar "The Creaturely" at the School of Criticism and Theory in 2006 contributed to the thrill of the final hours.

Daily life would have been impossible without many of the friends named above with whom I have shared the joys and pains of remaining grounded in this world. Whether at the beach or farmers' market, over meals or hikes, in Paris, Ithaca, or Berkeley, Kristin Hanson, Rayna Kalas, Mark Larrimore, Karin Schlapbach, and Catherine Witt have been bearers of happiness in a quotidian key. Traces of conversations begun in graduate school and sustained since lurk in these pages and may find their way back to Elise MacAdam, Charles Mahoney, Eun Min, Matthew Parr, Ginger Strand, Suzanne Yang, and Sarah Zimmerman. Susan Bernofsky and Charlie Kronengold have continued in the role of ministering angels ever-ready to resume the conversation and read a draft at a moment's notice; I'm not exaggerating when I say the book owes its readability to them.

Finally, I wish to thank my family—my parents, my sister Emilie and her family, Doug, Isabelle, and Stephanie—for their enduring love and support, for the relief they provided from unfinished academic work, and for their patience when I nevertheless brought it with me on holiday visits. The book is dedicated to my parents—to Nancy, who taught me the spell and dance of written words, and to Jean-Charles, who showed me how to play with them.

Preface

Comme si la fatigue devait nous proposer la forme de vérité par excellence, celle que nous avons poursuivie sans relâche toute notre vie, mais que nous manquons nécessairement, le jour où elle s'offre, précisément parce que nous somme trop fatigués.

—Blanchot, *L'Entretien infini*[1]

It may do good to others though not by effort or may simply be a good end in itself (or combining these, may only be able to do good by concentrating on itself as an end); a preparatory evasion of the central issue about egotism.

—William Empson (on Shakespeare's summer flower, which "is to the summer sweet, / Though to itself, it only live and die")

I have been in the habit of describing this book as a study of novels and poems in which "nothing happens," but it might be more accurate to say, reprising Auden's words about poetry, that they "make nothing happen" since the phrase allows us to hear the full range of ambiguities in the idea of "nothing" as an event made or allowed to happen. The works in question—Mme de Lafayette's *La Princesse de Clèves* (1678), Jane Austen's *Mansfield Park* (1814), and poems of uncounted experience by William Wordsworth, Emily Dickinson, and Thomas Hardy—all articulate attitudes that define themselves against the many figures we have for action, whether this is understood in the dramatic sense of public performance, in the moral sense of intervention, or in the economic sense of materialization and productivity: Mme de Lafayette's heroine withdraws from the court, leaving her passion unconsummated; Austen's Fanny Price "cannot act"; the terse, elliptical poems of Wordsworth, Dickinson, and Hardy elide the time of action. By their passivity and inconsequence, the subjects of these works might appear to be bound to a self-punishing eth-

---

1. "As if weariness were to hold up to us the preeminent form of truth, the one we have pursued without pause all our lives, but that we necessarily miss on the day it offers itself, precisely because we are too weary" (Blanchot, *The Infinite Conversation*, xiii).

ics of chastity, renunciation, and waste. Yet rather than read these novels and poems as narratives of denial and denials of narrative, I argue that they make an open secret of fulfilled experience, where the term *open secret* refers to nonemphatic revelation—revelation without insistence and without rhetorical underscoring. Exemplifying a mode of recessive action that takes itself away as it occurs, the novels and poems in question locate fulfillment not in narrative fruition but in grace, understood both as a simplicity or slightness of formal means and as a freedom from work, including both the work of self-concealment and self-presentation. The protagonists of these texts do not withhold themselves from the public scene: they present the difference they make as an open secret, a gift that does not demand response but is there for the having, as readily taken up as it is set aside.

Put in polemical terms, this book contests the normative bias in favor of the demonstrable, dramatic development and realization of human powers characteristic of, but not limited to, the capitalist investment in value and work and the Enlightenment allegiance to rationalism and unbounded progress. This continued faith in the unambiguous good of articulation and expression appears in everyday speech in the difficulty of using terms such as *frankness, directness, transparency,* or *self-expression* without normative effect or without presuming a desire for such qualities; perhaps more unexpectedly, this same confidence in the value of exposure undergirds the hermeneutics of suspicion informing many of our most prized methods of literary criticism and cultural theory, where the quest for the "new" or materially different takes the form either of the recuperation and recovery of something previously overlooked, neglected, undervalued, or, on the contrary, of the demystification and exposure of the secret ideological workings of power. Neither of these critical models, I argue below, is prepared to accept something that does not require either the work of disclosure or the effort of recovery: the reception of the self-quieting, recessive speech acts and hardly emitted announcements or reports on self of the heroines of the psychological novel and the speakers of the Romantic and post-Romantic lyric of missed of declined experience.[2]

2. In accordance with standard critical practice, even if at the risk of thereby reinforcing a false distinction between positively demarcated empirical history and free-floating theory, I will capitalize the words *Romantic* and *Romanticism* when referring to the literary movements of the historical period bound, in the

Yet I should clarify from the outset that this book is not simply a defense of "romantic" over rational or instrumental ways of accounting, nor is it a celebration of the quiet reception of deep internal meanings over against the Enlightenment's prizing of visibly measurable and productive difference. Instead, by tracing an ethos of nonappropriative contentment in a group of well-known but "minor" (minimally expressive) texts both at the center (Wordsworth's "Lucy poems") and at the far edges of the Romantic canon (Lafayette, Dickinson, Hardy), the book seeks to identify an alternative to the aesthetics of sublimity—of the inexpressible and nonrepresentable—characteristic of romantic investments in the heroic work of imagination—and to retrieve the "noninstrumental" from the concept of infinite, never-to-be-satisfied ethical responsibility found in the romantic sublime's postmodern heirs. It is true that one way to make sense of my seemingly odd assortment of primary texts—together unclassifiable according to a single literary period or genre—would be to read them under the rubric of apologia for the contemplative life and, more particularly, as exercises in that freedom from instrumentality that for many post-Enlightenment and Romantic writers makes of aesthetic experience what Geoffrey Hartman once called "the 'green belt' of an increasingly industrialized, action-oriented, and deprivatized world."[3] To be sure, critiques of what Shelley called the "unmitigated exercise of the calculating faculty," or of the avidity for "getting and spending" against which the speaker of another Wordsworth poem defends his "wise passiveness," by no means begin with the Romantic response to Western capitalism's scientific and industrial revolutions; there is a long and varied tradition within religious and nonreligious moral discourses of censuring and curbing the human animal's supposedly "natural" cupidity and impatience for demonstrable yields. The specificity of postsecular, "Romantic" attempts to rescue imaginative play from the hold of instrumental reason—as distinct from earlier stoic, Christian or monastic apologies for the contemplative life—would seem to lie, first, in the critique not of some supposedly innate, "instinctual," or "animal" appetite, but of reason's own arrogance—of whatever might be excessive or unstoppable in the mind's

---

British context at least, by the French Revolution on one end and the ascent of Queen Victoria on the other, and I will use the lowercase everywhere else to refer to the polyvalent concept and adjective.

3. Hartman, *The Unremarkable Wordsworth*, 186.

own will to seize—and, second, in the new role assigned aesthetic experience in freeing desire from the demands of goal-oriented action and forming it to laws of its own. Yet precisely here, I will want to distinguish (or at least keep open the relation between) the ethos of minimal realization adumbrated in my textual examples by figures whose passivity with respect to what it is in their power to do and ask for flies in the face of Enlightenment rationalism, and what might seem to be this ethos's closest ally: the turn, in Romanticism and elsewhere, toward aesthetic experience as a respite from the rushed action of a modernity so bent on bringing about the future that it leaves no time for the taking—deferral or postponement—of time.[4] For, as has been amply demonstrated by critics of "aesthetic ideology" as divergent as Paul de Man, Jerome McGann, Terry Eagleton, and Marc Redfield, the aesthetic, at least in its Schillerian incarnation, does not simply provide a refuge from the blindly transformative, acquisitive drives of Western capitalist development; as the locus of autoformation or *bildung*—of that process whereby the organism, whether artwork or human protagonist, is said to develop as much according to its own internal logic as by arbitrary determination—the aesthetic is also the chief repository of fantasies of self- and world-transformation, realization, and adequation.[5] Because in the pages that follow I will sometimes

4. For Hartman the "aesthetic" names a different because backward-looking (slower? more melancholic? more patient?) relationship to the "inertial force of the past" than that allowed by "action":

If the characteristic of action is to insist on a specific end, on change rather than interpretation, and to consume itself in achieving this end, it does not have to respect the inertial force of the past, or try to sublate it. Though it may have to respect the past provisionally to gain its purpose, action ideologizes interpretation and keeps moving relentlessly toward an all-consuming point which is the new regime, the new order. The alliance philosophy can make with art, through what we have learned to call the "aesthetic," is always characterized, therefore, by a structure of postponement; the doubting or delaying of closure, the insistence on remainders or of a return of the past, and—more problematically—on a concept of elation that embraces both the reality of history and freedom of mind. (Hartman, *The Unremarkable Wordsworth*, 186)

5. See, e.g., McGann, *The Romantic Ideology*; Eagleton, *The Ideology of the Aesthetic*; de Man, *Aesthetic Ideology*; and Redfield, *Phantom Formations*. Redfield's book, in particular, demonstrates the centrality of the concept of aesthetic *bildung* as self- or autoformation to modernity's narratives of history as the self-

have recourse to the concept of aesthetic play as the most readily available category for thinking "uncounted experience," it is important here to distinguish the aesthetic project of adequating desire and means (whether by circumscribing and calibrating the one or refining and expanding the other) from what I will be calling in a few Wordsworth, Dickinson, and Hardy poems and in the Lafayette or Austen sentence of narration "reticent assertion": the report of a minimal contentment often indistinguishable from a readiness to go without (answer), something that, translated into a psychological ethos, might look like accommodation to a world that promises one no return. Such complaisance without hope, akin to the mildness of the disappointed lover who bears his disappointer no ill will, differs from the tranquillity of stoic self-sufficiency and the stoniness of silent protest, although it can easily pass for either. More importantly, however, it represents something more modest, wearier, and less redemptive than the aesthetic project of reconciling duty and inclination and regaining via art the immediacy of nature, a project most explicitly developed in Schiller's *Letters on Aesthetic Education* but present whenever the artwork is described in terms of a free submission to formal necessity.[6]

------

production of humanity and fulfillment of the "human": "If aesthetics invents autonomy as the condition of the artwork, and disinterestedness as the condition of the perception of the artwork, it also defines art as the sign of the human, the human as the producer of itself, and history as the ongoing work of art that is humanity" (11). See also Schiller's claim: "For [the pedagogic or the political artist] Man is at once the material on which he works and the goal toward which he strives" (Schiller, *On the Aesthetic Education of Man*, 19).

6. While Schiller is the chief expounder of "aesthetic education (*bildung*)" as the means of forming man so that he would be "led by his very impulses to the kind of conduct which is bound to proceed from a moral character" (17), and of the hopes of restoring "by means of a higher Art the totality of our nature which the arts themselves have destroyed" (43), the theme of reconciling necessity and freedom, duty and inclination, echoes throughout the Romantic tradition, often taking the less secular form of a reprisal of Isaiah's apocalyptic vision of the wolf and lamb feeding together; see, for example, M. H. Abrams's comments on "the apocalyptic marriage" in *Natural Supernaturalism* (37–46). As de Man has argued, this dream of conforming to the law of reason without sacrifice to nature usually hinges, in Schiller at least, on what is itself a rhetorical figure of reciprocity, whereby two opposed principles ("nature" and "reason," or the "formal" and "expressive drives") mutually concede power to one another. See de Man, *Aesthetic Ideology*, 129–62.

Whereas aesthetic ideology often promises desire a reflective relationship with the world, even if only in the form of an echo or image of its unattainability, the strange mode of patient or benevolent abandonment I wish to describe gives up on precisely such fantasies of mutual fulfillment—of fulfillment as mutuality. "Weariness (la fatigue) is generous," asserts one of the interlocutors in the prefatory dialogue to Blanchot's *Entretien infini*, and it is an odd resignation that having given up on the world as a source of completion—as what would fill lack and make complete—now stays with it, whether from habit or fatigue.[7]

Two brief examples, neither of them exactly representative of such an attitude, may demonstrate some of the possible ratios of expectations to their concession/fulfillment (where fulfillment may have the feel of concession and vice versa) defining this—or rather these (since they are multiple and contradictory)—moods of "enoughness." The first comes from Austen's account, in the concluding chapter to *Mansfield Park*, of Edmund's easy transfer of affection from Mary Crawford to Fanny:

> Scarcely had he done regretting Mary Crawford, and observing to Fanny how impossible it was that he should ever meet with such another woman, before it began to strike him whether a very different kind of woman might not do just as well—or a great deal better; whether Fanny herself were not growing as dear, as important to him in all her smiles, and all her ways, as Mary Crawford had ever been; and whether it might not be a possible, an hopeful undertaking to persuade her that her warm and sisterly regard for him would be foundation *enough* for wedded love.[8]

Given that the preceding clauses refer to Edmund's settling on Fanny as a compensation for the loss of Mary, a careless reader might easily take the word *enough* as epitomizing the psychology of curtailment to which both Edmund and realist novel submit, and might thereby mistake for this novel's "foundation enough" the smooth functioning of the "reality principle"—that principle of accommodation whereby the subject, disappointed in his ideal, learns to tailor desire to the limits of the possible or, less cynically, take happiness where he finds it.[9] Yet the joke unperceived

7. Blanchot, *L'Entretien Infini*, xi.
8. Austen, *Mansfield Park*, 319 (emphasis added).
9. The difficulty here lies in distinguishing the project of "re-forming" desire to make it compatible with available object choices—an essentially "aesthetic" project, whatever its guise as a tough-minded, disenchanted "return to reality"— from the less heroic "happen-stance" of taking one's good where one finds it.

by Edmund, as he forms "a possible, an hopeful undertaking" to win a hand he already possesses, is that Fanny makes no sacrifice and no compromise (not even on the incest taboo): far from requiring persuasion to make do with less and settle, as he must, on a second object choice, she is getting all she wants and more: such love might as well walk on air. The sentence's ironically weightless "thud," as Edmund misses Fanny where he finds her, may cause you to clap your hands in glee at the fairytale ending and boldness of Fanny's unnoticed coup suspending the law of exchange (Edmund will exert himself to naught and still believe in the success of his persuasive endeavor), even as Austen thereby robs you of the illusion of a marriage founded in mutual understanding. Delight at the surplus underwriting Edmund's cautious "enough" by no means precludes, and indeed may well take the form of, dry-eyed despair at its inevitable missing.

My second example of an oddly satisfying reprieve or "letdown" from teleological expectations is a story Roland Barthes recounts at the end of his entry on "waiting" in *Fragments d'un discours amoureux*:

> Un mandarin était amoureux d'une courtisane. "Je serai à vous, dit-elle, lorsque vous aurez passé cent nuits à m'attendre assis sur un tabouret, dans mon jardin, sous ma fenêtre." Mais, à la quatre-vingt-dix-neuvième nuit, le mandarin se leva, prit son tabouret sous son bras et s'en alla.[10]

> [A mandarin was in love with a courtesan. "I will be yours," she told him, "when you will have passed one hundred nights waiting for me, sitting on a stool, in my garden, under my window." But at the ninety-ninth night, the mandarin got up, took his stool under his arm, and went away.]

Doubtless, psychology can readily solve such apparent inconsequence by interpreting it as a matter of self-imposed frustration and neurotic postponement: the mandarin is afraid of the moment of possession and will not stay to have reality puncture his ideal; he has fallen in love with waiting, and it now suffices him. Or the mandarin may be less of a lover than an athlete for whom only the test of endurance matters, not the promised fruit, and who departs having done what he came to do; or perhaps, on the contrary, he knows no other way to prove to the courtesan his unconditional love for her. Yet in all these rationalizations there is a hint of the nonpsychological satisfaction afforded by the anecdote itself, by its koan-like self-containment (refusal of narrative complexity, detail, or develop-

10. Barthes, *Fragments d'un discours amoureux*, 50. Except where indicated otherwise, all translations are my own.

ment) and its briefly, unhesitatingly assertive *passé simple*. So direct and nonexplicative a completed action ("and went away") has the effect not so much of redeeming the ninety-eight previous nights from the bargain that held them hostage—only the courtesan can do that—as of setting time to naught, as if, with one period reached, all narrative and erotic entanglements were to go "pouf."

One waits, and waits, and then gives up—such a movement yields a temporal sequence set loose from the ordering energies of the quest for possession and freed from the pendulum of anticipation and (non)fulfillment. In this book I will be interested as much in the rhythm of so inconsequent a sequence as in its possible, often contradictory, value-laden affects—the betrayal of apostasy, disappointment, relief, surrender, irony, elation. I offer these preliminary examples not simply to underscore the worldliness of these modes of divestiture—modes that include, importantly, habits of taking, and of taking without seeming to, as in the case of *Mansfield Park*'s Fanny, who helps herself to more than she is credited for—and not simply to distinguish such appropriative minimalism from modernity's image of self-sacrifice as guilt-driven and dutybound, if not regressively religious. My more oblique hope is that these examples may clarify why, in framing this project, I have not availed myself more readily of the rubric "Romantic pastoral" (although I certainly invoke it in my individual chapter readings). To the extent that pastoral is the justifiably maligned genre in which you point to poor people *and* say how good they have it, then this book sits uncomfortably close, even if the poverty in question here is not of the material kind.[11] But with the category "Romantic pastoral"—a term whose affinity with the suspension promised by aesthetic experience is already suggested by Hartman's metaphor of the "green belt"—come tales of redemption: hopes, if not for the restoration of lost Edens, then for the continuation of modernity's revolutionary proj-

---

11. William Empson's idiosyncratic account of pastoral remains in this sense a fundamental source of inspiration and critical model for this project insofar as his "versions of pastoral" refuse the standard "Christian" idealization of poverty as somehow purer because emblematic of self-sacrifice and recognize instead the worldliness or ambition or assertiveness or whatever we wish to call what is not self-denying in the making of minimal claims. Thus the "good" of Shakespeare's "summer's flower"—"poor" in the sense of not owning itself, being given up to the summer—lies in its continued vulnerability, its openness to danger and moral staining from without. See Empson, *Some Versions of Pastoral*, 89–115.

ects on milder grounds.[12] As I suggest more fully in the next chapter with respect to postmodern reprisals of Pauline dispensation, among the many ironies vexing the question of Romanticism's relation to the French Revolution (and to everything that in modernity seeks definitively, if not violently, to break with the past for the sake of bettering humankind) is that the attenuation of revolutionary violence—the turn toward less "formal," less "spectacular," less "dramatic," less "overt" modes of effecting change with which Romanticism is often associated—goes hand in hand with a radicalization of its ends: dreams of total expression, infinite perfectibility, and interminable progress accompany the slowing down of modernity's imagined break with the past. Thus quite apart from the by now familiar and often too narrowly construed debates about whether Romantic apostasy constitutes a falling away from, or more gradual realization of, the quest for, in Abrams's words, "the renovation of the world and of man," one of Romantic pastoral's more ambiguous and enduring legacies is the hypercathexis of figures of the ordinary, common and indistinct, making even the lightest of "letdowns" readable as a redemptive dream of "coming down to earth," and charging all deflationary or "leveling" rhythms with democratizing, universalizing ends.[13] Because it can endow the most modest, circumscribed, and contingently determined assent with the power to ratify, legitimate, or save an unjust world, this—the Romantic habit of crediting with universal import precisely those modes of speech that refuse a public stance—poses perhaps as great a rhetorical challenge to a book of this kind as the irony of publishing a book about reticence, or that which resists, or rather does not require, foregrounding. I can of-

12. Thus, according to Lore Metzger, "pastoral most frequently functions in English Romantic poetry to articulate radical ends of social reform attenuated by an insistence on conservative means" (*One Foot in Eden*, xiv). M. H. Abrams's essay "English Romanticism: The Spirit of the Age" presents probably the most succinct version of the account of "Romanticism" (for which read "Wordsworth") as a downward turn from the Miltonic/revolutionary epic level of "overt action and adventure" to "the more-than-heroic grandeur of the humble, the contemned, the ordinary, and the trivial" (118), a turn that Abrams explicitly links to New Testament pastoral themes of the divinity found among the poor and humble.

13. Abrams, "English Romanticism," 118. For an alternative account of Romantic disappointment, as a deflation that is not recuperated as a "sublime" fall into depth, see Quinney, *The Poetics of Disappointment*.

fer no solution except to acknowledge the challenge and to remind readers of a number of alternative genealogies for "appropriative minimalism" in traditions less saturated with globalizing political ambitions and less marked by pretensions to universal exemplarity: from the defense of dissimulation (defined as passively letting oneself be taken for what one isn't) as an *occasionally* appropriate tactic found in late Renaissance manuals on courtly manners; to the Jesuit allowance for mental reservation or silent disclaiming; to the kind of "minor ownership" (menue propriété)—attachment to minor things that "signals retreat," "doesn't show" (qui ne se voit pas) and "doesn't concern others"—that Barthes links in *Le neutre* to the Taoist search for "a right [or balanced] relation ("rapport juste") to the present, attentive and not arrogant" (118, 186); or again, to Blanchot's idea of a benevolent or generous relenting that would have no higher source than tiredness.[14] The minimalism of such practices consists in part in their willful circumscription; their refusal, to the extent possible, of a dogmatic posture; and their nontransmissibility as moral examples.

14. For better or worse (as I might sooner have been relieved of the need to do anything but point and cite), it is only in the final stages of revising this book that I became fully acquainted with Barthes' 1977–78 seminar "Le neutre" (or, as he would have had it "Le désir de neutre"), published both in audio and digested-note form in 2002. Among the many points of connection is Barthes' tracing across a number of different figures—"benevolence," "tact" ("la délicatesse"), "sleep," "retreat"—of an odd sort of sociability on the part of those who do not particularly seek out the company of others, or who have no strong inclination toward extroversion, a quality he invokes at one point by quoting one of Suzuki's definitions of the Zen term *sabi* as a "familiarity singularly tinged with aloofness," which in the French reads "familiarité étrangement mitigée de désintéressement" (*Le neutre*, 65)—a familiarity strangely mitigated by disinterestedness. Such easygoing disinterest presents the inverted form, as it were, to the quiet laying claim to a few possessions that Barthes wants to distinguish from the more typical arrogant "will-to-grasp." Quick to acknowledge the class-constructedness of this "attachment to minor belongings" as a "petit-bourgeois attitude," he nevertheless prefers it to the false choice between pure appropriation and pure asceticism that too often causes Westerners to misinterpret the Zen monk's restriction to a bowl and robe as mere deprivation rather than as the right to a few possessions (*Le neutre*, 186, 194).

OPEN SECRETS

§ 1 Toward a Theory of Recessive Action

i. open secrets: an overview

> Wem die Natur ihr offenbares Geheimnis zu enthüllen anfängt, der empfin-
> det eine unwiderstehliche Sehnsucht nach ihrer würdigsten Auslegerin, der
> Kunst.
>
> —Goethe, "Maximen und Reflexionen"[1]

An initial if ultimately inadequate working definition of the open secret
might be "a way of imparting knowledge such that it cannot be claimed
and acted on." Such a definition would correspond to the relatively familiar uses of the concept on the part of critics as divergent as Eve Kosofsky
Sedgwick and Frank Kermode. So, for example, describing the epistemology of the closet, Sedgwick has called an "open secret" an essentially preventative or conservative mode of communication that reveals to insiders
what it simultaneously hides from outsiders or, more specifically, protects
them from what they do not wish to know, from what it is in their power
to ignore.[2] Indeed, the term is frequently linked in both Sedgwick's and

1. He to whom Nature begins to disclose her open secret feels an irresistible
longing after her worthiest interpreter, art.

2. Writing on *Billy Budd*, Sedgwick describes the expressive challenge posed
by mutiny, a concept whose inherent explosiveness makes it, like homosexuality,
a "crime" committed at the instant of its thought—a possibility that merely to
verbalize is already in some sense to realize: "the terms [in which mutiny] can be
described must be confined to references that evoke recognizant knowledge in
those who already possess it without igniting it in those who may not" (Sedgwick, *Epistemology of the Closet*, 101).

D. A. Miller's critical idioms with that peculiar exercise of power that consists not in a knowledge claim, as a crude Enlightenment logic might have it, but in the privilege to ignore—the right to go on not knowing or pretending not to see.[3] Epitomized by the rationally incomprehensible, doubly unjust promise of Luke 19:26—"That unto everyone which hath shall be given; and from him that hath not, even that he hath shall be taken away from him"—the "open secret" so defined is another name for the tautological hermeneutics, familiar from Kermode's work on biblical exegesis, dividing those who can *read* the Gospels' latent "spiritual" sense from those who, caught by the image of the parables' manifest sense, can only "see but not perceive."[4] Yet my interest in the paradox of a disclosure that only opens the eyes of the seeing and closes the eyes of the unseeing lies less with its enforcing a hierarchical division between readers and nonreaders than with its presenting the critic with the formal problem of

3. Thus Sedgwick's analysis of the epistemology of the closet begins with the example of Reagan's not needing to learn French to communicate with Mitterand (4), an example that resonates today not only with the complacency of the parent who greets her child's "coming out" with "Why didn't you tell me before?" as if the burden of making known were all on the teller, but also with the continued presumption of American "innocence," as if this were a right to historical unconsciousness, audible in the post-9/11 question, "Why do they hate us?" D. A. Miller's account of "the sly logic of the Open Secret," on the other hand, emphasizes the inseparability of the interpellation of a subject supposed-to-know from that subject's release from the obligation to demonstrate the knowledge imputed to him; according to this logic, "while no reader is so indigent in received ideas as not to know what all these well-classified, even 'classic' reticences are driving at, every reader is simultaneously accorded the privilege of *not having to know he knows it*" (Miller, "Foutre! Bougre! Écriture!" 511).

4. Kermode cites the verse from Luke in the opening chapter of *The Genesis of Secrecy* as part of his argument for the essential (rather than accidental or historically contingent) hermeticism of the interpretive tradition. His gloss—"Only those who already know the mysteries—what the stories really mean—can discover what the stories really mean" (3)—highlights not only the tautology of such distribution but the paradoxical impossibility of history for the Christian witness who can no longer wait on time for revelation and for whom nothing can happen if it hasn't already. Pascal's thought—"Tu ne me chercherais pas, si tu ne m'avais trouvé" (you would not seek me if you had not found me)—gives the full measure of the despair and consolation afforded by such sated—immobilized—questing, although the intimacy of the familiar second-person address slants toward the consolatory (Pensée 553 in Pascal, *Oeuvres Complètes*, 1313; here and throughout, I refer to Pascal's pensées by their Brunschvicg numbers).

how to evaluate, recognize, and name a dramatic action so inconsequential it yields no *peripeteia* and seems to evade the Aristotelian definition of plot. Rather than either dismiss this movement of recessive disclosure as a nonevent whose sole effect is defensive—to bar change and ensure that nothing happen—or, on the contrary (but this amounts to the same), recognize it as the magic act essential to the effective workings of social relations—this book focuses on the ways in which the open secret as a gesture of self-canceling revelation permits a release from the ethical imperative to *act* upon knowledge.[5]

Even so, a defense of inconsequence such as the kind proposed here will perhaps inevitably look like a fetishization of virginity, of the blank page on which commitment is forever deferred in the name of limitless potential. Indeed, popular psychology affords us the ready label of "passive aggressive" for protagonists such as Austen's Fanny Price or Wordsworth's Lucy or the numerous figures in Dickinson's poetry, who keep themselves quiet and exert ways of being in the world without seeming to make demands. As for Lafayette's heroine, who but a secretly vindictive hysteric whose only yes is a "no" would confess to her husband her love for another man and then refuse to act on this desire when left free to do so by her husband's premature death? So, from false modesty to aggressive self-effacement, one might inventory the arsenal of ready stereotypes pathologizing unpursued desire, motivating noninsistence, and denying the possibility of weightless claims to attention. To the fetishist of Goethe's aphorism, whom an ungenerous reader might accuse of di-

5. If "acting on" includes "owning" and "demonstrating" knowledge, then, in a sense, I might be taken as defending the right to apparent obtuseness, whether feigned or real, that, as I suggest above, Sedgwick in her early work reads as a trick of hegemonic power—the blindness that erases more effectively than any censure. I can only answer "weakly" in the sense that Sedgwick herself uses the term in her more recent work when referring to "weak"—localized, particular, circumscribed—theories of reading—by reiterating my interest in the rhythm of such a relation between insight and action—the taking in of x and the leaving it at that—rather than in the generally disciplinary or evasive effects of such passive reception. This release from the obligation to pursue knowledge to demystifying ends may in fact belong to what Sedgwick herself has recently called "reparative" reading. See the partially self-critical chapter "Paranoid Reading, Reparative Reading" in her *Touching Feeling* (123–51), in which she identifies alternatives to the hermeneutics of suspicion, which has tended to make "exposure" criticism's only goal and, ironically enough, its one unquestioned "good."

verting his eyes toward art at the first glimpse of nature's disclosure, and the neurotic who won't have her fingers burnt by actual possession, highbrow philosophical discourse might add the Hegelian "Beautiful Soul" who saves herself for the day that never comes, rejecting each suitor for materialization as deficient in the negating, self-canceling power that is all she has to express;[6] the Kierkegaardian ironist who speaks so as to have said nothing, thereby retaining "the subjective freedom that at all times has in its power the possibility of a beginning and is not handicapped by earlier situations"; the Kierkegaardian "knight of resignation," who can make up his mind to loss but cannot bear to have his love returned; the Nietzschean "man of *ressentiment*," who "understands how to keep silent, how not to forget, how to wait, how to be provisionally self-deprecating and humble."[7]

Recent critical approaches to the open secret have generally echoed these popular skeptical diagnoses in their tendency to read the figure as one of disavowal—a denial that does not so much abandon as put its ob-

6. Its antecedents in Goethe and early German Romanticism, Hegel's Beautiful Soul "lives in dread of besmirching the splendour of its inner being by action and an existence; and, in order to preserve the purity of its heart, it flees from contact with the actual world, and persists in its self-willed impotence to renounce its self which is reduced to the extreme of ultimate abstraction, and to give itself a substantial existence, or to transform its thought into being and put its trust in the absolute difference [between thought and being]" (Hegel, *Phenomenology of Spirit*, §658/400). The figure of the beautiful soul whose confessions make up the sixth book of Goethe's *Wilhelm Meister*, and who quietly allows her engagement to the man she loves to be dissolved because he will not accept to live on her conditions, presents an especially interesting case for the figures of "weak" renunciation studied here; for her sternness derives precisely from her mildness—from her refusal to proselytize and contribute to others' conversion—as from her own unworldliness. Her piety not only keeps her from marrying the man she loves but also from putting pressure on him to persuade him to conform to her wishes. See Goethe, *Wilhelm Meister's Apprenticeship*.

7. See Kierkegaard, *The Concept of Irony*, 253; Kierkegaard, *Fear and Trembling*; and Nietzsche, *On the Genealogy of Morals*, 38. As I argue below, there is a self-reflexivity to these demystifying charges against reticent assertion, for in suspecting of "bad faith" any expressed readiness to leave power unused or potential unactualized, they too cannot *accept* their object at face value and thus are "guilty" of the same spirit of discontent—adolescent refusal or avoidance of actualized desire—they attribute to flirts and prudes.

ject in reserve—or as an ideological trick ensuring the neutralization, containment, and uneven distribution of the power supposed to come with knowledge. In post-Marxist, psychoanalytically informed ideology theory, the "open secret" becomes a trope for the implicit workings of ideology itself—for the way in which the ideological not only gains assent without show of force and polices imagination without explicit censorship, but occupies the space of the blank page from which it can produce a consensus that no actually written document could ever yield.[8] Like the Queen who, in Lacan's analysis of Poe's "Purloined Letter," does nothing to dress or cover up her lack except "keep herself immobile in [the] shadow [of the sign of woman]," the figure of the open secret evokes the "emperor-has-no-clothes" syndrome, frequently discussed by Slavoj Žižek, whereby a particular system of power is able to "lie in the guise of truth" and continues to work even when—and indeed only because—no one believes it anymore.[9] Such "cynicism," according to which no one is expected to subscribe to the explicit rhetoric of a dominant regime, signals the limits of the traditional "Enlightenment" approach that once trusted to the efficacy of exposing the fraudulence of claims to power. On another level, as a figure of ellipsis—of the set that no determinate content can fill and whose ends trail off into the implicit and nonspecifiable—the open secret also corresponds to the *secret* of *openness* or the fetish of nonclosure to which Žižek repeatedly draws our attention in his numerous accounts of how the symbolic order of Western modernity turns out to be premised on a gap it posits as having to remain empty or unfilled, always capable of accommodating one more articulated content, whether in question are human rights or the reasons of desire.[10]

8. See, for example, Althusser's comments on the obviousness with which ideology imposes itself or rather does not impose itself at all except as that which one already knows: "It is indeed a peculiarity of ideology that it imposes (without appearing to do so, since these are 'obviousnesses') obviousnesses as obviousnesses, which we cannot *fail to recognize* and before which we have the inevitable and natural reaction of crying out (aloud or in the 'still, small voice of conscience'): 'That's obvious! That's right! That's true!'" (Althusser, *Essays on Ideology*, 46).

9. See Lacan, *Écrits*, 31, my translation; and Žižek, "The Spectre of Ideology," in Žižek, *The Žižek Reader*, 61.

10. "Mind the gap!" one reads in the London underground, an imperative studiously observed in the following of Žižek's analyses: the cynic referred to

In other cases the figure of the open secret is understood as itself an instance of ideological mystification, and the critical work consists of unmasking one of the two antitheses—"open" or "secret"—as the illusion hiding the truth of the other. Thus the claim to openness, nondifferentiation, universality, or accessibility may be revealed as the illusion masking—either to protect or to deny—the existence of the invisible minority and secret of unmarked difference (Sedgwick follows Proust in mapping Jewish and gay identities onto one another as invisibly stigmatized Others in anti-Semitic and homophobic societies, themselves ironically informed by the trope of "the stranger in our midst" of the Christian story and drama of election). Or criticism may target a naive Enlightenment belief in the power of communication to set us free; thus Bataille, Foucault, and, more recently, Michael Taussig and Jodi Dean have all emphasized

---

above remains aloof from the discourse he nevertheless allows to represent him; the economy of phallic desire works only as long and insofar as it can imagine as eluding its grasp an enigmatic feminine *jouissance* (Žižek, "Death and the Maiden," in Žižek, *The Žižek Reader*, 214); and the subject of self-consciousness is rewarded with the potentially limitless power to "signify nothing"—"to relate to itself as to an empty 'bearer'"—in exchange for recognizing as contingent the "empirical features which constitute the positive content of his particular 'person'" (Žižek, *Tarrying with the Negative*, 29). In "The Spectre of Ideology" Žižek designates as the operation of "ideology at its purest" the ploy of suspending positive statement so as to produce the illusion of "depth" or of some "'truly essential dimension' about which we need not make any positive claim"—a ploy he links to the game of the Lacanian "Master-signifier" or "signifier without signified" (*The Žižek Reader*, 69–70). Yet in the same essay Žižek also claims that critique is only possible from a space that must remain similarly free of determinate content: "the place from which one can denounce ideology must remain empty, it cannot be occupied by any positively determined reality—the moment we yield to this temptation, we are back in ideology" (70). The apparent contradiction, no doubt traceable to the ambiguous status of Kantian transcendental idealism in Žižek's work, is less interesting to me than what may be Žižek's own constitutive antipathy toward a discourse that might, like reverie, simply drift or trail off into silence. Compare, for example, Barthes' pages on the "pensiveness" of the "classical text" at the close of *S/Z*; Barthes is equally critical of the ideological strategy of "signifying the inexpressible" by colonizing the space of the unsaid, even while refusing to fill it, and yet, in his affective register, he is far more attuned to what is seductive in the drift of such suspension. See Barthes, *S/Z*, 216–17.

the degree to which disclosure, far from defusing, only recharges the fetish power of the public secret that loves to "spend itself" in revelation.[11] Or secrecy itself may be the show; indeed, as D. A. Miller cannily reminds us, it requires a show.[12]

On the other hand, as Goethe's image of nature as the "offenbares Geheimnis" suggests, the open secret also has a long-standing place in Judeo-Christian thought as the image for the "secular" or "worldly" correlative to the trope of divine revelation: "the open book of nature"—"that universal and publick Manuscript that lies expans'd unto the Eyes of all"[13]—at stake in which is not simply the idea of another mode of access to the Law supplementing the written Word of God but a figure for its givenness— there for all to see—that no degree of wealth or power and no technology of reading, however sophisticated, can increase.[14] This trope informs al-

11. See Taussig, *Defacement*; and Dean, *Publicity's Secret*.

12. Miller's "Open Secrets, Secret Subjects" exposes the manufacturing of secrecy as the illusion that novelistic characters perform to give the impression of hidden psychological depth, thereby at once protecting themselves from prying eyes and, more importantly, defining themselves as impenetrable subjects. See Miller, *The Novel and the Police*, 192–220.

13. Sir Thomas Browne, *Religio Medici*, 1643, pt. 1, sec. 16, cited in Hartman, *Wordsworth's Poetry, 1787–1814*. Hartman's note reads: "The idea of nature as an open mystery, i.e., as a mystery-religion paradoxically open to all mankind (just as St. Paul had opened the Old Dispensation and transformed Judaism into Christianity) is linked to a persistent concept in the history of ideas, that of the Book of Nature, 'that universal and publick Manuscript that lies expans'd unto the Eyes of all'" (379n).

14. One can imagine that with the advent of print culture and the development of a reading middle class, this "second" book's "openness"—its capacity to be received by all, regardless of power—would have lost much of its democratizing valence relative to the closed or sealed book of the Word of God. On another level, however, to Browne's "universal," "publick" "expans'd," it isn't even necessary to add the expected countervailing "silent," "unfathomable," "incomprehensible," for that there may be nothing to do before such "presentness" suffices to suspend movement and guarantee this open secret's aporetic structure. Indeed, only the counterbalancing image of nature's obscurity—transformed into the perception of an initial but by no means final illegibility—prompts the development of modern science as the *work* of its decipherment. In *The Politics of Aesthetics* Jacques Rancière offers salient reflections on the "equality" of access of the printed page, "available as it is to everyone's eyes"—an "equality" that "destroys

most all of Heidegger's lexicon of unconcealment, as well as Kierkegaard's and Levinas's attempts to think beyond the self-generating, self-realizing progress of enlightenment, the concept of revelation as something that reason itself cannot produce or comprehend. Yet, as I argue below, precisely as a "naturalization," the open secret also implies a shift in the kind of attention that "revelation" (*Offenbarung*) demands, an attenuation of revelation's stakes, a license to take the revealed for granted. Section v of this chapter ("Stop here, or gently pass!") will describe the ways in which I have conceived this project as an indirect response to the language of limitless duty, impossible exigency, and heroic responsibility that, however passively inflected, continues to inform the Heideggerian work of disclosing Being and, more explicitly, post-Heideggerian ethical thought. "When I hear talk of enigma, I prick up my ears," Jean Laplanche asserts with that oddly phlegmatic, Dupin-like verve we've come to hear as the distinctive mark of the analyst's cool. Yet there are many such ears on alert if we are to judge by the acuity of attention bestowed in a number of postsecular contexts—psychoanalysis, Heideggerian-inspired ontology, Levinasian ethics—on a type of revelation whose enigmatic dimension cannot be traced to some omitted x but survives, indeed inheres in, its disclosure—a message it may take "forever" to heed, not because it is hard to decipher but because what such address or disconcealment calls forth is not on the order of observable action and measurable response.[15] Of

---

all of the hierarchies of representation" and "establishes a community of readers without legitimacy, a community formed only by the random circulation of the written word" (Rancière, *The Politics of Aesthetics*, 14).

15. See Laplanche's essay "Time and the Other," in which he distinguishes between a "riddle," whose solution is "in the conscious possession of the one who poses it," and an "enigma," which "can only be proposed by someone who does not master the answer" (Laplanche, *Essays on Otherness*, 234–59). If the enigma is thus defined as a site of nonmastery and nonpossession, precisely its passivity of emission elicits the receiver's interpretive activity and guarantees it enduring, indeed immobilizing, resonance long after its emitter's passing, as the recipient-patient-subject is stuck wondering "What does the Other want of me?"—the Lacanian question that Laplanche here helps to render more precisely as—"What does the Other want insofar as she is other to herself, unconscious of the messages that she bears and that I interpret as demands concerning me?" Laplanche's critique of the "ipso-centrism," by which Freudian and Kleinian theory tends to stop at the first-person subject as the originating source of fantasy,

recent theorists, Eric Santner has perhaps made most explicit the connection to the theological concept of "revelation," comparing the "enigmatic messages" that, in Laplanche's account, "set the child the difficult, or even impossible task of mastery and symbolization," to what Scholem once called "the nothingness of revelation" confronting Kafka (and perhaps secular Jews of the early twentieth century in general)—where "revelation appears to be without meaning, in which it still asserts itself, in which it has validity but no significance."[16] Whether ontological or historical, Santner's examples tend to define as essentially traumatic this proximity to opacity and state of being delivered over to something that refuses itself; in this they run the risk of being misread as instances of a "fallen" mode of revelation as if by contrast with some earlier, more generous and less unyielding openness. Part of why I wish to risk so oxymoronic, and perhaps also so naive, a term as *natural revelation* is to underscore, by contrast, the sense in which the muteness or mildness of the open secret as I'm using the term is not experienced as defective or constitutive of a lack; my examples refer to the reception of an address so light it is hard to know how one is concerned by it, but this uncertainty need not be experienced, as it is, in Santner's account of Laplanche, as setting the recipient to what he calls the "never-ceasing" work of decipherment and symbolization (*On Creaturely Life*, 33).

"A mode of expressivity that our available modes of acknowledgment

------

rather than recognize the degree to which the subject is caught up in a circuit of the other's long abandoned and never possessed messages, has recently been picked up by thinkers such as Judith Butler wishing to relocate ethical agency and responsibility in precisely those relationships where the subject seems least an "agent"—most given over to the other's unchosen, enigmatic address (Butler, *Giving an Account of Oneself*, 54, 76–78).

16. Santner, *On Creaturely Life*, 33, 39; Santner quotes from Laplanche, *New Foundations for Psychoanalysis*, 130; and Benjamin, *The Correspondence of Walter Benjamin and Gershom Scholem, 1932–1940*, 142. Santner's other examples of this paradoxical "exposure to an 'arresting opacity'" (11, 39 [the phrase is Heidegger's]) sometimes describe a general human condition (Heideggerian boredom) and sometimes refer to historical crises specific to modernity (the imperative of assimilation, simultaneously declared to be impossible, addressed to German Jews in the nineteenth century; the "exposure to an 'outlaw' dimension of law internal to sovereign authority" [Santner, *On Creaturely Life*, 29] by which subjects under the state of exception continue to be addressed without protection by the law).

and interpersonal engagement can't take up" is Santner's recent formulation for what it was Freud's originality to begin to listen to—a formulation that I'm tempted to steal for the "open secret," except insofar as the
very term *expressivity* automatically produces a duty to bear witness, and
so precludes the question that I would want to add: what if we were to try
"setting down" rather than "taking up" a gift itself indistinguishable from
its abandonment? Thus, in contrast with the restless vigilance and tireless
chivalry usually if paradoxically elicited by the enigma's own weakness
on the scales of positive representation, its opacity to itself, or incapacity to state its demands, Wordsworth's line "Stop here, or gently pass!"
scandalously grants permission to pass, implying an indistinct continuity
between the act of stopping to listen and acknowledge and that of letting
lapse or fall behind.[17] Similarly, one might read Goethe's seemingly faithless, inconsequent swerve to art not as a regressive fetishistic retreat from
modern science's exposure of nature's secrets but as a facing up to the
freedom implied by the open secret—as if the only "free" response to such
unsolicited revelation consisted not of taking advantage of it by trying to
see more but of giving an image, a shadow, a back, to the very gratuity
with which "nature" gives "herself up." While everyone across the critical
spectrum, from critics of ideology to historians of the "ordinary" to phenomenological thinkers, seems to take for granted the moral imperative
not to take anything for granted, least of all the given, the open secret,
as I define it in section v, constitutes a gift of revelation so transmuted
it's taken for granted—absorbed into the ground of the ordinary—before
being perceived as such, buried as part of its reception rather than repression.

   Thus one way of summarizing my departure from ideological approaches
to the open secret would be to say that if they uncover the work open secrets perform even in appearing to do nothing, I take seriously the release
from critical energies and sense of something simply there for the asking
implied by the various senses of *open* in "open secret." *Open*, for example,
can mean all of the following: awaiting enclosure—undetermined and
open to change—a site of potentiality; exposed—vulnerable—defenseless;

17. "The Solitary Reaper." Except where otherwise noted, Wordsworth's poetry is quoted from *The Poetical Works of William Wordsworth*, eds. Ernest de
Selincourt and Helen Darbishire, 5 vols.

public—held in common—known to all or to some.[18] Just as a poem can sometimes offer a sense of quiet, inexplicable but by no means threatening or extraordinary, mystery—the sense not that critical work is unnecessary but that no one will be at fault if the mystery remains unmastered—the action of the novels and poems studied in this book might be called "gratuitous," not in the common pejorative sense but according to the word's full range of meanings: "freely bestowed; granted without claim or merit;

18. Giorgio Agamben elaborates in *The Open* on the ambiguities by which "open" may slide into "exposed to" and "absorbed in," on the one hand, and "free," "released," "open to the 'that there is' of possibility," on the other, with respect to Heidegger's analyses of animal "*benommenheit*" (captivation) and human boredom. According to Agamben, for Heidegger what appears to Rilke in the Eighth Duino Elegy as the animal's "openness"—its unconstrained, unbarred absorption in what surrounds it—in fact keeps the animal closed to the possibility of the world's being revealed to it or not and excludes it from the "strife between concealedness and unconcealedness" ambiguously "proper" to Dasein. Agamben is less interested, however, in maintaining and reproducing the animal/human distinction than in obsessively tracing the dimension in Heidegger's thought that assigns Dasein the difficult task of bringing forth into the open precisely that which rises up as "self-secluding" or "undisclosable" to itself (whether this is the earth in the "Origin of the Work of Art" or the animal in its exclusion from the conflict between "concealment and unconcealment"). Yet, as if following the movement of Heideggerian "*Gelassenheit*," Agamben seems to recognize that this is a task that to complete is also to abandon, suspend, or let go of. Thus at times he strikes the starkly disenchanted tone of the teacher whose own boldly revelatory turns can save us from the illusion of a beyond-to-animal-being: "The open and free-of-being do not name something radically other with respect to the neither open-nor-closed of the animal environment; they are the appearing of an undisconcealed as such. . . . The jewel set at the center of the human world and its *Lichtung* (clearing) is nothing but animal captivation; the wonder 'that beings *are*' is nothing but the grasping of the 'essential disruption' that occurs in the living being from its being exposed in a nonrevelation. . . . The openness at stake is essentially the openness to a closedness, and whoever looks in the open sees only a closing, only a not-seeing" (Agamben, *The Open*, 68). Toward the book's end, however, Agamben appears to put into question this very project of awakening (and remaining starkly awake) to a blindness: referring to the etymological sense of forgiveness in the Latin verb *ignoscere*, he credits with ethical valence a lighter indifference to the project of disclosing what is itself indifferent to its nonknowledge (91).

provided without payment or return; costing nothing to the recipient; free" (*The Oxford English Dictionary*, Second Edition; hereafter referred to as *OED*). My argument in this sense gives free rein to the inevitable slippage across semantic registers—ontological, theological, aesthetic, economic, and ethical—by which the open secret continues to resonate with the religious and aesthetic concepts of grace and to evoke the related trope of the "gift" of natural revelation as opposed to the work of reason.

Central to this effect of grace in the novels in question is their mode of recessive narration allowing subjective perceptions to assert themselves with the simplicity and flatness of objective truths; so self-contained they can hardly even be said to occur, these states of mind at the same time more closely resemble decisions than reflections, insofar as they can only be briefly narrated, rather than articulated, vocalized, or elaborated in cognition.[19] In fact, I would like to round off this preliminary exposition of the "open secret," which began with the example of the strangely opaque transparency of biblical parables, with a brief excursion on the topic of third-person narration of subjective or "first-person" experience—the narrative method whose development defines both Austen's and Lafayette's contribution to the history of the modern novel. Such a discussion seems pertinent, first, because this unobtrusively intimate narrative mode holds a key to what "we moderns" might consider the Holy Word's secular equivalent—the inner lives of "other people"—and, second, because the critical debates surrounding the "impersonal" narration of "personal" or private experience (from the question of the narrative voice's relation to the characters whom it shadows without resembling, to that of whether one is even justified in positing "a narrator" "speaking behind" the sentences of narration) tend to reproduce in miniature the range of responses to the "open secret" just described.[20] Indeed, the case of

19. In my third chapter I address the different ways in which the first-person voice of lyric poems can also be felt to quiet itself even as it speaks—inconsequently, unobtrusively presenting itself without announcement, often coming out of nowhere and receding as quickly.

20. From Ian Watt's account of how Austen, following Frances Burney, "dispensed with the participating narrator" of a Fielding or Richardson as a means of achieving "psychological closeness to the subjective world of the characters" (thereby making "closeness" independent from mimetic identification), to D. A. Miller's recent analysis of Austen as a "stylothete" who achieves the transcendence of "Style" only by renouncing the finitude and coupledom enjoyed by her

unvoiced or unclaimed language, of a report not structured and directed as communication, is as scandalous to the hermeneutics of suspicion (and its underlying rationalist premise of a closed economy and law of just returns) as the idea of a "free gift" or of an avowal that, like the Princesse de Clèves' famous *aveu*, would "disclaim" or "un-claim" love (claim it so as to leave it untouched) and still not amount to disavowal in the sense of a denied, unconscious, or evasive affirmative.[21] The case of inward states and mental decisions being materialized for the first and last time by this strangely agentless mode of report can also clarify the "uncounted experiences" of my subtitle, in which *uncounted* refers less to an absence of narration or failure to acknowledge than to an action of "uncounting" (even "dis-counting"—making light of, depositing to leave unclaimed—if this could be taken nonpejoratively) comparable to the Penelope-like work of undoing, unthreading, unraveling with which narrative itself has come to be identified.

Not surprisingly, the study of the novel has featured prominently in

---

novels' characters, critical readings of Austen have often centered on the ambiguous nonrelation Austenian narration sustains to the characters whose turbulent inner lives it represents without participating in. See Watt, *The Rise of the Novel*, 296–97; and Miller, *Jane Austen, or the Secret of Style*. More generally, theorists of the novel have long understood the curious fact that "introspection" need not involve "self-confession" insofar as the novel develops techniques of "objective" or "unobtrusive" narration at precisely the same moment it reintroduces, in Dorrit Cohn's words, "the subjectivity of private experience . . . this time not in terms of direct self-narration, but by imperceptibly integrating mental reactions into the neutral-objective report of actions, scenes, and spoken words" (Cohn, *Transparent Minds*, 115). In addition to Cohn, see Ricœur and Hamburger. For the argument that to posit a narrator "voicing" the sentences of narration is inappropriately to impose a "communication model" of language on narration (and an assessment of the counterarguments) see Banfield, *Unspeakable Sentences*, 12.

21. Thus for ideological criticism, the impression of a floating, groundless, unaccountable presence—in Flaubert's famous phrase "everywhere felt but nowhere seen"—produced by thoughts that are neither in the first-person voice of the character to which they appear to belong nor directly attributable to a narrative voice, represents an ideological illusion—both symptomatic and mimetic of the universalism, obfuscation of agency, and erasure of particular perspectives effected by hegemonic discourse. See, e.g., Finch and Bowen, "'The Tittle-Tattle of Highbury'"; and Frances Ferguson's discussion of their essay in Ferguson, "Jane Austen, *Emma*, and the Impact of Form," 161.

the debunking of the pseudoromantic myth of interiority as property irreducibly mine, unique, and nonevincible—demanding original expression even while remaining essentially beyond it. Following the lead of the Foucauldian critique in the 1980s of inwardness as a not particularly special effect of discursive practices, a number of important studies in the last two decades have continued to develop nuanced accounts of the "commonness" of psychological interiors, often focusing on the circulatory dimensions of practices of reading "in private" in the periods immediately preceding the nineteenth century's consolidation of bourgeois individualism.[22] Such criticism often invokes "free indirect style" metonymically as a figure for narrative techniques in general that assume no direct correspondence between the subject of an experience and the agent of its verbalization. In this context free indirect style is said to relieve characters from the work of self-representation—from the burden, as Frances Ferguson has recently put it, both of having "thoughts that rise to the level of the expressible" ("The Impact of Form," 167) (as characters in a play must) and of constantly reporting on themselves (as the perpetually writing protagonists of epistolary novels do). It frees characters, in other words, first from the work of speaking for themselves, giving accounts, and making themselves legible to others that constitutes the right and duty of Habermasian individuals and then from the no less onerous burden of having to signal "deep" or unfathomable emotion.[23] The allusion to traditional Enlightenment values of proprietary responsibility and public accountability is not irrelevant, as will become clearer below. For it is precisely these values—as well as the very gulf they assume and, in many ways, reinforce between the mystery of inchoate private experience and the formal articulation of public life—that dictate the privileging of communicative speech as the upper limit toward which subjective, reflective experience supposedly tends, evident in the phrase "thoughts that *rise* to the level of the expressible."[24] By contrast, free indirect style records

22. See, e.g., Miller, *The Novel and the Police*; Lynch, *The Economy of Character*; and Pinch, *Strange Fits of Passion*.

23. So, for example, Lynch writes of *Sense and Sensibility*: "Through free indirect discourse Elinor's inner life is delivered into the safekeeping of an impersonal narrator, who takes up the burden of that language of sentiment and self-expression, which, with near-fatal results, Marianne has clamorously made her own" (Lynch, *The Economy of Character*, 214).

24. For an exemplary expression of the Enlightenment commitment to com-

experiences no less realized or complete for not concretizing themselves *out loud* in addressed verbal expression; the "failure" of such moments to result in spoken communication need not, although it may, signify their elision, undervaluing, or mystification.[25]

"Yes,—he had done it." So Austen in *Persuasion* punctuates Anne Elliot's wonder at how Wentworth has "quietly obliged" her into his sister's carriage, the suspensive dash at once lengthening and completing the pause of breathlessness produced by the perfectly executed male act. The end-stopped sentence—itself taking note of a fully achieved action—can exemplify the exhilaratingly disarticulative effects of free indirect style, even if the sentences immediately following this one both thicken and trouble the basis of Anne's psychological contentment with Wentworth, as she silently ruminates on the meaning of his taking the trouble to put her in the carriage, without considering the fact he may simply wish to be rid of her so as to be at greater liberty to pursue his flirtation with Louisa Musgrove:

> Yes,—he had done it. She was in the carriage, and felt that he had placed her there, that his will and his hands had done it, that she owed it to his perception of her fatigue, and his resolution to give her rest. She was very much affected by the view of his disposition towards her which all these things made apparent. This little circumstance seemed the completion of all that had gone before. She understood him. He could not forgive her,—but he could not be unfeeling.[26]

The passage, of which I quote only a part, exemplifies Anne's capacity to fill the tiny space of the carriage with the workings of her self-persuasion and might easily be taken as typifying the compensatory work of

---

munication as the telos of thought and its resulting suspicion and disappointment with an unexpressed, unshared, or rather unaddressed intellectual life, see Carl Friedrich Bahrdt's 1787 assertion that "communication is not only the principal goal of thought, it is also a universal need the satisfaction of which only makes the right to think enjoyable" (quoted in Schmidt, *What Is Enlightenment?* 102).

25. Effectively separating meditative from confessional experience (as "self-absorbed" from "self-presentative"), third-person psychonarration in a sense does for the epistolary novel what Michael Fried has shown painting does for the theater. See Fried, *Absorption and Theatricality*.

26. Austen, *Persuasion*, 61.

making up for a deficiency of presence or purchase on the other person's consciousness that the retreat into inwardness is supposed to perform. Austen's indirect narration accompanies this retreat from direct exchange so that Wentworth and Anne will "have it out" with each other only at the novel's end; until then Anne might be accused by a strict Enlightenment Kantian of "infantilizing" Wentworth by doing *for* him the work of self-explanation *to* herself. But even as it prolongs the postponement of the moment when the other will have to explain, excuse, account, and speak for himself (importantly, Wentworth will write his own first-person account in Anne's presence), such narration also stops short of doing for Anne what Anne does for Wentworth; it refrains from playing with the meditative character the game this character plays when seeing past the other's blind spots and filling in and interpreting the other's silences. What did Austen understand about Anne in writing "She understood him"? Neither simply shorthand for "she thought to herself, 'I understand him,'" nor exactly satire on the pleasure Anne takes in thinking she understands Wentworth and in thinking about herself, "I am she who understands Wentworth," a sentence of this kind works in part by letting its subject hang herself. Whether economy of judgment, or abstinence from it altogether, this contentment with the least said remains weirdly congenial with, even as it ironizes, the strangely abstemious if overactive consciousness of one who does not so much deny herself the fantasy of imagining the other spending his hours regretting her loss but, on the contrary, prefers to imagine him as having (only) a minimum of regard for her. Indeed, before we can even raise the question of whether Anne's richly interpretive because retroactive assent to Wentworth's act merely compensates for the failure of direct address, the first sentence's declarative "Yes" has not only expressed but afforded a satisfaction of its own. Rather than simply "echo" or give a secondary, ghostly voicing to speech that has already been vocalized, or, on the contrary, failed to take place, such sentences make available for silent reading experiences that may not want, need, or be capable of louder articulation; in Volosinov's formulation, free indirect style translates or puts them into silence, so that the "action" such narration asks us to imagine does not confer actuality on the previously latent, as most models of action assume, but effects a transfer from one "full" or even empty silence to another.[27]

27. Volosinov's formulation makes represented speech and thought "especially congenial to irony because it 'is bound up with the transposition of the larger

Thus the usual emphasis in criticism has been on the correspondingly magical access that readers enjoy to the "transparent" subjectivity of such characters, an access that, as Dorrit Cohn reminds us, they enjoy nowhere else.[28] Lynch's *The Economy of Character* recasts this access as the secret privilege of bourgeois readers *and* the discipline by which they learn to be "good," discerning readers of interiority, capable of seeing past surface appearances and suspicious of "easy," external signs of value. But such readers, I would add, can only exercise their cultural capital over "other" blind characters who, although in a book, are ironically limited to the stubbornly opaque and deceptive surfaces of life outside books. With respect to other readers their capital is nil, for now it suddenly appears to be universally granted, free and there for the taking; they do not know where it comes from and cannot say how they know what they know about quiet, noncommunicative characters such as Elinor Dashwood or Anne Elliot.[29] In other words, I wish to emphasize—contra Lynch but, more importantly, contra a certain Romantic genealogy of the paranoid, penetrating, critical, or "spiritual" reader who "earns" her prized insights by tunneling below the surface of the letter—the degree to which reading remains an experience of the surface when third-person narrative styles allow nonmanifest, "inward" truths to circulate in the open of the text. Here there is perhaps no more exemplary instance than Lafayette's *La Princesse de Clèves* for bringing this exquisite irony to a pitch: the Prince de Clèves is not especially "blind," obtuse, or dull-witted like those char-

---

prose genres into a silent register, i.e., for silent reading, destined to be read not spoken. Only this 'silencing' of prose could have made possible the multileveledness and voice-defying complexity of intonational structures that are so characteristic for modern literature'" (quoted in Banfield, *Unspeakable Sentences*, 222).

28. See Cohn, *Transparent Minds*. The originality of Cohn's argument, as I understand it, lies in refusing the superficial opposition between realism and attention to inward or psychological action (nothing of which shows up by external measures) so that for her the novel's "realism" is never mimetic but consists of naturalizing an otherwise never-experienced access to other people's minds.

29. Indeed, Frances Ferguson has suggested that the fact that anyone can see supposedly private states of mind is precisely what irks us about Flaubert's late style, where discerning inwardness is no longer the privilege of lovers and special readers. ("When Speech Becomes Ridiculous: Free Indirect Style and Its Impact on Speech," Narrative Conference, March 27–29, 2003, University of California at Berkeley.)

acters that weigh down Burney's and sometimes Austen's novels. (Lafayette makes them all aristocrats, so there can be no question of class privilege separating discerning characters from blind ones within the text; the
problem for the "unseeing" lies elsewhere.) Yet, or rather indeed, there is
no way the prince could have perceived (or indeed would ever have intu-
ited) his wife's secret had she not simply told him. What difference, then,
for readers who never for a minute doubt her feelings for Nemours? Very
little, except Lafayette's own limpid, transparent, "perfectly French" classical prose, so that although they know infinitely more than the prince,
they can no more congratulate themselves on their insight than he can
fault himself for his failure to see.

Finally, the formal problematic of third-person narration—and in
particular, the critical discourse around free indirect style rather than its
actual practice—anticipates the book's overall thematic project of desub-
limating the making of minimal claims on the world (by which I mean
both releasing these from an aesthetics of the sublime and a psychology
of sublimation) insofar as the very problem of indirect narration represents one of the few places in which talk of "unclaimed" experience need
no more signify "traumatic" experience than "unvocalized" experience
need signify "unrealized" experience (or disclaimed disowned, for that
matter).[30] For, in accordance with the decentering, displacing, slightly
distancing or "neutralizing" effects about which Blanchot has written so
movingly, the third-person narrative *il* introduces no real uncertainty as to
whose thoughts we are reading but opens up the question of the protagonist's relation to these thoughts—would he or she claim them? own up to
them? actually say them aloud?—and makes possible otherwise logically
scandalous phenomena such as enigmatic frankness, lucid self-deception,
weightless lying, passive agency, innocent—unpunishing—self-knowledge. Far from affording the "closest," most exhaustive, but still secondary picture of a protagonist's secret inner life, free indirect style, as in the
case of the blind spot constituted by "She understood him," or the more
famous instances of Flaubert's *Madame Bovary* and James's *What Maisie*

30. Thus Banfield's *Unspeakable Sentences* does not dwell on the apparent
scandal of its title, in part because it is a scandal only if we ignore the specificity
of literary experience and follow the general assumption, which Banfield dis-
putes, that "subjectivity in language is properly located within a theory of communicative act and intention" (7).

Knew, makes available experiences that may entirely elude their subjects.[31] Indeed, as numerous exemplary readings would attest, free indirect style unlocks a range of relations of identification and nonidentification, possession and nonpossession (between protagonist and the represented experience of which she is the ostensible subject, as between readers and protagonists, and narrative or authorial presences and the characters they often designate possessively as "my" or "our") that complicate the traditional liberal subject's claims to self-authorization in ways perhaps comparable to the expropriating action of trauma or limit-experience.[32] Our sense that it is good that the self-possessed subject of liberal individualism, whose claims to mastery and comprehension have inflicted so much historical and metaphysical violence, be disabled, inevitably colors the reception of trauma theory in postmodern criticism, as well as accounts of narrative dispossession such as Blanchot's. His metaphors describing the action of narration as a making or rendering passive (we would need to coin a new word—the equivalent of "activation" for the root "passive") highlight the close parallels between an ethical suspension of the subject's claims to mastery and appropriative powers, and trauma itself, often described as entailing the loss of the ability to assimilate experience to first-person narratives:

Dans l'espace neutre du récit, les porteurs de paroles, les sujets d'action—ceux

31. See, for example, Erich Auerbach's famous statement about the discrepancy between Emma's limited capacity for self-accounting and Flaubert's articulative intelligence (cited in Banfield, *Unspeakable Sentences*, 187). Making available to the reader an inner life that it also leaves, in some sense, unlived by the protagonist, free indirect style might be called "derealizing" rather than simply expressive or concretizing—an effect movingly captured by D. A. Miller: "In the paradoxical form of an impersonal intimacy, it grants us at one and the same time the experience of a character's inner life as she herself lives it, and an experience of the same inner life as she never could" (Miller, *Jane Austen, or the Secret of Style*, 60). Similar to a voice catching in the throat, the sentence's concluding "never could" sounds the barest note of mourning for a selfhood structured as a potential that exceeds the power of its fulfillment.

32. Foucault defines "limit-experience" through the work of Nietzsche, Blanchot, and Bataille, writers for whom, he claims, "experience has . . . the task of 'tearing' the subject from itself in such a way that it is no longer the subject as such, or that it is completely 'other' than itself so that it may arrive at its annihilation, its dissociation" (quoted in Jay, "The Limits of Limit-Experience," 66).

qui tenaient lieu jadis de personnages—tombent dans un rapport de non-identification avec eux-mêmes: quelque chose leur arrive, qu'ils ne peuvent ressaisir qu'en se désaisissant de leur pouvoir de dire "je," et ce qui leur arrive leur est toujours déjà arrivé. (Blanchot, *L'Entretien infini*, 564)

[In the neutral space of the narrative, the bearers of speech, the subjects of the action—those who once stood in the place of characters—fall into a relation of self-nonidentification. Something happens to them that they can only re-capture (literally, seize again) by relinquishing (unseizing themselves of) their power to say "I." And what happens (to them) has always already happened.] (Blanchot, *The Infinite Conversation*, 384–85, translation modified)

Yet, as I will argue in the following pages, the readiness to accede to a claim if one can do so quietly and the willingness to let pass at a cost what one would happily accept for free differ significantly from the figuratively similar inability to "claim" experience except indirectly characteristic of trauma insofar as this is survived before it is lived, experienced for the first time only in its repetition. As I argue in Chapter 4, Austen's voice seems at times to reserve for her heroine a mildly satiric but gently maternal protectiveness—as if she were willing to take her, where others weren't, as long she didn't have to take her too seriously; similar to the relation Lafayette sustains toward her heroine, this casual and qualified possessive-ness also marks reticent assertion's difference from the defensive irony of inverted quotation marks: it wishes to make a claim lightly—not so as to be disbelieved or protected from its consequences but because lightness is part of the claim.

ii. contesting the ideology of improvement

> And I was afraid, and went and hid thy talent in the earth: lo, there thou hast that is thine.
>
> —Matthew 25:25

> You are a great poet—and it is a wrong to the day you live in, that you will not sing aloud. When you are what men call dead, you will be sorry you were so stingy.
>
> —Helen Hunt Jackson to Emily Dickinson, October 1875

> "'Not a report' need not entail 'not an activity.'"
>
> —Iris Murdoch, *The Sovereignty of Good*

Some years ago, in an essay on Weber, Heidegger, and Arendt, George Kateb claimed that "Western humanity is and has always been at war with given reality. The world, as given, is disliked; it is disliked in large part just because it is given."[33] This book proposes to identify within Western literary modernity a countertradition to this spirit of discontent. As I argue in Chapter 4, "improvement," in its earlier sense of "the turning of a thing to profit or good account" (*OED*), is precisely what the figures of empty-handedness that I examine do not feel the need to make on their experience of the world, others, or themselves. Instead, the works in question share an ethos of attending to unobserved, not-for-profit experience rather than results entered on the public record, of defining action as a matter of timing and form rather than consequence, and of measuring difference not by what an action materially produces but by the imaginative possibilities revelation may either open or eclipse. Their propensity for narrative waste—or readiness not to make event x a cause for a subsequent event y—has its ethical analogue in the suspension of the impulse to take revenge on the given and decry transience as a deprivation; in such a mood one recognizes instead that the lapse between life's premise and its fulfillment constitutes no more of a cheat than the Other's difference from oneself.

Inasmuch as the historical endpoints of the literary texts studied here—Lafayette's *La Princesse de Clèves* (1678) and Hardy's *Poems of 1912–1913*—roughly correspond to the age of European capitalist expansionism and

33. Kateb, "Technology and Philosophy," 1241.

the rise of bourgeois liberal individualism, the book situates the example of those who would accept the risk of going unnoticed and returning empty-handed in response to the modern ideology of improvement that cannot admit the waste of unexploited powers. But, as I suggested earlier, the normative presumption favoring the articulation of human potential and implicitly conflating "enjoyment" with articulation, although it may coincide historically with a corresponding pressure to "develop" (and exhaust) natural resources, is not simply historically linked to the productionist, colonizing, and instrumentalizing ethos of modern Western capitalism. It continues to dominate our cultural landscape and critical horizons, often determining the meliorist—whether recuperative or demystifying—bent of much current scholarship in the humanities and, more specifically, facilitating the problematic slippage that Foucault's work warns us against from a hard-won *right* to speak and/or enjoy to a compulsive *duty* to speak, take possession of, and enjoy, evident in popular "consciousness-raising" and "liberating" productions such as HBO's *Sex and the City* or Eve Ensler's *Vagina Monologues*.[34] The forms of reticent assertion defended in this book express neither prudence nor prudery but a different kind of idealism, one that seeks to remain faithful to the open-endedness of thought, and to preserve the delicacy of the relation between the having of a desire and its externalization, or the making of a wish and its accomplishment. Attuned to the experimentalism and provisional nature of human desires, this ethos, far from negating, keeps alive the possibility of imaginative exercise and remains to this extent truer to the Enlightenment project of realizing human potential than do more programmatic responses to the license to make of the world what you will.[35]

34. I am thinking here of Žižek's repeated claim that in "our time" the super-egoic Father's only command is "Enjoy!" as well as an observation by Celeste Langan made to me in informal conversation on the ways in which *Sex and the City* enforces late capitalism's law of overarticulated enjoyment. Another instance of this assumption of a "duty to transgress" would be Jane Campion's answer to French *Elle* when asked about why she thought viewers were upset by the sex scenes in her film *In the Cut*: "Well, they're probably annoyed because they go home thinking, 'What now I have to do that in bed as well?'" See, as well, Barthes' discussion of anorexia as a response to a society that does not so much "prohibit" as "dictate desires," and "obliges us to satisfy them"—demanding that we eat even when we are not hungry (Barthes, *Le neutre*, 198–99).

35. Drawing on Adorno's example in *Minima Moralia* of the person who,

Perhaps nowhere is the persistence of this pressure to claim, develop, and make a return on one's given potential more evident than in the abiding influence of the biblical parable of the talents on Western moral and literary imaginations. Found in Matthew and Luke, cited by Weber in *The Protestant Ethic and the Spirit of Capitalism*, and repeatedly alluded to in Puritan sermons, the story of the unprofitable servant who, for having buried his one talent in the ground, lost even that, epitomizes the anxiety over wasted or undeveloped powers—the guilt of leaving the given untransformed—that attends the right to be judged by an end of one's own making.[36] (Before leaving on a journey, a master entrusts five talents to one servant, two to another, and one to a third; through good trading and investments, the first servant turns his five into ten, the second his two into four, and both are duly rewarded on the master's return; but the third simply buries the talent in the ground until the master's return, for which "nonaction" he loses "even that which he hath [not]" [See Matthew 25: 14–30].) If we remember that Matthew and Luke condemn as equally perverse and unthinkable the act of lighting a lamp only to put it in a secret place—under bed or bushel—rather than on a candlestick

---

wronged in love, discovers a right—"a demand not to be blinded"—which he nevertheless must refrain from invoking ("for what he desires can only be given in freedom" [Adorno, *Minima Moralia*, 164]), Judith Butler has thus recently defined as "ethical capaciousness" (rather than "paralyzing contradiction") the unwillingness to claim a right one nevertheless recognizes, and wishes to have recognized by others, as valid (Butler, *Giving an Account of Oneself*, 101–3). Butler's and Adorno's comments together point to the sphere of "tact"—that sphere of spared shame and declined revenge well-known to the protagonists of Lafayette's and James's novels—as an area in which the link otherwise often automatically assumed between the recognition of a potential and its actualization is momentarily suspended, and we are invited to think the relation between having the right to claim x and actually claiming x otherwise than as that of maximization and fulfillment. Thus precisely in not making his right felt and not claiming his due, the slighted lover may be, oddly enough, acquitting the debt owed to his and the other's dignity, even if such a "passing up" may often look like ascetic self-denial or a passive aggressive forcing of the other's hand.

36. See Weber, *The Protestant Ethic and the Spirit of Capitalism*, 162. I deliberately cite here and elsewhere from the 1611 King James Version to signal this text's specific formative impact on English literary imaginations in the "modern period."

for the world to enjoy and see by, the image of the buried talent left to languish in the dark comes to stand for not just a failure to develop, increase, and multiply one's God-given capital but a violation of the project of enlightenment itself.[37] In this section I'd like to make a brief survey of various expressions, both historical and contemporary, of this prevailing identification of virtuous action with the production of a concrete, manifest difference for the better, and the related emphasis on the good of exposing, disseminating, and making public one's "goods."[38] It is easy enough, especially for those of us wedded to the study of literature, to follow Adorno and Horkheimer in lampooning the philistine instrumentalism of an "Enlightenment" that cannot conceive of "unapplied" science and can only tolerate intellectual activities yielding measurable results and immediately shareable returns.[39] We become warier, however, of aban-

37. Here it is worth noting that the *OED* associates "the parable of the talents" in Matthew 25:14–30 not with the first and oldest definition of talent as an "ancient weight or money," but with its third definition of talent as "mental endowment, natural ability" appearing sometime in the first half of the fifteenth century (*OED*). The sense of talent as "power or ability of mind or body viewed as divinely entrusted to a person for use and improvement," current between the mid-fifteenth and mid-nineteenth centuries, and which has now given way to the more value-neutral "special natural ability or aptitude," best reflects the ideology I am referring to—the idea of my having a duty of stewardship toward the natural abilities I am given, of their not being "mine" to keep but only to make something of. It is, of course, precisely this notion (of personal abilities as a gift from God that won't have been dutifully received if denied a chance to flourish) that indicts aristocratic class privilege as not only arbitrary and unjust but as a sin against God; witness the complaint that under precapitalist aristocracy there is no "career open to talents" cited by William Empson with reference to Gray's "Elegy in a Country Churchyard" (see Empson, *Some Versions of Pastoral*, 4).

38. Giorgio Agamben provides a succinct definition of this conception of acting as "doing": "According to current opinion, all of man's doing—that of the artist and the craftsman as well as that of the workman and the politician—is praxis—manifestation of a will that produces a concrete effect. When we say that man has a productive status on earth, we mean, then, that the status of his dwelling on earth is a *practical* one" (Agamben, *The Man Without Content*, 68).

39. In the opening pages to their *Dialectic of Enlightenment* Horkheimer and Adorno attribute to Francis Bacon the pronouncement, "knowledge that tendeth but to satisfaction, is but as a courtesan, which is for pleasure, and not for

doning faith in the consequential good of enlightenment or "efficacy of knowledge per se" (Sedgwick, *Touching Feeling*, 138), when this demand for return (or expectation of a critical payoff) is recast, not as the crass, calculating "masculinist" worrying of time for material gain, but as the willingness to pay patient attention, whether in the hopes of opening the eyes of others to their ideological mystification, or of fostering recognition of previously neglected literary traditions, or even of correcting the misperception, indeed nonapprehension, of "queer," unaccountable practices such as the pointedly asocial, onanistic gesture of lighting a candle only to put it under a bed, a perversity that Mark, Matthew, and Luke all evoke only to dismiss as "impossible," but of which Helen Hunt Jackson appears to have found Dickinson all too capable.[40] Indeed, according to an irony of which this project is itself only too cognizant, the heroic, articulating energies of the enlightenment project never burn more intensely than when animating critical practices likely to be gendered "feminine" by the sensitivity of their attention to everything instrumental reason consigns to the trash heap of history as minor, nugatory, unworthy, insignificant, unreal. It is the power of the minor to fuel our gothic or, in Sedgwick's term, "paranoid," critical imaginations that prompts me to say that the texts about which I've written a book don't exist, or at least

---

fruit or generation" (2). The editors of the English translation refer to Bacon's "Valerius Terminus: Of the Interpretation of Nature," in which Bacon writes: "For I find that even those that have sought knowledge for itself . . . have nevertheless propounded to themselves a wrong mark, namely satisfaction, which men call truth, and not operation . . . which is the reason, why the learning that now is hath the curse of barrenness, and is courtesan-like, for pleasure, and not for fruit" (see Bacon, *Miscellaneous Tracts upon Human Philosophy*, 279–80). In the original German edition Adorno and Horkheimer only paraphrase Bacon as follows: "Das unfruchtbare Glück aus Erkenntnis ist lasziv für Bacon wie für Luther" (*Dialektik der Aufklärung* [Frankfurt am Main: Suhrkamp, 1984], 20–21).

40. "No *man*, when he hath lighted a candle, covereth it with a vessel, or putteth [it] under a bed; but setteth [it] on a candlestick, that they which enter in may see the light" (Luke 8:16; my emphasis). But apparently at least one woman did. In a letter from 1884 Jackson again exhorts Dickinson to allow her poems to be printed: "It is a cruel wrong to your 'day & generation' that you will not give them light. . . . I do not think we have a right to with hold from the world a word or a thought any more than a *deed*, which might help a single soul" (Dickinson, *The Letters of Emily Dickinson*, letter 937a, Sep. 1884).

remain unrecognizable on our critical radars, a claim I explain in section iii through a reading of Simone Weil's "unachieved" play *Venise sauvée*.

A later section of this chapter will address what might be thought of as the legacy of the countervailing command to do good only in secrecy, in ways unknown even to oneself: "But when thou doest alms, let not thy left hand know what thy right hand doeth. / That thine alms may be in secret; and thy Father which seeth in secret himself shall reward thee openly" (Matthew 6:3–4). This surprising vindication not simply of secrecy but of "unknowingness" finds an echo in the ways in which Western culture has historically defined feminine virtue as not knowing (modesty) and not doing (chastity), an issue I address most explicitly in my concluding chapter, on *Mansfield Park*.[41] At the same time, as a scandalous exception

41. It is perhaps this book's own open secret that it is often implicitly but rarely explicitly and certainly never singly a question of "woman" as disappearing act—of Western culture's figuring of femininity as that which appears only to disappear. One excuse for this overdetermined reticence is that I've wagered on the hope that the work of an earlier, more object-determined feminist criticism showing the inextricability of gender from other categories of difference has brought us to a point of no longer needing to name "woman" when assuming (or critiquing) the perspective of certain routinely feminized figures. But another reason I haven't drawn on gender as a separate analytical category when framing this project is that my intention has been less to expose the gendering of a certain passiveness of display—a habit of taking cover in the open and a negligence with respect to either showing or not showing—as the site of an oppression of which women have been both victims and perpetrators (especially insofar as sexual modesty has also been coded "white" and "middle-class" and public indifference deemed a "noble" prerogative)—than to trace the odd conjunctures of opportunism and virtue that emerge when one maps the often theologically inflected ethical reclaiming of passivity (in discourses on "grace," "love," "wise passiveness," etc.) onto its sociohistoric feminization *and* identification with aristocratic privilege. My own critical obliquity aims to keep in touch with the ironies by which least expectations meet greatest demands and what might seem heroic turns out to be effortless or unhelped, as when, for example, a position naturalized as feminine—say, the silence by which the "full," pensive classical text in Barthes' *S/Z* quietly solicits only to decline interpretation—is, in a different context, revalued as the suspension of the appropriative violence of claims to mastery and knowledge, or when the call not to count is addressed to a subject also interpellated as feminine so that it's as if she were suddenly called on to perform as the highest good, the most exacting sacrifice, precisely what she'd always been told was all she could do "by nature."

to the Greek imperative "know thyself," this strange call to heedlessness—
"do not advertise; do not add up; above all, do not count—remember to
forget"—not only momentarily suspends the usual identification of moral
conscience and consciousness, but presents the aporia of a command to
obliviousness, which to heed is to betray and to forget is to obey, and in
this it has obvious affinities with the often similarly vexed reclaiming of
passivity and nonmanifestation as the site of the ethical found in certain
strains of post-Enlightenment thought. Indeed, the suspension of relation
between the two hands, which releases the gift of alms, however temporarily, from the circuit of exchange (anticipation and return, sacrifice and
reward) in which charity is usually caught, might be taken as a figure
for the numerous tropes of passive agency, singularity, and nonrelation
informing postmodern ethical thought.[42] "Postmodern" insofar as they

42. In addition to Levinas, I am thinking of Blanchot's Levinasian-inflected
resistance to daylight modes of "appropriative comprehension"—what Blanchot
himself might nonpejoratively call the "obscurantism" of his Orpheus-like attempts to remain in a nonspecular, nonmimetic relation with the other in the
dark (without the security of cognitive orientation)—audible in the paradoxical quest to bear witness to the "obscure" in its "obscurity" or unavailability to
representational mastery (see "How to Discover the Obscure?" in Blanchot, *The
Infinite Conversation*, 40–48). The suggestion in the verse from Matthew that
one hand might do "unawares" more than the concerted effort of two together
also speaks to Blanchot's and Levinas's theorization of a "non-power that would
not be the simple negation of power" (ibid., 44) and, more generally, to the
trope of doing in weakness—from penury (Luke 21:4) or lack—what no degree
of strength, richness, or masterful forethought could achieve, a trope which Ann
Smock has recently movingly traced in Blanchot, Melville, des Forêts, and Beckett: "What is called for is different from anything you can do. But doesn't the
call appeal also to something you are unable *not* to do? Answer ahead of time,
that is, in advance of the question? Doesn't the call also call for a response you
are powerless to refrain from giving—a swift answer given impatiently, a heedless
answer that escapes you?" (Smock, *What Is There to Say?*, 5).
    Another obvious reference for the questioning of the priority of public acts
and calculable obligations is Derrida's work on the secret of ethical responsibility via Kierkegaard's reading of Abraham's decision (see Derrida, *The Gift of
Death*). But it is the Kierkegaard of *Works of Love* who explicitly links the verse
from Matthew to the concept of an infinite, incalculable debt (178), and who
confronts us with the irony that the struggle to free "love" from historical consciousness only entails another kind of ever-waking vigilance, similar to that

reject the evangelist's counterbalancing assurance of divine omniscience less on secular grounds than out of a kind of resolute despair of final judgments, these "antiocular" discourses sometimes risk, by the very austerity of their protest against calculability, hyperbolizing as a mode of secret heroism the readiness to go unrecorded. In section v I will address more explicitly the problem of infinitization, whereby the very call not to publicize and not to count "accomplished deeds" produces a discontent and restless vigilance more harrowing than the master's demand for manifest returns on the talents he has entrusted to his servants.

But lest readers fear I am moving toward a simple binary, opposing an ethics based on "good works" (associated with the parable of the talents) to one founded on "grace" (exemplified by Matthew 6:3), let me begin this survey of the various judgments that Western modernity passes on the servant's "failure" to do more than return the loaned talent as it was given him, by noting that only a philistine reader would reduce the parable to a crude legitimization of the acquisitive principle underwriting capitalism or positivist application of the biblical command, "Be fruitful and multiply." For the master's provisional distribution of talents to his servants is a gift conditional on the servants' making something of it; the servant who does no more than return unchanged exactly what he believes he has been given for safekeeping errs not in failing to obey instructions but in failing to write the law for himself. Imagination, license, and free play belong instead to the first two servants, who recognize the master's gift as one of absence, not presence—not the talent itself, but the chance to stray across boundaries, to decide for oneself where one's person and property stop and the other's begins. In this respect we can easily imagine how

---

which sustains the very precision of Derrida's own indefatigable questioning of available modes of responsibility: "there must be eternal vigilance, early and late, so that love never begins to dwell on itself, or to compare itself with love in other people, or to compare itself with the deeds that it has accomplished" (Kierkegaard, *Works of Love*, 179). Whatever the irony of this "call not to count," this last formulation makes particularly clear the ways in which these writers include as an essential moment within ethical responsiveness the dropping of the burden of historical memory—the refusal to decide on what is called for by comparison with past deeds, etc.—and in this sense, it is not surprising that a historian—Dominick LaCapra—has been one of the sternest critics of this turn toward "patience" and what he calls the "transcendent sublime" (see LaCapra, *History in Transit*, 148–51).

much this parable urging an expansive spirit of self-reliance and initiative must have spoken to the secularizing and democratizing project of early modernity. Indeed, in his essay "Modes of Political and Historical Time in Early Eighteenth-Century England," J. G. A. Pocock describes the transition toward a speculative economy based on credit and public debt, under which it became impossible simply to do as the "unprofitable" servant does: "Since a credit mechanism was an expansive and dynamic social device, the beliefs men had to form and maintain concerning one another were more than simple expectations of another's capacity to pay what he had borrowed, to perform what he had promised; they were boomtime beliefs, obliging men to credit one another with capacity to expand and grow and become what they are not."[43] The momentum of Pocock's sentence here captures wonderfully the sense of possibility opened up by the affirmative humanist promise that the world need not be as we find it, that nothing is determined at birth, and that everything may come of anyone, even as his argument exposes the economic conditions necessitating the belief in "the progress of the arts" and the development of "an ideology . . . of [a] secular and historical future"—"something society had never possessed before."[44]

This idea of a "secular and historical future," of which only other humans will be the judge, may in fact account for why the question with which one might suppose the master to meet his servants upon his return—"what do you have to *show* for your time?"—returns so urgently in the positivist assumptions of mid-twentieth-century behaviorist and analytical models of ethical action, as described by Iris Murdoch close to forty years ago: "Nothing counts as an act unless it is a 'bringing about of

43. Pocock, *Virtue, Commerce, and History*, 98.
44. See also Habermas's related argument, in the first chapter to *The Philosophical Discourse of Modernity*, linking the unprecedented experience of "the pressure of time" to modernity's "expectation of the differentness of the future" (6): "Whereas in the Christian West the 'new world' had meant the still-to-come age of the world of the future, which was to dawn only on the last day . . . the secular concept of modernity expresses the conviction that the future has already begun: It is the epoch that lives for the future, that opens itself up to the novelty of the future" (5). Michael McKeon's discussion of Weber's thesis in relation to the dialectical effects of Protestant soteriology's initial rejection of "mediation by external signs and powers" is also relevant here (see McKeon, *The Origins of the English Novel, 1600–1740*, 190–200).

a recognizable change in the world'"; "salvation by works is a conceptual necessity"; "self-knowledge is something which shows overtly."[45] A similar tendency to attach guilt to unused powers or uncommitted acts—to insist on the trauma of having had the power to do *x* and not having done it, or having seen *x* and not having made it available to others—marks, I argue in my third chapter, the new historicist criticism of Romantic lyricism. The positivist skepticism according to which the reality of our experiences depends on our establishing their continued existence within a represented whole, corresponds, I argue there, to the historicist unwillingness to allow anyone to go uncounted—excluded from public space, first in the sense of being denied decision-making power, then in that of being left out of the testimony of representative cultural figures. Such criticism reflects the premise, central to secular modernity's progressive humanism, that in the absence of a recording angel of history, inner conviction requires declaration just as knowledge compels action—that rather than keep our observations and insights to ourselves, we should act in light of what we know, and only in that light, or risk the charge of moral and political quietism.[46] In other words, if the new historicist project of expos-

45. Murdoch, *The Sovereignty of Good*, 5, 15, 16. Murdoch's book is particularly useful to this project in its emphasis on the morally active dimensions of mental acts such as perception, reflection, and acknowledgment. These states of continuous mental activity are not easy to dramatize as single outward events; the difference they make in outward behavior is never obvious, for the way in which a person thinks about or looks at an other may or may not correspond to the way in which she treats that other. But as Murdoch reminds us, "'Not a report' need not entail 'not an activity'" (24). She gives as an example the story of "M," the mother-in-law whose outward treatment of her daughter-in-law, "D," is from the beginning what it should be, but whose regard for "D" changes over time from carefully hidden dislike to unfeigned love.

46. I cite—somewhat at random, to give a sense of the continued currency of this attitude—Martha Nussbaum's recent faulting of Bernard Williams for his lack of demonstrative anger at the world: "Contempt, world-weariness, cynicism, even an irritability linked to the world-weariness, but never just *anger*, the sense that wrong has been done and that one had better go out and right it. I think his non-angry attitude to tragedy was of a piece with his critique of the Enlightenment: doing good for a bad world did not energize him, because his attitude to the world was at some level without hope. The world was a mess, and there was no saving or even improving it" (Nussbaum, "Tragedy and Justice," 39).

ing hidden violences and rescuing silenced voices is often weighted with a Benjaminian redemptive cast and a sometimes naive, self-important faith in the moral efficacy of representation, it is precisely because, incredulous of divine justice and disabused of any hope of redemption through world revolution, it can no longer afford to credit Benjamin's speculative claim that "one might . . . speak of an unforgettable life or moment, even if all men had forgotten it."[47]

In contrast to the positivist models of action criticized by Murdoch as excessively restrictive, late-twentieth-century developments in critical theory have significantly broadened our conception of what counts as action by focusing our attention on the potency of immaterial speech acts and on the very tangible effects of merely virtual, inoperative powers held in reserve. Queer theory, for example, has highlighted the limits imposed on gay identity by the policing of knowledge rather than of behavior per se; as Sedgwick has argued in *Epistemology of the Closet*, the "closet" is defined by the release or containment of volatile information rather than by the performance of sexual acts.[48] Thanks to the popularizing work of Žižek in articulating the political ramifications of Lacanian psychoanalysis, we have gotten used to thinking of ideological, phallic power in the feminine—as precisely that which does not actualize itself but remains *effective* only insofar as it keeps itself in reserve and holds the place of an absence.[49] More than forty years ago J. L. Austin was already correcting the tendency "to assume" that "ethics are . . . simply in the last resort *physical movements*," and in her *Excitable Speech* Judith Butler returns to the "tran-

47. "The Task of the Translator," in Benjamin, *Illuminations*, 70. For a more recent expression of the ethical imperative to count (and an exemplification of the logic by which narrative representation becomes synonymous with the "actualization of a human being" within the context of the democratizing impulses of nineteenth-century bourgeois individualism), see Alex Woloch's *The One vs. the Many: Minor Characters and the Space of the Protagonist in the Novel*. Woloch phrases his study's axiom in terms of the following question: "How can a human being enter into a narrative world and not disrupt the distribution of attention?" (Woloch, *The One vs. the Many*, 25, 26).

48. See, in addition to Sedgwick, Leo Bersani's provocative redefinition of the struggle for gay liberation as a group's attempt to "make itself unidentifiable even as it demands to be recognized" (Bersani, *Homos*, 31–32).

49. See Žižek's figure of the master as "impostor . . . [one] whose whole consistency hinges upon the deferral, the keeping-in-reserve, of a force that he falsely claims to possess" (Žižek, *Tarrying with the Negative*, 160).

sitivity" of language implied by Austin's title *How to Do Things with Words* to argue that the "wounding power" of "injurious speech" is not only real but exceeds traditional juridical models of accountability.[50] Similarly, the psychoanalytic theorization of trauma, as a wound whose original failure to transpire occasions its repeated "(re)occurrence" within the subject, has taught us to recognize the paradox of an event that takes place only after first failing to take place, a drama constituted as such by an original failure of presence or, in Lacan's terms, an "encounter" that happens not despite its being missed but only insofar as it is missed, missed at the time itself and then again after the fact, when retroactively experienced by the subject for the first time as a repetition.

One of the questions raised by these attempts to take into account the psychic, political, and ethical consequence of "merely" ideational states is whether they only reinforce the empiricist tendency to define action by its measurable consequence. (Butler's work renders the limits of the empiricist assumptions vividly apparent by arguing that language, when it "wounds," does not do so in a way "attributable to a singular subject and act" [*Excitable Speech*, 50].) Indeed, we may have moved so far in the direction of registering the political reverberations of even the most singular, nongenerative—in French one might say *insolite*—of gestures, that we cannot believe anyone ever *simply* buries her talent in the ground. Yet these critiques still leave us wondering where to put thoughts and desires to which we cannot or will not give consequence or empirical result. This project has emerged, in part, as a response to this problem—as an attempt to consider, at least for a moment, never-acted-upon passions and uncounted experiences not as *no*s disguising incipient, concealed, or denied affirmatives but rather as aimless, innocent, minimal, all but negative, contented affirmations.

In seeking to cut a way between the crude consequentialist positivism that denies the evidence of things unseen and our more familiar gothic critical imagination that reads for hidden meanings and lost histories, thus far I have chiefly presented the ethos of "making little happen" as an

50. See Austin, *How to Do Things with Words*, 19; and Butler, *Excitable Speech*, 43–69 ("Burning Acts, Injurious Speech"). This by no means exhaustive sketch of the critical work done on the rhetoricity of power, the violence of language, and the material effects of symbolic acts, might also include thinkers as disparate as Derrida, Foucault, and Kenneth Burke.

alternative to the overly narrow definitions of action as production and articulation associated with Western modernity's ideology of improvement, and I can easily imagine a skeptical reader saying at this point, "All well and good, but haven't we already heard this critique, whether of instrumental reason's demand for measurable results and fruits on the hour or of logocentrism's demand for manifest, positive presence?" (A more serious objection would be "Why assume the deferral of metaphysical presence has any oppositional value in a culture of perpetually deferred satisfaction?") In the following sections, I want to suggest more precisely how "reticent assertion" differs from the recuperative ethos of deconstruction-inspired feminist and melancholic new historicist critical models that work under the assumption that what we take for presence is really hollowed out by absence and that what we dismiss as absence or lack is the effect of self-withdrawn, hidden presence.

"You can never be melancholy enough"; "you can never be paranoid enough": so, following Žižek and Sedgwick, one might render the clichéd slogans of our critical moment.[51] The structure of negated or absented positive presence shared by melancholy and paranoia presents perhaps no stronger instance of the repudiation of teleological energies and positivist demands on time within the experience of capitalism itself.[52] Thus, according to Žižek the melancholic is tacitly commended for not getting over her loss, for refusing easy closure and remaining instead attached to the loss of the lost object, secretly faithful to an essentially and permanently nonpresentable ideal and thus wedded to the aftermath of teleological history characteristic of late capitalist (post)modernity. Similarly, like those PowerBar-consuming joggers who choose to run in the midday heat as if in advance of the duress of global climate change, the paranoid reader, as presented by Sedgwick, makes a virtue of scarcity, feeding off the slightest indications to confirm both the continued hidden presence of a plotting hand and the reader's own knowing relation to it: "Paranoia is of all forms of love . . . the most ascetic, *the love that demands least from its object*" (*Touching Feeling*, 132). In this respect, Sedgwick's paranoid

51. See Žižek, "Melancholy and the Act," 658; and Sedgwick, *Touching Feeling*, 127.

52. For one such argument putting melancholic divestiture at the center rather than at the contestatory margins of capitalist consumerist culture, see Levinson, "Object-Loss and Object-Bondage."

reader shares with Kermode's strong "spiritual" reader, as with Lynch's well-trained reader of novelistic inwardness, the expansive, fertile powers of an interpretive imagination capable of filling in the gaps and making *much* of the simplest, barest, least promising text, a power that differs, I want to suggest in the following pages, from the practice of making *do* with little.

Happily devoid of "tangible products and demonstrable profits," Lafayette's heroine and the speakers of Wordsworth's, Dickinson's, and Hardy's poems might appear to be, and certainly have often been read as, melancholics and paranoiacs.[53] Yet just as paranoia, on Sedgwick's account, does not defend against negative affect per se, only the *surprise* of pain (as of joy, Wordsworth might add), so too our paranoid habits of reading these figures as paranoid (or melancholic or passive aggressive, etc.) may protect us from registering the surprise of the open secret's simple "thereness." The following sections will present instances of a type of strangely immaterial, virginal, negative or renunciatory "act" of desistance or leaving untouched: an action particularly difficult to recognize as such, because, even as it does not constitute the expansion, development, or realization of latent potential (as in the model of productive action I associate with the parable of talents above), it also does not simply perpetuate the deferral of endbound realization as melancholic divestiture might.

iii. chastity belts for trees

In its earliest incarnation, in fact, this book began as a thought-experiment prompted by the strange value accorded to "doing nothing" or "as little as possible" within popularly inspired Thoreauvian environmentalist discourse. Working in the mid-1990s out of a Greenpeace canvassing office, I was struck by the insouciance with which, in apparent contrast with the Puritan work ethos, popular environmentalist slogans such as "tread lightly on the earth" or "take only pictures and leave only footprints" seemed to commend rather than punish planetary sojourners for making

53. Sedgwick's description of paranoia as a "monopolistic strategy of anticipating negative affect" and "forestalling pain" (*Touching Feeling*, 136–37) invites comparison, for example, to the apparent defensiveness of the Princess of Clèves' assertion that she would rather not marry Nemours than see him fall out of love with her, a comparison difficult to refute except through attention to the lightness with which she assumes the certainty of this contingency.

no difference and returning as they began—all but empty-handed. Yet these negative, minimizing directives, together with the virgin-baiting evident in the rhetoric of "pristine" ecosystems to be left untouched and undeveloped, quickly pointed to the political limitations of an environmental activism kept perpetually on the defensive because unable to articulate its demands except in the negative, or to offer an alternative to human action conceived as the violent appropriation, harnessing, and inevitable exhaustion of natural resources.[54] Like the modest woman of eighteenth-century conduct books, we conservationists could do no more, it seemed, than resist, deny, limit, mitigate, and delay, but never in the end escape, the rapacity of modern economic development, so tenacious was the habit of thinking of positive action as the actualization of potency.

At the very end of the twentieth century, critical works of quite different persuasions and orientations, from Kaja Silverman's *World Spectators* to Shierry Nicholsen's *The Love of Nature and the End of the World: The Unspoken Dimensions of Environmental Concern*, revived the insights of early-twentieth-century phenomenology into the "work" of disclosing Being—the creative act of letting the other appear; these works have made us more willing to acknowledge the "half-creative, half-perceptive" activity involved in environmental consciousness, something an earlier positivism would have dismissed as either "merely" passive perception or all-too-active projection. In the mid-1990s, however, the bias toward pictorial mimesis defining the activism of the culture wars and identity politics still meant that to exert power was to take up representational space, and there was little room for crediting the agency of the act of bearing witness to the given, an action difficult to show as such even if it is itself what makes

54. Andrew Ross had just published his *Chicago Gangster Theory of Life*, accusing environmentalists of being the new Puritans invoking the authority of Nature to curb human activity, appetites, and desires. Bruno Latour's *Politiques de la nature* provides a possible response to the charge; for Latour, the revolutionary power of "political ecology" lies precisely in its refusal of the binary separating politics as the sphere of human deliberation from nature as the realm of "indisputable nonhuman laws"—the same binary between action and being that, according to Hans Blumenberg's early thesis on Western modernity, put human creative energies at war with the given and caused progressive scientific inquiry and artistic exploration to take the form of a "violent countermovement" or backlash against the weight of the natural world (see Blumenberg, "'Imitation of Nature'").

the visible possible. The thought-experiment with which I began, then, was to ask whether one could imagine a counterexample to the act of taking possession of a territory and declaring it "mine," which Rousseau famously allegorized as the origin of civil society—a countermove that would be more than mere inaction, more than the indefinite avoidance of taking of positions of power, whether theoretical, symbolic, or physical, and postponement of claims: a double turn in the lock of nonpossession, a pointing that would give notice of an unrealized x and, just as surely and swiftly, put it irretrievably "off limits," beyond development.[55]

The results of this somewhat quixotic quest to radicalize ecologically minded nonintervention involved comparing the mild stealth of the hiker, who enters the forest to leave it more or less as he found it, to the stronger if equally invisible artistry of the eco-activist, who comes to drive nails into trees, not to harm them but to raise to the point of deterrence the cost of cutting them down: the one comes to change nothing or as little as possible, the other to change everything, except nothing actual, only the old-growth forest's potential market value. Tree-spiking—Earth First!'s controversial, often ineffective, and now abandoned practice of driving ceramic nails into old-growth trees so that they would, if logged, damage logging machinery—was indeed my first example of the open secret, in the first place because it allowed me to think *as an act* the disappearance or cancellation of unused potential, and in the second place because, in ideal circumstances, it exemplified an act complete at the moment of its being publicized.[56] Indeed, as an action requiring announce-

55. In the *Second Discourse on the Origin and Foundations of Inequality Between Men*, Rousseau gives the following parable for the origin of "civil society": "The first who, having enclosed a piece of land, bethought himself to say '*this is mine*,' and found people simple enough to believe him, was the true founder of civil society" ("Le premier qui, ayant enclos un terrain, s'avisa de dire: *Ceci est à moi*, et trouva des gens assez simples pour le croire, fut le vrai fondateur de la société civile" [*Discours sur l'origine et les fondements de l'inégalité parmi les hommes*, 107]).

56. In *Confessions of an Eco-Warrior* Dave Foreman summarizes the dialectic of publicity and hiddenness splitting in two the time of the act's occurrence—the moment of its being done and that of its taking effect: tree spikers act covertly but must give notice of—literally in most cases, flag—their acts after the fact if these are to be effective:

First, ecodefenders should recognize spiking as an extreme measure, to be

ment—but of a kind so slight it can bear no rhetoric of persuasion and must be immediately credited as such (otherwise, the swiftest means to test the spiker's word would be to cut down the tree)—the example of tree spiking can help distinguish what I'm defining as reticent assertion from a simple refusal or deferral of verbalization. By arming trees with a power to harm that she hopes they will never actually have to use on chain-saws, the tree spiker obviously does something more than the hiker who merely minimizes his impact, but the "what" of this "something more" escapes our usual methods of accounting. On one level, the tree spiker appears simply to render further untouchable—a little more beyond reach—something already experienced as differently inaccessible, to the extent that the environmentally conscious hiker relates to the redwood as something beyond human powers. We might say that by treating the tree unsentimentally, not as a living being but as a potential market value or dead wood, the spiker brings home the thought of its mortality. In fact, there is, I think, something Wordsworthian about the attempt to imagine

------

used only when other means fail. However, the safest time to spike a potential timber sale is years before it is to be cut. There is less likelihood of encountering forest rangers or timber bidders in the sale area then, and spiking years in advance allows the tree to grow bark over the spike, disguising it and making its discovery and removal more difficult. . . . If conventional means later stop the timber sale, fine; if they don't, then the spikes are already in the trees, and a warning can be made. (159)

This amazing image of trees growing bark over their spikes, so naturalizing their man-made defenses that the difference between spiked and unspiked trees becomes imperceptible and bark itself the sign of a hidden spike, still remains to my mind an extraordinary evocation of the politics and poetics of indistinction; the indistinctly spiked tree is the forests' equivalent to the trope of the stranger among us or God-made-man. Indeed, one of the means Foreman suggests for warning the Forest Service and companies of spiking is to "flag a spike high in a tree to warn of high, unflagged spikes in other trees in the stand." The flagged tree calls attention not so much to itself but to its likeness to other trees; forest-ers are meant to assume that spikers might have flagged all the trees they spiked but didn't or, in effect, that trees always show less than they have. But the sur-rounding trees might have been spiked ten years ago or they might not have been spiked at all; the same ambiguity allows spikers indefinitely to extend the ground they claim to have covered and to claim more in effect than what they have actually performed.

or live experientially the difference—the "before" and "after" of a spiking of towering redwoods. For being put out of reach, the trees are quite as suddenly brought nearer in that one gets a sudden sense of the possibility of their death avoided. The very thought of trees being spiked might thus produce the sudden realization that one is living in a museum, but is nature felt to be more or less alive, more or less mortal for now being artificially preserved?

The literary works to which I turn in the chapters to come furnish perhaps less far-fetched examples of this type of minimally inflected transition from the latency of unactualized, dormant possibility (with its attendant, residual temporality of suspended hope and quiet waiting) to "more" absolute privation—a change difficult to show as such from the presence of something missed, left unrealized, to its actual disappearance.[57]

57. Another way of putting the quest to believe in (and skepticism about) environmentalist practices of "letting alone" and "leaving untouched," with which this project first began, would be as the question, "How do you know when something, say a lost love-object, has *really* been given up?" In his 1926 essay "The Problem of Acceptance of Unpleasant Ideas—Advances in Knowledge of the Sense of Reality," Sándor Ferenczi evokes "the behaviour of . . . rotiferae which remain dried up for years waiting for moisture" (on contact with which they are suddenly resuscitated) to describe a common psychological response to loss that "looks like adaptation" but in fact involves an "attitude of interminable waiting and hoping for the return of the 'good old times'" and only amounts to a "provisional" recognition of loss—an "obedience under protest, so to speak, with the mental reservation of a *restitutio in integrum*" (Ferenczi, *Further Contributions to the Theory and Technique of Psycho-Analysis*, 376). I am grateful to Rei Terada for pointing me to this passage.

iv. *"Untouched by morning -/And untouched by noon -"*

Like a book at evening beautiful but untrue,
Like a book on rising beautiful and true.

—Stevens, "Auroras of Autumn"

Earth has not anything to show more fair:
Dull would he be of soul who could pass by
A sight so touching in its majesty:
This City now doth, like a garment, wear
The beauty of the morning; silent, bare,
Ships, towers, domes, theatres, and temples lie
Open unto the fields, and to the sky;
All bright and glittering in the smokeless air.
Never did sun more beautifully steep
In his first splendour, valley, rock, or hill;
Ne'er saw I, never felt, a calm so deep!
The river glideth at his own sweet will:
Dear God! the very houses seem asleep;
And all that mighty heart is lying still!

—Wordsworth, "Composed upon Westminster Bridge"

I turn now to Simone Weil's unfinished play *Venise sauvée* (begun in the summer of 1940 and left unfinished at her death in 1943), as an example of a drama that a positivist empiricism would have difficulty recognizing as such but that even the most expansive psychological narration would not render more obvious. According to Weil's unpublished drafts, the play would have ended as follows:

Sur la mer s'étend lentement la clarté.
La fête bientôt va combler nos désirs.
La mer calme attend. Qu'ils sont beaux sur la mer,
Les rayons du jour!
Rideau[58]

[Light slowly extends over the sea.
The feast will soon fulfill our desires.
The calm sea awaits. How beautiful they are on the sea,
The rays of daylight!
Curtain]

58. Weil, *Poèmes, suivis de* Venise sauvée, 134. The English translations are my own.

Light spreads over the sea in the absence of enlightenment, unmarred by the traditional reversal and recognition of Aristotelian tragedy. The sun rises as usual on a city delivered from a danger it has not even known to fear. Not only saved, but saved unawares, Venice awakens to a beauty it has not lost the power to take for granted. Weil appears to have shared with Madame de Lafayette a talent for the imaginative exercise of considering the present—the status quo in all its surface visibility and exposure to the naked eye—not simply as the fruit of history but as the (non)record of events that failed to transpire. For this play about an averted coup (we might call it *a coup de grâce* if the term retained its more literal meanings) dramatizes the deflection rather than unfolding of a plot; it bears witness not to the manifestation of a transformative will but to its recession—the kenosis or movement of self-contraction by which the present is granted what it almost already has—power for one more day.[59]

Briefly the plot of the play is as follows: a group of Spanish mercenaries have prepared to seize the city of Venice for the Spanish crown.[60] The Venetian authorities suspect nothing, and the plan is guaranteed complete success. Even a minor hitch—at the last minute the leader of the group is unexpectedly called away on other business—appears to turn to good effect as it gives the leader an occasion to show his best friend, Jaffier, his trust by ceding him his place. The Venetians for their part are hardly likable as unsuspecting targets of violence; taken in what Kant would call their pathological particularity, they have no more claim to justice and virtue than do the band of mercenaries. Thus Violetta, who speaks the play's last words, will never hear the brash hollowness of her joyful familial and civic pride.

On the evening of the planned coup, Jaffier watches the sun set over

59. As I show in Chapter 2, Lafayette's historical fiction similarly does not depart from the official record, positing no expansive counterfactuals—only innocent supplements explaining how *x* or *y* failed to take place.

60. Weil acknowledges as her source the Abbé de Saint Réal's *Conjuration des Espagnols contre Venise en 1618* (1664). See also Otway's *Venice Preserved* (1682); and, for a similar if "insider" plot of thwarted conspiracy and betrayed allegiances, Byron's *Mario Faliero* (1821). Central to Weil's reprisal of this plot in the summer of 1940 would have been the French decision earlier that spring not to resist the Nazis' entrance into Paris in order to spare the city destruction. See John Williams's account in *The Ides of May: The Defeat of France, May–June 1940* (London: Constable, 1968).

the naked city and reflects on how the city already lies unsuspectingly in the palm of his hand—as exposed to his power and will as it is to the setting sun's nearing rays. In the next scene we hear Jaffier announce to one of the co-conspirators that he will "execute what he has decided"; the curtain falls, and act 3 opens on the following morning. In between, Jaffier has confessed the plot to the Council of Venice, demanding only immunity for his friends by way of reward, a request that the council has initially agreed to honor and then ignored by having them all arrested. As Weil herself describes it, the third and final act is structured as a chiasm, alternating between Jaffier, who cries for his friends' release and whom no one answers, and the friends, who, condemned to torture and execution, imprecate Jaffier as a traitor and whom he does not answer.

Significantly, rather than enacting it in speech, Weil offers only a summary report of the scene of disclosure; when asked his motivation for the revelation, Jaffier is reported to have said "pity." Weil's narrative reticence makes sense when we consider that even my rudimentary paraphrase of Jaffier's soliloquy on the fatal evening already gives the active reader too much to work with by way of psychological detail; we may, for example, imagine that Jaffier pulls back out of a latent ambivalence over the exercise of power—perhaps he finds its touch intolerable, or, to follow Winnicott, he suffers from an unbearable fantasy of omnipotence because he lacks a sense of the world's resilience, having never tried to destroy it as a child. Or he may secretly resent his friend's generous act of trust and cannot stand being thought so "good."

However Weil might finally have chosen to dramatize Jaffier's decision to "save" Venice and alert the authorities, the lines probably would have elicited comparable overinterpretation. The extant version toys with, only in the end to shun, melodramatic convention. Thus if Violetta obviously corresponds to the conventional love interest, who comes between and divides homosocial alliances, the play abstains from using even these flimsy devices to generate the crisis: Jaffier responds to no tearful appeal to his conscience on Violetta's part; all Violetta does is assert the confidence that Venice's beauty is its own defense, in response to which Jaffier first articulates his act as a historical impossibility, unheard of in human affairs: "Child, don't you know that a city never was preserved by an enemy's pity?" Otherwise no scene of agonized conflict between two sorts of loyalties leads up to his decision, for it is essential that nothing or all but nothing prompt his desistance from a plot he has only to carry out.[61] Even so, for all the script's concerted minimalism, only the brief notations to the projected play that Weil made in her personal notebooks seem able to render, without psychologizing, the revolution that takes place when Jaffier cedes before the consciousness that Venice exists:

> Acte II. Faire sentir que le recul de Jaffier est surnaturel.
> Jaffier. Il est surnaturel d'arrêter le temps.
> C'est là que l'éternité entre dans le temps.
> Croire à la réalité du monde extérieur et l'aimer, ce n'est qu'une seule et même chose.
> En fin de compte, l'organe de la croyance est l'amour surnaturel, même à l'égard des choses d'ici-bas.
> Dès que Jaffier s'aperçoit que Venise *existe* . . .
> Croire qu'une chose existe et la détruire, il faut un devoir vraiment impérieux. (47–48)

> [Act II. Make (the audience) feel that Jaffier's retreat is supernatural.
> Jaffier. It's supernatural to stop time.
> That's where eternity enters time.
> To believe in the reality of the external world and to love it, are one and the same thing.
> In the end, the organ of belief is supernatural love, even with respect to earthly things.
> From the moment that Jaffier realizes/notices that Venice *exists* . . .
> To believe that something exists and to destroy it, takes a truly imperious duty.]

Projecting the unwritten play into the abstract present of interpretation, these notebook entries better "realize" Weil's vision of a barely perceptible arrest of—and skip in—human time, just as her failure of execution at the level of composition mirrors the negative action—a staying of the hand of history—it attempts to represent.[62] As Weil's notes make clear,

61. When I recount the play to filmmaker Cathy Crane (whose film *Unoccupied Zone: The Impossible Life of Simone Weil* [2005] is about the time Weil spent in Marseille during the war), she laughs in disbelief at the idea of a playwright who creates the dramatic disruption necessary to plot simply by having her hero "change his mind"—a cop-out so easy it is difficult for the skilled dramaturge to imagine.

62. This arrest *and* immediate resumption of time presents the greatest stumbling block to the pseudonymous Johannes de Silentio of Kierkegaard's *Fear and*

the difficulty of making a plot of Jaffier's "recul" lies, in part, in its being decided by a mere act of perception—something that would seem both below and beyond the temporal scale of human effort, that must either always have been possible or never at all. Nothing more than his taking notice of Venice's existence causes Jaffier to change his mind and stay his hand, and nothing or very little prompts this taking notice. Weil's attribution of the capacity to make the observation "that x exists" to the power of divine love only underscores the non-epiphanic, unplottable nature of such revelation: the perception of sufficiency requires supernatural force, precisely because nothing has happened—nor can happen—to give Venice any more reality than what it already has.

I offer this consideration of Weil's *Venise sauvée* as my first reading of a literary text to make as vivid as possible the difference between the interest of the authors included in this study (and my own) in perceiving the present as the effect of a desistance (a fully consummated act, however negatively inflected as withdrawal) and a more "romantic" or recuperative historicism whose searching gaze continues to scan the present for traces of unfinished histories. Weil forestalls the surface-depth dialectic

---

Trembling, as he meditates on a similar story of a wordlessly averted sacrifice. Indeed, in class discussions of Kierkegaard's text I've found there invariably comes a moment when students wonder out loud at the uneventfulness of faith: how could Abraham receive again what he never thought to lose? Or, on the contrary, and this is de Silentio's question, how could he get Isaac back in any real sense after having drawn the knife to sacrifice him? Either Abraham wins back only what he already had or, in the opinion of the more tragically minded who do not accept the "undo-ability" of the movement of resigning Isaac to God, loses a son he must never have taken for real. How, otherwise, could he so wordlessly give Isaac up and then just as impassively get him back? Perhaps Abraham needed, in Silentio's words, "no preparation and no time to rally to finitude and its joy" upon Isaac's release, because, as a student suggests, he never believed in Isaac's reality except as a gift from God (Kierkegaard, *Fear and Trembling*, 37). This seems wrong to me if understood as saying that the miracle of Isaac's belated birth, which made Sarah laugh, also prevents Abraham from granting him the solidity of autonomous existence, so that Isaac never becomes more than a chimera, an in-itself-bracketable sign of Abraham's relation to God. But we come closer to Weil's sense of supernatural love's making possible belief in earthly things if, on the contrary, we understand Abraham's "faith" as the power to take Isaac as less than a miracle and credit him with finite actuality.

typically structuring interpretive practice; the expected irony of dawn rising on the bloody last act with the heroes' corpses strewn across the stage is precisely what is averted here; but so is the effort to go behind the day's beauty and demystify it as the illusion masking unseen human suffering, for if that beauty occurs at all, it is not in spite of but only thanks to, and as the very cause and fruit of, the play's action. The arguments of theorists of the novel—according to which novel readers are taught to see more than meets the eye and to exercise a kind of depth of vision, mining blank, unpromising, "impassive," and "incommunicative exteriors" for signs of hidden interiority—may shed light on Weil's choice to write *Venise sauvée* as a play, a genre weighted toward the simply visible, even though its plot hinges on an internal change of mind—a renewed perception of the world—to which no one in the play, not even Jaffier himself, bears witness. Imagination continues to supplement vision, but not, as usually happens, to long for or bring back what might have been, but to perceive the miraculous evacuation rather than fulfillment of historical possibility.[63]

In this sense Weil might simply have used Wordsworth's "Westminster" sonnet for Jaffier's soliloquy and the play's concluding lines, for her plotting of how the sun was permitted to rise on a city as usual appears almost to provide the objective correlative to the breathlessness of near escape— the quieted urgency and happy relief of the quotidian exception—informing the speaker's ecstatically whispered hyperboles in the face of the city's waking sleep. What shocks in both Wordsworth's sonnet and Weil's play is the apparent unwillingness to disturb or penetrate below the surface of a city's unthinking serenity. Rather than unmask as false consciousness the illusion of safety in London's heedlessly enjoyed existence, Wordsworth's

63. In her reading of the play, Ann Smock has captured this difference from our more "normal" interpretive habits most clearly:

> What clear eyes see here—eyes, that is, that just give up, turn away and close—is not more but less, miraculously less than there might have been by a miracle: a sun left to shine and rain left to fall on the righteous and the wicked alike, tides left to ebb and flow, waves left to curl and crash over broken ships, left to their unhesitating, shapely movements by a weak and bleeding God who leaves himself to die under the sun, under the sun which that very day causes crowns and scepters to glitter beautifully just as on the day before. Likewise, the world transfigured by grace is the world minus this very marvel. (Smock, "Doors," 851–52)

speaker is content to register the strange mixture of vulnerability and impudent self-display in the city's trusting openness to the skies. Similarly, Weil's title *Venise sauvée* indicates only the fruit of a finished action and nothing of the time of its happening; the city undergoes no transformative test or experience but is simply given back to itself; its blessing, as Smock suggests, is to have been doubly spared, saved from actual destruction and saved the very need to be grateful for such saving—in Dickinson's words, "Untouched by morning - / And untouched by noon -."[64]

So complete an annulment of plot and elision of even the knowledge of the averted threat presents a scandal to enlightenment-oriented readers, especially when contrasted with the much more typical role routinely assigned literature: that of registering the aftershocks of a rhetorical or self-retracted violence that penetrates the psyche all the more effectively the more it remains "merely" imagined or virtual.[65] It is as if these texts—and here I'm also thinking of the movement of temporal doubling between stanzas of "A slumber did my spirit seal" or "Safe in their Alabaster Chambers"—were attempting to present temporal succession—the passage from dawn to day, from one day to the next—as something other than either

64. All references to Dickinson's poetry are to R. W. Franklin's edition of *The Poems of Emily Dickinson*; poems are generally referred to by their first lines. When quoting Dickinson, I follow Franklin's adoption of her sometimes unorthodox grammar and spelling, and I reproduce her variants, when relevant, at the bottom of quoted passages, indicating with asterisks the words to which they correspond in the poem. Smock echoes Dickinson's lines from "Safe in their Alabaster Chambers" when she writes: "In Simone Weil's tragedy, *Venise sauvée*, the sun that rises every day, perfectly indifferent to the city's fortunes, bathes with its lovely light a city which has come through the night miraculously unscathed. In the bright morning Venice awakens exactly as it does every morning: not only unmoved by grief but untouched by gratitude. Unenlightened. The miracle does not make the slightest difference. The city is perfectly innocent—of its salvation, which just leaves it alone, all its polished hardness intact, its worldly splendor immaculate" (Smock, "Doors," 852).

65. One has only to think, for example, of Keats's "This Living Hand" or Dickinson's "'Twas like a Maelstrom" to remember the sufficiency of imaginative exercise in inflicting and receiving violence. Hyperbolic assertions of the irrevocable, lingering power of imaginative identification, these poems perform the impossibility of "reprieve" by giving the last word to the sumptuous psychic dispossession that leaves the addressed "You" incapable of taking her life back when offered it.

the continuation or the correction of a blindness, and were asking us to imagine what it would feel like to receive something from time if this did not take the usual form of a disruption of illusion and infliction of the violence of temporal difference but were also not reducible to the merely temporizing deferral of that violence, to a "buying of time" and only momentary preservation of experiential blankness.

v. "Stop here, or gently pass!": hurtless light, weightless touch

> The story of trauma, then, as the narrative of a belated experience, far from telling of an escape from reality—the escape from a death, or from its referential force—rather attests to its endless impact on a life.
>
>   —Cathy Caruth, *Unclaimed Experience*

> And he said, I beseech thee, shew me thy glory.
>   And he said, I will make all my goodness pass before thee, and I will proclaim the name of the LORD before thee; and will be gracious to whom I will be gracious, and will shew mercy on whom I will shew mercy.
>   And he said, Thou canst not see my face [*panim*]: for there shall no man see me, and live.
>   And the LORD said, Behold, [there is] a place [*makom: place, home, room, whithersoever, open, space, country*] by me, and thou shalt stand upon a rock:
>   And it shall come to pass, while my glory passeth by, that I will put thee in a cleft of the rock, and will cover thee with my hand [*kaf: hand, palm, hollow, sole*], while I pass by.
>   And I will take away mine hand, and thou shalt see my back parts [*achory—back(s), backward, behind, hinder-parts, afterwards, hereafter*]: but my face shall not be seen.
>
>   —Exodus 33:18–23

In their readiness to imagine that which lies dormant otherwise than as waiting or refusing to come to consciousness, Wordsworth's and Dickinson's poems and Weil's play go against the grain of dominant critical habits, in particular the tendency to read unknowingness as a latent, disavowed desire to know (or not). Scandalously, and yet in a way perfectly consonant with the emphasis on a "missable" God-event within the Judeo-Christian tradition of revelation, they present receiving something from time as synonymous and continuous with abandoning it, making this abandonment a part of its reception rather than avoidance, repression, or sublimation.[66] So, for example, in the book of Exodus, God's promise of a shielded revelation at once barred and accomplished through touch receives no further direct mention (it is simply followed by God's second delivery of the law to Moses in chapter 34), yet the absence of its narration, direct or indirect, would be no reason to doubt God kept his appointment. To make and then let drop such a promise is, in some sense at least, already to realize it, since part of its good lies in relying on the recipient's imagination rather than seeing it through for him. For the lines announce an event that to experience would be to miss and that can have no time of its own, only the tense of a hope or memory. "See, there is a place near me" ("Look, there is a place with Me"), God says to Moses, and with his passing, known only as a "not yet" or a "too late," teaches the sufficiency of spatial and temporal *nearness* as a mode of knowledge.[67]

In this last introductory section, or *aperçu*, I wish to shift the discussion away from the performance of a materially innocuous, preservative act to the reception of an eventless experience by returning to the question of the open secret as a trope for secondary, supplemental, naturalized revelation—revelation that one is free to take for granted. As I suggested earlier, this shift also means moving away from traditions of thought emphasizing, with the parable of the talents and the image of the lighted candle in Matthew 5:15, Mark 4:21, and Luke 11:33, the publicity of ethical action, to those that instead follow Matthew 6:3 in privileging its secrecy or unwitnessable nature—a move that, as I also noted earlier, appears to map onto the heuristic if ultimately inadequate binaries: active/passive; "good works"/"grace"; masculine/feminine; modern/postmodern; Enlightenment/Romantic. If my examples of "nothing happening" or "nothing being allowed to happen" so far include a desistance from projected violence and the (non)reception of a (greater) chance to be left as before, I have for the most part been addressing the problems these escapes or near misses pose for positivist conceptions of action that would simply dismiss them

66. In Weil's play, to be sure, the Venetian authorities violently suppress even the trace of the foiled plot, but there is another sense in which Venice escapes internalizing the history of the hurt averted and good done it, a sense in which this noninternalization, far from implying that good's missing or denial, becomes the only way to receive a blessing not addressed to the city's merits.

67. For these translations, see Sarna, *The JPS Torah Commentary: Exodus* (214) and Alter, *The Five Books of Moses* (505), in that order.

as nonoccurrences, nonexperiences. I turn here to another example of "uncounted experience" that also has the structure of an escape from difference or deflection of change, this time reading it against or in dialogue with the sublime cast of much postmodern (nonpositivist, dialectically informed) literary theory, according to which the only experience that "counts," "matters," or "signifies" and deserves ethically positive valuation is negative, subjectively nonappropriable or missed experience.[68] I take this promise of an essentially recessive appearance as my third example of the open secret, in part because its very burial within the Judeo-Christian canon is typical of the simultaneously minor and canonical status of the works included in this study—minor *and* canonical or even minor because canonical: brief, slim, lightweight, as easy to access as to overlook, at times deceptively simple in diction but also actually or simply simple.[69]

68. For an account of postmodern theory's simultaneous discrediting of subjective experience and rehabilitation of "limit-experience" as that which exceeds the subject's appropriative powers absolutely, see Jay, "The Limits of Limit-Experience."

69. As I address in more detail below, this burial is deceptive, however, since the law against seeing God ("no man may see me and live") both echoes and, in some sense, interprets the commandment prohibiting graven images, and is at the origin of the iconoclasm defining the sublime cast of Judeo-Protestant aesthetic and ethical traditions; thus Kant could find "no more sublime passage in the Jewish Law" than "Thou shalt not make unto thee any graven image, or any likeness of any thing that is in heaven or on earth, or under the earth, &c." According to Kant's famous comment, far from a limitation or binding to the (dimly? partially?) revealed world as sufficient, the proscription on graven images—reinterpreted as a ban on conceiving of God or the moral law after the likeness of visible things—frees or "unbinds" the imagination: "when nothing any longer meets the eye of sense, and the unmistakable and ineffaceable idea of morality is left in possession of the field, there would be need rather of tempering the ardour of an unbounded imagination" (Kant, *The Critique of Judgement*, 127). It is precisely this canonical reading, whereby moral duty is infinitized by its unrepresentability, that I would like to bracket for the moment, by reading the sightless revelation—the gentling, tempering, or toning down by which God comes down to Moses's limitation—as calling forth not a comparable infinite within Moses but a capacity to be met in his finitude. Reading the episode against the grain of its traditional interpretations, I want to separate the capacity to receive the gift of a "still small voice" from the power of *limitless* imagination. I am grateful to Steve Goldsmith for reminding me of the passage in Kant's *Third Critique*.

Repeatedly evoked by Kierkegaard and Levinas, this example of a deferral become definitive can also clarify both my project's indebtedness to and its departure from the Levinasian-Derridean critique of the logocentric quest for self-presence, manifestation, and plenitude.[70] For this study proposes to inflect the reception of knowledge as something from which to walk away—the dispensation of "merely" parenthetical experience and nontransmittable insight—somewhat differently from earlier critiques of enlightenment[71] that have put the emphasis on interpretive undecidability, epistemic impasse and rational breakdown.[72] Rather than rehearse

70. On the one hand, God's promised passage constitutes a future anterior, a past that will never have been present, never known except as a trace; on the other hand, it affords thought the dream of a perfectly innocent experience that would leave no trace—no substantive scar or sign of itself. Is God's announced deferral of presence a future-directed, protective withdrawal or an irreparable irruption of absolute difference? This was Derrida's question thirty years ago: how to think "différance" simultaneously as an "economic detour"—a mode of diversion or deferral that preserves the fantasy of one day recovering the fullness of deliberately withheld presence—and "différance" as a "relation to an impossible presence, as expenditure without reserve, as the irreparable loss of presence, the irreversible usage of energy, that is, as the death instinct, and as the entirely other relationship that apparently interrupts every economy?" (Derrida, *Margins of Philosophy*, 19). ("Comment penser *à la fois* la différance comme détour économique qui, dans l'élément du même, vise toujours à retrouver le plaisir où la présence [sic] différée par calcul [conscient ou inconscient] et d'autre part la différance comme rapport à la présence impossible, comme dépense sans réserve, comme perte irréparable de la présence, usure irréversible de l'énergie, voire comme pulsion de mort et rapport au tout-autre interrompant en apparence toute économie?" [*Marges de la philosophie*, 20]). Yet, as the history of deconstruction suggests, the preference given the second alternative makes impossible the question's own closure, and precisely this absence of closure ironically ensures the endless productiveness of deconstructive reading as an interminable performance of a never sufficiently realized loss.

71. The awkwardness of this phrase is necessary to its meaning, insofar as "enlightenment," as the end of rational inquiry, and "The Enlightenment," as the Age of Critique, are both the object and agent of these critiques.

72. Given the horrific history of mass exterminations with which the dialectic of Western Enlightenment culminates in the twentieth century, it is not surprising that the most prominent of these critiques have made historical trauma the centerpiece of their rejection of naive economies of representation, recuperation, and totalization. One unfortunate consequence, however, has been an easy slip-

the poststructural theme of the eruption of a nonconvertible (non)value incapable of contemporaneousness, presence, or manifestation except as excess or lack, I wish to focus on scenes of impracticable instruction (or all but noninstruction) that afford a message of little or no communicative content, one that to receive is to be left free to take up, as if all it had to communicate or impart were precisely this freedom of response and follow-through.[73] Since God promises to mitigate the encounter in the name of Moses's future, one cannot say that the event has no reference beyond itself, yet its own status within the larger narrative that it enables remains deeply ambiguous. The questions with which one might imagine Moses to be left—How is he to know anything has happened? What weight is he to accord so self-contained an exchange? And how should he go on in light of it?—are also those that repeatedly arise for the readers and protagonists of the works included in this study, as they labor under the open secret's weightless burden.

Moses asks to see God's glory, in response to which God promises to turn his back on him: the deity meets only to chasten the man's desire, with a gesture that puts down as much as it takes up and makes the deferral of response a part of acknowledgment itself. Moses is to be left intact, his eyes, like those of the Pascalian believer who "sees enough to know that he has lost," uncovered only in time to see God's "back parts." The ostensibly protective spirit in which God denies Moses the full experi-

_____

page between the unrepresentability of specific historical traumas such as the Shoah (which we are ethically required to think both despite *and* in its very unthinkability and excess of our "normal" conceptual powers and representational abilities) and a more generalized "trauma" of nonrepresentability as a crisis to which we cannot bear witness enough. The "literature of uncounted experience," I want to suggest, simply desists from this latter crisis, not in a cynically despairing mood but, on the contrary, by way of fidelity to experiences, usually personal, intrapsychic, or intersubjective rather than historical, whose fulfillment does not require more than passing witness.

73. "Car enfin cet aveu n'aura point de suite" (for in the end this admission will have no sequel), the Princesse de Clèves will declare, laying down an interdiction by the same gesture that she confesses her love (Lafayette, *La Princesse de Clèves*, 171). As I propose to show, precisely this emptying of consequence on the part of the giver calls on the recipient to "donner suite" in the literal sense of the French phrase—to *give* sequel—rather than simply and automatically follow the speaker's lead.

ence of divine glory resonates uneasily with the arbitrary spirit by which the lady of courtly love withholds herself from her suitors; both might seem to express the spirit of perverse denial and gratuitous prohibition that drives Western asceticism to excess. Yet one aim of this study is to contest the urge to decry the near-miss as a cheat, whether on the part of niggardly fortune or of an ambiguously protective Other. For as the passage from Exodus remarkably illustrates, the ellipsis by which experience remains below the threshold of representation and unavailable to discursive knowledge is constitutive of experience itself. Precisely that by which Moses misses God's passing before him—his placement in the cleft of the rock, the hands that cover his eyes, the glimpse of God's "back parts"—occasions an imageless intimacy between them; the very gentling or lessening of human experience—its diminishment to all but nothing— constitutes a more penetrating gift than the vision denied.[74]

The idea of an experience from which one may walk away because it remains below the threshold of representation perhaps cannot but conjure the famous example from Freud's *Moses and Monotheism* of the person who "gets away [die Städte verlässt], apparently unharmed, from the spot where he has suffered a shocking accident, for instance a train collision."[75]

74. Indeed, just a few verses earlier God has been described as speaking with Moses "face to face"—a fact that makes inexplicable the promised "missing" of God's face, except as a further gift to rather than denial of Moses. Sandwiched between God's dispensation of the law to Moses and Moses's writing it upon the tables, the passage finds its echo in Exodus 34:29, when Moses comes down from the mount with the two tables of testimony and "wist not that the skin of his face shone while he talked with [God]"; Aaron and the children of Israel will not draw near him until he veils his face. I cannot do justice to the complexities of this double echo/reflection here. Suffice it to note that even here the biblical writer remains faithful to the prohibition against graven images by retaining the structure of an epiphanic experience Moses can hardly claim for himself: his face reflecting the light of God, Moses cannot see that to which he has been exposed except by reflecting on others; if Aaron and the others perceive and fear his glory, we as readers recognize his "innocence" from the way in which he must learn or infer—from the response he elicits from others—what he has received from God.

75. Freud, *Moses and Monotheism*, 84 (cited in Caruth, *Unclaimed Experience*, 22). Missed at the moment of its occurrence, the "meeting" between God and Moses has the structure of a traumatic event, but experienced as a sufficiency, it engenders no compulsion to repeat, as does the traumatic event with its "unas-

Indeed, just as earlier it was a question of "melancholic" or "paranoid" theoretical perspectives affording the readiest diagnosis for the renunciation of materialized desire and falling away from actualization, here the psychoanalytic theorization of trauma represents the expected critical paradigm for such *lightened* experience (Geoffrey Hartman might say "elated," lightened to the point of being missable, unnoticeable) insofar as trauma theory admits of no easy distinctions between the escape from— survival and missing of—an event and the event itself.[76] And here again my response is to ask, "Are we able to read weightless experience otherwise—otherwise than as the 'unbearable lightness' of surviving a failed or unborne death?" In choosing to focus on a story about Moses, the figure Freud famously associated with the latency of experience itself—with its continued impact, effectiveness, or "realness" in the absence of its leaving any apparent trace, marking, or wound—my polemic is not against psychoanalytic criticism per se but against the tendency within psychoanalytically influenced postmodern theory to reduce experiential possibilities to what Caruth has described as "the oscillation between a *crisis of death* and the correlative *crisis of life*: between the story of the unbearable nature of an event and the story of the unbearable nature of its survival" (7).[77]

---

similated" surplus. Here there is no failure of presence on Moses's part—nothing he could have done to be a "better" or more "prepared" witness to it. By contrast, in Caruth's account of Freud's *Moses and Monotheism*, the gentling or toning down of experience by which it "leaves no scar" remains merely, and at the same time falsely, protective, since, thereby unclaimed and unremembered, the latent murder of the father with which Freud identifies Moses is condemned to keep on repeating itself.

76. In her reading of this passage, Caruth locates the "event of the accident" not simply in the "shock of whatever happened at the time of the accident" but also "in the fact that the person 'gets away'": "The leaving of the accident . . . is not only the unexperienced event of the crash but the non-experiencing of the fact that the person has indeed remained 'unharmed'" (Caruth, *Unclaimed Experience*, 71). Thus the fact of survival itself returns as part of the repressed—often the last truth to which one awakens.

77. Caruth herself is careful to distinguish between the two crises so that, although the escape from destruction is a wound or trauma of its own, there is also no easy equating of death and survival. In fact, the movement of doubling she describes—from one kind of unborne/unbearable experience to another—closely resembles the movement of doubling in time between states that are neither identical nor agonistically opposed that I am trying to describe in nontraumatic contexts.

In a sense then, I am asking whether our critical habits can sustain a reading of the biblical passage in terms of the beautiful rather than the sublime, remembering that the discourse of the beautiful traditionally emphasizes the sufficiency or adequacy of the subject's representational and experiential powers (even and especially in the absence of a determinate object or positive content to that experience), and asserts, as scandalously as it does lightly, the "fact" of satisfied desire—of eyes that have their fill, possess their object, and, nevertheless, miraculously, continue gazing.[78] The "beautiful," especially as it fades into the hum of bored contentment and feminized domestic habit, represents one alternative to the despair of absolute presence shadowing the Western (anti)metaphysical tradition—the despair that Kateb calls Western humanity's dislike of the "world as given" and that Stanley Cavell refers to as philosophy's "repudiation" of language's "everyday functioning."[79] Similar examples of an accepted satisfaction oddly indistinguishable from a willingness to let fade or pass by might also be drawn from the deflationary, earthbound tendencies of Romantic natural supernaturalism or from the resolutely antitragic traditions of Humean skepticism and American pragmatism (with their antifoundational, uncapitalized "nature"-talk). It is through the perspectives afforded by these traditions that we can read the passage from Exodus 33, not as a formalization of the irremediable split or gap between human and God, subject and Other, experience and presence, but rather, according to the decline of an embrace that sets down more than it takes up, as an instance of the downward movement sometimes called "secularization," "humanization," "internalization," or "naturalization," but thereby misnamed, not simply because such terms evoke residual binaries (sacred/profane, divine/human, transcendent/immanent, supernatural/natural) that the movement itself makes unintelligible, but because at stake in such domestication is the abandonment of anything identifiable as critical, dramatic change. Here too, we are obliged to for-

78. I realize this image borrowed from Valéry may strike readers as a bizarre way to describe the reception of a promised deflection/denial of vision, a promise itself no sooner made than let go of, but oddly enough, perhaps only the so-called instantaneity and immaculateness of visual perception can convey the sufficiency of imagined presence and the adequacy of a promise fulfilled at the moment of its making.

79. See "The Uncanniness of the Ordinary," in Cavell, *In Quest of the Ordinary*, 153–78, esp. 154.

age for strange, counterintuitive phrases—*aufheben* in reverse; leveling, evening transcendence; Stevens's "cure of the ground" or Barthes' *fading* into love—so as to understand these processes as involving both more and less than the transfer of authority from one site to another: a shift in the kind of attention revelation demands, an attenuation of its stakes, a license to take the revealed for granted.[80]

> Gratitude - is not the mention
> Of a Tenderness,
> But it's still appreciation
> Out of Plumb of Speech -

Thus Dickinson admits, only to leap over, the impasse of our incapacity to verify or judge reception, as if glossing both the silence with which Moses receives God's promise and the hiatus of the biblical narrator's chapter break. Crucially, the promised "Tenderness" itself comes in response to an earlier and equally ambiguous pause of indeterminate length—the silence of gratitude or discontent? confidence or disbelief? understanding or incomprehension?—with which Moses punctuates God's reiterated promise "to go before him" and lead the people of Israel into the promised land. (Since this promise also implicitly reminds Moses that he will not see this land himself, dissatisfaction might well inform his mute [non]response.) Indeed, careful reading of the passage reveals that the play of inferred meanings and merely guessed-at desires, and the reliance on the other's imagined but *necessarily* unconfirmed responsiveness begin before and continue after Moses's half-burial in the place "near" God. For Moses never actually asks to see God face to face but more euphemistically to see his glory,[81] in response to which God reiterates the general assurance

80. "Content of fading / Is enough for me - / Fade I unto Divinity"—asserts one (falsely) modest Dickinsonian speaker. Conventional reading, of course, takes her modesty as false, since she makes her willingness to fade contentedly—to die? disappear? go unnoticed? lose perceptibility?—conditional on these terms' transcendent cancellation in the divine. Perhaps only Blanchot would conceive of "divinity" such that the last clause would read not as a qualifying condition annulling the threatened annulment of value but as a continuation of the fading.

81. *Kavod*—the Hebrew word for dignity, for the gravity and momentousness of God's person, that the King James translates as "glory"—belongs to a metaphorical register of weight, rather than light or luminosity, so that when God

of divine power and leadership in verse 19; only when Moses appears to falter, by forfeiting his turn in the dialogic exchange of quid pro quo, does God, without himself appearing to skip a beat, then reinterpret the request as a cry for love, a desire for epiphany or closest contact imaginable: "And he said, no man may see me and live."[82] As Robert Alter points out, the repeated tagline "And he said" usually indicates a switch in speaker, but since here both verses 19 and 20 belong to God's speech, the otherwise redundant "and he said" of verse 20 allows us to infer an unmarked response of silence on Moses's part taking place between the verses (Alter, *Five Books of Moses*, 505). The elided break and reprisal together mark a shift in registers away from the diplomatic game of mutually exchanged signs of commitment and trustworthiness toward more intimate address, as God appears to interpret Moses's lapse as a call for "time out" from their public, historical roles of negotiating a people's destiny.

Perhaps it is only by dropping the burdensome names of "God" and

---

promises to cover Moses with his hand, he may be taking Moses at his word and promising to make Moses feel the weight of his presence, and this by the very gesture that ostensibly nullifies the experience, making indeterminable the way in which it is to "matter" to Moses. In his commentary on Exodus 33, Robert Alter notes *kavod*'s literal sense of "weightiness," while also remarking on the unusual "conjunction of the verb 'shield' (or 'screen') with *kaf*"—"the inside" or "tender part of the hand"; Alter follows earlier commentators in suggesting this may also be "an assimilative spelling of *kanaf*, 'wing' (or 'border,' of a garment), a noun elsewhere idiomatically associated with shielding or protection" (*The Five Books of Moses*, 505). I am grateful to Alter for generously consulting with me on the Hebrew text prior to the publication of *The Five Books of Moses*.

82. That it should be God who attributes to Moses the desire to see His face, whether to recognize the desire ahead of its articulation, as I suggest above, or to accuse him of the same need for visible manifestations of presence that just one chapter earlier resulted in the Golden Calf, complicates the traditional reading of the denial of Moses's wish as a lesson in iconoclasm. As Leslie Brisman has suggested, idolatry in this context consists not of worshipping other gods but of needing and using representations to worship divine being. But the textual uncertainty as to whether Moses is actually "guilty" of asking to see God's face highlights the ambiguity of the demand for visible presence too often reduced within dominant Judeo-Protestant narratives of the progress of human spirit to an infantile failure of faith, an immature dependence on the image, rather than an expression of too much love. See Brisman, "On the Divine Presence in Exodus," 116.

"Moses" that we can hear the extraordinary delicacy of G.'s imputation (after how long a silence?) to M. of an unvoiced protest and self-quieted, still-kept desire for unmediated vision. On this reading, the declaration "no man can see me and live," spoken into a stillness that neither accuses nor demands but simply waits, derives its pathos from first articulating for M. expectations he had not himself formulated in speech, not even to renounce, and assuming for M. a loss he did not claim to suffer. This is not, or not simply, the familiar knot of a law that first creates by articulating the desire it prohibits. For in taking it on himself, unsolicited, to lay down the law, G. is neither limiting nor censuring, nor even coyly inviting transgression, but addressing himself to legitimate dissent regardless of its ever coming forward to articulate itself as such, as if to say at once and without contradiction—"I know what you're thinking of; I can't grant you that wish; it would have been within your rights to conceive it." In a sense the difficulty of capturing the tone of quiet resolution/ resignation and nontriumphant decisiveness with which a person might thus draw the line ahead of all testing is akin to the question, How can a person admit to limitations, confess to failing or being failed by the other in such and such a demand, when no charge has even been made, and *not* be perceived as aggressively defensive?

The precariousness of such anticipatory gestures—the potential for shame, exposure, misprision risked and averted in imagining what the other wants—might fill the pages of a Jamesian novel, but in the end James remains on this book's peripheries, in part because, unlike the compulsive interpreters found in James's fiction, the subjects of the works included here simply walk away from the vertigo of doubt, uncertainty, and interpretive second-guessing opened up by the other's subjectivization. In this sense the expansive, protracted inner workings of James's late style provide a foil to the gently stern decisiveness of Lafayette's and Austen's prose. As I've been arguing, God leaves Moses at the chapter-end of Exodus 33 in the position of saying *without irony*, "Thanks for nothing," and the near impossibility of hearing these words nonironically perhaps dooms to failure all psychologizing readings of this scene, however ripe it may be for interpretation because, in Erich Auerbach's famous words, "fraught with background."[83]

83. Auerbach, *Mimesis*, 12. In this respect, however, Brisman is especially good at giving full play to the ambiguities of the friendly détente between God and Moses; he makes particularly evident the closeness of "keeping with" and "aban-

In fact, neither of the standard critical responses to the near miss Moses is promised under God's cover appears able to accommodate the possibility of such nonironic "thanks" or reception on Moses's part. On the one hand, the impatient instrumentalizing rationalist I imagined earlier cannot see the point of such taunting (if there is nothing for M. to receive, the whole thing might as well be skipped). On the other hand, and this corresponds to the more canonical interpretations, the renunciation of the face-to-face in exchange for Moses's continued life, far from leaving him intact, allegorizes the human subject's entry into history and into language; it represents, in Lacanian terms, his initiation into the symbolic and submission to the law of sacrifice and substitution, internalized authority, and permanent deferral. Indeed according to most Talmudic readings, the passing of divine presence whose missing is promised at the end of Exodus 33 *does* occur and *is* recorded in the following chapter when God *appears as a voice* naming himself before Moses and reciting the divine attributes that become part of the Jewish liturgical prayer:

> And the LORD descended in the cloud, and stood with him there, and proclaimed the name of the LORD.
>
> And the LORD passed by before him, and proclaimed, The LORD, The LORD God, merciful and gracious, longsuffering, and abundant in goodness and truth,
>
> Keeping mercy for thousands, forgiving iniquity and transgression and sin, and that will by no means clear [the guilty]. (Exodus 34:5–7)[84]

------

doning"—and the difficulty of knowing which is kinder—by reminding readers that Yahweh's earlier promise *"Panai yelechu vahanichoti lach"* usually translated as "My Presence will go before you, and I will give you rest," could also be heard by Moses as "My Presence will go [go away]; I will leave you alone" ("On the Divine Presence in Exodus," 118). Here again the promise tests the recipient's worthiness of it by assuming in him a power to trust and to supply implied meanings—in this case the implied "with you" alongside the ambiguous verb "go."

84. According to Talmudic exegesis, the "back" or "back parts" Moses is told he will catch sight of in Exodus 33:23 refers to the knot formed by the straps of the phylacteries containing liturgical prayers on the back of God's neck. Leslie Brisman remarks on the extraordinary transumption or reversal of temporal and divine hierarchy performed by this reading, as it not only imagines God himself praying but makes "the liturgical adaptation—i.e., a later historical development" the "source" for Exodus 34:5–7 (Brisman, "On the Divine Presence in

On this reading, far from leaving everything as before, the episode could not be more historically and psychically definitive as Moses is taught to accept the verbal law of prayer in the place of either a visual or tactile experience of divine presence. So allegorized—as a weaning from dependence on visible manifestation and a lesson in living in the shadow of Being's back—this seeming parenthesis thus suddenly becomes absolutely central to Western modernity, its legacy evident in the loneliness of the Kantian subject before the Law he must give himself, as well as in the figure of the never finished call of interpretive responsibility so critical to later iconoclastic theories of the (non)event of ethical subjectivity.

So, for example, as Martin Jay reminds us, Levinas makes the deflected theophany emblematic of his ethical philosophy's rejection of the face-to-face recognition of Enlightenment moral positivism, with its inevitable reduction of the Other to an image of self and narrowing of duty to a finite set of publicly executable acts. For Levinas, the event's minimization to all but nothing—what we might call its virtuality or hurtless (non)fulfillment—neither indicts nor accommodates Moses's limited ability to withstand the fullness of divine presence but, on the contrary, derives from the god's own powerlessness of imposition (left for the recipient to take up), just as the related figure of the miraculously unconsumed burning bush does not concern the finitude of human powers but the daily infinite of the continual, forever unfinished, practice of the law.[85]

Exodus," 110). Brisman also comments on the ambiguity of the Hebrew word *naqah*, appearing in the biblical text as "will by no means clear [the guilty]" and in the prayer as "wiping the slate clean," and meaning "clear" both in the sense of "wipe away, annihilate, destroy" and of "cleanse, purify, etc." (121). If we follow Brisman's claim that the interpolated "guilty" in Exodus 34:7 (along with that verse's entire conclusion) represents a later addition, then the last attribute of God's goodness or virtue—the claim that "he will not utterly clear . . ."—would consist of an essentially negative power to spare, to leave intact, *not* to destroy, etc. These same ambiguities, of course, also inform the simultaneously protective and destructive movement of the Hegelian term *aufheben* as to surpass and leave intact, suspend and carry over, keep and cancel in the same breath, put under erasure.

85. In "Revelation in the Jewish Tradition" Levinas offers the following gloss on the burning bush:

The idea that the other is the enemy of the Same is an abuse of the notion; its alterity does not bring us to the play of the dialectic, but to an incessant

Repeatedly Levinas figures the Other's recessive approach as something that does not register on the phenomenal world's scales of experience—an unceremonious announcement followed by as inconsequent a retraction: "First a revelation, then nothing"; "[the enigma's disturbance] enters [the given order of things] so subtly that it has already retired unless we retain it. . . . It remains only for him who is willing to take it up."[86]

---

questioning, without any ultimate instance, of the priority and tranquility of the Same, like an inextinguishable flame which burns yet consumes nothing. And the form of this flame, surely, is the prescription of the Jewish Revelation, with its unfulfillable obligation. An unfulfillable obligation, a burning which does not leave any ash, since ash would still be, in some respect, a substance resting on itself. The "less" is forever bursting open, unable to contain the "more" that it contains, in the form of "the one for the other." . . . Can we convert transcendence as such into answers without losing it in the process?" (Levinas, *The Levinas Reader*, 209)

86. Levinas, *Collected Philosophical Papers*, 66 ("Il y entre d'une façon si sub-tile qu'il s'en est déjà retiré, *à moins que nous ne le retenions. . . . Il ne reste que pour celui qui veut bien lui donner suite*" [*En Découvrant l'existence avec Husserl et Heidegger suivie d'essais nouveaux*, 290; emphasis added]). In this 1957 essay, "Enigma and Phenomenon," Levinas poses the "enigma" as an alternative to "the indiscreet and victorious appearing of a phenomenon," defining it as "this way the other has of seeking my recognition while preserving his incognito, disdain-ing recourse to the wink-of-the-eye of understanding or complicity, this way of manifesting himself without manifesting himself" (Levinas, *Collected Philosophi-cal Papers*, 66). ("Cette façon pour l'Autre de quérir ma reconnaissance tout en conservant son *incognito*, en dédaignant le recours au clin d'œil d'entente ou de complicité, cette façon de se manifester sans se manifester, nous l'appelons—en remontant à l'étymologie de ce terme grec et par opposition à l'apparoir indiscret et victorieux du *phénomène*—énigme" [*En Découvrant l'existence avec Husserl et Heidegger suivie d'essais nouveaux*, 291]). Levinas defines the other's intervention as a disturbance so absolute it cannot be reintegrated or reabsorbed by the exist-ing order—not because it opposes to that order anything positive or substantive, but only because it has already of itself lapsed back into silence, "shattering" the order of reason, not by violence, not by visible effect, but only by leaving nothing to take its place: "Disturbance is a movement that does not propose any stable order in conflict or in accord with a given order; it is [a] movement that already carries away the signification it [was bringing]: disturbance disturbs order without troubling it seriously" (*Collected Philosophical Papers*, 70; transla-tion modified).

This thematization of a missed encounter whose missing does not enter the account books, not even as a loss or deprivation, is no mere exercise in irony or bitter complaint at the fatal noncoincidence apparently structuring human experience as a "not yet" or "too late." On the contrary, if Levinas repeatedly returns to the figure of the disappearing god known only by and in his retreat, it is as to a scene that initiates and founds the passion of the Other—the "primal" scene of exposure to the naked and suffering Other that, far from impinging on or limiting the subject's freedom (as it would if the ethical relation were conceived on the model of correlation, intentionality, contract, or mutual obligation), brings the subject (as a capacity for infinite and undetermined response) into being as such.

My point in thus evoking the Levinasian trope of the other's inconsequent *nondisruptive* interruption is not so much to rehearse the crisis of passivity by which the other escapes my grasp (precisely by not opposing any concrete obstacle to my power to seize), but to use the substitution of "trauma" for "drama" in these stories of parenthetical disclosure to illustrate the almost inevitable slippage in our critical habits from understatement to hyperbole and undermeaning to overmeaning. Levinas's concept of the "enigma" obviously bears interesting affinities with this book's preoccupation with forms of uncounted experience and unremarkable virtue (those nonassertive ways of being in the world I am designating by the term *open secrets*), particularly insofar as his examples suggest how such weightless, minimally assertive, nonemphatic encounters open up the question of how to survive or follow up on an experience (the gift of grace, divine love, the Other's retreat), the essence of which is for the recipient not to know how she is concerned by it. At the same time, Levinasian ethics, or at least a certain popular reception of it, risks foreclosing this question by substituting for this indefiniteness the call on the recipient to be responsible to what the Other does not ask her, to what remains unfathomable in the Other's demand. There is, then, a recurring oscillation between the extremes of "nothing" and "all"—a seesaw between unsubtle absolutes ultimately exclusive, I am suggesting, of the reception of weightless experience—evident in the apparent contradiction above between defining the Other's recessive approach as a historically *innocuous, harmless, impotent* movement and my calling it "foundational" in analogy with the "primal scene" of psychoanalysis: on the one hand, the disturbance adds nothing positive to history understood in naively referential terms; on the other, the gift's content *is* its calling forth of undetermined response (an appeal to the recipient's license and interpretive freedom or "subjectivity" as to something she would never otherwise have had).[87] Hence the interpretive pattern familiar from analyses of trauma as from the poetics of the sublime, in which an initial dearth of signifiers gives way to a surplus of meaning: the promise of a passing blessing—God's covering Moses's eyes as he passes—becomes the story of a "blessure" or bloodless wound from which there is no recovering. Reading itself would appear fated to oscillate between stark, equally *thankless* alternatives: either there is no transformative parousia or there is only education in lack or both at once: Moses missed seeing God, *and* this "escape" was an illusion.

Again, I offer this sketch of the movement of (non)choice between finite loss, on the one hand, and infinite debt, on the other, less as a "reading" of the Levinasian notion of the Other's antiepiphany or revelation-in-withdrawal than as a comment on the quickness with which, following a certain vulgarized habit of deconstructive reading, we are liable to absolutize the minimal and turn a contingent missing into the revelation of ontological guilt.[88] In this sense, one "casualty" of post-Hegelian theories of

87. Although Levinas wants to keep before us alterity's "inoffensiveness," his very metaphors of "disturbance," "rupture," and "interruption" continue to echo the phallocentric logic (which he would resist) that conceives of action as the penetration, arousal, and occupation of dormant, empty feminine space. This, in turn, invites reading the "non-offense" according to the logic of trauma as a wound all the more shattering and constitutive of identity for having withdrawn itself before it could take place.

88. In the last decade, even if only in passing comments on Levinas, Žižek and Santner have been articulating a critique of this overemphasis on limitless responsibility and infinite debt as the expression of "a punishing super-ego" (Santner, *On the Psychotheology of Everyday Life*, 65) and as the condition for permanent dissatisfaction with the world. See Žižek, *The Fragile Absolute*; and Santner, *On the Psychotheology of Everyday Life*. Given that Žižek explicitly frames his critique as a choice "for" Christianity over "against" Judaism's insistence on a permanently unredeemable "indivisible remainder" (*The Fragile Absolute*, 98), we might compare his critique to Habermas's earlier characterization of Derrida as a strangely Puritanical figure who, by "renew[ing] the mystical concept of tradition as an ever delayed event of revelation," need never come to rest and is assured endless interpretive work to do (Habermas, *The Philosophical Discourse of Modernity*, 183).

the event has been the "casual" itself or the ability to distinguish between minimally articulated experiences and traumatizing traces of a withdrawn presence. Indeed, I have perhaps perversely chosen the overcharged example of God's promise to pass by his human witness, or simply pass him by, precisely because it illustrates the strange convergence, via the tropes of proximity and nearness, of the language of immanence—of implicit, tacitly assumed, forgetful day-to-day fulfillment—the passing, the quotidian, the uneventful and anticlimactic—and the figure of transcendence—the unassimilated, parenthetical exception whose violence is both to leave and not leave everything as before. The brush with God or glancing touch (passing hand) that Moses is promised in lieu of sight is both literally and figuratively "tangential"—at once touching and "going off 'at a tangent'; erratic, divergent, digressive" (*OED*). Like the one passed by, the tangent is not worth stopping over but not for that worthless. But this sense of experiences, places, encounters *sufficiently* marked by only the slightest (and slighting) of caresses, whose cherishing need not take the form of formalization, ultimately remains foreign to the high stakes of ethical thought (even and especially when reduced to the passivity and nonpositivity of Levinasian ethical responsibility) and belongs instead to an ethos of ordinariness perhaps better instantiated in "freely" grounded aesthetic inattention, or in the ecologist's awareness of more than one species in the "background," or in the type of mildly amorous companionship once conjured by the term *Boston marriages*.

If we read "the capacity to take for granted" nonpejoratively—not as indifference or as a failure of imagination but as a positive absence of any felt need to imagine the world differently—then this license implies as well a release from the duty to improve.[89] The open secret is a dispensation, then, in the double sense of a providential event or ordering of events—the dealing out of blessings and afflictions—and of a relaxation or suspension of the law, an exemption, a remission or release from obligation. Again it would be difficult to underestimate the pervasiveness, on today's critical horizon, of the trope of this ambiguous gift of a destiny fulfilled at the moment of its lapse.[90] Indeed, much in postmodern thought

89. For the implications of such a release for current debates over biotechnology and genetically engineered foods, see my "'O happy living things!'"

90. Particularly resonant with my own project here is Santner's metaphor of "unplugging from the rule of the talents" (*On the Psychotheology of Everyday Life*, 18) to describe the psyche's release from its drive to know and make itself

bears witness to the demagnification, minimization, and rendering passive
of the ethical act (as of the political event): its emptying out of positive
content, visible difference, and measurable consequence; its release from
master narratives of progress and revolution; its reduction to all but nothing as in the Lacanian/Heideggerian forced "choice of 'freely assuming'
one's imposed destiny."[91] This "coming down to earth" of the time of
the law's fulfillment, its simultaneous dispensing with positivist criteria
of change and calling forth of the barest, most nugatory, already present
offerings, thus appears in a number of recent negative or apophatic the-
ologies of the "this-worldly," the immanent, the phenomenological and
everyday ("bare life" and the state of permanent exception in Agamben;
"the fragile absolute" in Žižek; "worldly spectatorship" in Silverman; the
daily exposure to the proximity of the Other's insistent enjoyment that
for Santner constitutes "the psychotheology of everyday life"; even the
permanent imminence of militant action from within "a vital and in-
eluctable participation in the set of social structures, with no possibility
of transcending them" that Hardt and Negri call "joy of being").[92] And

---

knowable to other minds, a release that Santner defines as essential to, rather
than exclusive of, the acknowledgment of others. Yet Santner's account of Freud
and Rosenzweig's ethical projects can sometimes make it sound as if the self is
"unplugged" from the "life of the talents" (the pursuit of scholarly, professional,
institutional recognition, etc.) only to be "plugged" into the never-finished "obligation to endure the proximity of the Other in their [*sic*] 'moment of *jouissance.*'" This is an obligation to bear witness to everything in the Other that
remains unrecognizable to himself and others, what Santner calls "the Other's
touch of madness, . . . the way in which the Other is disoriented in the world,
destitute, divested of an identity that firmly locates him or her in a delimited
whole of some sort" (82). Far from effecting a "release," Santner's metaphors of
"endurance" and "exposure" to the Other's "insistent expressivity" often seem
to carry over what he calls the rigid uncanny animation or "undeadness" of our
worldly pursuits. If, unlike the Levinasian Other, the Other in Santner's account
of Freud and Rosenzweig, always "insists," even and especially in his or her unconscious ipseity, my project wants instead to ask about how we are to think our
"obligation" to those forms of life, human and nonhuman, that simply do not
insist, neither through conscious formal demands for recognition nor through
their unconscious enjoyment of themselves.

91. Žižek, *The Ticklish Subject*, 18.

92. See Agamben, *Homo Sacer*; Žižek, *The Fragile Absolute*; Silverman, *World
Spectators*; Santner, *On the Psychotheology of Everyday Life*; Hardt and Negri, *Em-*

yet, as I've been arguing, inasmuch as it is determined by an aesthetics of the sublime, much in this deflationary tradition also tends to elevate the infinitesimal to the status of an impossible and absolute ideal, making the release from heroic, goal-oriented energies conditional on a call to permanent vigilance and ever-readiness, and thereby reproducing the oscillation I've been referring to between paralysis before the "nothing" left to do and renewed energy at the endless urgency of its task.[93]

─────

pire, 413. These are obviously widely divergent critical orientations, and their salience for the contemporary moment would have to be explained, however violently and reductively, through "reference" to what deconstruction asks we imagine differently than as a point of reference and to what in fact increasingly presents itself in its own ontic dimensions as a groundless, placeless vacuum occurring without normal frames of reference, including the scope of the polis or political life: "contemporary history" insofar as it is defined by the so-called end of history (the collapse of the Soviet empire, the triumph of neoliberal global capitalism, and rise of religious fundamentalisms), and marked by the imminence of global ecological disaster.

93. The contemporary force of this compulsion to radicalize thought by seizing on the least bearable, least hospitable extreme appears more clearly when we compare Giorgio Agamben's recent commentary on the Pauline notion of a law suspended and canceled in its very accomplishment—which he reads through the Schmittian notion of the *foundational* nature of the state's suspension of law and illustrates with the example of the Nazis' 1933 suspension of the German constitution—and a different if equally "Hegelian" form of Pauline antinomianism—the reading of Romanticism as the internalization of quest romance popularized by an earlier generation of literary critics (Bloom, Abrams, and Hartman). Agamben's reading hinges on the Greek verb *katargeō*—to make inoperative, to deactivate, suspend the efficacy of—and on Luther's remarkably fateful decision to translate it as "aufheben." See Agamben, *The Time that Remains*, 95–108. The most salient contrast would be with Geoffrey Hartman's reading of a movement of fulfillment in Wordsworth similarly constituted as the lifting of a burden that does and doesn't leave all as before. In *Wordsworth's Poetry* (50, 352) Hartman points, for example, to Wordsworth's transmutation of the promise from I Corinthians 15:51—"we shall all be changed" to "Home at Grasmere"'s "all shall survive"; and there is a further echo in the lines from "Hart-Leap Well"—

> She leaves these objects to a slow decay,
> That what we are, and have been, may be known;
> But at the coming of the milder day
> These monuments shall all be overgrown (173–76)

—whose rhymes implicitly collapse the coming to legibility and full disclosure

One way that *Open Secrets* differs from these recent theorizations of passive agency and meditations, direct or indirect, on the Pauline promise "my strength is accomplished in weakness" (II Corinthians 12:9) is in its departure from their tendency to radicalize and unsettle the norm (whether as the site of a secret and permanent exemption from the law or of potential insurrection or of the Other's monstrous enjoyment), thereby disallowing and exposing as false consciousness the power to take anything for granted. Instead, the protagonists included in this study show their colors, sometimes to shocking effect, by what they are prepared to accept and settle on—if not as "normal" then as "sufficient." Alternatively, but without contradiction, their difference appears in the way they demand—of themselves, of the world, of their neighbors and lovers—the impossible as the very least ("la moindre des choses"), refusing to take it if it does not come as such—as the most natural thing in the world.[94]

---

of human history with its reabsorption into the ground: the same movement that leaves time for the reading of history—nature's abandonment of things to their "slow decay"—already belongs to "the milder day" of that history's redemption. That what gets described as "naturalization" in Wordsworth should have the same structure as permanent alienation in Agamben is perhaps itself an expression of the Romantic dialectic of the "uncanniness"—we might now say "inhospitality"—of the "ordinary."

94. As I suggested in my preface, the oddly feminine boldness and unassuming grandeur of an attitude that will not press for what it would happily take for free, account for the privileged place of "pastoral" and pastoral themes in my readings of Lafayette, Austen, and Wordsworth, in particular. For pastoral is precisely the place, genre, or mode in literature where people of limited means and no social entitlements become expressive of the aristocratic and feminized ethos of doing as little to persuade others of one's worth as to press home demands on them.

§ 2 *L'aveu sans suite*: Love's Open Secret in Lafayette's *La Princesse de Clèves*

> Il ne faut pas qu'il ne voie rien du tout; il ne faut pas aussi qu'il en voie assez pour croire qu'il le possède; mais qu'il en voie assez pour connaître qu'il l'a perdu. . . . Quelque parti qu'il prenne, je ne l'y laisserai point en repos.
>
> —Blaise Pascal, Pensée 556[1]

> . . . that he might see and know, and yet abstain.
>
> —Milton, *Areopagitica*[2]

i. retractive gifts

Toward the end of Madame de Lafayette's *La Princesse de Clèves* (1678), the heroine, now a widow, discovers that the man she loves has rented a room next to her apartment and has been watching her without making himself known to her; troubled by this discovery, she seeks solitude in a park where she comes upon him sitting lost in reverie, doubtless thinking of her. He is so self-absorbed that he doesn't see her to recognize her but, startled by the noise of her entourage and wishing to avoid contact with others, bows so low he doesn't see her and leaves. She in turn lets him go without making herself known:

> elle vit un homme couché sur des bancs, qui paraissait enseveli dans une rêverie profonde, et elle reconnut que c'était M. de Nemours. Cette vue l'arrêta tout court. Mais ses gens qui la suivaient firent quelque bruit, qui tira M. de Nemours de sa rêverie. Sans regarder qui avait causé le bruit qu'il avait entendu, il se leva de sa place pour éviter la compagnie qui venait vers lui et tourna dans une autre allée, en faisant une révérence fort basse qui l'empêcha même de voir ceux qu'il saluait.[3]

1. Pascal, *Œuvres complètes*, 1282. (He must not see nothing of the whole; nor has he to see enough to think that he possesses it; but he must see enough to know that he has lost it. . . . Whichever side he takes, I will not let him rest.)
2. Milton, *Complete Poems and Major Prose*, 729.
3. Lafayette, *La Princesse de Clèves*, 166–67. Except where indicated otherwise, I supply my own translations, done in consultation with those of Buss, Lyons, and Mitford.

[She saw a man lying on some benches, who appeared absorbed in a profound reverie, and she recognized M. de Nemours. This sight stopped her short. But her attendants who were following her made some noise that pulled M. de Nemours out of his dream. Without looking at what caused the noise he'd heard, he got up to avoid the people coming toward him and turned into another avenue, making a bow so deep he didn't even see whom he was saluting.]

Occurring in the aftermath of the heroine's fateful *aveu* but before her final rejection of Nemours, the episode does not move the plot forward but exemplifies a form of narrative action so chaste that, in retrospect, it might as well not have happened. Valincour, the novel's early critic, thus found the scene not only implausible but strangely, perversely pointless:

> Ce qui m'a semblé de plus étrange dans cette aventure, c'est de voir combien elle est inutile. . . . On tire Madame de Clèves de sa solitude; on la mène dans un lieu où elle n'a pas coutume d'aller; et tout cela, pour lui donner le chagrin de voir sortir Monsieur de Nemours par une porte de derrière.[4]

> [What struck me as strangest in this adventure, is how much it is useless. . . . Madame de Clèves is drawn from her solitude, brought to a place she doesn't usually visit; and all this, so that she can be given the pain of seeing Monsieur de Nemours leave by the back door.]

The impatience of Valincour's reaction has something of the bitterness of a frustrated lover and typifies the dismissal that Lafayette's flouting of rationalist narrative standards easily solicits. Indeed, the anonymous "on" who, in Valincour's paraphrase of the scene, engineers this useless exercise in mutual frustration, might easily pass for a flirt toying with the idea of consummation by bringing Nemours and the princess together only to have their meeting *not* take place. But in imputing the thwarting of his expectations to the workings of a demonic and controlling agent, whether Author or Mistress Fate, Valincour misses the point that no circumstance prevents their meeting. The scene belongs, on the one hand, to the topos of waste: condemned to remain buried, unregistered and unevidenced, the excursion's only effect is invisibly to sustain the status quo—to conserve the characters' mutual inexperience of one another. On the other hand, as an acting out of unmet potential, this chance *rencontre* or encounter dem-

4. Valincour, *Lettres à Madame la Marquise*** sur le sujet de "La Princesse de Clèves"* (published anonymously six months after the novel's first printing), 61.

onstrates a remarkable efficiency of structure: nothing, except themselves, intervenes to keep apart Mme de Clèves and Nemours. The fantasies by which they possess each other in mind effectively bar them from ever sharing the same physical space; the characters themselves provide the safest barrier, keeping each other intact and separate, even as their unspoken mental life makes redundant any physical action between them.

Unkind to readers who value fulfillment, Lafayette's novel thus reproduces the negative power of its heroine, who abstains from, even as she meets, desire. Like the minor, essentially negligible episode described above, the novel's plot only supplies the characters with the means by which to ignore their own narrative experience. By way of sealing her faith to her husband, a woman confesses to him her love for another man and, in the process, unwittingly assures this other that he is loved. Tortured by a jealousy he would never have conceived on his own, the husband soon dies, leaving the woman free to marry the man she loves. But, blaming herself for this death and seeing her virtual lover as its means, she refuses his offer of marriage, retires from the court, and dies shortly thereafter. Through almost no fault of her own, things happen in such a way that she can hold herself responsible for the death that liberates her, and she is stopped from proceeding by the very thing that opens the door for her. Her husband profits so little from her faithfulness to him that, where he is concerned, she might as well have committed the physical act of adultery. As for the lover, he is no closer to possessing her for knowing himself loved or for seeing the husband dead. Her virtue is as free of effect as her passion is innocent of consequence. In terms of the plot, her not acting on her desire makes as slight a difference to her husband as her speaking it does to her lover.

Thus if plot summary cannot justify the princess's refusal to act on a desire that she does not mind making known, it does register just how much her abstinence looks, in its final effect, like indulgence and her indulgence like abstinence. For, as must be emphasized, she does, in her own retractive way, indulge desire in the double sense of giving in to her own passion and of forgiving Nemours' illicit expression of his. But as her ultimate confession of love to him makes explicit, she does so only when it appears to cost her little: "cet aveu n'aura point de suite," she stipulates: this avowal will have no consequence; nothing will follow from it. Until then, she allows Nemours to infer her meaning, rather than telling it to him outright, and gives her assent only to actions that she cannot prevent and need never assume as her own. Her decision to do nothing (except let him have it) when she catches Nemours in the act of stealing her miniature portrait is, in this sense, exemplary: "Enfin elle jugea qu'il valait mieux le lui laisser, et elle fut bien aise de lui accorder une faveur qu'elle lui pouvait faire sans qu'il sût même qu'elle la lui faisait" (92). Thus when she is not avowing to disavow desire (as in the *aveu* to the prince and in her final admission to Nemours that she does indeed love him, another *aveu* which she promises will remain without consequence), she is passively assenting to it, but so passively as to make her "yes" weightless.[5] Even the *aveu* to her husband, which readers might well argue constitutes an exception significant enough to suspend all talk of passiveness, initially consists of no more than a silence sufficiently prolonged, as the princess simply keeps quiet long enough for the prince to guess the truth: "'You do not answer me,' he went on, 'and this is as good as to say that I'm not mistaken'" (122). By her own account "unprecedented," and only ambiguously called for by the circumstances, this revelatory act opens a hole from which we, like the prince and Nemours, are challenged to walk away—a report on another's inner life we are invited to take note of and leave without follow-up.

With the same lightness, Lafayette allows others to think the book her own, as long as she does not have to claim it for herself. Pressed by friends to admit to having engendered it, she admits that she is happy to let herself be associated with it but would not want to have to defend her claim: "Pour moy, je suis flattée que l'on me soupçonne et je croy que j'avoûrois le livre, si j'estois asseurée que l'autheur ne vînt me le redemander." (As

---

5. Refusing to engage in contractual exchange with Nemours, Mme de Clèves exemplifies a mode of gift giving that in its passivity and erasure of accountable, identifiable agency comes close to meeting the impossible conditions of Derridean gift giving described in *Donner le temps*. There Derrida plays on the two senses of *percevoir* (to perceive and to cash) and *reconnaissance* (recognition and gratitude) to insist on the gift's absence from either donor or receiver: "Pour qu'il y ait don, *il faut* que le donataire ne rende pas, n'amortisse pas, ne rembourse pas, ne s'acquitte pas, n'entre pas dans le contrat, n'ait jamais contracté de dette. . . . Il faut, à la limite, qu'il ne *reconnaisse* pas le don comme don. . . . *A la limite, le don comme don* devrait *ne pas apparaître comme don: ni au donataire, ni au donateur*" (24–27). According to this logic, in making a necessity of her free gift and not letting him see it as such, the princess frees Nemours of any debt to her.

for myself, I'm flattered that people suspect me of it, and I think I would admit [to having authored] the book, if I were assured that the author would never come to ask it back of me.)[6] Her sustained refusal to claim authorship for the novel thus takes the form of leaving open, without actualizing, the possibility of her having engendered it—an "I would if I could" that reproduces the ambiguities of her heroine's refusal either to give up or to claim her passion. Theoretically, anyone may come forward and claim the book, yet in effect no one can, because this mode of disclaiming without foreclosing is so much in the style of the princess, who says "yes" only when she cannot do otherwise, that we cannot doubt Lafayette is the author, however much we take it on faith. The open secret of her authorship thus presents readers with an experience that we will see repeated in this chapter—that of an absolute certainty that, however absolute, one can never demonstrate, bring forth, or act on.

Critical attention has long centered on this peculiar and equivocal mode of affirmation shared by both heroine and author: a mode of presenting in such a way as to withhold, of giving in such a way as to neutralize the value of the gift. Indeed, in thus beginning with an assessment of *La Princesse de Clèves'* potential kindness or unkindness to fulfillment-seeking readers, I am deliberately reproducing the implicitly misogynist tendency to approach this text as if it were a mistress capable of granting or withholding favors to her suitors, a tendency that Lafayette herself may have ironically encouraged by allowing its heroine's to be the book's only name.[7] Seeking to reverse this tendency, late-twentieth-century readers

6. Lafayette, *Correspondance*, 2:63.

7. The notice to the reader says that the author omitted his name so that the book might be judged on its own terms. Ironically this shared namesake has instead made it impossible to dissociate the book from its heroine, and from the earliest criticism on, readers have focused their critical energies on her, through attacks or defenses of her two most problematic acts, the *aveu* to the prince and her final refusal of Nemours and retreat from the court. We can only speculate whether in withholding her name from the published text, Lafayette anticipated this inevitable slippage between the bewilderment and frustration the princess produces in her male auditors, and readers' responses to a story of missed encounters, vows kept in vain, and profitless exchanges. My sense is that Lafayette may actually have expected readers to associate the impersonality of the narrative voice with the princess's reticence, may have wanted them to hear in it a gender-inflected indifference, coldness and distance, precisely so as to dramatize their experience of reading as one of being left empty-handed, thwarted, with nothing to claim but a relation of aesthetic disinterest or nonpossession.

have frequently defended the novelist's and heroine's famed elusiveness as deliberate evasions of oppressive and unsatisfying norms of happiness, accountability, or authorial identity—necessary strategies by which to regain control over the transmission of their gifts.[8] In this chapter I approach the question of these disowned, unclaimed legacies somewhat differently by reemphasizing instead the peculiarly passive quality of their making—a passiveness that undermines the very concepts of intentionality and gainfulness we commonly associate with the agonistic economy and ambition of "plot." The princess's reserve exemplifies, I argue, a *nonappropriative* assumption of the weight of circumstance. For even as she seems to remove herself from her most affirmative acts, she appears, in another light, to assume too much responsibility for the outcome of a chain of events she may have set off but in no way intended: "Je sais que c'est par vous qu'il est mort et que c'est à cause de moi" (I know that it is by you he died and because of me) (172), she tells Nemours when explaining why she cannot marry him. So strong an inscription of the *moi*, especially blatant for so self-effacing a heroine, is indeed a strange way of claiming authorship,

8. See, in particular, Joan DeJean's seminal essay, "Lafayette's Ellipses," to which any reading of the princess's "open secret" must remain indebted for its close attention to the work performed by the novel's omissions. As her title indicates, DeJean reads these withholdings—both Lafayette's enigmatic "nonsignature" and her heroine's enigmatic relation to desire—as affirmative negations, "attempts to avoid the loss of authority that accompanies every public appropriation of fictionalized female desire and to create enigma from the protection of privacy, thus generating new privileges of anonymity" (246 [887]). DeJean argues that the princess achieves her desire to be "outside of story, to be unnarratable . . . by rejecting Nemours and life in society, by scripting a negative plot that resists accountability" (264 [897]). But by thus reassigning a liberating agency to both author and heroine, this claim risks missing the fully paradoxical nature of the heroine's participation in her own story, a participation that effectively leaves her unable to pursue this story: by Mme de Clèves' own logic, had she played no part in her husband's end, she would have been free to take Nemours up. For another account of the negativity of "what the princess left," see Alliston, *Virtue's Faults*, chap. 2. According to Alliston, by discharging her debt to her husband with a story of her inner life (rather than with an image others might verify and guarantee), the princess both exceeds and eludes the demand of "maternal inheritance," an inheritance that, in contrast to the "hard" property of patrilineal inheritance, is conditioned on the daughter's willingness to receive—by reproducing herself in its image or "living up to"—the mother's "exemplary representation" (38–39).

without intent and only after the fact. But the real surprise lies in the simplicity with which she admits to the causal connection but walks away from the guilt it might imply.[9]

ii. the difference within

The princess makes her untouchable, nongenerative legacy against the backdrop of courtly romance, where the lady, object of the hero's erotic and epistemological quest, acts by doing nothing, her silence confirming an inaccessibility that the hero is more intent on proving than overcoming.[10] Feminine action so defined distinguishes itself from inaction only minimally, not by its outcome but by the meaning it gives to the hero's final possession of a body that he might from the start have had by force. Just as content cannot determine the difference between gift and theft, only the form that this action takes in her mind, not its end, can mark (as well as leave unmarked) the difference between the heroine's passive surrender and freely given hand. By beginning where romance usually ends—with the heroine's marriage—*La Princesse de Clèves* limits the significance we can attach to this kind of end as an indicator of feminine action and builds into its formal structure a truth that eighteenth-century novels to come will be at pains to communicate, namely that the only significant object of the heroine's giving and withholding is news

9. Here I want to suggest an alternative to reading this announcement as an inscription of guilt and spectralization of the real, as Peggy Kamuf does in "A Mother's Will." The strangeness of this novel's contribution to the modern construction of interiority is that its heroine insists on the difference made not by subjective intentionality or degrees of hidden suffering but simply by the shape that events have taken in her mind, if not in the eyes of the world. For a psychological heroine she is surprisingly aesthetic in this attention to form rather than sentiment.

10. Thus Lacan's verdict on courtly love: "C'est une façon tout à fait raffinée de suppléer à l'absence de rapport sexuel, en feignant que c'est nous qui y mettons l'obstacle" (*Encore*, 65); and Žižek's gloss: "external hindrances that thwart our access to the object are there precisely to create the illusion that without them, the object would be directly accessible" (Žižek, *Metastases of Enjoyment*, 94). The open secret as I use the term designates the way in which the princess undoes this illusion. See also the rich insights of Henri Rey-Flaud's *La névrose courtoise*.

of her inner life. Hence the centrality of heroine-centered fictions such as Lafayette's to the rise of the psychological novel, with its simplicity of action and emphasis on introspection.[11]

Courtly sexual relations already locate the woman's agency less in what happens to her body, the passive object of male claims, than in the presence or absence of her mind to this action, a presence or absence that can give the same material events very different moral valences. But whereas Mme de Clèves' court society is prepared to accept as sufficient the mere appearance of feminine compliance to the institution of marriage, her "singular" example relies on readers to recognize, without mystifying or sensationalizing, psychic states that remain beyond public notice and without public consequence. As I argue in the next chapter, this new ethics of feminine subjectivity may have less in common with the novel of sensibility than with the antiheroic and subdued relation to self that appears in a later strain of Romantic lyricism. For unlike the eighteenth-century sentimental novel that will work hard at representing sentiment convincingly through expressions of immediacy and authenticity, Lafayette's fiction teaches readers to accept a priori the nonevincibility of moral difference: her characters do not paint pictures of themselves in the first person but forgo the attempt to convince by demonstration. Rather, "how it is with me inside" announces itself without insistence or protestation and thus achieves the intractability of impersonal fact.

Lafayette's heroine consents to marry the prince only by default, when a series of aborted proposals have made it unwise for her to reject him, and with the admission to her mother that while she would marry him with less distaste than she would another, "she was not particularly attracted to

---

11. As Frances Ferguson has argued, the peculiarly psychological nature of heroine-centered action is particularly evident in the example of a rape—a crime whose event only insight into psychological states can establish and whose very articulation, if not prosecution, Ferguson argues, requires the development of the psychological novel (see Ferguson, "Rape and the Rise of the Novel"). Ferguson's argument draws attention to the perverse collusion between the structural passivity of the female body and the development of a subjectivity conceived as autonomous from and unknowable by the body. Insufficiently indicated by the body's actions, the mind grows both autonomous and irrelevant to this "action." (Since the feminine body tells us nothing because it lacks the capacity to "say no" even if it wants to "say yes," voice must reside elsewhere.)

him."[12] This intractable neutrality continues to characterize her relations to the prince after marriage, minimizing for him the difference between her married and unmarried state:

> La qualité de mari lui donna de plus grands privilèges; mais elle ne lui donna pas une autre place dans le cœur de sa femme. Cela fit aussi que, pour être son mari, il ne laissa pas d'être son amant, parce qu'il avait toujours quelque chose à souhaiter au-delà de sa possession. (52)

> [The status of husband gave him greater privileges; but it did not give him a greater place in the heart of his wife. Thus for being her husband, he did not stop being her lover, because he always had something more to wish for beyond possession.] (Buss 44)

With the prince, as with her general auditors, the princess undoes an economy of appropriation by her capacity to engage in a form of exchange that seems to leave her unchanged and looks, in effect, like a nonexchange. On her first appearance at the court, she is described as receiving compliments with "so noble a modesty that she didn't seem to understand them, let alone be moved by them" (avec une modestie si noble qu'il ne semblait pas qu'elle les entendît ou, du moins, qu'elle en fût touchée [43]). Punning on the two senses of *entendît*—"hear" and "understand"—Lafayette lets the reader infer from initial appearances a deficiency of understanding, indeed a psychic vacancy, in her heroine. Thus to Valincour the princess appears an "innocente" who "ne sait que répondre à ce qu'on lui dit; les moindres choses sont au-dessus de ses connaissances" (She doesn't know what to say to what one tells her; the slightest things are above her cognitive powers) (*Lettres*, 37). By seeming not to know, she anticipates the game of eighteenth-century conduct-book heroines of modesty, for whom virtue will lie in sustaining the "assault" of masculine communication without injury to their minds. But whereas eighteenth-century and, after them, Victorian conventions of feminine morality promote abstraction as a means to avoid sexual knowledge, the joke in Lafayette's novel is that the princess's deflection of words addressed to her and capacity to ignore them as if they did not really concern her (in this first instance, evidence of the social grace with which she receives

12. Lafayette, *The Princesse of Clèves*, trans. Robin Buss, 39; hereafter referred to as Buss. "Mlle de Chartres répondit qu'elle lui remarquait les mêmes bonnes qualités; qu'elle l'épouserait même avec moins de répugnance qu'un autre, mais qu'elle n'avait aucune inclination particulière pour sa personne" (50).

compliments) will, as the plot unfolds, function as the measure of how much meaning her mind in fact takes in, and of how much she implicates herself in seemingly neutral, free observations. Far from signifying a blank and vacant mind ignorant of human desire, her capacity to listen as if she weren't supplies the condition for a proto-Jamesian "intercourse" in which every utterance has penetrating power, however indirect its address, and that nevertheless leaves interlocutors free of one another's knowledge.[13]

iii. the inconsequence of knowledge

Like many heroine-centered fictions, then, Lafayette's novel under-stands intimacy between people as potentially objectifying and intrusive and presupposes the pessimistic view of intersubjective knowledge af-forded by the analogy of psychological knowledge to carnal—to a sexual possession that can never absolutely establish its difference from violation. But if the generic heroine trades in her autonomy for the passive condi-tion of being known by another, the princess refuses to choose between the two. Lafayette uses the ambiguity of gift giving—the minimal differ-ence between giving and giving up, between self-bestowal and self-aban-donment—to make it impossible to claim the heroine's gift and convert the knowledge she bestows into power. Thus if the norm of action in courtship novels is a progress that brings the lover within reach of his mis-tress, Mme de Clèves' confessions are antiacts that prevent such progress and undo the equation between greater knowledge and greater possession. Self-revelation as she practices it—as an open secret—is not an occasion

13. Thus whereas the princess receives without appropriating compliments addressed to her, young British and American women a century or so later will be taught to receive without registering insults to their sexually pure minds: "when [a young female] hears an indelicate allusion: she ought to appear not to understand it, and to receive from it no more impression than if she were a post" (William Cobbett, *Advice to Young Men, and (Incidentally) to Young Women in the Middle and High Ranks of Life* . . . [London, 1829], letter 3, para. 90 [cited in Yeazell, *Fictions of Modesty*, 56]). As Yeazell argues, this language of "unknow-ing" and "insensibility" usually only increases the knowing consciousness of their young female addressees (57–58). In contrast, French *pudeur*, as it works in La-fayette's novel, never pretends to be anything but the means by which characters know their own minds and "handle" their emotions, but as if these were foreign, almost aesthetic objects.

for appropriation, and through her, Lafayette makes paradigmatic speech acts that ought to be the basis for some kind of claim, some hold, but in fact prevent any taking at all.

"I am putting this information into your hands so that you may do nothing with it." So one might sum up the tenor of the princess's famous *aveu*. By it the princess merely presents the prince with something he will need to overlook. "I am trusting you with the secret of my illicit feelings for another man—a secret that you will do best by me to ignore as I do." *Ignore* acquires its active sense of "overlook"—an action that demands some degree of effort; otherwise, Mme de Clèves is simply asking M. de Clèves to act toward her as before: "Je vous demande mille pardons si j'ai des sentiments qui vous déplaisent" (I beg you a thousand times to forgive me if I have feelings that displease you) (122). Unable either to deny or to alter these feelings, she simply asks that he excuse them, although whether or not he does so will not change her behavior toward him. In this sense her act calls his autonomy into play, and the more she relies on his generosity, the less she seems to want or expect anything of him. In his initial response to her *aveu*, he himself articulates their relationship as one of mutual overlooking; at best, they can provide one another with the deaf walls on which to record their impossible demands, even as they pay one another no attention: "Refusez-moi toutes les fois que je vous demanderai de pareilles choses; mais ne vous offensez pourtant pas si je vous les demande" (Refuse me each time I ask you such things; but do not be offended that I ask them of you) (124–25).

Through the princess's *aveu*, we can define the open secret as a paradigm for trust: just as she promises faithfulness precisely by her acknowledgment of her withheld *power* to be unfaithful, the open secret asks that one accept as sufficient and real facts that may never become operative and of which one may have no direct, empirical evidence.[14] Though

14. In Alliston's words, the princess "demands credit: credit for the truth of an incomplete narrative that lacks evidence other than its own lack of completion and the openness, sincerity, and freedom with which it is offered" (*Virtue's Faults*, 59). According to Alliston, Lafayette's novel and heroine together introduce an immaterial form of evidence—what she describes as the substitution of the "private narration" of "truthfulness," which only a "private public" of readers can "credit," for the public image of wifely fealty once supposed to guarantee the legitimacy of patrilineal inheritance. But as something for which only the princess can supply the evidence, this new type of truth also produces a different relation

he could not have asked for surer proof of fidelity than the one he is given, M. de Clèves dies of jealousy less because of anything he believes Nemours and Mme de Clèves have done together than because he cannot bring himself to credit those feelings in her—credit them as psychic capital that can be no "loss" to him—just as he cannot make the formal fact of her faithfulness real to himself. She acts toward him on principle, and trusting him to do likewise, she does not try to make him believe her. Only when pressed to persuade him before he dies, does she tell him in her defense that she never did anything that she wouldn't have wanted him to see—in other words, that she always acted in his absence *as if* he had been present. "Je n'ai jamais fait d'action dont je n'eusse souhaité que vous eussiez été témoin" (162–63). But the prince has no way of testing this *as if,* and the past conditional tense names only a forever unrealized potential. The princess's readiness to be judged by an outside party, in this case the prince, in fact corresponds to her ability to do without his actual presence. Even her faithfulness to him amounts, in this sense, to a form of autonomy from him. By promising him that "at least her actions will never displease him" (du moins je ne vous déplairai jamais par mes actions [122]), she indirectly retains control over her own mind; faithfully if minimally fulfilling her marital obligations to him leaves her free to pursue her own thoughts.

A similar language of continence informs her plea that he be "*content*" with the assurance "that none of [her] actions have revealed [her] feelings and that nothing has been said to [her] from which [she] might have

---

to time: predicated on the continuance in time of the very power she declines to use—the freedom to act independently of the prince—the aveu asks him to accept as sufficient a truth that can never be guaranteed once and for all but only assumed from one day to the next, as long as she remains alive and capable of "falling like other women." Something of this capacity for incompletion—this readiness to trust and lend credit in advance of definitive conclusion—informs even the novel's last sentence declaring the princess's life, like those of the historical figures surrounding her, a "bio teleio": "Et sa vie, qui fut assez courte, laissa des exemples de vertu inimitables." On Alliston's reading, this offhanded legacy left to no one in particular completes Lafayette's (and the princess's) "fictionalization" of feminine virtue: its openness of address—the absence of a designated recipient for the "inimitable examples of virtue" and uncertainty even of their reception—undoes the definitiveness of its deposit as narrated fact. See Alliston, *Virtue's Faults,* 57–59; 73–75.

taken offense" (124). Faithful to him in form and deed if not in mind, she asks that he accept as sufficient this formal chastity and to credit her a purity of word and act that has had no bearing on the actual state of things. For whatever her silence, her feelings are suspected, and without giving offense, Nemours has made his passion known to her. The inoperative nature of the truth—the absence of direct external evidence for how things really are—forces the issue of the characters' capacity to trust one another. Ineffective in preventing knowledge between her and Nemours, the princess's purity is a truth for which the prince must simply take her word. Conversely, if what she says is true and no words have passed that could have given her offence, only the princess can testify to the passion of which she speaks. This passion not only excludes M. de Clèves as an actor but bars him from even being its witness; it remains cognitively inaccessible to him, not something he could have seen or even suspected on his own.

That the prince should accept the truth of his wife's fidelity to him (truth that, after her *aveu*, should have been self-evident) only on his deathbed figures the very unworldliness—the inappropriable, impractical, even unlivable nature—of the truth dispensed by the open secret of her chaste passion. His wasted enlightenment is not simply a perverse twist of fate by which he learns the truth too late to profit by it but rather the measure of a truth that is, as far as he is concerned, only good for death:

> Je me sens si proche de la mort que je ne veux rien voir de ce qui me pourrait faire regretter la vie. Vous m'avez éclairci trop tard; mais ce me sera toujours un soulagement d'*emporter la pensée* que vous êtes digne de l'estime que j'aie eue pour vous. (163; emphasis added)

> [I feel so close to death that I don't wish to see anything that might cause me to regret life. You have enlightened me too late; but it will always be a relief to me to *take away the thought* that you are worthy of the esteem that I've had for you.]

Accepting or being convinced of the truth is conditional, it seems, on withdrawal from life; the prince can only take away with him the *thought* of the princess's worthiness, while refusing its translation into lived reality. Readers unsympathetic to the prince are quick to suggest that his avoidance of her truth in life only serves his ambition: certain that *with these words*, dead, he will cast a greater shadow over her than alive, he finds, like Mme de Chartres before him, a way of leaving the princess without leaving her free. Victim only of an uncommitted crime, he produces his death as material evidence of her guilty conscience.

But his death also materializes the nonpossessive relation he *should* have maintained toward Mme de Clèves in life; in dying he only takes away the thought of her faithfulness. On this reading, his willingness to recognize her fidelity and yet still to die makes him a paradigmatically non-exploitative reader capable of crediting a truth in which he cannot hope to participate. His acknowledgment includes the recognition of its own irrelevance: by it, he does nothing for her. In thus crediting the princess an inner experience inaccessible to his gaze and always already hers—both her passion and her refusal to consummate it—M. de Clèves adumbrates, however belatedly, an ethic of recognition premised on accepting and acknowledging, above all, the limits to what we can claim to know or have the right to know of one another.

In the same way, Nemours can do little with the knowledge he receives when overhearing her *aveu* to the prince, and the full sense of her words quickly takes back the initial joy they give him:

Il s'abandonna d'abord à cette joie; mais elle ne fut pas longue, quand il fit réflexion que la même chose qui lui venait d'apprendre qu'il avait touché le cœur de Mme de Clèves, le devait persuader aussi qu'il n'en recevrait jamais nulle marque et qu'il était impossible d'engager une personne qui avait recours à un remède si extraordinaire. (125)

[At first he abandoned himself to this joy; but it was short-lived, as he realized that the same thing which had just informed him that he had touched Mme de Clèves' heart ought also to persuade him that he would never receive any sign of it, and that it was impossible to engage a person who had recourse to so extraordinary a remedy.]

The very words that give Nemours unassailable proof that he has touched the heart of Mme de Clèves also assure him, on another level, of the impossibility of engaging her; loved, he has nothing to hope for from this love. As in the Pascalian epistemology of God, to know *x* is to know *x* as unrealizable.[15]

15. As presented through her aveu, the potency of the princess's love for Nemours corresponds to a Pascalian essential possibility, as Lucien Goldmann uses the term in his *Le dieu caché* to describe the absent presence of Pascal's God—a possibility that works all its effects as such. Commenting on Pascal's

But the *aveu* is perhaps most dispossessive to the princess herself, as her first reflections on it afterward suggest: "Elle trouva qu'elle s'était ôté elle-même le cœur et l'estime de son mari et qu'elle s'était creusé un abîme dont elle ne sortirait jamais" (125). The crucial reflexivity of "s'était ôté" makes the sentence difficult to translate. "Elle-même" refers to the princess as the subject and reemphasizes the horror of finding that she has just, by herself, without anybody else's help, done exactly what actually being unfaithful to the prince would have done.[16] Meaning to take away, to withdraw, to remove or cut out, the verb *ôter* suggests a singular, lightning-quick act of dispossession, itself difficult to undo. While the verb's subject is usually different from its object, the true strangeness of the sentence is not the verb's reflexive use but this reflexive use being combined with an indirect object: the princess does something to herself with her husband's heart and esteem. What she does is not exactly a self-mutilation or self-removal but a causing to withdraw of another person's property or investment in her. Effecting a passage from the *not yet* to the *never to be*, this disinvestment confronts us with the novel's paradigmatic form of action, difficult to take into account because it affects only a virtuality.

iv. unburdened reception: the open secret

As discussed in the previous chapter, Sedgwick's work on the epistemology of the closet defines the "open secret" as an inherently *conservative* form of potent knowledge that, without active denial, allows its subjects to continue to ignore, and hence contain, this potential. Along similar lines but to different effect, I have been using the term to refer to the

---

fragment 559, "S'il paraît une fois, il est toujours" (If he appears once, he forever is), Goldmann writes: "Pour la pensée tragique, [ces mots] ne représentent qu'une possibilité essentielle mais qui ne se réalise jamais. . . . Pour Blaise Pascal qui écrit le fragment 559, Dieu est toujours et ne paraît jamais, bien qu'il soit certain . . . qu'il puisse paraître à chaque instant de la vie sans qu'il le fasse jamais effectivement" (For tragic thought, this fragment represents only an essential possibility that never realizes itself. For Blaise Pascal who writes fragment 559, God forever is and never appears, even though it's certain that he could appear at any moment in life without his ever in effect doing so.) (*Le dieu caché*, 46).

16. Lacking the reflexive form, a faithful English translation would have to go something like, "She found that she had herself deprived herself of her husband's love and esteem."

perfect impracticality of a knowledge that works in the novel to inhibit action of one kind and displace it with another. As I suggested earlier, Sedgwick's open secret is conservative because crucially redundant in its articulative as well as disarticulative effects: it communicates information to those who already possess knowledge and keeps this same information from those who don't. But whereas Sedgwick's early work tends to emphasize only this first direction, concentrating on the open secret's disciplinary effects in keeping knowledge impotent because never admitted, I want to pay closer attention to what the open secret enables, namely a strangely passive, all but agentless and guiltless, exchange between people. Thus in *La Princesse de Clèves* characters know one another in ways that both prevent and make unnecessary direct physical contact and explicit communication between them. The open secret is not simply a retractive mode of expression—a way of making something about oneself unavailable, burying it in the very means of its revelation; it is also a way of letting oneself be known without even seeming to, calling into play the interpretive powers of one's auditors and engaging their moral freedom.

Thus the "secret" of "open secret" need not mean hidden or unstated but simply unavailable, untouchable, nonpossessable, implying a relation to the beloved that neither appropriates nor denies. In a context where the norm for fulfillment remains sexual possession, it describes a chaste and chastening mode of interaction: chaste in the double sense of bearing little or no material consequences and of belonging to those who engage in the least possible intercourse, chastening in the sense of limiting anyone's power to do more than leave and be left alone. This chasteness also refers to the open secret's perfect economy of means: for both its revelation and concealment, it uses no more than already available channels of communication.[17]

17. In the self-sufficiency with which its characters repeatedly dramatize only to leave suspended a failure to meet for which there is no external solution, the novel invites comparison to the "nondramatic nature of Racinian drama" as Claudia Brodsky discusses it in "'The Impression of Movement.'" Brodsky argues that Racine's tragedies not only "render superfluous the revelatory impulses of literary interpretation" by their "wholly explicit or self-explicating quality" (164), but they also reject "the transformative power of their own medium, literary language" (170–71). "[Racinian texts] present an atectonic dissonance, a tension in relations, which no action can resolve or recast as past history. . . . Just as the measured clarity of Racine's alexandrines gives irresolvably unstable

Defining the open secret as a form of knowledge that allows—indeed asks—me to ignore what I know, as I have done in this preliminary overview, suggests that it puts pressure on the difference between knowledge and acknowledgment, a difference that Stanley Cavell invests with moral significance in his work on skepticism and the problem of knowing others.[18] This difference has nothing to do with degrees of cognitive certainty but is a question of whether my knowing has any practical and moral value, of whether it counts and for whom. "Acknowledgment," Cavell writes, "goes beyond knowledge, not in the order, or as a feat, of cognition, but in the call upon me to express the knowledge at its core, to recognize what I know, to do something in the light of it, apart from which this knowledge remains without expression, hence perhaps without possession" (*The Claim of Reason*, 457). But contrary to the suggestion that "doing something in light of what I know" is the only right way to receive knowledge, Lafayette's novel defines another kind of faith or fidelity to what one knows. It is commonly assumed that knowledge without acknowledgment is worthless, not only inconsequential but morally void because the truth (whether the truth of your suffering or of the way I distort my relation to you, to use Cavell's examples) asks to be met—demands acknowledgment; knowing and not saying that I know represents a failure to meet my truth—take "possession" of it—and hence a moral shortcoming toward myself and others.

The open secret in *La Princesse de Clèves*, however, complicates these assumptions by suggesting that there are truths, or knowledges between humans, that do not ask to be so met. The novel provides a crucial insight into the *passiveness* by which people come to know and be known by one another. In the novel, taking action means saying, "You can't know me," but doing nothing means presenting oneself to be known to anyone who has eyes to see, and "having the eyes to see" represents serious moral work on the part of interpreters. The same passivity structures one's relation-

---

relations the impression of being at rest, the nondynamic structure of the dramas gives classical or fully articulated form to events whose own logic insists that they cannot be so contained" (173, 174). Brodsky's articulation of the surprisingly *architectural* effects of Racine's literary texts throws light on the comparably mysterious effects of Lafayette's impersonal narration, which presents subjective experiences as discrete, immutable events that seem never to have known a time of genesis or occurrence.

18. See "Knowing and Acknowledging," in Cavell, *Must We Mean What We Say?* See also part 4 of Cavell, *The Claim of Reason*.

ship to oneself and to a desire one can neither seek out nor hide from; significantly, the princess comes closest to meeting her desire when she is not trying to claim it, face up to it. In short, *La Princesse de Clèves* offers an alternative to the common moral framework in which leaving what you know unsaid counts as dishonesty and not acting on what you know constitutes either conscious hypocrisy or unconscious denial, for the novel suggests that *right*, morally free knowledge between humans demands just this kind of avoidance. The princess is not a hypocrite, nor does she hide from her feelings; on the contrary, the "open secret" names the utter simplicity with which she meets the unmeetable in herself and others.[19]

Readers have often noted the analogy between the seemingly contradictory over- and underassumption of responsibility, by which the heroine seems both to write herself in and out of the picture, and Lafayette's elusive historical style, where agency and causality are similarly dissociated in the sense that "no one speaks" or takes credit for the recounting, which is content to pose, without elaboration, a causal relation between successive events.[20] Indeed the simplicity with which the princess delivers

19. Cavell's own title to the final chapter of *The Claim of Reason*—"Between Acknowledgment and Avoidance"—suggests the need to negotiate a form of acknowledgment that would not betray this passivity and hence would look, initially at least, more like avoidance. Cavell identifies in human subjects what is both a reticence toward and openness to being known and, without contradiction, takes this openness as the marker of their privacy and unknowability. It is this openness that can make inappropriate, indeed dangerous, direct, explicit forms of recognition and questioning: "It is true of a great deal of what goes on in me that normally if it is to be known I must tell it, or give expression to it. But for nothing in me is this absolutely true. . . . About human beings there are only open secrets, open questions" (459).

20. Mitchell Greenberg, for example, identifies in "the prevalence of negative sentence formations" a "hysterical gesture of advancing an idea, an image, a form of sexuality in order immediately to recall it" (Greenberg, *Subjectivity and Subjugation in Seventeenth-Century Drama and Prose*, 206). Greenberg reads this structure of giving-so-as-to-withdraw shared by feminine text and heroine as a "refusal of [the law of] circulation and castration" demanded by the symbolic (208), and an undermining of the "novel's supposed Classical clarity" or "éclat" (206). In contrast to the general tendency, exemplified here by Greenberg, to treat the gaps, litotes, and other modes of feminine "aphanisis" in Lafayette's and Mme de Clèves' discourse as primarily a mode of resistance and refusal, whether of presence, phallocentric logos, or the symbolic, I'm putting the emphasis on what their cutting terseness allows them to meet.

herself to her husband's judgment and thereby escapes it—the strangely
noninsistent, passing assertiveness with which she announces a guilty
passion (to the prince) or judgment (to Nemours) and leaves it at that,
without self-justification, because the announcement alone is enough to
empty the guilt—finds its parallel in the lightness with which Lafayette's
passé simple disposes of a death or a life. "Withdrawn from spoken French
. . . its function [in Barthes' words] no longer that of tense" but to rid
time of its experiential fullness, the preterite belongs, according to Benveniste's famously contested distinction, not to discourse but to "historical utterance" (or *récit* in Genette's terms), where it contributes to the
illusion of "no one speak[ing]" and "events seem[ing] to narrate themselves."[21] Lending to her narration the cool with which it delivers psychological experiences as historical truths—without stopping to comment
on these nonobservable events, let alone justify the "narrator's" knowledge of them—Lafayette's employment of "the tense of the event outside
the person of the narrator" might in this sense seem of a piece with the
heroine's apparent double withdrawal—first from the messiness of psychological experience and personhood, then from the scrutiny of public
accountability.[22] Yet far from representing a throwback to a threatened

21. Benveniste, *Problems in General Linguistics*, 208. Paul Ricœur discusses the
critical reception of Benveniste's distinction in *Temps et récit* (2:118–21). Barthes'
critique of the preterite as an illusion of order that empties lived experience of its
density—"part of a security system for Belles-Lettres" and a "formal pact made
between the writer and society for the justification of the former and the serenity
of the latter"—appears in *Le Degré zéro de l'écriture*, 46–52; *Writing Degree Zero*,
30–34.

22. Neither Lafayette nor Madame de Chartres, who sometimes takes over
as the intradiegetic purveyor of historical anecdotes, divulges the sources that
might ground or "authorize" their narration; in Kamuf's words, "Mme de Lafayette's narrator presents no credentials underwriting the validity of what is
told about that which, by definition, is meant to be hidden" (Kamuf, *Fictions of
Feminine Desire*, 67). According to Kamuf, the "obfuscation of the origin of this
knowledge" displaces the production of knowledge from any particular narrating
agency onto an "all-knowing source which comprehends [the characters'] necessarily limited knowledge" (68). Kamuf's analysis with respect to Lafayette shares
obvious features with the broader critique usually leveled at the third-person
"omniscient" but nonmanifest narrator—"felt throughout but never seen"—as
pure ideology effect. Yet rather than treat the silence of Lafayette's narrators on
their sources as the mark of withheld or insufficient enlightenment—a covering

ideal of classical decorum as if in retreat from both the opacity of subjective interiority and the demand to make oneself intelligible to others, the unhesitating incisiveness of Lafayette's prose allows the novel to bypass, as I've been arguing, the skeptical crisis produced by the sentimental realism of the eighteenth-century epistolary novel, where the value of internal states only grows with the increasing sense of their inability to manifest themselves to convincing or persuasive effect.[23]

Read through the precise terms of the "least said" required by the *aveu* to the prince, the style of minimal articulation whereby both Lafayette and her heroine hardly stop to explain what they pose thus becomes leg-

---

up of tracks and a covert assumption of universality awaiting demystification and exposure—I'd like to ask what Lafayette's self-silencing narration permits by producing knowledge while eliding the moral categories of "person" or "agent" to which it may be assigned. For the resulting difficulty that readers have justifying, explaining, and claiming their knowledge effectively renders them innocent of it and belongs to the novel's overall hindrance of applied knowledge.

23. Gérard Genette's recognition in Lafayette, as in Stendhal, of an "accent of truth" that has nothing to do with psychological realism, but accompanies "a fully assumed arbitrariness that hardly even tries to justify itself," remains in this sense as salient as ever: "L'accent de vérité, à mille lieues de toute espèce de réalisme, ne se sépare pas ici du sentiment violent d'un arbitraire pleinement assumé, et qui néglige de se justifier" (Genette, *Figures II*, 77). Genette's analysis has the advantage of distinguishing Lafayette's "extreme reserve of commentary and all but complete absence of general maxims" (78, my translation) from what it at the same time looks like—the economy of the "récit vraisemblable" (78), which also does not justify itself because it relies on "everyone's" implicit knowledge of probable behavior. By drawing on the lexicon of romantic genius—invoking the "savage individuality" that "renders great actions (and great works) unforeseeable" (77)—Genette reinflects this reserve, oddly enough, not as secrecy but as an *openness* without explication not reducible to ideology's naturalization into muteness of what "everyone is supposed to know." His account of Lafayette's text as oscillating between the classicism according to which nothing needs explaining (and that which does is not worth doing) and the "modernism" (we might say "romanticism") according to which great actions do not admit of explanation (or even representation), might seem to follow a familiar dichotomy opposing the normative and the singular, the common and the sublime. But his comments in fact suggest that Lafayette and Stendhal may be at their most "modern" when not treating the secret of action as an unfathomable mystery or as something only legible in terms of psychological depth.

ible as something other than mere dogmatism or indifference to persuasion—a trust in the sufficiency of announcement in matters where no
degree of positive demonstration would ever be enough. Indeed, the unhesitating quality that inheres in the princess's assertions announcing an
otherwise unevinced inner life is perhaps best read in accordance with the
Kantian irony that it takes less time and effort to ascertain the demands of
self-imposed duty than to calculate one's world-determined good.[24] While
it may be perceived as mild self-righteousness, and however much she
may inwardly suffer, resist, delay, or withhold, only this quality of not-
waiting—as an absence of calculating prudence and heedless presumption
on the other's confidence without first testing its limits—allows her to
find her innocence in the act of avowal and not before. The specificity of
Lafayette's contribution to the psychological novel lies, accordingly, less in
its privileging of hard-to-represent, always potentially nonmanifest mental
acts of consent or demurral, than in its emphasis on how little such acts
may require, let alone result in, so that the qualification—"*Not nothing,
but an inner activity or exchange that externally might pass as nothing*"—can
stand as the paradigmatic hermeneutic response that the novel repeatedly elicits. Thus even as the cursory dimensions of Lafayette's prose may
school us to see better—to pay more attention and become more careful, delicate readers of a minimally gestural subjectivity—the novel also
disabuses us of the illusion that interpretive vision is capable of technical
improvement. For if the prose presents an "all but nothing," this is less as
a measure of the contingent material inconsequence of a subjective decision, which may or may not show up on the plane of observable results,
than as a sign of the essential paucity or minimalism defining subjective
acts insofar as they are, on one level, easily discharged, not hard to complete, not a matter of violent interpretive work on the self.[25]

24. "What is to be done in accordance with the principle of the autonomy of
choice is seen quite easily and without hesitation by the most common understanding; what is to be done on the presupposition of heteronomy of choice is
difficult to see and requires knowledge of the world; in other words, what *duty*
is, is plain of itself to everyone, but what is to bring true, lasting advantage, if
this is to extend to the whole of one's existence, is always veiled in impenetrable
obscurity" (Kant, *Critique of Practical Reason*, 33).

25. Reference to the dimension by which Kantian *Vernunft* (reason), usually
understood as what lies beyond ordinary understanding, speaks with a plainness,
openness, and accessibility unavailable to the measured and measuring work of

In this respect it may be worth returning to the scene of the stolen miniature in which the princess lets Nemours have what he has already taken and what in any case is not hers to give (technically the portrait belongs to the prince and signifies his possession of the original), as an instance of the way in which Lafayette's itself unhesitating, often trenchant, third-person narration can transmute the *durée* of psychological hesitation and moral confusion (marked by the *imparfait* or progressive past tense) to the instant of a decision as lightly posed as it is assumed, strangely free of agent-guilt, because given in the *passé simple* or tense of completed action. Recording an otherwise imperceptible subjective decision (imperceptible "from the outside" since it is a decision to let pass, to do nothing, to choose what already is), Lafayette's impersonal style also passes lightly over it and so appears to double, on the level of narration, the release from responsibility that, on the moral level, reduces the princess's *faveur* to all but nothing—the very release that, far from devaluing the act, lends it the gratuitousness of a gift:

Mme de Clèves n'était pas peu embarrassée. La raison voulait qu'elle demandât son portrait; mais, en le demandant publiquement, c'était apprendre à tout le monde les sentiments que ce prince avait pour elle, et, en le lui demandant en particulier, c'était quasi l'engager à lui parler de sa passion. Enfin elle jugea qu'il valait mieux le lui laisser, et elle fut bien aise de lui accorder une faveur qu'elle lui pouvait faire sans qu'il sût même qu'elle la lui faisait. (92)

[Mme de Clèves was not a little embarrassed. Reason would have had her ask for her portrait; but to ask for it publicly was to apprise the whole world of the feelings the prince had for her; and to ask for it in private was all but to engage him to talk to her of his passion. In the end she judged that it was better to leave it him, and she was quite pleased to accord him a favor which she could do him without his even knowing that she was doing it him.]

---

empirical *Verstand* (understanding), can also lend a different, less critical valence to Barthes' account of the *passé simple* as the "operative sign whereby the narrator reduces the exploded reality to a slim and pure logos, without density, without volume, without spread, and whose sole function is to unite as rapidly as possible a cause and an end" (*Writing Degree Zero*, 30–31). I am suggesting we reread the lack of weight or density of the juncture simply and fleetingly effected by the *passé simple* between events a and b, not as a trick of art designed to rob time of its manifold complexity or as the mark of subjective destitution but, on the contrary, as the measure of the lightness with which subjective autonomy can assert a causal relation to x and the next moment find itself acquitted.

The scene invites comparison with the more famous scene of open theft in Poe's "Purloined Letter," where the Queen is powerless to stop the Minister from taking the letter she has counted on the King not to see, insofar as both dramas give nothing, or very little, to the external spectator to see; here, as there, "narration," to borrow Lacan's words, "doubles the drama with a commentary" without which the scene's "action would remain invisible [to the public]" (*Écrits*, 12). Following Lacan's analysis, one might explain this "nothing to be seen" as indicative of the chain of intersubjective gazes, whereby the possession of the portrait—in itself a dead material thing Nemours can now look at to his heart's content—matters less to him than knowing, and letting the princess know that he knows, that he has been seen—and even blessed—by her in the act of taking her portrait.[26] Yet what interests me here is less the heroine's inter-

26. "Giving in love what she does not have" is Lacan's phrase for the woman who sustains (and by the unconditionality of her gift risks losing) phallic desire in the gap between unconditional demand and gratifiable needs (Lacan, *Feminine Sexuality*, 84). Lacanian analysis, with its critique of rationalist, ego-oriented ways of thinking about desire as brute acquisitiveness undetermined by the question of what the Other wants, might thus usefully explain the more "delicate" mode of aggression, by which Nemours is not content to "objectify" the princess—to acquire her tangible representation—but insists on gaining her subjective complicity—on letting her know that he has perceived her perception—even as he knows (or prefers) not to wait for her first-person response:

M. de Nemours, perceiving her embarrassment and half-guessing its cause, approached and whispered to her:

"If you have seen what I've dared to do, have the goodness, madam, to let me believe that you ignore it; I don't dare ask for more."

And with these words, he withdrew and did not wait for her response. (92)

In effect a declaration that he counts on her to lower her gaze so that he may enjoy her where she is not, this strange address (strange, because it reminds the princess of the very thing it asks her to ignore) might seem, on the one hand, to support Greenberg's claim that both characters are caught in the "narcissistic hold of the imaginary register" where "no reciprocity of passion is possible except as representation . . . in the masturbatory fantasy of seeing oneself being loved" (Greenberg, *Subjectivity and Subjugation in Seventeenth-Century Drama and Prose*, 203). On the other hand, by addressing her precisely as the one who need say nothing, such an address also presupposes the autonomy of response for proof of which it declines to wait. As the least form of attention to the other's power of response, the gesture in this sense fleetingly suggests an alternative to—

pellation as an interpretive subject into a possibly infinite series of "I see that you have seen me see" than the ease with which Lafayette's impersonal style disposes of available alternatives and bottoms out the protagonist's own subjective impasse, so that the latter appears to find her choice in the precise time it takes to decide to do nothing. Indicating the ongoing agony of embarrassment as experienced by the character, the imperfect tense of the verbs *voulait* and *n'était*, belongs to those telltale linguistic signs of absorption in the near but not quite first-person perspective associated with free indirect style.[27] Yet the joke in the sentence "enfin, elle jugea . . . " is that judgment itself appears to yield an unexpected felicity occurring in the time of a smile—as soon (but also only as long?) as the princess "concludes the time to understand" that she can do nothing better than what she is in any case quite content—*aise*—to do: play dumb and entrust her gift to the other's possible imperception or power not to see.[28]

---

only to disappear between—both the closet of imaginary mimetic relations and the "phallic role of having the 'word,' of manipulating and controlling the Law" that Greenberg claims is denied Nemours (205).

27. See, e.g., Banfield, *Unspeakable Sentences*, 104.

28. The swiftness of Lafayette's narration helps, in other words, "dialectically reduce the moment of *concluding the time for comprehending* to last but the *instant of the glance*" (Lacan, *Écrits: The First Complete Edition in English*, 173). The formulation comes from Lacan's early essay "Le temps logique et l'assertion de certitude anticipée," where he uses the problem of the three prisoners who must decide the color on their backs out of a possible three white discs and two black, to challenge the supposed "timelessness" of logic, according to which logical solutions are deemed instantaneously available and time plays only a contingent role—a question of how long it takes the subject to figure them out. Here, except in the easiest scenario where B and C each wear black discs and A immediately knows he must be wearing white, the dilemma makes essential to its solution the passage of time in which the prisoners notice that none of them (yet) possesses the solution since none is moving toward the exit. In the second scenario, if A sees black on B and white on C, then A will say to himself, "If I were wearing black then C would be moving toward the door, solution in hand; but he is not moving, therefore I must be wearing white." The third scenario involves A displacing this thought exercise onto his neighbor: if A sees white on B and white on C, then he will say to himself, "If B were seeing black on me then he would be saying to himself 'If I were wearing black then C would be moving toward the door, but he is not moving, therefore I am wearing white—I will move toward the door,' but since B makes no such movement and neither does

The chiastic play between the singular *durée* of heedlessly uncounted time of the imperfect progressive past, on the one hand, and the *passé simple*'s power to level or make time as nothing, on the other, finds a more terrifying exemplification in the episode of the betrayed mistress's letter, whose facsimile Nemours and Mme de Clèves together attempt to forge for the queen's eyes and on the Vidame's behalf. Here a series of verbs in the imperfect past registers the simultaneous sense of hours flying and time not mattering as, closeted together, forgetful of their purpose and the worldly interests that wait on them, the two write to no effect: "Elle ne sentait que le plaisir de voir M. de Nemours, elle en avait une joie pure et sans mélange qu'elle n'avait jamais sentie: cette joie lui donnait une liberté et un enjouement dans l'esprit que M. de Nemours ne lui avait jamais vus et qui redoublaient son amour" (She was feeling only the pleasure of seeing M. de Nemours, taking from it a pure and unmixed joy which she had never felt before; this joy gave her a freedom and lightness of spirit that M. de Nemours had never seen in her and that redoubled his love) (117). That these few misspent hours—founded in illusion and devoted to fabricating illusion—will be of decisive and fatal consequence to nearly everyone concerned, causing the Vidame's downfall and leading directly to the princess's *aveu*, does not lessen their immateriality or uncountability—what one might call, with the poorly copied letter itself, their inachievement ("Enfin, à peine, à quatre heures, la lettre était-elle achevée" [At last, at four o'clock, the letter was hardly finished])—just as the brutal resumption in the following paragraph of the *passé simple*'s

---

C, I [A] must conclude that B and C are, like me, seeing two whites, therefore I am wearing white." Thus, the solution occurs in the time of hesitation during which each discovers that "in the inertia of his neighbor he holds the key to his own problem" (qu'il tient dans l'inertie de son semblable la clef de son propre problème [205]). The connection I wish to make with the passage in Lafayette lies in the way the very interval of waiting eventually makes movement possible, just as in the scene of the stolen portrait, the mere realization of an impasse frees something else up—not only makes decision possible but renders it superfluous. In an unpublished essay "Precipitation: Poetry and the Rain of Information," Celeste Langan remarks that the word "certain" in Lacan's phrase "after a certain time" (Après s'être considérés un certain temps [198]) works precisely to name the impossibility of determining exactly how long this interval must last, in the same way that Dickinson's famous "certain slant of light" opens unto a certainty "nearly indistinguishable from randomness, from a principle of uncertainty."

level flattening or making even of the fates of minor characters is only the obverse to the lovers' choice to make nothing of time.[29] An hour given up to play may be fatal, but (and, perhaps, because) time is as nothing for the aorist past as it levels whole years and decades to come within the course of a few short sentences, as in Dickinson's reduction of the downfalls of the Doges of Venice to fallings "Soundless as dots - on a Disc of snow -."

In recounting these unhappy fates, Lafayette's narrator gives enough details to suggest that, where the Vidame is concerned at least, this downfall was in any case already unavoidable, thereby implying that the parenthesis in time represented by the fictitious letter remains, in an important sense, supplementary to what it produces, and making it more difficult simply to extrapolate from the episode a moralistic condemnation of love as an idleness pernicious to the interests of the community. Indeed, more strongly than the familiar critique that would accuse the lovers of failing their peers by idling away their time and ignoring the serious business of history, the episode conjoins history as waste and love as vanity—as a feint from which one does not recover: the letter the princess mistakes as addressed to Nemours might as well have been, for however causeless, or rather precisely as causeless, the jealousy that burns through her ("cuisantes douleurs" [119]) is sufficient as such to void the blank space of pre- or anticipated consummation of its potential, so that later, when, during their final interview, she invokes the "certainty of no longer being loved by you as I am now" (173), the void from which she speaks is not abstract

29. "[La reine] demeura convaincue, non seulement que [la lettre] était au vidame de Chartres, mais elle crut que la reine dauphine y avait part et qu'il y avait quelque intelligence entre eux. Cette pensée augmenta tellement la haine qu'elle avait pour cette princesse qu'elle ne lui pardonna jamais et qu'elle la persécuta jusqu'à ce qu'elle l'eût fait sortir de France.

Pour le vidame de Chartres, il fut ruiné auprès d'elle. . . . Leur liaison se rompit, et elle le perdit ensuite à la conjuration d'Amboise où il se trouva embarrassé" (118).

[The queen remained convinced, not only that [the letter] belonged to the vidame de Chartres, but she also believed that the dauphiness had a hand in it and that there was an understanding between them. This thought so augmented her hatred for this princess that she never forgave her and persecuted her until she caused her to leave France.

As for the vidame de Chartres, he was ruined by her. . . . Their liaison was broken off, and she brought him down afterward on the occasion of the Amboise conspiracy in which he was implicated.]

or pre-experiential but is already blocked or traversed by the prolepsis by which she will have lived his loss. It makes little sense to call the princess a virginal idealist shying away from the pains of mortal experience or avoiding contact with history out of fear of having her fingers burnt, when "engagement" with history takes, as it does here, no more real or concrete form than being burned by its "white heat." Whereas the nineteenth-century novel of ambition will make plot the instrument and figure for what Peter Brooks has called "the self's tendency toward appropriation and aggrandizement," Lafayette's novel repeatedly defines narrative temporality as the minimal, all but imperceptible passage from one kind of blank to another—as the princess begins untouched in the sense of as yet unscathed by experience and ends untouched in the sense of scathed by a blank or hole in time—in this case the letter and its misprision as addressed to Nemours—a mistaking of the other where he isn't—become definitive.[30]

---

30. Brooks, *Reading for the Plot*, 39.

v. "they toil not neither do they spin"

> Avec une vertu qui fût imaginaire
> (Car je l'appelle ainsi quand elle est sans effets.)
>   —Corneille, *Nicomède*[31]

> "All is vanity" is the beginning and end of ethics. The only genuine way to be good is to be good "for nothing" in the midst of a scene where every "natural" thing, including one's own mind, is subject to chance, that is, to necessity.
>   —Iris Murdoch, *The Sovereignty of Good*

> To deal with the world by condemning it, by withdrawing from it and shut-ting it out, by making oneself and one's mode and principles of life the very center of existence and to live the round of one's days in the stasis and peace thus contrived—this, in an earlier age, was one of the recognized strategies of life, but to us it seems not merely impracticable but almost wicked.
>   —Lionel Trilling on *Mansfield Park*

> It is only in degree that any improvement of society could prevent wastage of human powers; the waste even in a fortunate life, the isolation even of a life rich in intimacy, cannot but be felt deeply. . . . Anything of value must accept this because it must not prostitute itself; its strength is to be prepared to waste itself, if it does not get its opportunity.
>   —William Empson, *Some Versions of Pastoral*

It becomes apparent, then, that to begin by assessing the novel's delib-erately unsatisfying ends is a kind of false start that alerts us to the impru-dence of expecting actions to justify themselves by their outcomes. Suffer-ing the pain of abstinence while paying the price of sin, the princess will always fail readers who, using the standards of Corneille's *Nicomède*, seek to prove her virtue by its effects. Nicomède's demand for some good to come of virtue before he will call it real corresponds to normative expec-tations of profit at the economic level, of consummation and progeny at the sexual, of creditable knowledge at the epistemic, and of progress at the level of narrative; at each of these levels *La Princesse de Clèves* repudiates fulfillment and assaults instrumental reason and its corollary, the hope of completion or possession. Unrewarded virtue, frustrated sexual desire, thwarted epistemological powers, wasted verbal and narrative economies:

31. "With a virtue that was imaginary / (For I call it so when it is without effects.)" Quoted in Stanton, "The Ideal of 'Repos' in Seventeenth-Century French Literature," 86.

on not one but many parallel fronts Lafayette withholds the expected or desired end. In this sense, we do well to pay attention to the ungenerous reader who would accuse the princess of a double cheat in robbing herself of her husband's trust only to deny herself her lover's hand. For, initially at least, this reader's perspective offers a more acute insight into the exhaustiveness of the novel's sustained production of waste than do interpretations that defend the princess's rigor, either on the basis of the purity of her principles (Kantian ethical defense) or by questioning the desirability of the heterosexual union she rejects (feminist defense). Feeling her cheat on two fronts, the ungenerous reader does justice to the severity with which the novel whips our hopes of gain, first here then there.[32]

The disappointingly similar results of virtue and unfaithfulness—the dead end that in any case awaits us in the *dénouement*—thus suggests two interpretive responses, both of which I want to pursue: (1) this sustained thwarting of expectations, the withholding of any fruit, is Lafayette's meaning; (2) we should look for the meaning of actions in *La Princesse de Clèves* elsewhere, not in the final effects that all can see but in the form that actions take in the minds of the characters involved. Insofar as actions taken fail significantly to change the course of events, or at least to produce different outcomes than their opposites would have (i.e., Mme de Clèves' faithfulness might as well have been adultery), the novel testifies for the internal experience of knowing that x is in fact the case and not y, a knowledge that one cannot justify by appeal to outward evidence.

"Car enfin cet aveu n'aura point de suite" (171).[33] So in her final interview with Nemours the princess seals what might have been her one unambiguously open admission of love. The point-blank announcement works as a self-fulfilling prophecy, for with these words she again immediately qualifies the joy Nemours feels on hearing himself loved; the words take back the expected import of such an admission, while leaving the admission itself intact. So disclaimed, neither enlightening Nemours of

32. In its practical ineffectiveness and in the simplicity with which she maintains it regardless of its public recognition, the princess's virtue indeed anticipates Kant's notion of a moral will whose value resides within itself, whatever its impotence at the hands of "unfortunate fate or . . . the niggardly provision of stepmotherly nature" (Kant, *Grounding for the Metaphysics of Morals*, 7-8).

33. "For after all, nothing will follow from this admission"; "For in the end this admission will lead to nothing" (Buss, 166); "for certainly this avowal will have no consequences" (Lyons, 102).

something he doesn't already know nor bringing him any closer to possession, her final declaration becomes yet another event that, *for all the good
it does*, might easily be ignored or left off the record. Coming in place of
the conventional heroine's final surrender, this promise to remain childless, weightless and without future, represents all that vexes the question
of the princess's generosity, makes ambiguous the "good" of her virtue and
problematic her legacy to others. She gives news of her love, and adds that
it will be as nothing. This readiness to reveal an inner state but not to act
on it, to name something about herself that she will not concretize, as if
speech and action were incommensurate and indeed incapable of coinciding, is supposed to have prompted one of Valincour's female friends to
dismiss her as the "most coquettish prude and prudish coquette":

> D'ailleurs . . . à quoi bon faire une si longue déclaration à un homme qu'elle
> aimait, et qu'elle avait résolu de ne pas épouser? Si elle avait assez de force
> pour surmonter son inclination, pourquoi n'en avait-elle pas assez pour la
> cacher? L'étalait-elle aux yeux de Monsieur de Nemours, pour avoir un té-
> moin de la victoire qu'elle en prétendait remporter? En vérité, il lui eût été
> bien plus glorieux de ne rien dire. Si elle ne cherchait qu'à se faire estimer de
> Monsieur de Nemours, il ne fallait point lui parler comme elle fait; il en savait
> assez pour juger de la violence qu'elle se serait faite en cette occasion; au lieu
> que tout ce qu'elle lui dit ne sert qu'à témoigner qu'elle a de l'amour, et qu'elle
> ne peut s'empêcher de le faire paraître. (Valincour, *Lettres*, 120)

> [Indeed . . . to what end make such a long declaration to a man whom she
> loved and whom she had resolved not to marry? If she had enough strength
> to surmount her inclination, why didn't she have enough to hide it? Was she
> laying it out before Monsieur de Nemours' eyes to have a witness to the vic-
> tory she was claiming over herself? In fact, it would have been more glorious
> to say nothing. If she'd simply been seeking Monsieur de Nemours' esteem,
> she shouldn't have talked to him as she did; he already knew enough about
> her inclination to appreciate the violence she would have been doing herself;
> instead all she says to him only makes evident that she loves and that she can't
> help herself from showing it.]

To his rejoinder that "it is difficult to keep in one's heart such violent and
such legitimate feelings as were those of Mme de Clèves," Valincour tells
us that his friend replied:

> Il fallait . . . suivre ces sentiments jusques au bout, si elle les croyait légitimes;
> ou les étouffer, et ne les point faire paraître, s'ils ne lui paraissaient pas in-

nocents: au lieu que voulant faire tous les deux, elle ne fait ni l'un, ni l'autre. C'est une femme incompréhensible que Madame de Clèves: c'est la prude la plus coquette, et la coquette la plus prude que l'on ait jamais vue. (Valincour, *Lettres*, 120)

[She should . . . have followed her feelings through to the end, if she thought them legitimate, or suppressed them and not let them appear if they did not seem to her innocent; instead of which, wanting to do both, she does neither one nor the other. Mme de Clèves is an incomprehensible woman: she's the most coquettish prude and the most prudish coquette that one has ever seen.]

In its conception of love as a form of intrigue and vying for positions of power, the voice behind this passage articulates the perspective of the novel's court, where "love was always allied to politics and politics to love" and where "no one was untouched or unmoved: each considered how to advance, to flatter, to serve or to harm" (Buss, 34). The commentary accurately presents the heroine's action as a choice between showing and hiding—"faire paraître, étaler, témoigner, cacher"—but remains unable to make sense of this choice except through a semiotic economy in which to give a sign (*une marque*) is to give (away) a unit of value.[34] By equating a woman's words with loss and making silence her only means of gain, this logic remains blind to the open secret's possibility of a nonremunerative communicative act, a possibility according to which Mme de Clèves' communications to Nemours constitute gifts precisely because they cost her almost nothing.

Here only the freedom with which she acknowledges her love gives this acknowledgment any value for Nemours; whereas the form of her first *aveu* had curtailed his ability to enjoy its content, here not the content of her words but only their form—the fact that they come directly and freely from her and that she wants him to have them—matters to him:

—Je ne vous apprends, lui répondit-elle en souriant, que ce que vous ne saviez déjà que trop.

—Ah! madame, répliqua-t-il, quelle différence de le savoir par un effet du hasard ou de l'apprendre par vous-même, et de voir que voulez bien que je le sache! (171)

34. "Resonating with the princess's own practice of acutely perceptive self-analysis, Valincour's commentary suggests the continuities between Lafayette's creation, considered the original *roman d'analyse*, and the exquisite dissection of psychological states perfected by the *précieuses* of Lafayette's youth. For a discussion of these continuities see Fabre, *L'art de l'analyse dans "La Princesse de Clèves."*

["I'm only informing you of what you already knew too well," she answered smiling.

"Ah! Madame," he replied, "what a difference there is between knowing it by chance and learning it from you and seeing that you would like me to know it!"]

In a certain sense, Valincour's friend is absolutely right: the princess's decision not to marry means that she isn't required to tell Nemours anything of her love. But precisely because they are gratuitous, by her words she does him a kind of grace; only that they are gratis and free from any economy of obligation makes possible the easy smile, itself no more than a parenthesis, with which she blesses them.[35]

35. The princess's smile brings her closer to Barthes' figure of "la bienveil-lance" or "benevolence," an attitude that, while not necessarily possessed by de-sire, also does not censure it, or at least bears it no ill will: "*Benevolentia* est en retrait sur *Ti voglio bene*, et correspond paradoxalement à son mot à mot: je veux bien ne pas être bloqué par ta demande, ta personne: je ne refuse pas, sans forcé-ment vouloir: position exacte du Neutre, qui n'est pas absence, refus du désir; mais flottement éventuel du désir hors du vouloir-saisir" (*Le Neutre*, 40–41). Closely related to the profane ideal of "repos" discussed by Stanton, Barthes' elaboration of this figure of openness to eventuality without the will-to-seize, like his emphasis on Pyrrhonism as a practice not of *apatheia* or insensibility but of *douceur* (66) or mildness with respect to alternative propositions—not a radical refusal of choice but a disinvestment from disinvestment itself—can help us understand the equivocation that seems to mitigate or temper even the prin-cess's sternest statements as something other than coquetry or fear of conclusive choice. Also relevant here is Agamben's discussion in *Potentialities* of the skeptic's suspension of preference, even of the choice to prefer suspension, according to which his own "'no more than' [as in the statement 'providence is no more than it is not'] is no more than it is not" (Agamben, *Potentialities*, 256). Agamben reads the skeptic's suspension of propositional claims as a mode of "announce-ment"—something more than mere indifference to whether x is the case or y—a way of experience, even enjoyment, of potentiality as such, presumably distinct from (although never securely so) the neurotic's temporizing deferral of actual-ization. Modestly, minimally announcing by negation only what is already the case—delivering to Nemours "no more than" he already knows—the princess would seem at first take to have little in common with this experience of poten-tiality if by it we understand an expectant waiting on possibility; yet precisely in this reticence toward acting on the present as the premise for something yet to come, as the stuff out of which to make a future, the princess can highlight the antispeculative dimension of Pyrrhonian skepticism.

For Valincour's friend, the princess contradicts herself by giving voice to feelings that she does not consider legitimate enough to act on. This criticism understands speech as a mere prologue to and lesser form of action and cannot conceive of a passion's guilt or innocence except as an absolute, predetermined condition, whereas, in the princess's mind, by not acting on her feelings, she ensures the innocence of their expression. For Valincour's friend, this "illogic" produces the political and moral vanity of the princess's actions: she partakes of both coquette and prude, the two least charitable feminine stereotypes of the time, exposes herself to the insult of both, but in such a way as to take no benefit from either. The conceptual havoc she wreaks is, like her defeat of political purposes, a form of waste, and the unanswered question, "A quoi bon?"—"To what end?" or "For what good?"—a sign of her inherent evasion of most forms of public accountability.

Indeed, the fatal if inadvertent effects of the princess's earlier *aveu* to the prince—she speaks her mind, and within months he dies—inevitably qualify the claim, "cet aveu n'aura point de suite," and lend credence to the view that speech carries the same weight as action. The princess may mean, in effect, "this avowal, unlike my first, will be without consequence." In penance for the prince's death, as if to compensate for the cruel efficiency of her first speech act, she chooses to empty her words to Nemours: they will not be marriage vows. Or ignoring the irony, she may be speaking to Nemours in the same spirit in which she spoke to the prince: "this avowal will be the last you hear of the desire expressed therein; the feelings to which I give voice will not change the course of my actions." As she would have wished the prince to do, she continues to separate ideational and real states, to entertain thoughts without implementing them, and to maintain the inconsequence of representations as opposed to acts, a causal "innocence" that the novel's plot thoroughly puts into question but never directly denies.[36] Signaling her refusal of Nemours

36. As the only evidence of the princess's passion, the prince's "causeless" death is proof that mental states, however divorced of action, do indeed make a difference. But the plot gives no instance of the sequential linear causality implied by the word *suite*; no one, including Mme de Clèves, can assign or claim responsibility for anything that happens in the novel except through figuration—through an elision of the sequence of facts. She can never, for example, say, "I killed him," but can only claim passive and retroactive agency, as in her assertion to Nemours, "Je sais que c'est par vous qu'il est mort et que c'est à cause de moi," where "being the cause of something" appears as a structural position that requires no psychological presence. (Indeed such figuration elides the psychological absence of the causal agent to his or her effects.)

and retreat from the court, the princess's final nonbinding avowal—her gift of words that imply no commitment—marks the strange indirection with which she fulfills social responsibilities but escapes being held to account. This antipromise—an announcement that "I have the power to . . . but will do none"—parallels the strange innocence of Lafayette's fictional supplement to history: as a historical novel, *La Princesse de Clèves* makes only a negative contribution to the public record, supplying the reasons why *x* or *y* didn't happen and explaining material events in light of projects that never came to fruition.

In this section I read the princess's ultimately deceptive withdrawal from the scene of history in terms of the parallel problems of potential and the burden to realize it, and private experience and the pressure to make it count on public scales of value, at issue in the various passages quoted above from Trilling, Empson, Corneille, and Murdoch. Taken together, the passages help frame the problem of waste as (1) a question of what value, if any, to accord thoughts to which one cannot (or will not) give empirical content and (2) the problem of unused capacities and untapped powers and their paradoxical "action" on those who recognize them.[37] Close readings of two of Mme de Chartres' historical anecdotes will then show the extent to which the princess, in fact, belongs to history as Mme de Chartres retells it, as a story whose meaning lies not in the end result but in the form that action takes, and that presents "change" or "progress" as, at most, a difference in potentialities. In dramatizing the element of nonexchange—of noncoincidence and nonreciprocity—at the core of most forms of exchange, Mme de Chartres' history lessons do more than

37. For a pertinent analysis of the efficacy of possibility as such—its capacity to produce effects independently of actualization—see Slavoj Žižek's recapitulation of Hegel's understanding of possibility in *Tarrying with the Negative*: "The status of possibility, while different from that of actuality, is thus not simply deficient with regard to it. Possibility as such exerts actual effects which disappear as soon as it 'actualizes' itself" (159). For Žižek's Lacanian example of castration anxiety, we can substitute the princess's *aveu* as the moment at which the threat of her adultery "takes precedence over its actuality" and the imagining of a potential loss displaces its production. Here the princess's acknowledgment of the real possibility of her unfaithfulness secures the categorical impossibility of its actualization (something the prince should have known) but supplies the effects of actual unfaithfulness (something the princess might have expected).

For a more precise discussion of the distinction between the possible (as opposed to the real) and the virtual (which may be real without being actual), see also Deleuze, *Bergsonism*, 96–98.

comment on the irony of fate or prepare readers for the strangeness of
the princess's "interactions": they define an oddly worldly ethos of non-
exploitativenss and minimal appropriation, by ascribing moral value to
those types of taking and giving between moral agents and the world that
go unpunished and almost unnoticed; such an ethos does not so much
censure worldly activity, as vain pursuit or exploitation, as it does value
exchange precisely insofar as it takes a minimal, barely noticeable form.

In her final choice of a devotional life tinged with solipsism and in
the burial of her own desire in the name of her *repos*, the princess inscribes herself within a long-standing debate, central though not peculiar
to French seventeenth-century intellectual history, about the moral value
of *repos* (rest) over worldly activity. In her essay "The Ideal of 'Repos' in
Seventeenth-Century French Literature," Domna Stanton discusses the
term's polyvalence in seventeenth-century Stoic, Epicurean, skeptic, and
Jansenist schools of thought where it uneasily combines elements from
the classical ideal of *otium*, the Christian ideal of unworldly contempla-
tion, and the skeptic's desired *ataraxia* or suspension of judgment.[38] As
Stanton notes, Lafayette retains the ideal's secular meaning and, I would
argue, its purposefully superficial, limited moral content. Thus the princess uses the term to name a responsibility to herself distinguishable from
her moral duty to others; as she admits to Nemours, the call of duty
alone would not be sufficient to guarantee her against him, without the
additional and separate dissuasive force of the "interest" of her *repos*: "Ce
que je crois devoir à la mémoire de M. de Clèves serait faible s'il n'était
soutenu par l'intérêt de mon repos; et les raisons de mon repos ont be-
soin d'être soutenues par celles de mon devoir" (What I believe I owe the
memory of M. de Clèves would be weak if it weren't sustained by the
interest of my ease [peace of mind], and the cause of my ease needs to be
sustained by that of my duty) (175). In the end neither her duty to her
dead husband (who also stands in for the dead mother) nor her concern
for her peace of mind has final determining force; the princess simply

38. Repos "was a profound ethical concept and, at the same time, a common-
place. . . . The ideal of repos always remained as much a secular as a religious
concept. . . . In the Bible, as in the earliest periods of French literature, the
meaning of repos is both serious and superficial, sacred and profane" (Stanton,
"The Ideal of 'Repos' in Seventeenth-Century French Literature," 80).

defers her decision, asking Nemours "to wait and see what time will do." In thus leaving things to run their course, she realizes the passive, recessive quality of her own ideal of *repos* and confirms its essential modesty as a moral goal of only limited relevance to others, perhaps best attained without the asking.

Stanton gives as the "final meaning of [the princess's] *repos*"—"freedom from all externally imposed rules and directives"—and claims that Lafayette's heroine "is, in the end, physically independent, emotionally and morally self-sufficient" (101). But such autonomy comes at the cost of great simplification, and to readers who share Trilling's modern wariness of "stasis and peace thus contrived," the princess's ideal of *repos* will always appear both dangerously ascetic and strangely indulgent. In many ways the strength of the novel is to leave room for what this choice of *repos* looks like to other people—emotional escapism, onanistic seclusion, life-poisoning protectiveness—by juxtaposing the traditional ideal of moral and emotional self-regulation with the more troubling concept of psychic or imaginative autonomy and developing the parallel between living a life of retreat, away from others, and living in one's mind, without others.

Thus psychoanalytical readings have taken a different perspective on the quiet "self-sufficiency" that Stanton celebrates as liberating, seeing in its stead the repressive self-control of a psyche intent on conjuring its demons as specters so as not to meet them in the flesh. "The certainty of no longer being loved by you as I am now," Mme de Clèves admits to Nemours, "appears to me so great a misfortune that even if I hadn't insurmountable reasons of duty, I doubt whether I could make up my mind to *expose* myself to such unhappiness" (173; emphasis added). Peggy Kamuf points to this defensive fantasy as part of the princess's vain struggle to "keep safe the fiction of the invulnerable self" (*Fictions of Feminine Desire*, 96). The difficulty with such readings is that they risk overlooking the sense in which the princess's peculiar honesty does in fact expose her to experience and its losses. In this case her surmise allows her to share with Nemours a pain that, lived, she could never have let him see, and to spare them both the ugliness of living his eventual interest in other women as a direct affront to her. In avoiding one kind of certainty, she lets drop— both acknowledges and underinflects—the simple fact of knowing herself "loved as she is now." The chasteness with which she lives this fully op-

erative certainty, parenthetically and unassumingly announcing it, corresponds to the difficulty of according the present any other kind of place
in the novel.[39]

The calm forthrightness with which Mme de Clèves here announces
and meets her fears makes her more than merely evasive, and the relation
that she sustains to Nemours' certain abandonment—crediting this inoperative certainty precisely so as not to assume its burden empirically—reproduces in miniature the nonpossessive relationship she sustains to her
passion. If, as it seems, she habitually meets in thought realities that she
avoids in "lived" experience, the trope of the open secret allows us to
reevaluate this strange habit as something more complicated than mere
evasiveness—a different kind of moral realism. That marital infidelity can
take strange and unexpected forms is, after all, the novel's central conceit,
an insight that the princess extends in inverted form, by bringing into
focus rejection—the choice to decline actualization—as a peculiar way
of knowing and sustaining a relation to—keeping faith without claiming—the world.

The princess's final withdrawal serves as a metonymy, then, for the
way in which, throughout the novel, she names a potential that never
materializes but only makes itself known nonempirically, by means at
once strange and intimate; unevidenced, it simply asks to be assumed
and so lays itself open to the Corneillean charge of waste: "Avec une
vertu qui fût imaginaire / (Car je l'appelle ainsi quand elle est sans effets
. . .)" (2.3.640–41). Stanton cites Nicomède's impatience with his brother's inactive virtue as evidence of an early-seventeenth-century "faith in

39. The sentence is so worded that "la certitude" seems to refer less to what
she might already know of Nemours' inevitable fickleness (an abstract certainty
she might have about all men, at all times) than to the event—the specific condition of knowing herself, beyond doubt, no longer loved (an epistemic *malheur*
she could only encounter in marriage). As a state of consciousness imagined
as an event, "la certitude de n'être plus aimée de vous, comme je le suis," has
the simple, definitive weight of fact and yet belongs to no one and to no real
time. If, as it turns out, "time and absence" eventually do "extinguish Nemours'
passion," this death cannot touch the princess. She has gone ahead to meet as
thought an abandonment that will never enter her experiential register, except
as it once already has, as mere, all too efficacious illusion. Significantly, Kamuf's
translation simplifies the princess's sense to "the certainty that I have of one day
losing your love" and drops the parenthetical "comme je le suis." See Kamuf,
Fictions of Feminine Desire, 95.

the human potential for grandeur and glory," and indeed the Corneillean imperative to act on what one has, and to bring potential to effect, rests on an optimistic view of human history.[40] But whereas Mme de Clèves' willingness to pose her potential without following it up may feel like a tease to her lover and look like irresponsible stewardship to a Nicomède, the perspective of Empsonian pastoral helps legitimate such "readiness to waste oneself" as a different kind of trust—faith that right "opportunity" can and should come without the asking: "the waste even in a fortunate life, the isolation even of a life rich in intimacy, cannot but be felt deeply. . . . Anything of value must accept this because it must not prostitute itself; its strength is to be prepared to waste itself, if it does not get its opportunity." Through the image of prostitution, Empson warns against trading in an innate but unconfirmed sense of value for unambiguous but untrustworthy validation from without (the untrustworthiness of any such acknowledgment deriving from one's having had to ask for it). Borrowing from Gray's lines—

Full many a gem of purest ray serene
The dark unfathom'd caves of ocean bear:
Full many a flower is born to blush unseen,
And waste its sweetness on the desert air.
("Elegy Written in a Country ChurchYard," 53–56)

—he identifies in the experience of waste a peculiarly feminized virtue, the antithesis to ambition and self-promotion, a reticence toward bringing about a success one would happily receive at the hands of fate, and

40. In Corneille's hardly tragic tragedy, Attale, Nicomède's half-brother and passive tool of Arsinöé's political machinations, ultimately does defend himself against the charge of "vanity" by the action he takes, in the final act, to foil the plot against Nicomède. Until then, Attale's passivity makes him morally untrustworthy and Nicomède seems justified in refusing to credit—admit as relevant—his as yet untested and effectless virtue. Attale's intervention "comes out" in due course because it is successful; his good work immediately evident with Nicomède's restoration to the throne, he does not need to assert the fact that he took the measures he did as he might have had to in the face of failure. But whereas characters in Corneille's world can trust the end to tell them something about how each has acted, effects in the princess's world tell us nothing about actions themselves, which consequently have to be known on their own, independently of the way things turn out.

fidelity to a special form of value that diminishes as soon as one has to assert it.[41] Passive and immobile, flower and gem cannot be more present to the world—wasting "its sweetness on the desert air," the flower holds nothing back—yet they do not in any usual sense change or interact with the world; they only take from it what it offers. Such figures combine a weird self-sufficiency with vulnerability to external powers, whether of fate or of others; as a passiveness toward fulfillment, their trust—a form of dependence on the world—looks strangely like the absence of any expectation from it.[42] If flower and gem carry a secret value, regardless of whether anyone discovers them, they also carry it regardless of anything they do; the flower's beauty is no more than the superfluity of its brief life. The intuition of innate worth thus yields almost immediately to the sense of unearned value, and the antithesis to exchange value is also beyond use—unavailable and unknown to its own bearer. Condensed in four lines here is the entire problematic of agency for feminine virtue, in the question of how to reconcile a goodness so passively produced, a virtue so painlessly and unknowingly exercised, with conventional notions of moral responsibility, self-knowledge, and self-discipline.

By opposing virtue to self-promotion, Empson's pastoralist makes inevitable the risk of waste (identified via Gray's "Elegy" as historical obscurity or absence from the scene of history), even as he mitigates its cost by questioning the desirability of any recognition for which one has to

41. Gray's lines are quoted from *The Complete Poems of Thomas Gray: English, Latin and Greek*.

42. Trust, as Annette Baier has defined it, involves relying on the world—giving up full control and acknowledging the power of others to "do their part"—but it also looks, in effect, like its opposite—the absence of any formal demand on others as one leaves them to do what they will toward one. "Trust . . . is accepted vulnerability to another's possible but not expected ill will (or lack of good will) toward one. . . . Trust is accepted vulnerability to another's power to harm one, a power inseparable from the power to look after some aspect of one's good. . . . Trust is acceptance of vulnerability to harm that others could inflict, but which we judge that they will not in fact inflict" (Baier, *Moral Prejudices*, 99, 133, 152). Trust presents an instance of a potential—in this case, to do and receive harm—that is already fully effective and significant as *potential* and whose value has nothing to do with its being realized. Indeed a relation of trust only has value when the other has real power to harm (in Empson's examples of waste, power to ignore) and yet does not use this power.

apply.[43] In the same way, Lafayette both completes and qualifies her as-sault on end-driven action by reserving for her characters a measure of unsought attention and unhoped-for gain, even as she denies them what they seek. In her dialectical critique of ambition she does more than teach readers to expect nothing from direct attempts to control fate and exploit the world; she displaces the question of how much or how little is gained or achieved, with close attention to the form that success or failure takes, and makes the effortlessness with which one secures a public position a measure of its value. Her heroine may in the end retreat from the court, but she never quite shuns the world or denies the value of holding a place in it; instead, her success lies in readily accepting a place in the minds of others (whether a place at the court, in history, or in another's heart) for which she has not had to and would not want to fight.

vi. absent histories

Whether readers understand the princess's final retreat as a simple rejec-tion of worldly interests or, through the lens of Mme de Chartres' ambi-tion for her daughter, as the only means of securing a place in a court that asks exactly nothing—a blank reputation—of feminine virtue, the novel's historical subplots echo the Jansenist and Epicurean arguments that, ac-cording to Stanton, would have discouraged engagement in worldly activ-ity following the disappointments of the Fronde.[44] Lafayette's fidelity to

43. Thus Empson's gloss on Gray's lines, "a gem does not mind being in a cave and a flower prefers not to be picked." Pastoral so defined provides the necessary brakes to an Enlightenment that too quickly and uncritically identifies progress with the recuperation of lost potential and full development of latent capacities. As Empson notes, the lines evoke a waste one would not want to prevent and give the "Elegy" its ultimately conservative import. The waste of talent among the poor and uneducated "is stated as pathetic, but the reader is put into a mood in which one would not try to alter it" (Empson, *Some Versions of Pastoral*, 4).

44. Stanton points to a serious questioning of "the value of worldly activity" "after the Fronde . . . and in the wake of Louis XIV's domestication of the nobil-ity" ("The Ideal of 'Repos' in Seventeenth-Century French Literature," 86). The idea that retreat from the Court would have been practiced not only by ethical or religious choice but as itself a politically motivated strategy and because of the absence of any other viable options, is also implicit in Lucien Goldmann's account in *Le dieu caché* of the political origins of Jansenism.

the known historical facts of Henri II's court parallels Mme de Clèves' fidelity to her husband, inasmuch as the narrative deviates from the record
only in ways that don't or aren't supposed to matter. Thus the historical
narrator can surmise with impunity both Nemours' plans to make an offer of marriage to Elizabeth I of England and her heroine's role in abort-
ing these plans. Distracted by Mme de Clèves and wishing to make her
the symbolic sacrifice of a crown he has yet to possess, Nemours delays
putting these designs into execution. Indeed he puts off his planned journey to England so long that the offer of marriage, once a latent, as-yet-
unacted-on potential, becomes even less than that—simply impossible;
time simply passes, making it indecent for Elizabeth I even to consider his
offer were he finally to make it. (The ambassador sent ahead to prepare
Nemours' journey writes back that he "can no longer make excuses to the
queen for Nemours' delays and that she is beginning to be offended by
them, especially as while she had given no definite response, she had said
enough for him to hazard the journey" [81].) The minor episode sums
up the effect of much of the action in the novel—the passage, obviously
difficult to record historically, from latent possibility to categorical impossibility, in this case effected by the mere passage of time.[45]

  Skepticism of the wisdom of all human enterprises, initiatives, and
endeavors to make or change history underlies, in particular, Mme de

---

45. In *Revising Memory*, Faith Beasley takes issue with "modern critics" who
have typically explained away Lafayette's inclusion of a historical backdrop as
a mere convention meant to ensure *vraisemblance* and to facilitate the slippage
from fact to surmise, as if to say, "Since this much we know was true, that might
have been as well." Beasley draws attention to Lafayette's displacement of male-
authored and male-centered history with "feminocentric history": "by subsum-
ing the official, well-known events of the past into the inner life of the court and
positing affairs of the heart and mind as affairs of state, [Lafayette] transforms
particular history into universal history" (Beasley, *Revising Memory*, 193, 202).
Beasley's attempt to recuperate through Lafayette a history of which women are
the principal actors raises the problem that the more recorded history includes
of private and particular histories, the less it can claim universal accessibility.
Knowledge of "the inner life of the court" requires not only privileged access but
the power to surmise mental states that will have left no traces of themselves—in
effect the writing of fiction. For a different perspective on the question of who
writes the historical record in Lafayette's novel see Alliston's argument discussed
below, according to which we should remain skeptical of an epistemology based
on husbands' public testimony of their wives' private experience.

Chartres' education of her daughter—even if this education is itself an exercise in worldly ambition.[46] The historical anecdotes she tells to fill in the princess's picture of the court of Henri II contain numerous examples of actions that, even when successful in themselves, do not, as it were, pay off. Thus at the origin of Diane de Poitiers' rise to power, we discover an aborted exchange of sex for life. Recounting how the young Poitiers used her favor with François I to have her condemned father pardoned, Mme de Chartres says, "She did so well she *obtained* her father's life," and euphemistically implies—"(I don't know by what means)"—that Diane prostituted herself in the bargain. As it turns out, she did so in vain, her father's life (the object of her ransom) having already been taken from him:

> Il fut condamné à avoir la tête tranchée et conduit sur l'échafaud. Sa fille, dont la beauté était admirable, et qui avait déjà plu au feu roi, fit si bien (je ne sais par quels moyens) qu'elle *obtint la vie* de son père. On lui porta sa grâce *comme* il n'attendait que le coup de la mort; mais la peur l'avait tellement saisi qu'il n'avait plus de connaissance, et il mourut peu de jours après. Sa fille parut à la cour comme la maîtresse du roi. (56; emphasis added)

> [He was condemned to be beheaded and led to the scaffold. His daughter, whose beauty was remarkable and who had already pleased the late King, did so well (I don't know by what means) that she obtained her father's life. His reprieve was brought to him as he was awaiting only the deathblow; but fear had so seized him that he did not recover his senses, and he died a few days later. His daughter appeared at court as the mistress of the king.]

Taken as emblematic, this compressed narrative alone defines the novel's

46. The dialectical nature of pastoral's and Lafayette's attitudes toward ambition might be resumed in the contradictory advice: "don't seek but take right opportunity when it comes"—a contradiction inscribed in the very question of "feminine" ambition whenever feminine virtue is restricted to a question of marital fidelity and decided not on the basis of a woman's contribution to history—of the use that she makes of her talents—but on her (non)reputation—on the (blank) images that others have of her innermost self. The possible absence of relation between a woman's own actions and her public image—her nonparticipation in constructing this image—produces the paradoxical dependence on receiving the right reader marking Empson's strange figures of value. For the reduction of feminine virtue to a matter of the "appearance of legitimacy," an appearance over whose interpretation women themselves have no control, see Alliston, *Virtue's Faults*, 45–46.

world as one in which people do act on one another but in which the strongest exchanges—the taking and giving of word, of life—are merely virtual, having the effect of *coups—de grâce/de la mort*—without the form (and vice versa). The story conforms to the novel's recurring chiastic pattern, according to which the weight of the real is shifted onto the unreal and a final determining force given mistaken or unconfirmed beliefs. So-called real actions are taken to no effect and might as well not have been, while private mental states, though they may correspond to an objective reality, have a final, determining effect, independently of rather than through this correspondence.

Typifying the elliptical style that Valincour and, since him, Genette, DeJean, and others have identified as Lafayette's own, Mme de Chartres' narrative economy here is central in conveying this chiasm, as a crossing implied precisely in not being spelled out: "On lui porta sa grâce comme il n'attendait que le coup de la mort." Grace is brought as the deathblow would have been, and has the same effect. On one level this is a story of a message gone awry, a communicative act failing to take place: Diane de Poitiers' actions miscarry, because word of her father's pardon comes too late to reach him. While the sentence's verbs—*porta, attendait* (brought *x*, was awaiting *y*)—present its actors—*on, lui/il*—in the act of giving and receiving, what happens is that something is never received. The *on* and *il*, in fact, never meet, so absolute is the noncorrespondence between what the condemned was to be told and what he was prepared to hear.

Yet at the textual level, another kind of meeting comes to displace, and compensate for, the failure of the intended communicative exchange. Diane's intervention has one effect: it causes grace to be substituted for death as that which the anonymous, unlocatable subject *on* brings her father. Rather than effecting a radical revision, however, the grammar implies that things have been too perfectly interchanged—taken for one another and to no effect. The first irony that "on" brings exactly the opposite of what he expects is superseded by the second—that it amounts to the same thing, as if what counted was not what they brought, but that it was *on*, and that what they did was *porta*. Or putting the determining accent on "him," whatever they bring *him*, the bringing means death. Going ahead of his death-dealers, the would-be recipient has put himself beyond reception. The solipsism of fear has shut him off from contact only to leave him utterly exposed in a state where anything may serve as the final blow. Insofar as either sentence—death or the granting of life—depends on the same messenger, recipient and means of execution, it is as if both were in effect the same, as if, that is, this structural, formal identity were enough to annul any difference in the content of the sentence, whether grammatical unit or verdict. There is, then, not only failure of communicative exchange but also, and in place of such exchange, analogy of failure: grace is brought (never to be received) in the same way that the blow is awaited (never to be given).

Judging solely by the consequences, they might as well have killed him; Diane might as well have done nothing. The only difference is a formal one, but as I'm arguing, form is that by which everything takes place, and this difference in form has a moral significance, even if it has no bearing on the outcome. It guarantees innocence for all, or what becomes all but synonymous with innocence, noninteraction, as each plays his or her discrete part without aid from the other. In being killed by his own defenses, Diane's father offers a mirror image to the autonomy with which *on* delivers him his grace, without waiting for and regardless of its being received: even unregistered, the event occurs in the definitive simple past. That it will never be his to assert does not change the fact that grace has been given him. And just as they are innocent of his blood, so he remains innocent of Diane's actions, actions that, had he lived to learn, might have been supposed to add to the burden of his life and conscience. Instead, although Diane has prostituted herself for him—for his sake, for him—in his now darkened mind—she will never have done so. While the object and cause of her actions, he is also the only subject for whom she will not have acted. The daughter he had to himself he takes to his grave, while she "parut à la cour comme la maîtresse du roi."

Indeed, in the story's final turn of the screw, Diane's public appearance as the king's mistress displaces what would have been her father's public execution. Had he lived, Diane's secret maneuvers might have been kept behind closed doors; instead, her new relation to the king comes to light as simple fact. In a chiasm that resonates with the novel's central plot, what was to be hidden comes out; what was to come about never happens. But this strange turn of events effectively renders Diane's inner motivations inscrutable: she may have been acting on her father's behalf, but *it looks as though* he merely served as her pawn to glory. Judging by appearances, and from the standpoint of a history conceived of as the record of manifest results, she was not the means to his end; he was the means to hers.

Mme de Chartres, indeed, tells this story to illustrate her dictum that "if you judge by appearances in this place, you will often be deceived" (Buss, 46). The story warns against taking the manifest at face value and accepting final effects as culminations, as in the expression "the rest is history"—a saying that implicitly identifies history with the materially operative and the publicly acknowledged. As that part of the story that prevailed in the end and now counts for the present, "history" so defined needs no special telling nor supplementing with insider information. In the case of Diane de Poitiers' story, however, what comes to light is only the residual and unintended aftereffect of something that, however intended, did not come to pass. If her story is exemplary, then behind every new appearance on the scene of history is a thwarted attempt to change the course of history. Not only is history not the whole story; it may not even be the essence of the story. One can assume no correspondence between private intentions and manifest results. Agents have only a passive relationship to the effects they produce.[47]

47. The moral of the anecdote might be phrased as follows: "History is the attempt to rewrite history that backfired." Or "Warning: Actions have unintended side-effects; they are usually the only ones that count." The story, like so much in the novel, asks that events be read not for themselves but against their grain, backlit as it were, as the only vestiges, the aftereffects or negative markers, of a potential that otherwise failed to materialize.

In thus exposing the relation between cause and effect as a retroactive illusion, Lafayette's subhistorical narratives appear to bypass the reductive causal linearity for which Thomas Carlyle, in his essay "On History," faults standard historical narratives. Skeptical of whether narrative history can even "recover" the "most important part" of "acted History," Carlyle writes:

> The real leading features of a historical Transaction, those movements that essentially characterise it, and alone deserve to be recorded, are nowise the foremost to be noted. . . . Men understand not what is among their hands: as calmness is the characteristic of strength, so the weightiest causes may be most silent. It is, in no case, the real historical Transaction, but only some more or less plausible scheme and theory of the Transaction, or the harmonised result of many such schemes, each varying from the other and all varying from the truth, that we can ever hope to behold. (Carlyle, *A Carlyle Reader*, 59)

Carlyle questions the adequacy of written records of "acted History" not simply on the basis of the limits of human observation but also on the basis of the inevitable asymmetry between "successive" observation and "simultaneous" action: "It is not in acted, as it is in written History: actual events are nowise so

Thus well before the princess denies Nemours the consequence of her final *aveu*, plenty has been told to chasten expectations of enjoying one's effects or reaping the fruits of one's actions. More is at stake, I would argue, in these stories of failures and setbacks than a simple warning about the perverseness of fate. For they also teach one to expect nothing from what the world sends back of oneself and, at the same time, to anticipate the final relevance of the world's misprisions of oneself. Mme de Chartres goes on to tell the story of how the duchesse d'Etampes once played informant to the emperor's army so as to ensure that France negotiate for peace. Her plans succeeded, and the peace treaty was signed. All along she was acting with one purpose in mind—that of promoting the duc d'Orléans's interests over the Dauphin's. As if reproducing the merciless "advance" of history, Mme de Chartres' narrative simply continues, without even a sympathetic "but" to mark fate's turn against the duchess: "this duchess did not long enjoy the success of her betrayal. Soon after, M le duc d'Orléans died, at Farmoutier, from a kind of contagious disease."[48]

---

simply related to each other as parent and offspring are; every single event is the offspring not of one, but of all other events, prior or contemporaneous, and will in its turn combine with all others to give birth to new. . . . Narrative is linear, Action is solid" (59–60). To the extent that Lafayette addresses this problem, it is less by supplying what the definitive record leaves out than by teaching readers a kind of skeptical modesty or awareness that what they hold is only a fragment of the "whole story."

For a related, Althusserian-inflected discussion of the "problematic status of history" as an "absent cause" at once unavailable to "such ordinary means of verification as sight or touch" and only knowable in its effects, see Liu, *Wordsworth*, 39. In her recent *Georgic Modernity and British Romanticism* Kevis Goodman also invokes "the difficulty of recording and recognizing history-on-the-move" or "recreating the historical process as a present participle" (3), suggesting that part of the heuristic work done by Raymond Williams's repeated references to "structures of feeling"—to "all that comes through [below the level of articulation] as disturbance, tension, blockage, emotional trouble" (Williams, cited by Goodman, 5)—would be to register the "cognitive noise" of this elusive "present participle" (7).

48. The mysteriousness of this contagious disease—the one thing the duchess forgot to count on—puts it in line with the unnamed mistress, whose existence is acknowledged immediately thereafter, as if the state of his sexual affairs, like his susceptibility to natural accident, were to become relevant only upon his death, in accordance with the unsuspected determining force of the "private."

Mme de Chartres then immediately passes on to the story of the duc d'Orléans's *unnamed* mistress:

> Il aimait une des plus belles femmes de la cour et en était aimé. Je ne vous la nommerai pas, parce qu'elle a vécu depuis avec tant de sagesse et qu'elle a même caché avec tant de soin la passion qu'elle avait pour ce prince qu'elle a mérité que l'on conserve sa réputation. Le hasard fit qu'elle reçut la nouvelle de la mort de son mari le même jour qu'elle apprit celle de M. d'Orléans; de sorte qu'elle eut ce prétexte pour cacher sa véritable affliction, sans avoir la peine de se contraindre. (59)

> [He loved one of the most beautiful women at the court and was loved by her. I won't name her to you, because she has since lived so virtuously and has even hidden with such care the passion she had for this prince that she has deserved to have her reputation preserved. As chance would have it, she received word of her husband's death the same day that she learned of M. d'Orléans's; so that she had this pretext to hide her true affliction, without having to make an effort to control herself.]

At a first level, in the duchess, whose advantage is no sooner won than lost, we have a typical instance of the brevity with which anyone "jouit" (has the pleasure) of anything in *La Princesse de Clèves*. Since Mme d'Etampes is eventually forced to leave the court in disgrace, her story, taken on its own, seems a homily on the pointlessness and danger of engagement in worldly intrigue; the world's contingency is such that little or no returns can be expected from any investment in it. But what might be a simple story promoting stoic abstinence from an essentially untrustworthy and unexploitable world is complicated by its juxtaposition with the story of the duke's mistress, who does, it seems, turn a profit on events beyond her control, albeit a remarkably circumscribed one. This second story both confirms and modifies the message of the first. Where success is not so short-lived as to be practically nonexistent, it is impressively muted, accepted rather than earned, and never broadcast as one's own.

The two stories sustain an interesting symmetry. The woman who takes matters into her own hands to force a particular outcome is punished at the hands of fate, while she who passively submits to fate is helped by it.[49] But the terms defining each agent's relationship to the world are not

49. Mme d'Etampes is not the only woman who makes a bid for power in *La Princesse de Clèves*. The presence of the queens and Diane de Poitiers, as well as the seventeenth-century's relatively progressive attitudes toward women (by

the same: whereas Mme d'Etampes's engagement is defined in terms of possible acts of interference in a dynamic course of events, for the duke's mistress the terms have become hiding behind or allowing appearances to speak for oneself; not what she does to the world but what it shields and reveals of her, defines her relationship to the world. As in the case of Diane de Poitiers' "success," the focus shifts from the course of history to the scene of history and from an ethics of actions and their consequences to an ethics of appearances and their interpretations. Virtue, that is, becomes a question of choosing among modes of self-presentation, self-disclosure, and self-concealment—some more passive than others. Thus the mistress gains exemplary value, not because of what she did or didn't do with the duke, but because of how, without any real act of deception or repression on her part, she was able not just to keep her passion but to keep it from the public.[50]

The mistress maintains this essentially conservative praxis by inflecting with the same passiveness her acts of giving as of taking; passively accepting what comes to her as if by right, she as passively gives out, or rather allows to be taken from her, false impressions—such as that she is mourning her husband or that she is an honest woman. This passiveness is such that hardly anything in this story counts as an explicit, volun-

---

comparison with later ages), make it difficult to know whether to read these stories for their antifeminist message. But in the eyes of later ages, it is hard not to see Mme d'Etampes's misfortune as punishment for having acted like a man and for having been doubly bold in tempting both fate and gender lines. Indeed one might argue that to the extent that of the two older women, the duke's mistress is clearly the princess's role model, the eyes that judge the duchess as transgressor and the mistress as keeper of woman's place are themselves part of the princess's legacy to eighteenth-century constructions of virtuous heroines.

50. Mme de Chartres' defense of an unnamed exemplum of discretion over an identified maker of history marks the shift, noted by Alliston and others, toward defining feminine virtue "in terms of the private" and limiting feminine moral activity to passive rather than active modes of engagement: the virtuous heroine is expected to withdraw from the public sphere, except, and this is crucial, as an exemplary object. Even as she stops engaging in acts directly shaping the future, her inner life or what she does offstage becomes the object of a special kind of moral attention, one that paradoxically acknowledges and accepts the inscrutability of what it looks at.

tary, agent-identified act of giving or taking, and yet some kind of exchange—one that both circumvents and confirms the rule that nothing is got for nothing—occurs.[51] At the most basic level, the woman is a simple recipient of news that she did not help to write. And, although in fact two men are taken from her *d'un même coup*, the news of her husband's death received with that of her lover's has the effect of a gift insofar as it spares her a double deception. By it, she is saved from having to pretend to feelings she does not have—grief for her husband's death—and allowed to give full vent to those she does have. Typifying Lafayette's taste for efficiency-driven narrative structures, this chiastic pattern allows every part to work for the other in such a way that, with the least possible output, the situation is exploited to the fullest and demands met on every front. As a feminine passiveness that takes only what comes to it, the woman's exploitativeness hides itself as such and appears instead as a kind of grace—a minimal investment and stake in how things actually turn out. She does not put out a lie but allows assumptions about her to be made that she cannot keep others from making. And what she takes from her husband's timely death is precisely the opportunity to hide the part she has in another's story. She takes advantage, and looks like she has taken nothing; "and" here expresses both temporal sequence and simple conjunction. Her taking (first of a lover, then of the opportunity to express her feelings for him) is free in the sense that it takes away nothing from the image the world has of her; to the extent that her "private" engagements do not diminish her presence in the world, they are never anything for which she has to pay the world.

Suggesting that the alternative to the duchess's meddling is neither, as one might think, abstinence from engagement nor indulgence in private acts without regard to their public effects, the duke's mistress hides nothing and yet also betrays nothing, and in this double fidelity figures the absence of sacrifice, either of private or public demands, suggested

51. The story's oddness, like much in the novel, lies in its meeting the condition of a blessing while remaining within a completely closed universe. It is as if the giving of a death (A) and taking of a life (B), freely given and taken without respect to the other, were mysteriously to coincide so as to balance the books and cancel any outstanding debt just as they would have if they had, in fact, been directly exchanged for one another. The complexity of side effects is such that A can be said to "pay" or make up for B but only secretly and independently of B.

in the term *open secret*.[52] In the effortlessness with which she keeps faith both with herself and with the world, she provides an early image for the weird felicity, the special freedom from repression or self-distortion, enjoyed by the princess in the production of her equally "inimitable examples of virtue." The comparison is useful for bringing into focus the open secret as a deferral not of knowledge per se but of its burden, and as an avoidance not of experience but of its consequence. The question of the innocence of her "cheat" anticipates in many ways that raised by the princess's immaterial semiotic "intercourse" with Nemours—namely, whether in reserving her thoughts for him, she keeps something that she owes the world and the prince. The mistress, at any rate, acts as one who has understood that what the world wants from her is nothing, or almost nothing, of herself. Playing *with* as much as by the rules of the game, she nevertheless does not play against them; unintelligible as subversion, her deviation does not want to be known anymore than the world needs to know it. Thus the lovers' separate space is contained within the boundaries of normative social space without the one affecting the other.[53]

Dramatizing the problem of being a party to an event in which what

52. True to her feelings, and true, if not to appearances then to the demands of appearances, the unnamed woman is able to meet two sets of claims at once; in this two-frontedness she comes close to realizing what Adorno describes as the ideal of tact: "Tact meant not simply subordination to ceremonial convention: it was precisely the latter all later humanists unceasingly ironized. Rather, the exercise of tact was as paradoxical as its historical location. It demanded the reconciliation—actually impossible—between unauthorized claims of convention and the unruly ones of the individual" (Adorno, *Minima Moralia*, 36).

53. Thus the mistress might say of Mme de Clèves that her mistake was (like that of Nicole Kidman's character in recounting her dream in Stanley Kubrick's *Eyes Wide Shut*) to "come out" to her husband. By inviting him to help her control her passion for another, she makes him responsible for feelings that are only her concern. She forgets that the "world" of which M. de Clèves is the primary representative may share exactly her own epistemological passiveness and may be prepared to tolerate what it need not acknowledge and ready to assent to whatever it need not confront. On this reading the princess is a precursor of Sedgwick's twentieth-century example of the potentially closeted individual whom society's courts punish not for the "protected and bracketable fact of [his or her] homosexuality" but according to the subject's "highly vulnerable management of this information" (Sedgwick, *Epistemology of the Closet*, 70). Whereas in its most well-known forms, gay political liberation rejects the closet as essentially

occurs is self-containment, these stories help make sense of the princess's own deeply ambiguous relationship to her public legacy; they typify the passiveness with which anyone "wins" or "takes" anything in the novel. Their paradoxical lesson thus includes the idea that nothing can simply and straightforwardly be taken from others' stories; experience is so constructed that no one is the more advanced for it. The woman's fulfillment of her passion, for example, includes the quieting of its having taken place. True to this negative exemplarity, Mme de Chartres' only indication of sympathy for the mistress is her refusal to expose her. But if Mme de Chartres cannot explicitly put forward the duke's mistress as an example whom her daughter should actively seek to emulate, the princess at least need not try to avoid a similar fate. Morally speaking, the story is one she ought never to seek to make her own. Yet it is also one that, were it hers without the asking, she might accept with impunity, with the same passiveness with which the mistress accepts the pretext offered her. Precisely here, in light of the impossibility of any direct, attempted imitation, we see both the intimacy and strangeness of connection between actors and readers produced by Lafayette's narrative structures. On the one hand, because interpretation mirrors the action recounted as a taking that hides itself as such (interpretively, a "taking in" of someone's meaning without acknowledgment that it has been so taken), actors and readers share a relation of identity; on the other hand, because no one actively "takes from" the other, everyone reserves the right to exercise what Sedgwick, in a different context, has called "the privilege of unknowing."[54]

---

inhibiting and restrictive, a necessary evil partially and temporarily put up with until the world learns to be more accepting, the moral crux of Lafayette's novel hangs on admitting the special value of privately enjoyed, publicly withheld experiences and on reasserting a qualitative moral difference between what goes on in the head and what goes on without. In *La Princesse de Clèves* a person doesn't keep socially unsanctioned thoughts to herself as a means of policing them; rather a person keeps for herself thoughts that, expressed, would have an entirely different value.

54. See the introduction to *Epistemology of the Closet*, as well as her essay on Diderot's *The Nun* in *Tendencies*. In the implied connections here between legacy making and exemplarity, I am once again drawing on Alliston's argument that women's exclusion from patrilineal inheritance of property makes feminine legacies a matter of the examples of virtue that women leave one another to emulate. The mistress's story makes particularly vivid Mme de Chartres' reliance on

vii. immaterial exchanges

Nowhere is this lightening of the burden of knowledge more evident than in the style in which Nemours and Mme de Clèves communicate, each giving what the other wants without seeming to know it. Theirs is a form of exchange as efficient in its self-canceling energy as the production of history in the pointedly minor episodes discussed above. Indeed, I would argue, it is only because Mme de Chartres' historical narratives train our eyes on historical action as essentially transmuted that we can recognize as productive of "change" perhaps the novel's simplest example of an open secret: the colors that Nemours wears at the tournament to signify the princess to herself while taking the thought of her away from the minds of others:

> M. de Nemours avait du jaune et du noir; on en chercha inutilement la raison. Mme. de Clèves n'eut pas de peine à la deviner: elle se souvint d'avoir dit devant lui qu'elle aimait le jaune, et qu'elle était fâchée d'être blonde, parce qu'elle n'en pouvait mettre. Ce prince crut pouvoir paraître avec cette couleur, sans indiscrétion, puisque, Mme. de Clèves n'en mettant point, on ne pouvait soupçonner que ce fût la sienne. (141–42)

> [M. de Nemours was wearing yellow and black, the reason for which was sought in vain. Mme de Clèves had no trouble guessing it: she remembered having said in his presence that she liked yellow, and that she regretted being a blonde, as she couldn't wear that color. He judged he could appear in it, without indiscretion, since, as Mme de Clèves never wore any, no one could suspect it of being hers.]

The example is simple first in the sense of being quite literally an open secret as the "message" consists of one primary visual color, there for all to see, and then in the more important sense of realizing a perfect efficiency, for the same color, yellow, serves the double function of message and smokescreen. Here, as throughout the novel, Nemours and Mme de Clèves understand one another by the very means that prevent others from associating them as a pair. This simplicity of means corresponds to

---

"insider" information to retell history; one wonders how she knows what she knows unless she herself is the widowed mistress, and readers themselves occupy the same position of not knowing how they know what they know, except internally. The analogy to Nemours' and the princess's comparably chaste intercourse should be obvious.

a minimalism of effort or work and produces the effect of a kind of grace, both moral and aesthetic, as Nemours and Mme de Clèves do with what is already given and avoid resorting to anything not already there.

In this efficiency and quietness of exchange, Nemours and the princess enjoy as a blessing what Valincour saw as the risk of Lafayette's and her heroine's linguistic brevity—"reduction" to the "language of angels":

> Je sais bien que la brièveté dans l'expression est un des grands agréments du langage; mais il ne la faut pas outrer jusqu'au point de rendre les phrases obscures, et d'en retrancher ce qu'elles ont de nécessaire. Sans cela, dit plaisamment Monsieur de Voiture, nous nous verrions bientôt réduits au langage des anges, ou au moins nous serions contraints de nous parler par signes. (*Lettres* 136)

> [I know that brevity of expression is one of language's greatest charms; but we should not push it to the point of making sentences obscure and omitting what is necessary (to their sense). For if we did, as M. de Voiture jokes, we would soon find ourselves reduced to the language of angels, or at least forced to speak to each other with signs.][55]

Nemours' and Mme de Clèves' expressive minimalism compels us to revise this famous criticism: it isn't that they omit what is necessary for meaningful exchange, but that they give no more than necessary to understand one another's meaning. The trope of a language of angels—a language between immaterial and transparent beings with little either to communicate or hide from one another—expresses the peculiar weight-

55. From the perspective of feminine virtue's commitment to an appearance of blankness and inaction, Valincour's charge of possible exclusion and omission cannot count as a criticism. Thus in "Lafayette's Ellipses" DeJean reappraises Valincour's comparison to "the language of angels" while leaving intact the content of his criticism—something is missing and has been withheld from Lafayette's language, something readers are invited—indeed have a duty—to restore: "When dealing with the princess, readers must read between the lines: they must interpret (verbalize) the unsaid and even the unsayable, for the language of Lafayette's heroine is a language of lack, of silence, of repression, of gaps" (251 [889]). DeJean understands this elliptical style as a voluntary, political act of resistance to representational structures that "[erode] female authorial status" (262 [897]). To overemphasize the princess's withholding, however, is to miss the point that she, in fact, holds nothing back—the signs that she puts out are there to see if one has eyes to see.

lessness—the imperceptible, nonfunctional, and nonprogressive character—of their exchanges.

Yet however much they conserve their energies, it is not exactly true
that nothing happens between Mme de Clèves and Nemours here; a communicative act takes place and by the same *coup* hides the fact of its occurrence. Insofar as the event is as much a blockage as a release of meaning, we cannot even say that nothing happens to the public whom this
act excludes. For if yellow names the princess to herself, it does exactly
the opposite to others: it takes her name away from the general public's
lips and spares her the spotlight of the inquiry over Nemours' inexplicable choice of colors. Positivist models of action do not allow for the
recognition of this kind of preventative, blocking action because it affects
only the likelihood of her being named; we cannot exactly say that yellow
deflects public attention away from the princess, as she is not in the first
place an object of suspicion. Rather, Nemours' choice of yellow, a color
no one will associate with her, makes it difficult for those who are not yet
thinking of her in connection with him ever to do so; it withdraws her
even as a *potential* thought from the minds of others. If before the tournament the princess's name is unspoken among the gossips, afterward it is, if
anything else, not even available to them, removed from their vocabulary.
Even as a nonsign that conserves the public's state of ignorance, then, yellow does more than not communicate: it disarticulates; its negativity of
action stronger and more complicated than mere inconsequence, it does
take something away, only nothing already operative within the present.
We have here another figure for the kind of weirdly retractive intervention
Lafayette asks us to think through with the princess's *aveu* to the prince:
an (anti)intervention that does not move the narrative action forward but
only removes the possibility of development.

Such interventions count as acts even if they don't bring about a recognizable change in the world; at the same time, they only have value
insofar as they leave open and accept the possibility of making no difference. Inasmuch as such a message serves no practical purpose of enlightenment, it puts no pressure on the recipient to respond; indeed, that
Mme de Clèves can ignore Nemours' gesture pleases her as much as the
gesture itself. Here the openness of the "open secret" refers not only to
its visibility but to its making available a significance that one *may* or
may not take in; its value, in this case, lies in reserving the possibility of
its nonreception. Nemours and the princess are *free* to pick up on one

another's meanings, precisely because in applying the slightest pressure
to preexisting public structures of significance, they leave it open as to
whether they are giving or taking—sending each other outwardly directed
messages or simply using these accessible structures symbolically to claim
for themselves the inaccessible object of desire. Thus, in Nemours' presence but really to whoever may be listening, Mme de Clèves volunteers
her preference for yellow and expresses a sorrow at being blonde because
this means she cannot wear it. That she cannot wear yellow gives her taste
for it the innocence and disinterestedness of an aesthetic relation where
possession is not an option. The casual, unsolicited remark is her way of
saying "Nemours" out loud, not only because it is an admission that she
wants what she cannot have, but because it typifies her ability to claim
something without taking it, without making it materially less available
to anyone else.[56]

The efficiency with which Nemours and Mme de Clèves here produce
meaning for one another, through the simple inflection of public speech
acts and appearances, also guarantees the chasteness of their "interaction,"
for this involves no previous agreement or contract between them. His use
of yellow remains, like hers, a kind of nonuse—as self-fulfilling, nonref-
erential, and nonappropriative. Through it, he does not affix her name to
his, as the other knights in the tournament do their ladies', as trophies for
their glory, but neither does he lend this glory to another mistress. The
open secret here designates not a covert communicative exchange but the
self-contained fulfillment of private fantasy (it isn't even clear whose) taking place under everyone's eyes. At the very heart of social grace, Lafayette
thus uncovers the containment of a profoundly asocial and nonreunipro-
cal activity; later nothing will please the princess more than the image
of her lover "songeant à la voir sans songer à en être vu" (seeking to see
her without seeking to be seen by her) (167). Nemours and the princess
"meet" and pay attention to one another as subjects, not by establishing
a secret contract for pleasure between them but only insofar as they ask
one another to ignore the private, inevitably objectifying "uses" that they
make of each other.

56. Calling out Nemours' name would have the same effect, as it too is both
the containment and negation of love: *ne* + [*a*]*mour*. To say it is to perform a
self-quieting naming of love or, more simply, to hush the name of love. Read
this way, as a voicing that cancels or quiets itself, his name alone provides the
paradigmatic "open secret."

viii. weightless legacies

"J'ai espéré au temps, je n'en dois plus rien attendre" (Time was my hope, I must expect nothing more from this) (157). As the only possible conclusion to his absolute but nonproductive certainty of being loved, these words express the paradoxically chastening effects of Nemours' second intrusion into the garden at Coulommiers, where he comes upon Mme de Clèves lost in reverie, winding yellow and black ribbons (colors that are as little and as much his as they are hers) around an Indian cane that belongs to him and gazing at his portrait. Perhaps more than any other scene in the novel, this one lays waste any attempt to take A as the first step toward B, and teaches the gazing reader forbearance from any demand to convert "experience" into transferable value, for the princess's mental preoccupation with his image provides Nemours with no basis for entering.[57] Nothing—no "experience"—can accrue to either virtual lover or mistress, as Lafayette transmutes, with remarkable wit, Nemours' intended penetration of the other's space into a moment of self-discovery and self-displacement: the woman he would surprise is already "taken" with the thought of him. Nemours may later vent his jealousy of his own image—"Regardez-moi du moins avec ces mêmes yeux dont je vous ai vue cette nuit regarder mon portrait" (At least look at me with the same eyes with which I saw you look at my portrait) (157)—and complain of his material irrelevance, but as Lafayette makes clear, he really cannot separate the joy of being present to her thoughts from this material absence: "Voir au milieu de la nuit, dans le plus beau lieu du monde, une personne qu'il adorait, la voir sans qu'elle sût qu'il la voyait, et la voir tout occupée de choses qui avaient du rapport à lui et à la passion qu'elle lui cachait, c'est ce qui n'a jamais été goûté ni imaginé par nul autre amant" (To see

57. Insofar as the princess's dwelling on his image is not preliminary to inviting Nemours in, it represents an action that refuses to justify itself by that to which it leads, and corresponds quite literally to the empty, nonproductive daydreaming from which the positivist philosophers cited by Murdoch wish to distinguish "thought." Twice Murdoch cites Hampshire's claiming that "thought cannot be thought as opposed to day-dreaming or musing, unless it is directed towards a conclusion, whether in action or in judgment" (Murdoch, *The Sovereignty of Good*, 5, 19)—as if instantiating "the repressive intolerance toward a thought not immediately accompanied by instructions for action" of which Adorno speaks in his essay "Resignation" (166).

in the middle of the night, in the most beautiful place in the world, a person whom he adored, to see her without her knowing that he saw her, and to see her completely absorbed by things connected with him and with the passion she was hiding from him—this is what no other lover has ever tasted or imagined) (154). Seeing her without being seen, he enjoys the consciousness of his absence from the scene as much as the recognition of his presence in her mind; pervading his vision of her winding knots around his cane is the awareness that she acts on her own free time, that she would give as much if he weren't there, and that she does not intend this gift: unsolicited, unprompted, and noninstrumental, her labor of love is in every sense free.

Dramatizing another elision of sexual contact, the scene would seem at first take to support those who want to read the princess as a hysteric desperately attempting to avoid her own desire. For when Nemours' scarf catches in the window as he attempts to enter the room, she turns to see not him but only the specter of her dream, and flees. But I would argue instead that Mme de Clèves simply refuses to be *made to pay* for her fantasy; what Nemours sees gives him no rights over her. As Michel Butor's impressive reading of the scene suggests, until then, their mutual preoccupation occasions a silence full, not with what might be, not with what waits to be said, but, on the contrary, with the containment of potential and impossibility of any future. Inverting the dynamics of the public tournament where outside observers have their potential to suspect the princess taken away from them, the scene leaves insiders nothing more for which to hope, while, as Butor points out, the outsider—M. de Clèves' spy—can imagine whatever he likes except that there is, in fact, nothing to hear: "For the spy, on the other side of the palings, who has neither seen nor heard anything, everything is possible: there must have been a conversation, a love scene, while everything happened in silence."[58]

For Nemours, on the other hand, the certainty of being loved means the evacuation of hope and enforces a passivity bewildering to one used to shaping his destiny:

> Car, enfin, elle m'aime, disait-il; elle m'aime, je n'en saurais douter; les plus grands engagements et les plus grandes faveurs ne sont pas des marques si assurées que celles que j'en ai eues. Cependant je suis traité avec la même

58. From *Répertoire I* (cited in Lyons's critical edition of Lafayette, *The Princesse of Clèves*, 158).

rigueur que si j'étais haï; j'ai espéré au temps, je n'en dois plus rien attendre; je la vois toujours se défendre également contre moi et contre elle-même. Si je n'étais point aimé, je songerais à plaire; mais je plais, on m'aime, et on me le cache. Que puis-je donc espérer, et quel changement dois-je attendre dans ma destinée? (157)

[For, after all, she loves me, he was saying [to himself]; she loves me, I can't doubt this, the greatest pledges and the greatest favors are no surer marks than the ones I've received. Yet I'm treated with the same rigor as if I were despised; I once had hope in time, I can expect no more from it; I see her always defending herself as much from herself as from me. If I weren't loved, I would think to please; but I do please, I'm loved, and it's kept hidden from me. What then can I hope, and what change can I expect from my fate?]

Apprentice to the chastening rigor with which his mistress surrenders her love without addressing it to him, he knows he has conquered and must leave his conquest there.

The freedom with which Mme de Clèves here gives herself up to thoughts that she will not put into practice or bring to fruition supports Sedgwick's claim that autoeroticism expresses a refusal to pass into history and threatens, in its relative tracelessness, "the orders of propriety and property" (Sedgwick, *Tendencies*, 111).[59] A final example of a gift that commits itself to waste, evades proprietary claims, and turns around the impulse to move past A to B, Mme de Clèves' unguarded labor exemplifies one last time Lafayette's sustained questioning of linear causality and agent-identified transmissions of value; in it we can recognize the seemingly contradictory double movement by which she repeatedly invites characters and readers to exercise their interpretive autonomy and imaginative license, but only as a power not to be taken up, a mode of discretion, a readiness to assume nothing or simply take on credit, not a faculty to exploit or develop. "The more we see, the more we must be

59. Enjoying, at most, a pleasure they neither can nor want to transfer, Lafayette's characters capture something of the asocial, noncontractual, and renunciatory dimension of nonreproductive sexuality that twentieth-century critics have tended to associate with Sadean pornography and/or homosexuality. See in addition to Sedgwick, Frances Ferguson's work developing Blanchot's and Bataille's readings of Sade (Ferguson, "Sade and the Pornographic Legacy"); as well as Leo Bersani's theorization of "homo-ness" as a "repudiation of sociality, of the social," and a renouncing of "the project of mastery for the sake of pleasure" (Bersani, *Homos*, 99).

able to imagine," Lessing famously claims in his praise for the Laocoön artist, who, by choosing to represent a moment just prior to dramatic climax, still leaves viewers something to imagine for themselves; modern hermeneutical practice, we might say, has certainly obeyed the dictum by learning to read between the lines, supply absent meanings, and approach surfaces as teasing veils, a game that most readers find *La Princesse de Clèves* plays only too well. Yet here it is M. de Clèves who, inferring the worst from his spy's equivocal report, presents the caricature of the strongly imaginative or speculative reader who can fill in the blanks and supplement a limited and partial body of evidence with his own surmise. He lacks only the imagination to imagine that there is nothing to miss, like Kafka's Ulysses, who, having plugged up his sensory ears, may lend his inner ear to "ditties of no tone" but cannot imagine that the sirens might simply have kept quiet. Butor's unnerving contrast between the spy, for "whom everything is possible" precisely for as long as he remains out of earshot, and the nugatoriness or paucity of what there actually was to hear, is suggestive of the minimal movement I've shown Lafayette repeatedly tracing—from a contingently determined silence or nonexperience to a definitive in-experience, or from an ear that imagines itself deaf, cut off by physical or historical or willfully imposed obstacles, to one that even in the midst of its nonperception remembers to imagine a soundless present. Insofar as "romanticism" names, among other things, a protest against secular modernity's reduction of that which is to that which is capable of articulation, observation, representation, and reproduction, for much of this chapter I have been emphasizing this early modern text's proto-"romantic" dimensions—its attunement to those modes of experience only poorly measured or reflected by their manifest results, and its readiness to credit that which does not materialize on the plane of history. Yet in its adumbration of a mode of minimal realization, where the slightness of what is realized—the little that occurs—is not a basis for complaint, not a limitation on enjoyment, but part of fulfilled experience as such, Lafayette's text also at times momentarily suspends the "romantic" critique of recorded history as a document of such repression and impoverishment that sensitive or imaginative counterhistorians, and especially practitioners of literature, can never do enough to supplement it.[60]

60. In *Practicing New Historicism*, Catherine Gallagher and Stephen Greenblatt give a lucid account of the shared attention to the "reality of unrealized

Après qu'elle eut achevé son ouvrage avec une grâce et une douceur que répandai[ent] sur son visage les sentiments qu'elle avait dans son cœur, elle prit un flambeau et s'en alla, proche d'une grande table, vis-à-vis du tableau du siège de Metz, où était le portrait de M. de Nemours; elle s'assit et se mit à regarder ce portrait avec une attention et une rêverie que la passion seule peut donner. (155)

[When she had finished her work with a grace and a gentleness that the feelings she had in her heart spread over her face, she took a torch and approached the big table facing the painting of the siege of Metz where there

---

possibilities" (54) by which "counterhistory," as the attempt to tell the story of everything excluded from and erased by official history's dominant narratives and methodologies, often joins the "counterfactual," as the attempt to imagine alternative outcomes to particular historical struggles (52–53). Gallagher and Greenblatt trace the origins of both modes of recuperating the "nonsurviving" to romanticism's attentiveness to those types of experience denied by and within modernity's enlightenment discourses, a denial all the more urgent to correct the more this same modernity makes representability a measure of experiential validity. Of Raymond Williams, they write: "[His] appeals to an 'experience' that cannot be described derive from a tradition of thought stretching back to English romanticism and defining the modern as a state of experiential lack or repression. That tradition is well suited to counterhistory, since both imply that a knowledge of modern times requires constant reference to, and imagination of, all that modernity leaves unregistered in consciousness. . . . The study of literature, therefore, allows us to extrapolate the unthought, the unfelt, from the tensions in the constraining structures of feeling" (64). Yet Lafayette's innocuous or innocent historical fictions seem not to carry the revisionist, redemptive charge Gallagher and Greenblatt find Williams attributing to literature, and appear pre- or anti-"romantic" in that they do not present the "gap between the articulated and the lived," of which Williams speaks, as a wrong done to the "lived." Somewhere between the two impulses—the counterhistorical attempt to recover all that the victors' representation of the past suppresses (including, in addition to lives lived but granted no representational value, thoughts that never found words for themselves and were therefore not quite thoughts, feelings that did not allow themselves to be felt, etc.) and the counterfactual attempt to imagine not what once was lived, however obscurely or anonymously, but what might have happened and almost did when the outcome of certain class struggles and political contests was still in play—her anecdotes of acts fulfilled even as they passed for nothing instead posit a world where an experience's failure to come to public light is not identical with its repression and where justice to potential may occur in the absence either of representational adequacy or actualization of possibility.

was the portrait of M. de Nemours; she sat down and began to contemplate this portrait with an attention and a reverie that only passion can give.]

When she had finished her work, she went and sat and contemplated her lover's image. The radiance saturating this extraordinary passage of happily completed if childless creation may disarm generously attentive readers by leaving them, like Nemours, nothing to dream of. "I have not done one thing of which I should not be glad to have you an eye-witness" (Lyons, 89). Such onanism—such spectacular contentment with one's completed acts—may be exhibitionist but not secretly so, that is, not in the usual sense according to which self-pleasuring might be exposed as the secret fantasy of being seen as self-sufficient. Rather, this shameless readiness to have left nothing yet to show (or still to come), this frank admission of having hidden nothing on the order of the observable or even imaginable, is consonant with the text's own unrepentant absence of regret over a virtue possibly not coming to light or a love not bearing fruit, because it does not wait on counterhistory to supply a better pair of eyes than the spy's, or even Nemours', to do justice to a time that to lose was already fully to spend.

The princess's throw-away legacy "of inimitable examples of virtue" hardly counts as an exception to this "nothing-left-to-show" or to the novel's sustained refusal of Nicomède-like demands for the conversion of mental labor into positive value; on the contrary, at once minimal and superfluous, it too only curtails, even as it surpasses, expectations: "Et sa vie, qui fut assez courte, laissa des exemples de vertu inimitables" (And her life, which was quite short, left inimitable examples of virtue) (180). Including as part of its action a renunciation of agency and deferral of responsibility, the verb *laisser* distinguishes this "legacy" from positive acts of willed transmission and generation that would extend a claim into the future, and registers the passiveness with which the princess, here as elsewhere, abdicates the very power that she puts forth and abandons what she gives, making it difficult to claim as such.

Lafayette's presentation of the princess's legacy thus ironizes the compensatory logic that would read the "examples" as reward for her unfulfilled life.[61] By emphasizing the possible absence of connection between the life and its final legacy, the neutral, appositive sentence structure not

61. The subject of much critical attention, the tone of the last line—ironic, melancholy, or blandly affirmative—is difficult to pinpoint. Kamuf takes the

only reminds the reader that the ageless examples cannot equal the brevity of the life, but inflects the novel's conclusion with the thought that the princess may not have "earned" the value of her examples. It is not just that her life, in and of itself, is mentioned only to be dismissed: its mention is its dismissal as if it were indeed so short, and being short so fragile, it could only be glanced over. Delicacy risks being mistaken for indifference here: both can equally be inferred from the refusal to pause. Yet the reader who does stop to pay the clause close attention will find that its tonal ambiguity derives, most of all, from the qualifier *assez*. *Assez* does not add anything on the level of content but makes vague what would otherwise be a definitive statement in a way typical of Lafayette's noncommittal style. This style resonates deeply with Mme de Clèves' own refusal to commit herself, and like hers, its deliberate indefiniteness—impersonal and detached as it may be—is not exactly neutral. In this case it has the ambiguous effect of making modest again what is already diminished. *Assez* deflects the question "how short?" with the answer "*quite* short—short *enough*," and the whole thing, translated as "and her life, which was modestly short . . . ," plays with the two senses of what it means to minimize—to reduce and to moderate. In the first sense Lafayette can be heard to be brushing off (again) a life so unmarked that it is not worth being specific about as if redundantly to reemphasize its blankness. But she can also be taken to be generously leaving room for doubt and naturalizing, softening, the fact of that shortness. The princess's life was short enough, unexceptional even in its briefness—not a matter of violent curtailment.

---

parenthetical clause given Mme de Clèves' life as further evidence of her final readiness to pass over her own life (and desires) to fulfill her mother's will; the clause's consummate brevity expresses the novel's ideological devaluing of life in favor of "insubstantial value": "Once again, a representation is saved from the fate of the representative, since the princess, as well, leaves a ghost as she departs the world: the insubstantial remains of an incomparable virtue. Her death, in other words, sustains and consolidates the construction of an unattainable, inimitable model. In its stead, the unmatched force of the heroine's desire, that cleft of difference which detaches the child from the mother, the reproduction from the model, expires without a trace" (Kamuf, *Fictions of Feminine Desire*, 96). At the same time, as Kamuf's own argument implies, the hint at mortality, even if confined to the parenthetical clause, cannot but undermine the supposed triumph of "insubstantial value."

As if gently chiding her for it, Lafayette thus rounds off her heroine's repeated claim to self-containment—"nothing will come from this"—but so simply and offhandedly that we feel just how little her own final legacy to others concerns Mme de Clèves and at the same time how much it resembles her. In not registering the contradiction between the character's choice to keep her life to herself and her legacy of "inimitable examples of virtue," Lafayette produces the remarkable appearance of passivity—of something effortless and agentless—in feminine moral action.

Just as Empson's feminized figures of value await recognition without soliciting it, the princess's only lasting claim on the public thus seems, like her other *aveus*, hardly to distinguish proper reception from being indefinitely ignored. In the same way, Lafayette's stories await but also defer integration into history. Both she and her heroine have a way of surpassing expectations without closing the gap of need. Such minimalism of assertion requires of recipients a comparable modesty and suspension of reception: "J'ai espéré au temps, je n'en dois plus rien attendre." Lifted out of context and freed of bitterness, these two paratactic statements express the virtue of one who understands the conditions of acceptance to be a giving up of the right to demand more and a willingness not to use one experience as the basis for another. As a patient withdrawal of all expectation, it presents a necessarily paradoxical stance, as affirmative as it is defensive—closed in on itself without closure. Mme de Clèves may retire from the court in the name of her *repos*, but the combined finality and indefiniteness of the never-fulfilled present-tense "dois plus" names the only kind of *repos* allowed by her open secret.

§ 3 Lying Lightly: Lyric Inconsequence in Wordsworth, Dickinson, and Hardy

Deposit: 1. To put or set down; place. 2. To lay down or leave behind by a natural process. 3a. To give over or entrust for safekeeping.

—*American Heritage Dictionary*

i. critical prologue

A. "PAS DE SUITE": LYRIC AND THE NOVEL'S ABANDONED QUEST

> En ce sens, et à condition qu'il ne soit pas dirigé vers une pseudo-immortalité conçue sur le modèle de l'avenir, l'amour qu'on voue aux morts est parfaitement pur. Car c'est le désir d'une vie finie qui ne peut plus rien donner de nouveau. On désire que le mort ait existé, et il a existé.
>
> —Simone Weil, *La pesanteur et la grâce*[1]

> And Enoch walked with God: And he was not.
>
> —Genesis 5:24

Narrative makes a gift of nothing, according to Walter Benjamin, who, in his essay "The Storyteller," identifies the "estate which the novelist administers" with the bequest named in Pascal's thought, "No one dies so poor that he does not leave something behind."[2] Nothing is expected of

1. In this sense, and as long as it is not directed toward a pseudoimmortality conceived by analogy to the future, the love that we will to the dead is perfectly pure. For it is the desire of a finished life that can give nothing more. We desire the deceased to have existed, and he has existed.

2. Benjamin, "The Storyteller," in *Illuminations*, 98. Benjamin is paraphrasing a response Pascal is said to have made in defense of his inveterate habit of giving charity to the poor, sometimes beyond his own means; the comment is reproduced in the "Vie de Pascal" included in the 1964 edition of his works:

Cet amour qu'il avait pour la pauvreté le portait à aimer les pauvres avec

one who dies destitute. Pascal's aphorism has the arrestive, countering force of an "and yet"—an "even so" that supplements and mitigates, if it does not deny, empty-handedness. Yet it offers so limited and ambiguous a consolation that even in affirming transcendence, the thought remains barely distinguishable from a simple statement of mortality.[3]

> une tendresse si grande qu'il n'a jamais pu refuser l'aumône, quoiqu'il n'en fît que de son nécessaire, ayant peu de bien et étant obligé de faire une dépense qui excédait son revenu à cause de ses infirmités. Mais lorsqu'on lui voulait représenter cela quand il faisait quelque aumône considérable, il se fâchait et disait: "J'ai remarqué une chose, que quelque pauvre qu'on soit, on laisse toujours quelque chose en mourant." Et ainsi il fermait la bouche; et il a été quelquefois si avant qu'il s'est réduit à prendre de l'argent au change, pour avoir donné aux pauvres tout ce qu'il avait, et ne voulant pas après cela importuner ses amis. (Pascal, *Œuvres complètes*, 1:588)
>
> [This love that he had for poverty led him to love the poor with such a great tenderness that he could never refuse to give alms, although he only did what was necessary, having few riches and being obliged to spend beyond his income because of his infirmities. But when his friends tried to remind him of this when he made a considerable gift, he would get angry and say, "I've noticed one thing—that however poor one may be, one always leaves something at one's death [literally, in dying or as one dies]." And this was his last word on the subject; and he has been sometimes so liberal that he's been reduced to borrowing, for having given to the poor everything he had and not wanting to importune his friends.]

I am grateful to Alain Cantillon for locating this reference.

3. Pascal's reported remark itself exemplifies an unhoped-for gift, not simply on the level of content—as a tacit reference to the corpses we are all fated to become—but also on the level of enunciation, where it turns on its head the familiar problematic of the gift given without hope of return. To the concern that he is giving away all he has, Pascal answers, not, as we might expect, "others have less than I do," but "even—especially—those to whom I give leave something." The surprise—what Derrida would call the gift of a truly responsible response not already predetermined by the question posed—comes with this assertion of a final, absolute remainder, as if Pascal were deflecting the interminable mise-en-abîme of the excess of charity, with a simple statement of justice—"I only give others their due / I am always paid back." There is a remarkable tact in this enigmatic assertion that at one stroke gives back to the poor their dignity and mortality; by it Pascal not only does in one line what Wordsworth seeks to do in hundreds—dispel the illusion of thankless, impersonal charity *and* underscore the slightness, arbitrariness of the signs attesting to a particular life—but

In this chapter I assign the role of registering this minimal bequest—a gift one might as soon ignore as acknowledge—not to the novelist but to two closely related lyric figures who recur in short Romantic and post-Romantic poetry: the reluctant mourner who abjures the heroism of loss, and the heedless lover who commits his love to inconsequence. In Wordsworth, Dickinson, and Hardy, these figures return to the scene of an original epistemic and moral lapse, yet they return to do nothing; they come back only to confirm the inevitability of a silence that once promised to be broken, and to continue indefinitely a slightness of address that once seemed temporary.[4]

The slightness of the hardly noticed gift in Pascal's aphorism means that its recipients receive no directions as to whether or how to claim or transmit it; they must invent their own mode of doing it justice.[5] This chapter

almost appears, as if in advance of Levinas, to found ethics in the simple fact of the other's exposure to death: "it is because my neighbor is abandoned to (and precisely not destined for) death, that he has a claim on me."

4. Of the three sets of poems in question, perhaps only Hardy's *Poems of 1912–13* unambiguously qualifies as an elegiac sequence, yet one whose departure from the traditional consolatory elegy is well known, while the Dickinson poems, as if continuing the erasure of "plot" begun in Wordsworth's Lucy cycle, make it more difficult to assign to the speaker a distinct role, even that of a lover abstracted in her love or a mourner muted in his loss.

5. In fact, "doing justice" here may include preserving the sense of just how minimally the "making" of such a "gift" distinguishes itself from a mere leaving behind or abandonment devoid of personal address, so that the uncertainty as to whether a debt has even been incurred can occasion a salutary lightening, as well as improvisation, of responsibility (rather than, as sometimes appears in Derrida's meditations on the gift, an unstoppable and irresolvable crisis of doubt). I hope readers will remember this whenever I refer to such a "gift," for the trope of heedless accounting—of receiving from time next to nothing—may well recall to some Bataille's figure of a "nonproductive expenditure"—sovereign because it takes no thought of what it does or doesn't acquire from time (Bataille, "The Notion of Expenditure," 117). The difference, however, lies not simply in the visual and affective contrast between the easy missability of a legacy left and received without the means and against all expectation, and the spectacular nature of Bataille's examples of the gift-as-excrement—the potlatch and its Western equivalents (jewels, racetracks, the sacrifice of Christ)—but in the irreducibly agonistic, competitive function that, on Bataille's account, these "magnificent deposits" fulfill, even and especially when their makers have no "real" means of

examines instances of such improvised acknowledgment in the deflective, leveling gestures by which the speakers of Wordsworth's, Dickinson's, and Hardy's poems set aside elegiac concerns with inheritance, generation, succession, and issue, and move beyond telos, from a register of grief and guilt into the posthumous space described by Weil of simple, constative, disinterested affirmation. The poems in question record as part of the same paratactic movement an appearance and disappearance, a taking in of unsought gain and its heedless setting aside. In thus leveling the difference between before and after, they generate an awareness of how close possession comes to dispossession, loss to gain, life to death, the other to oneself: the recognition of such differences takes the form of nearly missing them. My readings will seek to tease out these texts' implicit claim that this *should* be so—that the experience of such differences is not complete unless one's acknowledgment of them almost fails to take place or occurs only incidentally, gratuitously; the near miss is not simply a function of the limitations of human knowledge, a handicap to be put up with until such time as we can do better, but in a different sense fortuitous, because it reveals the contingency of our moral responses to others.

Indeed, the chapter's more difficult task will be defending this commitment to walking away from experience empty-handed. Several ethical and philosophical traditions, including tragic irony, might offer the terms for such a defense. To come away from morally instructive experience with a sense of how easily it might not have happened: this, within an antihumanist skeptical tradition such as the Jansenism often associated with Mme de Lafayette, might count as its own chastening instruction in the finitude of human judgments and arbitrariness of fate. Similarly, we might adduce the readiness to appear empty-handed at the hour of judgment to both Christian and non-Christian ascetic traditions suspicious of fruition and profit, although in its Romantic expressions this readiness is most often rhetorical—a refusal to be judged by outward show—and has

----

making them: that of expressing a capacity and "need for *limitless* loss" (ibid., 123; emphasis added). As I suggested in the first chapter, the affinities of the ethos adumbrated in this book lie elsewhere—with the minimal exertion and conservation of energies, the readiness to take as well as to leave that Barthes, for example, finds in the Taoist concept of "wu-wei" (nondoing), and the petit-bourgeois complacency in precisely those "moderate" (*Le neutre*, 116)—essentially finite and renewable—pleasures Bataille would dismiss as mediocre.

more to do with the Judeo-Protestant proscription of images than with a suspicion of fruition. Or we might locate an ethics of inconsequence masquerading under an aesthetics of the surface in the unrelenting ironizing spirit that, reacting to Enlightenment rationality, throws away its own good and makes imprudence a condition of delight. Finally, the sense of how easily *x* might also *not* have occurred—bringing with it a feeling for the palpable nearness of roads not taken—serves within liberal humanist ethics, existentialism in particular, not to chasten but to strengthen claims for human autonomy. The contingency that makes it a matter of indifference whether *x* happens or not leaves the agent alone with a duty she could easily ignore, and the value of her act lies not in its consequence but in the choosing of it. All of these traditions (skeptical, stoic, ascetic, ironic, humanist) make claims for inconsequence; how much they actually inform the poems' acceptance of waste depends perhaps less on the content of these claims than on the tone—absolute or qualified, heroic or tentative—with which they defend futility. In the conclusion to the chapter, I will seek to elucidate the particular ethical stance implied by Wordsworth's, Dickinson's, and Hardy's poems of weightless experience. But when suggesting that their speakers make a moral choice of what might seem an accidental slightness of remark, it will be important to shape this claim in accordance rather than in conflict with the speakers' own suspicion of programmatic and didactic ends.

In the previous chapter, I defined the *open secret* as the unwarranted and uncompelled act of divulging, as Lafayette's heroine does, a futureless secret—a knowledge that auditors and speaker alike are meant to continue to overlook rather than exploit. I argued that *La Princesse de Clèves* resists its own generic thrust—the novel's propulsion toward the end of desire—and redefines action as precisely that which leaves off questing and turns aside the agon of plot: the ethical act is not a decisive intervention but an announcement "qui n'aura point de suite" (of which nothing will come), made not so as to pursue desire but to assert one's freedom to then set it aside. Making deferral the sequel rather than prologue to the *rencontre* or recognition between lovers, the open secret fails to organize narrative time as the Aristotelian plot does, around the critical difference between the before and after of *peripeteia* and *anagnorisis*. It asks that we understand temporal succession as something other than teleological development, in terms as foreign to tragedy's cathartic climax as to the modern novel's

hypotactical ordering of time around the hero's unfolding identity.[6] To go
on after conversion (or marriage or renunciation) as if nothing had happened, leaving the event unmarked, implies an ethics of reading—of the
reception of narrative experience—unintelligible to novel readers except as
waste and disavowal. For even when known, the open secret continues to

6. For the purposes of this broad-stroked theoretical exposition, I use the
term "the novel" to refer to the set of generic expectations invested in the abstract
ideal of the novel of self-education, or *bildungsroman*, even if rarely met by any
particular instance of the genre. Some such caveat seems necessary, not simply
because one might multiply instances of nonconsummation, lapsed desire, and
evacuated plots in the novels of Stendhal and Flaubert, but also because, as Marc
Redfield has argued, the bildungsroman is an essentially "phantom genre," at
once "excessively available" (any narrative can qualify as some sort of formative
tale) and "hyperbolically absent" (no literary text appears to meet the aesthetic
criteria under critical scrutiny) (Redfield, *Phantom Formations*, 63–64). As Redfield's complex discussion usefully illuminates, references to the bildungsroman
in the abstract tend, ironically, both to elevate the genre as the site of modernity's
highest aesthetic project—the process whereby the human achieves its humanity
by forming itself—and to degrade it as the site of sordid ambition and petty ac-
cumulation—as the "genre seemingly built around a hero who, in Hegel's ironic
summary, 'in the end usually gets his girl and some kind of position, marries and
becomes a philistine just like the others'" (39).

It may also be worth remembering here that Wordsworth's and Hardy's "major" works belong to the genre of bildungsroman, and both writers have something to tell us about the ideal and failure of the Hegelian project of bildung
as defined by Gadamer: "In Bildung, . . . that by which and through which
one is formed becomes completely one's own. To some extent everything that
is received is absorbed, but in Bildung what is absorbed is not like a means that
has lost its function [not like a grammar book one can throw away once one has
assimilated the language]. Rather in acquired Bildung nothing disappears, but
everything is preserved" (quoted in Redfield, *Phantom Formations*, 47). If, as
Redfield's argument suggests, no instantiation of the genre achieves such happy
plenitude, if, on the contrary the dialectic between self-forming and self-copy-
ing, between making and reception, produces only a melancholy alternation between preservation without meaningful absorption and supersession without en-
riching preservation, then one might read even the "minor" texts studied in this
chapter as tiny, phantom bildungsromans. The only difference might lie in the
temporal experience of an arc of disappointment (of the forming and receding
of expectations) bent, folded, or dropped across a stanza break vs. one sustained
for hundreds of pages.

insist, at some level, on *not* mattering. A scene of instruction that asks us to bracket rather than give consequence to what we learn, the open secret occasions a narrative lapse in development that looks like a moral lapse of knowledge—a violation of the Enlightenment imperative that we act in light of what we know.

I turn at this point from an early example of the psychological novel to lyric poetry, because the latter's freedom from the energies of plot can help to distinguish the open secret's deflective, leveling action from a mode of renunciation and avoidance of experience—the two explanatory models invariably invoked by readers baffled by the princess's refusal to take her lover's hand in marriage. "Renunciation" invests the act of not taking with moral consequence, while "avoidance" inflects it with negative charges of evasiveness and fraud, but both insist on defining the act as loss. Thus either the princess sacrifices the immediate chance before her in the name of some higher ideal, whether it be her virtue, her reputation, her own peace of mind, or inasmuch as she never experiences the adultery for which she accepts to suffer, hers is the record of an unfulfilled, abortive life. Seen through post-Nietzschean and -Freudian lenses, her abstinence appears suspect, the sign of a repression that only redirects, without giving up, the will to power against the self. Indeed, however little the narration's own affective reserve might support this response, a number of epistemological habits and normative judgments we routinely associate with the realist novel—the tendency to conflate eros and telos, the empiricist bias grounding psychological life in the experience of the senses, the positivist suspicion of untested claims and investment in reaching conclusions that make a difference—all encourage the impulse to decry the open secret as an elision of experience and squandering of potential, the stamp of a life unlived.[7]

7. The "forward-looking movement" of the novel is central to Peter Brooks's argument in *Reading for the Plot*, where he describes the "ambition" of plot as "inherently totalizing, figuring the self's tendency to appropriation and aggrandizement, moving forward through the encompassment of more, striving to have, to do, and be more" (39). Wonderfully rational in its drive toward the productive, this Eros sounds on first take less like desire than like the instrumental reason of Adorno's and Horkheimer's *The Dialectic of Enlightenment* that in the name of progress "anathematize[s] the self-forgetfulness both of thought and of pleasure" (22–23). Brooks's own argument, however, goes on to call into question the presumed positivity of the desire that motivates narrative: "under

The same urge that goads the novel's development, and that constitutes a positivist demand for readily identifiable difference, frequently informs disappointed critical responses to a kind of lyric so uninterested in marking narrative difference that it, too, appears to miss its chance for worldly experience. "'Was Not' - was all the statement - / The unpretension stuns - / Perhaps - the Comprehension -"—Emily Dickinson's gloss on Genesis 5:24—"And Enoch walked with God: and he was not"—captures the minimalism of this kind of lyric interjection: a statement so free of inflection that it produces an open-ended "Perhaps" even as it reports the end of a life. For without the explanatory "For God took him," the biblical line's paratactic construction "and : and," like Dickinson's own dashes, doubly defaults on narrative's promise of temporalized identity in difference and continuity in change: on the one hand, the passage from time 1 to time 2, as from thesis to antithesis, could not be more stark or resistant to narrative mediation; on the other, the parataxis all but elides the difference, as well as the relation, between the two actions, so that in place of a sudden abruption and breach of presence, Enoch's "not being" seems continuous with his walking with God, parallel to it. In the seamlessness with which it passes from Enoch's presence to absence, the verse from Genesis exemplifies the kind of nonappropriative relation to experience sustained in the poems addressed in this chapter—poems that record only to set aside narrative gain.[8] Expressing a refusal to make anything of the

---

[the hero's] explicitly formulated demand for pleasure and fortune may lie that which can never be satisfied by the realization of explicit wishes: the more nearly absolute desire to be heard, recognized, listened to" (53). The so-called ends of narrative—the production of a "significant version of the life story" (54), like the acquisition of worldly possessions and "realization of explicit wishes"—turn out to be merely the means of compelling auditors to listen to one's story. Nothing more than the desire to be acknowledged by another subject produces the will to both action and meaning—the will to domination and objectification whose effects so utterly preclude the fulfillment of that original wish.

8. Thus Alan Bewell finds an echo to the verse from Genesis in the similarly arbitrary narrative lapse of Wordsworth's "Lucy Gray":

They follow'd from the snowy bank
The foot-marks, one by one,
Into the middle of the plank
—And further there were none.

On the one hand, the last line euphemistically and efficiently tells us to infer

reported experience, the clarity, indeed vacancy, of such a parataxis has the paradoxical effect of releasing the speculative into the constative mood: in the face of a negation that could not be more definitive, judgment is nevertheless suspended.[9]

What Dickinson calls the statement's "Unpretension" thus corresponds to the freedom from "the constraints of construction" that for Adorno links lyric parataxis to the antithetically Hegelian project of "tarrying with the negative" without hope of any systematic development—a surrender by which the mind, rather than say "so much for that, now for something else," gives itself up to a "desolation" from which nothing more may come.[10] This contrast to the expansiveness of the nineteenth-century

---

the worst—Lucy Gray never made it across the plank; on the other, as Bewell claims, the very absence of conclusive information "leaves us, like the parents on a bridge, in a state of surmise." Far from signifying death, the disappearance of the body and its writing, Bewell argues, corresponds to "an intimation of immortality." Yet just so, the historicist might complain, Wordsworth erases the body of evidence so as to preserve poetry as myth. I want to suggest instead that the poem is an intimation less of immortality than of the open-endedness of loss, of the ways in which loss may be absorbed into the sound of the wind rather than concretized in a single event:

O'er rough and smooth she trips along,
And never looks behind;
And sings a solitary song
That whistles in the wind.

Lucy Gray's, like Enoch's, is the story less of premature death than of the lapse of story itself. See Bewell, *Wordsworth and the Enlightenment*, 204–5. With the exception of "There was a Boy," poems from Wordsworth's *Lyrical Ballads* ("The Brothers," "Lucy Gray," "She dwelt among the untrodden ways," and "A slumber did my spirit seal") are quoted from the Cornell Wordsworth volume *Lyrical Ballads and Other Poems*, 1797–1800, hereafter abbreviated as *LB*.

9. As Avivah Zornberg points out, the Hebrew term *einenu*—"was not"/"is not"—is the same that will be predicated of the missing Joseph, and is both "apparently unequivocal—what could be more absolute than its declaration of not-being?"—and "strangely redolent with possibility" (Zornberg, *Genesis*, 298).

10. See Adorno's essay "Parataxis: Hölderlin's Late Poetry," in which he claims that the "passivity," "docility," and "diffidence" of lyric parataxis correspond to the nonappropriative and nonconstructive dimensions of the Hegelian project of "merely looking on" (Adorno, *Notes to Literature*, 2:134). See also the "Dedication" to *Minima Moralia*, where Adorno, to justify the book's aphoristic style,

bildungsroman is similarly implied in post-Adornian theories that have defined the lyric in terms of a power to "disclose the real without expropriating it for historical or structural ends."[11] If Adorno's account captures the tendency toward a melancholic divestiture from the world within the lyric's blankness of utterance, then these later theories enjoin us not to interpret its inconclusiveness as a failure to complete the work of mourning in the face of the absent one's irresolute fate; pointedly unsentimen-

-----

cites the now famous passage from Hegel's *Phenomenology* on "tarrying with the negative": "[Aphorisms] insist, in opposition to Hegel's practice and yet in accordance with his thought, on negativity: 'The life of the mind only attains its truth when discovering itself in absolute desolation. The mind is not this power as a positive which turns away from the negative, as when we say of something that it is true or false, so much for that now and now for something else; it is this power only when looking the negative in the face, dwelling upon it'" (*Minima Moralia*, 16).

11. This is Paul Fry's formulation for "lyric nonconstruction," which he develops following Käte Hamburger's contrast between "mimetic literature (narrative and drama)" and the nonmimetic lyric statement, whose only difference from "nonliterary statement" is that it "'has no practical purpose'" (see Fry, *A Defense of Poetry*, 17–18; and Hamburger, *The Logic of Literature*, 10, 13). If the metaphor of "expropriation" underscores the ethical value of this refusal to "make" "history" and "meaning," then Fry's last chapter, "The Ethics of Suspending Knowledge," testifies to the difficulty of articulating this Heideggerian-Adornian ethics of "letting nonidentity be" without either betraying its refusal to make claims or reducing it to banality. Thus Fry's suggestion that "the ostensive moment in literature" offers "a respite, a temporary release from significance, after which, when we return to the workaday world of meaning production, . . . we no longer feel that we are chained to the assembly line" (204) unwittingly invests the "ostensive moment" with a therapeutic and instrumental function ultimately complicit with the continued production of meaning.

For another important account of the ethical transformation promised the imagination by aesthetic formalism's suspension of conceptual and discursive knowledge, see the work of Robert Kaufman, in particular the essays "Negatively Capable"; "Red Kant"; and "Legislators of the Post-Everything World." That Kaufman should call "constructivist" the same paucity of discursive content that prompts Fry to describe lyric utterance as ostensive "nonconstruction" should not surprise, given Kaufman's emphasis on the revolutionary character of aesthetic noninstrumentality in enabling critical thought to escape from the determinism of already extant concepts.

tal, Paul Fry's term—"ostensive non-construction"—might well describe Genesis's passing record of Enoch's passing. In the blankness with which it leaves temporal lapse unexplained in terms of cause and effect, or premise and fulfillment, the verse from Genesis parallels what Margaret Mahar has referred to as the "innocence of rhyme"—the "innocence" whereby lyric declines to assume temporality as a burden of knowledge and produce a moment of recognition or *anagnorisis* out of the juxtaposition of time 1 and time 2.[12]

In her poem Dickinson dismisses the explanatory "For God took him" as a failure of "Negative Capability"—an inability to do without resolution or signification of any sort:

12. Contrasting the novel's "effort at sustained explanation of cause and effect" with the lyric's relative indifference to the reckonings of Aristotelian plot, Mahar refers to the "absolute and terrifying innocence" with which "rhyme voices the identity of accident" ("Hardy's Poetry of Renunciation," 304, 306). Of the rhymes that substitute for an answering consciousness in Hardy's "How she went to Ireland," Mahar writes: "What is significant is the degree of unreason which can be carried, so gracefully, within rhyme. The final 'Dora does not know' echoes 'Since she meant to go' and the echo seems nearly an answer to the poem's problem. . . . The effect of the form is to disclose and then dissolve the problem" (306)—a phrase richly resonant with the movement of a claim posed only to be set aside traced in this book. The deafness to—and of—irony with which the poem takes Dora's being shipped in a coffin to Ireland as the fulfillment of her wish to go there makes it a rewriting of Wordsworth's "She dwelt among the untrodden ways," without the fiction of a speaker capable of appropriating the difference between a "now" and a "then" (or a "go" and a "know") as a "difference to me." Mahar does not fault Hardy for defaulting on narrative's promise to organize and interpret time into a past of desire and a present of (non)fulfillment but, on the contrary, presents poetry's power to let "past and present face each other" across the "white space between" stanzas as more faithful than plot to the transience of temporal experience and more generous in its willingness to get less in return on life's expectations. In this, her essay has obvious affinities with the argument developed in these pages and also appears to anticipate Marjorie Levinson's more recent account of Hardy's poetry as reneging on "art's eternalizing, immortalizing aims," although Levinson frames the choice as one between the appropriative impulses defining the "self-integration" of Romantic lyric and the indifference to such self-organization in Hardy's poetry, rather than between narrative telos and lyric inconsequence. See Levinson's "Object-Loss and Object-Bondage," 576.

But lest our speculation
In inanition die
"Because God took him -" tell us -*
That was Philology -

*mention -[13]

Dickinson's terms align "poetry" with the unbearable lightness of "Speculation," the empty burden of imaginative license, and "Philology" with
relief from the threat of cognitive starvation. Yet traditional exegesis has
usually assumed God was protecting Enoch by sparing him the passage
from life to death.[14] In the same way Romantic lyricism's voiding of empirical detail has been construed as the effect of a defensive impulse intol-
erant of difference, and a corresponding resentment has grown up over a
shielding that denies the lyric subject the chance to withstand the test of
experience.[15] When in his essay "Lyric Poetry and Society" Adorno speaks
of the lyric's release of "something not yet distorted, not grasped, not yet
subsumed," it is not to evoke an untouchable, immutable principle of autonomy, but to present nonidentity in the image of mortality—as a pas-

13. Asterisks here and subsequently indicate Dickinson's variant word
choices.

14. According to Christian interpretation Enoch was spared the experience of
death and transported directly to God on account of his goodness in the eyes of
God, while in Jewish commentary Enoch was spared the test of life; thus Zornberg cites Rashi's claim that Enoch was "a righteous man" but "easily seduced to
return to evil ways," so that God thought it best to remove him from this world
rather than give him a chance to fall (Zornberg, *Genesis*, 299).

15. For one such response see Tilottama Rajan's essay "Romanticism and the
Death of Lyric Consciousness," 195. Rajan contrasts Wordsworth's "She dwelt
among the untrodden ways," where the "ideality of Lucy remains simple, protected from dismantling by the very brevity of lyric" (197), to the longer narrative forms of the later Romantic lyric, privileging the latter inasmuch as it
is "increasingly absorbed into larger structures which place it within a world
of difference" (195). The moral judgment implied here, aligning the brief lyric
with a solipsistic avoidance of experience and blindness to the reality of others,
including one's own otherness, recurs in critiques of Romantic lyricism as an
avoidance and denial of history. For a persuasive counter to these critiques see
Zimmerman, *Romanticism, Lyricism, and History*, in which Sarah Zimmerman
illustrates Romantic lyricism's "facility for registering diverse and ambivalent political impulses" and demonstrates the complexity and variety of the poetry's
engagements with history (6).

sive condition suffered from without, not a sign of individual redemption achieved from within: "The danger peculiar to the lyric . . . lies in the fact that its principle of individuation never guarantees that something binding and authentic will be produced. It has no say over whether the poem remains within the contingency of mere separate existence."[16] Yet in framing the difference between narrative and lyric as a choice between referentiality and abstraction, transformative purpose and intentionless abandonment, formalist and historicist critics alike have often seemed to hear in the singularity of the lyric's voice a protective withdrawal into a world apart, rather than, with Adorno, the cry of "the course of a particular"—a cry that may never get picked up or recuperated within any destiny.[17]

Indeed, if a novel such as Lafayette's leaves its characters in a terminal space beyond hope, with little to *show* for their experience, then according to a popular narrative of literary history, Romantic lyricism emerges to insist on private rather than public harvests, substituting for plot-determined progress a difference made within the self. (As materialist critics have long pointed out, the contradictory logic of the "social" under print capitalism is such that increases in mass circulation and anonymous readership in fact demand this apparent default on public meanings in exchange for an interiority only knowable to the poet himself: the figure of a self-reckoning without reference to the scales of public judgment is precisely what readers of print find most consumable.)[18] Thus a poet such as Wordsworth is said to articulate the consolatory and compensatory

16. Adorno, *Notes to Literature*, 1:38.

17. For an important critical revision of the new historicist critique of Romantic disengagement, however, see Marjorie Levinson's essay "Romantic Criticism," in which she does not so much withdraw her earlier materialist criticism of Romantic lyricism's tendency toward metaphysical abstraction, as use the poems' stubborn muteness in the face of such criticism to locate in them an intransigent resistance to the instrumental demands of Enlightenment reason.

18. So fifty years ago Raymond Williams pointed to the ways in which early industrial market conditions put the "Romantic artist" in the contradictory position of claiming as a personal specialty, rather than professional skill, the power to deliver a "common property of imaginative truth" (see "The Romantic Artist," in Williams, *Culture and Society*, 40). More recently, Virginia Jackson's *Dickinson's Misery* has offered a sustained critique of J. S. Mill's famous figure of the lyric poet singing to himself—performing a privacy which by virtue of being addressed to no one in particular becomes readable by everyone—and of its troubled legacy for twentieth-century reading practices.

fictions by which the self can redeem a life devoid of existential wealth.[19] Wordsworth's blankly redundant lines—"She liv'd unknown, and few could know/When Lucy ceas'd to be"—certainly resonate with the empirically impoverished and denuded character of the lives that make up for Benjamin the "sum total of the estate which the novelist administers" (*Illuminations*, 98).[20] In insisting "But she is in her Grave, and oh!/The difference to me," Wordsworth can be heard to be appropriating this legacy for himself and promoting himself as the one visionary who did have eyes to see. Yet in going on to rhyme *know* with the simple, weightless, and passing *oh*, Wordsworth does not simply pass from a public to private register; the echolike reduction of *know* to *oh* signals the transmutation of experiential knowledge conceived of as a proprietary inheritance either to be hoarded by the self or transmitted to others, into something even less than noncommunicable pathos, a nonappropriative relation to passing time. In the same way, the brevity of "A slumber did my spirit seal" does not preserve the "ideality" of the speaker's love, but testifies to how simply, casually, dispossession can follow on possession; the speaker passes from illusion to disillusion without dramatizing this passing as a morally instructive event.[21]

Each of the poets studied in this chapter offers insights into the way

19. According to Alan Liu, for example, Wordsworth's turn toward lyricism represents "a rush to escape history in which each transitional genre . . . harbors denied knowledge of the nation, family, and riches that must be left behind for the self to be free" (Liu, *Wordsworth*, 223). A critique of the language of "unaccountable" wealth—of riches deemed immaterial, incalculable and infinitely multipliable—pervading new critical and sometimes even deconstructive discourses on poetry, Liu's theory of lyric value describes by contrast a *closed* economy in which the lyric self grows only in the negative, in the place of others, and as the denial of history. Liu's own method of "denied positivism" seeks to register the violence of the denial necessary to become blind to "narrative agony" and complete the transvaluation of a Pauline-like hermeneutics: "the imagery of the hungry eye is 'rich' no matter the evidence of poverty strewn all around. It is full of itself" (223).

20. Benjamin describes this estate with a phrase from Arnold Bennett "about a dead woman in one of his novels—that she had had almost nothing in the way of real life" (Benjamin, *Illuminations*, 98).

21. In his reading of Goethe's "Wanderers Nachtlied" and "Ein Gleiches" in "Lyric Poetry and Society," Adorno describes a similarly elided instruction by which the setting aside of illusions coincides not with an Enlightenment awak-

in which "history"—temporal change—can thus take place as a passing out of existence, a trailing off or lapse, rather than as a concretization or production of significance. Wordsworthian characters tend to disappear without notice, arbitrarily and inconsequently, imparting the sense of how easily they might also have remained, and raising the question of the relationship one can maintain to loss when "things" are not "violently destroyed" but "silently [go] out of mind." Wordsworth uses the phrase in the "Preface to *Lyrical Ballads*," when assigning to the poet the role of bridging cultural and temporal distances "in spite of things silently gone out of mind, and things violently destroyed" (Wordsworth, *Selected Prose*, 292); here as elsewhere, whether consciously evoking "wise passiveness" or enacting the involuntary character of poetic memory, he appears to embrace the paradox that the poet may owe his recuperative, transcendent powers to nothing more than his openness, even defenselessness against such arbitrary loss and readiness to allow things to disappear without notice rather than seek to preserve them.[22] Repeatedly Wordsworth engages the pastoral topos of the shepherd whose watch barely distinguishes itself from inattentiveness or trusting abandonment.[23] So Vaudracour is said to allow his child to die "by some mistake / Or indiscretion" (*1805 Prelude*, IX.907–8); so Leonard's younger brother in "The Brothers," having fallen asleep among his flock, walks to his death over a cliff.[24] The somatic, agentless character of loss, according to which it might have happened at

---

ening but with the simple moment of falling asleep, and the realization of a promised reconciliation with the natural world takes place as a relinquishment of human claims over it. See Adorno, *Notes to Literature*, 1:41–42.

22. It is this readiness to accept gradual, unremarkable, nonviolent change, however destructive in effect, that has earned Wordsworth the charge of complacency and evasiveness from critics wishing to insist on the specific subjects of historical violence. See Marjorie Levinson's exemplary reading of his representational elision of the victims of industrial development in *Wordsworth's Great Period Poems*.

23. Willard Spiegelman has examined the uneasy and unresolved tensions in Wordsworth between the imagination's "wise passiveness," pastoral indolence, and an unthinkingness that repeatedly occasions accidental, gratuitous death or inadvertent moral lapse (see Spiegelman, *Majestic Indolence*).

24. Except where otherwise noted, passages from *The Prelude* are taken from the Cornell Wordsworth, *The Thirteen-Book Prelude*. In "The Brothers" the fact of James's not being found is initially a "circumstance / Of which [his companions take] no heed" (369–70 [1800]); their nonconcern is not simply dramatic

any time, makes its occurrence difficult to distinguish from the time of actual, undiminished presence.

Similarly, in his *Poems of 1912–13* Hardy will describe his dead wife Emma as having gone "without ceremony," but once he begins to remonstrate in "The Going"—"Why did you give no hint"—he realizes he must go all the way back: because they might have spoken at any time, they permitted themselves a silence that became definitive; their life together was always there for the taking; but, never used, this possibility diminished imperceptibly:

> Why, then, latterly did we not speak,
> Did we not think of those days long dead,
> And ere your vanishing strive to seek
> That time's renewal? We might have said,
>   "In this bright spring weather
>   We'll visit together
> Those places that once we visited."[25]

The familiar phrases capture the simplicity with which the invitation might have been extended but never was. The quoted lines' chiastic redundance ("We'll visit . . . that once we visited") and their attribution to a now impossible, and lately unused, common voice inclusive of either partner emphasize the ambiguously revisionary potential in "together" as all that would have been either different or the same a second time; the thrust of the revision—whether aimed at their recent alienation in marriage or at a still earlier absence to one another in courtship—remains unclear.

Hardy's ability to communicate the sense that one cannot specify the loss of this unused "might"—that, although now definitively lost, it never ceased at any particular moment to hold out decisive power—corresponds to the withdrawal without closure in "Lucy Gray" and to the open-endedness by which Wordsworthian characters are able to count the dead weight of inoperative tendencies among productive and vital states: so

------

irony but testimony to how ordinary, uninflected, how like any other day, the event of his disappearance remains:

> The Loiterer, not unnoticed by his Comrades,
> Lay stretched at ease; but, passing by the place
> On their return, they found that he was gone.
> From this no ill was feared. . . . (365–70 [1827])

25. All references to Hardy's poetry are from the James Gibson edition of *The Variorum Edition of the Complete Poems of Thomas Hardy.*

the girl in "We are Seven" continues to count her dead brother and sister within the family, and Michael continues to repair to the unfinished sheepfold, even if it is not to lift a single stone. Many of Dickinson's poems similarly define action (in particular, heavenly, transfigurative action) to include its own erasure or deflection: in the time it takes for "It sifts from Leaden Sieves" to reveal its conceit, the snow has gone; in the lightness with which it moves from metaphor to metaphor, "indifferent quite," the poem's own deferral of naming becomes definitive:

It sifts from Leaden Sieves -
It powders all the Wood.*
It fills with Alabaster Wool
The Wrinkles of the Road -

It makes an even Face
Of Mountain, and of Plain -
Unbroken Forehead from the East
Unto the East again -

It reaches to the Fence -
It wraps it Rail by Rail
Till it is lost in Fleeces -
It deals Celestial Vail**

To Stump, and Stack - and Stem -
A Summer's empty Room -
Acres of Joints, where Harvests were,
Recordless, but for them -

It Ruffles Wrists of Posts
As Ankles of a Queen -
Then stills it's Artisans - like Ghosts -***
Denying they have been -

  *Field -   **flings a Crystal Vail//On   ***Swans -[26]

The poem's anaphora reproduces the iterative "at-one-ment" of snow that reduces all it covers to the same blankness; indeed, readers, noting the way in which the poem makes the snow's blanketing and blankening ac-

26. Another variant to the poem reads:

It sifts from Leaden Sieves
It powders all the Wood
It fills with Alabaster Wool

tion its own, have taken the seemingly endless yet strangely self-absorbed generative power of the "It" as a figure for poetry's euphemistic powers of voidance and negation—at once couching and destructive, fatal and protective. Thus Sharon Cameron: "Dickinson avoids any naming but the absented referentiality, the mere pointing at an otherness, of 'It'. . . . The consequence is emptiness unable to recall that it ever had an alternative, the phenomenal world so subject to cancellation that it absorbs its own annihilation with deference. While there is no manifest violence in the picture, snow nonetheless gentles distinction out of existence."[27] If Cameron's language wonderfully renders the tone of submission, surrender, and annulment that makes such leveling of distinction something less than agon, her reading nonetheless insists on the violence of this empirical voidance in both its root cause—pain—and its anesthetizing effects. Yet no reading of the poem should ignore the lightness of the metaphors—"It Ruffles Wrists of Posts / As Ankles of a Queen -"—by which it feminizes as well as covers over the earth's recalcitrant, already diminished, "Stump, and Stack - and Stem -." Premised on transience, the poem accepts the superfluity of its artistry and awakens us to negation as to an action taking place in time: more than a suspension of empirical memory, a dispensation; more than an erasure of harvests, a kind of negative harvesting or gift received when it amounts to zero.

Anxiety over the experiential loss implied by so heedless a mode of marking time grows as the promise of a divine redemption of history recedes, and humans are left the task of securing their inheritance. Such

---

The wrinkles of the Road -
It scatters like the Birds
Condenses like a Flock
Like Juggler's Flowers* situates
Opon a Baseless Arc -
It traverses - yet halts -
Disperses, while it stays
Then curls itself in Capricorn
Denying** that it was -

*Figures   **Disputing

The proliferation of variants that cancel and replace without representing any advance over one another is another way of performing the indifference of succession that the poem is describing.

27. Cameron, *Lyric Time*, 175.

a secularist and participatory conception of history as an open-ended collectivist project accounts for the easy slippage between the political and pictorial senses of representation that have sometimes marked both the liberal critique of the Western canon, when it believes that pictorial representation can compensate for political disempowerment, and new historicist polemic, when it understands representational exclusion as a violent erasure doubling the original violence of political, social, and economic disenfranchisement.[28] Hence the vindicatory zeal with which the avowedly secular critic seeks to retrieve history from its denial at the hands of the lyric poet and return to Enoch that which he missed.[29] Yet this will to liberate the positive content of experience from its own shielding—to recover a "history" that the poet is supposed to have cloaked in time and to isolate narrative loss or gain from the blankness in which it has been covered and enfolded—threatens reception itself, for it means discounting as false and derisory the very form in which this experience has accrued.[30] Indeed in its refusal to take silence at face value and to accept a concluding blankness as the entire story, this critical posture in many ways responds to the same burden of stewardship—the reception

28. Thus John Guillory responds to an admittedly reductive version of the liberal critique of the canon as a demand for more inclusive possibilities of self-mirroring: "Are we obliged to say . . . that the pleasure experienced in works of art can always and only be reduced to the pleasure of seeing our social identities or beliefs mirrored in the work?" ("Canon," 237); see, as well, Jerome Christensen's critique of what he calls the "pictorialism" of Romantic new historicism in Christensen, *Romanticism and the End of History*.

29. If Liu and Levinson have followed Adorno in unmasking what he called the "demand that the lyric word be virginal" (*Notes to Literature*, 1:39) as the very symptom of historical trauma—itself the effect of the violence of alienated social relations that it would hide—they have sometimes left unquestioned their own demand for agon when insisting on the guilt behind a loss for which they would make restitution. As Liu himself has claimed, new historicism is marked by "a fear of the loss of loss" and seeks to avoid this metaloss by naming the specific content of historical violence. See Liu, "New Historicism and the Work of Mourning," 558.

30. As I have argued elsewhere with respect to Wordsworth's recognition of the gently and imperceptibly determining forces of "habit" and "custom," the effort to specify change is at odds with the open-endedness of an insensible formative process that, even as it eclipses possibilities and defines the self, remains

of a missed and bracketable legacy—that the lyric speakers in question choose to set down rather than take up.

Animated by a desire to rectify a history that unjustly denies some human talents their full expression, the historicist, in this sense, shares with the figure of the Romantic Promethean poet a strong sense of the malleability and nonabsoluteness of given conditions, even as her methodology begins, like the psychoanalytic theory of trauma, in the Romantic hermeneutics of the sublime and its pessimistic recognition of the inevitable noncoincidence and nonadequation of witness to event—the structural impossibility of ever being present to historical action as it unfolds, an impossibility that produces the logic of belated and symptomatic representation from behind.[31] This double parallel—on the one hand, a shared commitment to shaping and revising the course of human events, on the other, skepticism regarding the efficacy of human agency when it conceives of historical action as linear and nonrecursive—means that we need not pit poet and critic against one another, but we can rather read them together as embodying a range of only partially articulated attitudes, rather than full-fledged positions, toward the unfinished Enlightenment project of worldly responsibility.[32] Both critic and speaker are readers of

---

by its very gradualness difficult to declare final, definitive, absolute. See François, "To Hold in Common and Know by Heart."

31. Here I want to qualify the contrast Christensen makes between the historicist as "dead set on decoding the iron logic of past events" (*Romanticism and the End of History*, 2) and the Romantic poet whom he characterizes as specially attuned to accidents, near misses, and other events decentering the historical subject's relation to experience "as it happens." For Christensen, this attunement to the arbitrary does not result in a skeptical withdrawal from end-oriented action but, on the contrary, occasions a celebration of "opportunities for change"—evidence that the world need not be as we find it. The poems to be discussed here similarly keep alive the sense of the contingency of experience so that its nonoccurrence remains almost as palpable as occurrence, yet this contingency is not taken, as in Christensen's account, as an occasion to express "a principled frustration with the way things have turned out and a deliberate impatience to turn them right," nor, as on the reductive deconstructive reading, as a sign of the failure of agent-oriented interpretive practices, but, strangely, as both a reception and a lightening of something akin to fate.

32. Christensen's own Benjaminian account of Wordsworth as delivering to "us" a meaning unavailable to his own historical moment belongs at the optimistic end of this spectrum insofar as "the unrepresentability of the historical

experience in the sense that they are in a position to cast retrospective judgment and to take the measure of the fulfillment or waste of a life's potential; both face the problem of how to register, receive, and acknowledge not the fruits of experience, but its essentially recessive address, a task it is difficult not to invest with heroic energies.[33] Yet the poems in question here both record and accept a failure of telos profoundly at odds with this heroic quest as well as with the constructive project that Claudia Brodsky has called the "creation out of history of an acquisitive value."[34] In them the postponement of definition—of that which would allow the assignment of positive value—becomes experience itself.

B. UNCOUNTED TIME AND THE BURDEN
OF SECULAR HISTORY

"She lived unknown, and few could know / When Lucy ceas'd to be"; "Gone - as soon as known -" (Dickinson, "So the eyes accost and sunder"); "Forgotten, as Fulfilled" ("The birds begun at four o'clock"); "But

---

moment when it appears"—a phrase that should be heard as an echo of the psychoanalytic formulation of trauma as an event missed as it occurs—becomes for Christensen an occasion to further the enlightenment project of using the future to rewrite (and correct) the past: "Looking for something that one cannot find is looking for something in the future. . . . The evidence of Wordsworth's return to the past, a planned obsolescence, urgently solicits an attention that could not have been provoked earlier and which gives us (nothing but) hope in the project of literary history and criticism as a practice of something more than academic interest" (*Romanticism and the End of History*, 73). Again, the figure of an "untimely" call answerable only after its lapse invites comparison to Cathy Caruth's more pessimistic reading of the dream-call that awakens the father to his dead child's burning body as analyzed by Freud and Lacan. See her chapter "Traumatic Awakenings (Freud, Lacan, and the Ethics of Memory)," in *Unclaimed Experience*, 91–112.

33. Thus on Christensen's account, Wordsworth's *Prelude* remains for Liu "subject to a history that it thoroughly denies," saturated with a violence to which it remains blind, and in its blindness repeats, until the critic arrives to make such blindness readable. Even Susan Stewart's *Poetry and the Fate of the Senses*, a book that, far from emphasizing the lyric's abstraction from history, seeks to rematerialize poetry as a vehicle of sensory perception, continues to frame the poetic project as an Orphic quest to rescue the figure of the beloved from darkness and oblivion by recovering her perceptibility.

34. See Brodsky, "Contextual Criticism, or 'History' v. Literature," 94.

what they record in colour and cast / Is — that we two passed" (Hardy, "At Castle Boterel"). These minimal interjections share with Pascal's thought the attempt to register a hardly noticed passing; they repeat its gesture of remarking and in the same breath quieting an unsummoned legacy or unsought experiential difference. The open secret, a record of how something was almost not counted, thus begs the question of both its status for history and claim to futurity by accepting the risk of not counting a second time, or of making only an uncountable difference. Why?

The constellation of meanings centered on the root word *count* may suggest a preliminary answer even as it gives the question its particular force. Originally meaning simply to consider, *count* in both its transitive and intransitive meanings—to assign numerical value to and include within a set of similar objects; to matter, make a difference for the future by having an impact on other events—implies a mode of having reference to others. "Accountability" designates the legal and moral capacity not just to take responsibility for one's actions but to explain them before a public authority, while the act of "recounting" tests the representativeness of one's experiences for others; these terms further inflect "not counting" with the negative sense of failing in relation to others. The question, "Can I count on you?" seeks an affirmative and implies a set of expectations anchoring the person addressed in the future and protecting her from her own mortal weightlessness. Similarly, it is by counting them that we transform random occurrences into chapters of a single life; conventional marriage plots, in particular, betray the fear that experiences might remain less than real if we did not establish their continued contribution to a narrative whole. Aesthetes, flirts, and others who define their acts as play-acts, and speak only "off the record," invite, by contrast, the charge of not knowing how to value their object, because they seek neither to preserve nor transmit it to others. They do not speak seriously, if as Stanley Cavell claims, "To speak is to say what counts. . . . Something counts because it fits or *matters*."[35]

One premise of this chapter is that the moral exhortation to count gains its urgency through the historical process of secularization, as the passive mirroring of human value in timeless, divine authority comes to be replaced by its active if finite measurement according to fallible human

---

35. Cavell, *Disowning Knowledge in Six Plays of Shakespeare*, 205.

instruments—courts, history books, markets, polls.[36] The withdrawal of a sovereign judge issuing absolute judgments of value corresponds to the growing pressure to give a rational account of oneself, one's actions, and motivations before a community of like-minded peers. But in thus redistributing among peers the power to adjudicate moral worth, secularization has tended to define the moral life exclusively in terms of "acting beyond the self and making oneself intelligible to those beyond it."[37]

"Those beyond [the self]" in the above formulation are not gods gifted with the power of omniscience, capable of reading the soul's mysteries instantaneously, but near equals who have only limited powers of insight and who await some sort of demonstration from the self in question. Human audiences are in this sense more exacting than divine judges: a priori blind to one another, they expect to be *made to see* one another's moral experiences, whether through perceptual evidence or by sympathetic

36. In question here are not only actual historical developments but the paradigmatic narratives of emancipation embedded within the concept of enlightenment itself, famously defined by Kant as "man's leaving his self-caused immaturity" (see "What Is Enlightenment?" in Kant, *The Philosophy of Kant*, 132). The salient feature of this narrative for Kant is the individual's assumption of responsibility before the Law: where there once had been passive and blind obedience to commands perceived to come from without, the Enlightenment subject acts of his own accord in conformity with the law, which presents itself as "aris[ing] from his own will." This passage from heteronomy to autonomy (from foreign to home rule, as it were) does not so much change the content of one's actions as one's relationship to them; the authenticity of that relation is gauged by one's success in articulating it. According to Lukács, this is also the trajectory traced by "the inner form of the novel . . . as the process of the problematic individual's journeying toward himself, the road from dull captivity within a merely present reality—a reality that is heterogeneous in itself and meaningless to the individual—toward clear self-recognition" (Lukács, *The Theory of the Novel*, 80). As Žižek, following Adorno, has argued, twentieth-century psychoanalysis repeats, in the other direction, this attempt to "subjectivize," appropriate, and render intelligible injunctions initially deemed foreign, arbitrary, "nonsensical"; the patient is asked to recognize himself by articulating not the socially prescribed Law but that of his own repressed unconscious. See Žižek's commentary on Adorno's critique of Freudian analysis as an attempt to "de-psychologize" the subject, to free the subject of the "heteronomous rule of his unconscious," in Žižek, *Metastases of Enjoyment*, 16–22.

37. Cavell, *Conditions Handsome and Unhandsome*, 46.

identification or by appeal to custom or by the recognition of universally prescribed rational moral principles. It is a truism that the Enlightenment forgoes predetermined patterns of assigning value, of distinguishing the worthy from the undeserving, the innocent from the guilty, and agrees to overlook a person's origins in return for the right to judge her by her end. Secular, rational human judgments, in other words, take time; this is precisely the demonstrative, experimental use of time that the novel promises to make and that the poems I am grouping here as poems of declined experience, no sooner begun than ended, seem to miss. Moving from one kind of blankness to another, their unheroic subjects appear to forfeit the chance held out by modern liberalism's proclaimed willingness to count from zero—to bracket the question of origins and witness history in the making.[38]

Yet, even at its most negative, the skeptical despair of progress that one might hear behind Wordsworth's, Dickinson's, or Hardy's abortive exclamations does not necessarily take issue with democratic liberalism's generous impulse—the willing suspension of judgment and inclination "to see what time will do," as Lafayette's heroine puts it. Rather this skepticism

38. Historians of the novel have long recognized the intimate connection between the novel's developmental use of time to form character and establish meaning, and the historical expansion of temporal over preordained authority, of which the genre's ascendancy is a part. Thus Ian Watt's seminal *The Rise of the Novel* distinguishes the novel from "an earlier tradition of using timeless stories to mirror unchanging moral verities" and locates its appeal to an upwardly mobile reading public in its emphasis on the formative power of individual experience. Michael McKeon's *The Origins of the English Novel* also underscores the new role that temporal difference plays in establishing claims to "truth" and "virtue" in the late seventeenth century and early eighteenth, as the new objectivity afforded by print culture, which empowers individuals to test for themselves what they had previously accepted from the mouth of authority, parallels the new legitimation of class status on the "rational" grounds of a person's achievement in time rather than inherited privilege. In both cases humans are given license to judge for themselves, but they soon discover that the absence of fixed criteria means that there will be no end to judgment. If the novel, according to McKeon, develops out of this dialectic, Alexander Welsh's *Strong Representations* highlights instead the *conclusiveness* of narrative representations in the early novel: Welsh links the emergence of the genre to the growing use of circumstantial evidence in jury trials, which requires ordering seemingly isolated, unrelated facts in such a way that they amount to one conclusion and not another.

concerns the possibility of bringing such an experiment to term, given the uninterpretability of final effects. One has only to remember with Weber how quickly the opportunity to prove one's worth by increase becomes an interminable, never sufficiently achieved task, in order to reinterpret these poems' indifference to what time might actually bring as a plea for contentment. For just as Protestantism dismisses every particular "good" work as irrelevant to salvation, the new call to make the most of time expressed in Benjamin Franklin's equation "time is money" sacrifices lived time in exchange for its all but limitless potential: the loss of five shillings is that and all it could have turned into. To this the graveside loiterers and heedless passing lovers of Wordsworth's, Dickinson's, and Hardy's poems respond with their own *inverted carpe diem*: since what we could make of time is limitless, let us make nothing at all. The lyric timekeeper adumbrated by these figures thus does make use of time; time is, in fact, all he takes. He begins, like the Enlightenment judge, by withholding the conferral of value and suspending judgment on himself as on the other who is his *semblable*; only in time he decides simply to do without judgment and leave off questioning, rather than wait for a demonstration that, even when forthcoming, provides no more conclusive answer than what he himself might have supplied.

But is it possible to define a lyric subgenre simply in terms of a temporal gesture of desistance, in the course of which one waits and then gives up waiting? In terms of a cadence of lapse or recessive progress that may occur in a single phrase as in Dickinson's "Forgotten, as Fulfilled"? For what this otherwise seemingly random assortment of poems may most have in common is a temporal sequence in which time 2 both repeats and cancels time 1, as in the reception of unexpected gain taken in only to be just as quietly abandoned. Enforcing a double take or revisionary structure of reading, Wordsworth's, Dickinson's, and Hardy's poems appear at first to record a failure of *x* to have noticed *y*, or *y* to be differentiated from *x*: Lucy dies into Nature before her lover can realize her difference from him; Hardy's elegist cannot make himself feel the difference between his wife's absence in life and in death; the reception of experience in Dickinson often includes its own deflection, and contact recedes as informally, unceremoniously, as it occurs. In continuing to make light of a now undeniable difference, however, these lyric speakers come to suggest that the going without inflection was the missed event's way of happening, and underdetermined difference the loved one's way of making herself known. Because these characters do not understand experience as progress, whether from the hypothetical to the real or from illusion to disillusion, as they would if they were in a novel, they can accept the open secret's parenthetical action as complete rather than failed or elided instruction. In returning to the scene of the original epistemic and narrative lapse only to do nothing a second time, they affirm, by their very reticence, that they have *not* suffered a loss. This is, in fact, the charge most commonly made against them, but whereas the charge usually implies a crisis of affectivity threatening their capacity for moral response, as in "they have not suffered enough—they are not up to their loss," my argument insists on a different sense: "they received all they could—the slightness of the difference made did not constitute a loss." If they finish empty-handed, it is not that they have deferred, elided, or sacrificed experience, but that experience as such comes to very little.

In the following pages I propose to read Wordsworth, Dickinson, and Hardy as bearers of open secrets rather than private harvests. In keeping with the poems' own repeated evacuation of telos, I have not sought to give the argument a linear development but have divided the chapter into discrete sections, each organized around a particular constellation of poems. Since repetition is all that goes on in the open space beyond the end, readers will inevitably, although I hope not tediously, find themselves covering the same ground. I offer these readings less as contributions to the study of the particular poets than as articulations of a lyric subgenre—the lyric of inconsequence—variously worked out by three poets who themselves share a commitment to the possibilities of nonsequential connection opened up by lyric (as opposed to narrative) sequences or constellations.[39] At the same time, I hope that by the end of this chapter the quiet

39. M. L. Rosenthal and Sally M. Gall, for example, discuss the modern poetic sequence as a way of organizing time according to minor and readily forgotten epiphanic moments rather than narrative development, while Roland Greene emphasizes the blurring of "lines of priority and causality" in lyric sequences. See Rosenthal and Gall, *The Modern Poetic Sequence*; and Greene, *Post-Petrarchism*, 18. See also Sharon Cameron's intriguing suggestion that Dickinson may have chosen not to publish her poems, because she "could not decide whether to publish her poems in sequences or as lyrics"—an indecision that may well define the modern poetic sequence itself, in its latency of connection and free play of resonances between individual poems (Cameron, *Choosing Not Choosing*, 54). For what I consider the most lucid account of Wordsworth's Lucy poems as a

with which the poems in question here register only to let pass temporal difference will be distinct from the more widely theorized paradox of lyrical utterance as the "open secret" of "overheard speech"—a vocalization so intimate it hardly counts as externalization—according to John Stuart Mill's famous definition of poetry in opposition to eloquence, as "feeling confessing itself to itself."[40]

---

single lyric sequence or song cycle, see Ferguson, *Wordsworth: Language as Counter-Spirit*, 173–94. Ferguson's comparison of the poet's progressive renunciation of claims to knowledge to the quester's renunciation of possession of the love object in courtly romance remains important to any consideration of the poems in light of *La Princesse de Clèves*.

40. Mill, "What Is Poetry?" 12. Virginia Jackson's recent polemic in *Dickinson's Misery* against the lyricization of historically specific written address as timeless nonaddress appropriable by a potentially infinite set of readers compels me to add this remark. Jackson's book mounts a powerful critique of the decontextualizing violence done to Dickinson's writings by over a century's worth of printing and reading them as lyric poems, frequently extracted from the letters in which they originally appeared and abstracted from the particular, "familiar" addresses that once defined them. Jackson argues that such decontextualization has ironically contributed to making Dickinson's socially embedded writings exemplary specimens of the abstraction from referential contexts supposed to define the genre of lyric in general. Although this chapter will no doubt seem to perpetuate this decontextualizing interpretive tradition, Jackson's polemic helps clarify the question of the role of genre in my argument. For the peculiar traits that interest me in Hardy, Wordsworth, but especially Dickinson—an insouciance that dispenses with explanatory gestures, whether introductory or conclusive; an openness strangely devoid of sociability, as imperious as it is undemanding; a noninsistent revelation exposing all and desisting just as quickly—include a contentment with minimal self-accounting at odds with the confessional and expressive moods usually attributed both to lyric *and* epistolary modes. While these features may "pass" more easily by virtue of appearing in texts traditionally associated with the genre that famously teaches the reader to expect nothing except to be surprised out of ordinary expectations, such nonaccounting seems to me worth theorizing as distinct from (even if closely related to and easily mistaken for) the fiction of intimacy produced by lyric reading whenever the reader indiscriminately assumes the position of a poem's "I" or "you," especially when such an identificatory gesture becomes inflected as appropriative—precisely that which "lyric inconsequence" forswears. For the question of lyric intimacy and the ways in which the reader is invited to vocalize the lyric "I" as her own, see also Vendler, *The Art of Shakespeare's Sonnets*; and Greene, *Post-Petrarchism*.

The constellation of the first section provides a new context for reread-
ing perhaps the most famous nondialogic scenes of instruction in Romantic poetry—Wordsworth's "There was a Boy" and "A slumber did
my spirit seal"—two poems that have been critically overdetermined as
founding moments in Romantic selfhood's redirection and reabsorption
of the progressive, expansive energies of Enlightenment reason. Rhetorical readings of Romanticism have repeatedly focused on the poems for
the way in which they not only suspend these developmental energies
but also undercut Romanticism's own hopes of visionary transcendence
and transfiguration. Yet rather than read the doublings in these poems
as symptomatic of a compulsion to repeat by which the subject returns
both to atone for and complete a crucially unfinished, unachieved act,
I read them as expressive of a freedom to repeat in the very absence of
the promised return, which, whether as punishment for that earlier failure or as the high Romantic fiction of "abundant recompense," never
arrives. The poems' mood of minimal assertion or constatation signals,
in other words, their speakers' release from a psychic economy of debt.
Two modern, psychoanalytical figures of developmental impasse—the
shock victim who can only repeat, never appropriate, her trauma, and
the melancholic who cannot get over the loss of what he never had—offer
well-known models of subjects whose experience also puts them beyond
expectation. In the sections "'A Leisure of the Future': Dickinson and the
Reprieve from Narrative" and "'Without Ceremony': The Inconsequential Address," I consider poems by Dickinson and Hardy that more explicitly engage—although only to dismiss—the possibility of interpreting
the lyric of inconsequence according to these two narratives of impasse.
Neither, I argue, ultimately corresponds to the poems' mood of gratuitous

---

The problem with these Mill-inspired theories of lyric—sympathetic and critical
alike—is that by continuing to describe poetry as "speech," albeit "solitary," they
routinely project unto the type of verbalization involved in poetry (an instance
of language frequently encountered only in written or printed form) the communication model of language which can only conceive of its use as the sending
of a message from one user to another, a model, that Ann Banfield's work on the
unspeakable sentences of narration has taught us to reject. See her discussion of
Mill's distinction between "poetry" and second-person address, and her provocative claim that "the language of narrative . . . realizes most fully in its form and
not only in its intent the essence of the literary which has for so long been taken
to be the achievement of poetry" (Banfield, *Unspeakable Sentences*, 179-80).

reception, and in a third section, "Weightless Gain: Dickinson and the Passing by of Experience," I return to poems of Dickinson that make of repetition itself a mode of setting down rather than taking up the burden of temporal experience.

The quietly introverted voice of Wordsworth's poems has become so much a part of an informal grammar of mourning that it is difficult to get back to a point where these poems are not heard in the self-confessional mode that defines modern responses to grief and loss. Dickinson's lines about Enoch—"'Was not' - was all the statement - / The unpretension stuns -"—might also describe the generic "Unpretension" of many of Dickinson's poems as they begin and end "without ceremony," without commitment to any one set of readerly expectations, only confronting readers with a negation as unequivocal and weightless as an earlier affirmation. Unlike the elegist whose task entails a specific set of motivations and obligations—memorializing the deceased, exorcising the guilt of survival, proving through his rhetorical power the living's claim over the dead—Dickinson leaves undefined the occasions for and premises of her texts, whether because their inclusion in letters addressed to particular recipients would once have made superfluous further explanation or because such underdetermination, informality, and abruptness of address belong to their formal effects. By reading Wordsworth's "Lucy" poems together with Dickinson's poems, which do not in the first place create assumptions about what kind of experience is being described and what kind of affective response is expected, I wish to revive our sense of Wordsworth's tonelessness as a form of constative simplicity rather than as the stifled expression of a grief and guilt too strong to surface otherwise.

Hardy's explicitly elegiac *Poems of 1912–13* will provide a second counterpoint to Wordsworth inasmuch as they not only thematize anxieties about the work of mourning but express skepticism over the possibility and necessity of its achievement. They appear to set aside the burden of reinvesting the dead in a cultural or psychic economy, and distill in starker terms an insight already assumed in Wordsworth's poems—that the mourner's relation to the loved one in death may only barely distinguish itself from the one he maintained toward her in life since this relation never consisted in *doing anything* concrete. While the two poets remain vulnerable to the charge of denying agency to the love object in life as in death, I want to use their juxtaposition to suggest that the poems themselves already do much to deflect the force of this charge by enjoining us to accept that relations between people may obtain even in the absence of definitive action. Their speakers do not so much commit moral violence by what they fail to do—through objectification, erasure, or denial—as learn to stop conceiving of moral acknowledgment between persons as a decisive, explicitly manifest act. Hardy's poems, in particular, yield a sense of the ongoingness and open-endedness of the moral silences between persons, a sense that can guard against the temptation to read Wordsworth's poems as epitaphic attempts to mark, seal off, and ultimately abandon a failed relation to the other. The explicit antiheroism of Hardy's elegies will help cast into relief a more latent capacity for contentedness in Wordsworth, for whom the right moral response to experience lies in continuing to keep its news in parentheses and committing its secret to inconsequence.

ii. lyric abandon: atoning for "things silently gone out of mind"

Thus far the negativity of my examples—a failure of notice or incompletion become definitive—invites their being read according to a familiar Romantic paradigm: as symptoms of the traumatic sublimity and consequent sublimation of history. Even Dickinson's "It sifts from Leaden Sieves" raises the question of whether the mind would thus assent to the emptying out of the phenomenal world as to a "making right" if the ear did not hear it happening in the verbal impoverishment, internal rhymes, and aural repetitions by which the poem enacts the reduction of which it speaks ("mountain/plain/again," "Un-/Unto," and "East/East" in the second stanza). In his essay "Poetry as Menace and Atonement," Geoffrey Hill speaks of "the technical perfecting of a poem" as "an act of atonement, in the radical etymological sense,—an act of at-one-ment, a setting at one, a bringing into concord, a reconciling, a uniting in harmony."[41] His concept of poetic action as "atonement," which he is at pains to distinguish from a compensatory achievement of verbal mastery in the face of experiential destitution, is richly suggestive of the recessive action performed in these poems and can offer an alternative to the paradigm of sublime (a)voidance, inasmuch as the concept locates transformation in a redoubling of the same action, a coming to rest, rather than a constructive or destructive event. Hill's examples bear witness to how "intransitive attention" may nevertheless effect a transition from the stasis of a silent

41. Hill, *The Lords of Limit*, 2.

faith to the fullness of its confirmation. He cites, for example, Coleridge's marginalia to "The Ancient Mariner": "and the stars that still sojourn, yet still move onward; and every where the sky belongs to them, and is their appointed rest, and their native country and their own natural homes, which they enter unannounced, as lords that are certainly expected and yet there is a silent joy at their arrival" (12).[42] The "silent joy" at the stars' "unannounced" entry gives the only sign of a reception so awaited it does not need to be marked as extraordinary. *Atonement* in Hill's sense represents the affirmative counterpart to the disappearance "without ceremony" in Hardy's failed marriage poems and lapse of "things gone silently out of mind" in Wordsworth's, and helps explain why it is possible to speak of these lyric moments as acts of reception, even though their speakers are left with nothing to which to point. Indeed what these divergent passages together suggest is the fineness of the line between a stillness pregnant with expectation, a quiet unassumingness, and the abandonment of any attending consciousness whatsoever.

The indefinite tense of Coleridge's "enter unannounced"—once or every night?—finds its echo in the peculiarly recessive fulfillment of "would enter unawares" in Wordsworth's "There was a Boy," perhaps the most exemplary instance of a response so deferred it turns back, in the very process of meeting, the petitioner's anticipatory energies:

> There was a Boy, ye knew him well, ye Cliffs
> And Islands of Winander! many a time
> At evening, when the stars had just begun
> To move along the edges of the hills,
> Rising or setting, would he stand alone,
> Beneath the trees, or by the glimmering Lake,
> And there, with fingers interwoven, both hands
> Press'd closely, palm to palm, and to his mouth
> Uplifted, he, as through an instrument,
> Blew mimic hootings to the silent owls
> That they might answer him.—And they would shout
> Across the watry Vale, and shout again,

42. The lines recall the power of Shakespearean marriage not to disenchant but to confirm the rightness of love's consummation by making it a part of the course of things without lessening its cause for wonder (thus Othello to Desdemona: "It gives me wonder great as my content / To see you here before me" [2.1]).

Responsive to his call, with quivering peals,
And long halloos, and screams, and echoes loud
Redoubled and redoubled; concourse wild
Of mirth and jocund din! And when it chanced
That pauses of deep silence mock'd his skill,
Then sometimes, in that silence, while he hung
Listening, a gentle shock of mild surprize
Has carried far into his heart the voice
Of mountain torrents, or the visible scene
Would enter unawares into his mind
With all its solemn imagery, its rocks,
Its woods, and that uncertain Heaven, receiv'd
Into the bosom of the steady Lake.[43]

Like the boy who begins by, then gives up, calling forth response, the speaker begins with, only to let drop, an elegiac-sounding appeal for attestation, a call on the landscape to supply the pathos to the interjection—"There was a Boy . . . !" Rather than sustain this heightened commemorative address, the poem yields to pastoral and makes lateral rather than linear progress, multiplying choices as it goes—the stars might have been "rising or setting," the boy would stand "beneath the trees" or "by the glimmering Lake"—and establishing in a few lines a sense of duration in which time was lost, not counted. According to most readings of the poem, it is into this seamless, undifferentiated continuum that mortality irrevocably intrudes with "a gentle shock of mild surprize."[44] Yet, as these

43. Because of its standing in the critical tradition, I cite the version of "There was a boy" that appears as lines 389–422 of Book V of the 1805 *Prelude*. Among the many variants, the 1799 version's "Would carry far into my heart" is most relevant to my reading not on account of the first person but because of the use of a habitual verb tense in the place of "Has carried"; this variant is cited in *Lyrical Ballads*, 140.

44. Deconstructive readings of the poem have highlighted its multiple ironic reversals of the relation of before to after, anticipation to reception, demand to yield; for Paul de Man, for example, the poem is less retrospective than it is anticipatory of the older poet's death—a death experienced in the aporia between the "visible scene" that "enters unawares" and the boy's intent, progressless listening (see de Man, "Time and History in Wordsworth"). Although de Man's reading insists on the autobiographical character of the poem—claiming that the death intimated is the poet's own—his reading is also the least psychological,

same readings are quick to note, this violent intrusion is so deflected that it becomes its own iteration. In the alternation of weak and strong en-

for the temporal perspective yielded by the poem's metalepsis is precisely that which can never be "experienced" by the subject in the ordinary sense. See for this Cynthia Chase's comments on his reading in her introduction to *Romanticism* (17–22). In figuring the sound of mountain torrents as a "voice" that breaks the surface of aural perception and "enter[s] into" the boy's heart, the poem invites the identification of this deposit or penetration into the boy's perceptual field with his death. Wordsworth himself seems to have understood the poem as an observation about the phenomenology of perception and consciousness; see his note in *Poetical Works* 2:440 as well as Thomas De Quincey's report of his and Wordsworth's waiting for the midnight coach bringing the *Courier* from Keswick. De Quincey details Wordsworth's insight into the turning back of anticipatory energies reversing the ratio between expectations and their fulfillment such that something is received into consciousness only with the recession of expectant attention—in this case a "star," a visual phenomenon that, at once infinitely far and near, substitutes for an expected aural perception of the arrival of news of distant events—"some great crisis in Spain was daily apprehended":

> At intervals, Wordsworth had stretched himself at length on the high road, applying his ear to the ground, so as to catch any sound of wheels that might be groaning along at a distance. Once, when he was slowly rising from this effort, his eye caught a bright star that was glittering between the brow of Seat Sandal and of the mighty Helvellyn. He gazed upon it for a minute or so; and then, upon turning away to descend into Grasmere, he made the following explanation:—"I have remarked, from my earliest days, that, if under any circumstances, the attention is energetically braced up to an act of steady observation, or of steady expectation, then, if this intense condition of vigilance should suddenly relax, at that moment any beautiful, any impressive visual object, or collection of objects, falling upon the eye, is carried to the heart with a power not known under other circumstances. Just now, my ear was placed upon the stretch, in order to catch any sound of wheels . . . at the very instant when I raised my head from the ground, in final abandonment of hope for the night, at the very instant when the organs of attention were all at once relaxing from their tension, the bright star hanging in the air above those outlines of massy blackness fell suddenly upon my eye, and penetrated my capacity of apprehension with a pathos and a sense of the infinite, that would not have arrested me under other circumstances." He then went on to illustrate the same psychological principle from another instance . . . derived from that exquisite poem in which he describes a mountain boy. . . . (De Quincey, *Recollections of the Lake Poets*, 159–60)

jambments carrying the sentence over ten lines, we hear both the precariousness of going on when met with silence and the inevitability of continuing, as the "pauses"—moments of "uncertain" abandonment (reduced to caesuras)—make the deferral of response a part of its reception.

Indeed the lines figure all that one would expect to leave a mark and scar the boy for life—the deposit of nature's images—as a quiet intrusion, a stealing into that is also a coming to rest, as the boy is suspended in the exercise of a power to receive that puts him beyond all seeking. The mimic hooter, who initially seems to have nothing of his own, turns out to have unsuspected depths: the syntactical delay of the direct object in the lines "Has carried far into his heart the voice / Of mountain torrents" gives full measure to the distance traveled inward. Yet this internal progress takes the form of a strangely dispossessive gain, as the open-ended clause at once extends and quiets itself across three lines in a series of appositives that accumulate without increase and, never returning to the scene of exchange, achieve closure in the process of seeming to suspend it:

> With all its solemn imagery, its rocks,
> Its woods, and that uncertain Heaven, receiv'd
> Into the bosom of the steady Lake.

The deposit made in the boy's soul includes the disappearance of agency, whether of giver or receiver, for that deposit. Thus while revisionary in structure—in every sense a poem about echo and the flooding of first impressions by what comes after—the poem does not read as an advance of consciousness or blindness corrected; instead it presents growth as a diminishment—a diminishment of the very ability to say of what—to give positive content either to one's loss or gain. Registering no difference between the singular, definitive act of "has carried" and the iterative "would enter unawares," the variant lines present a typically Wordsworthian collapse of the irrevocable and the habitual.

As is evident from Geoffrey Hartman's readings of the poem, as well as from essays collected ten years ago in a special issue of *Studies in Romanticism* (volume 35, winter 1996) dedicated to Hartman (a number of which have been recently reprinted in a volume entitled *The Wordsworthian Enlightenment*), "There was a Boy" occupies a privileged place in articulations of the traumatic, delayed character of Romantic experience and, in particular, of the negativity of Romantic instruction in selfhood.[45] Hartman's original claim that the "child is moved gently and unhurt toward the consciousness of nature's separate life" (*Wordsworth's Poetry*, 19) has been picked up by a number of readers who have also understood the displacement of the owls' echolike response by the "visible scene's" more penetrating silence as a chastening education in otherness. These readings underscore the contrast between the boy's unexpected, gratuitous "education" and the rationalist programs of controlled intellectual formation that Wordsworth criticizes in Book V of *The Prelude*: the boy receives something on which he had not counted—instruction in the near presence of a nonmimetic nature not formed in the image of man.[46]

At the same time, however, the ambiguity of nature's "gentleness" is such that Hartman's readings also emphasize the boy's story as the failure or missing of transformative instruction: the boy experiences "no uprooting, no discontinuity" (*Wordsworth's Poetry*, 21–22); his "life was enclosed, a mere interruption of nature's silence" (*The Fate of Reading*, 183). It is this insularity that appears to justify Rajan's charge concerning the narcissistic and protective solipsism of lyric experience.[47] Yet the very agon denied by Hartman's terms also explains the tendency to posit at the core of the development of the Wordsworthian self an interruption so unspeakable and so catastrophic it leaves the mature self mutely suspended over his

45. For Hartman's readings see Hartman, *Wordsworth's Poetry, 1787–1814*, 19–22; and his later comments in "Wordsworth and Goethe" and "Self, Time, and History," both in Hartman, *The Fate of Reading and Other Essays*, 182–83, 284–93. For the revised essays by Elam, Fry, Goodman, and Lucy Newlyn, and an interview by Caruth, see Elam and Ferguson, *The Wordsworthian Enlightenment*.

46. See, e.g., Fry, "Green to the Very Door?" esp. 542–43; and Cavell's earlier, more theologically oriented reading of the poem in *The Claim of Reason*; for Cavell the note of rest struck in the lines " . . . receiv'd / Into the bosom of the steady Lake" corresponds to the skeptic's surprise at the world's "separate and silent existence," a relief that follows when the skeptic renounces his initial demand for absolute response from "Heaven" (Cavell, *The Claim of Reason*, 473).

47. See Rajan's reading of Wordsworth's decision to incorporate the episode into the "interdiscursive" *Prelude* as an attempt to break out of such monism ("Romanticism and the Death of Lyric Consciousness," 200).

own grave.[48] The *SiR* issue thus draws attention to the affinities between the aporetic structure of elided discontinuity, which Hartman assigns to Wordsworthian formative experience, and the Freudian model of traumatic experience as a meeting that in its initial occurrence appears to leave no mark on consciousness and is only ever experienced as the repetition of this missing, not despite but "in and through its inherent forgetting" (Caruth, *Unclaimed Experience*, 17). The blank space separating "receiv'd / Into the bosom of the steady Lake" from the moment at which the speaker picks up again in a tone of quiet, affectless reportage—"This boy was taken from his mates"—has thus been adduced as evidence of a catatonic shock that leaves both boy and mature speaker "Mute"—incapable of being present to their own experience and of laying claim to the fruits of their instruction:

> This Boy was taken from his Mates, and died
> In childhood, ere he was full ten years old.
> —Fair are the woods, and beauteous is the spot,
> The Vale where he was born: the Church-yard hangs
> Upon a Slope above the Village School,
> And there, along that bank, when I have pass'd
> At evening, I believe that oftentimes
> A full half-hour together I have stood
> Mute—looking at the Grave in which he lies.

The poet's suspended dreaming over the grave simply repeats the boy's muted suspense, neither compensating nor atoning for his premature death; this doubling has been so often noted that it is easy to lose all sense

48. In her introduction to the *SiR* issue Helen Regueiro Elam puts this crisis in terms that make particularly obvious its relevance for the skeptical crisis of acknowledgment discussed later in the chapter—the crisis by which the self comes to accept its contingency and forgo absolute confirmation from without: "The traumatic episode in the Boy of Winander is not the moment in which the poet is mute, 'looking at the grave in which he [himself] lies,' but just prior to it, when the echo stops. . . . The moment in which the echo does not return, does not return his voice to him, does not return the certainty of his self to him, is the moment in which the remembering and prefiguring of mortality become simultaneous" (505–6). The tendency to insist on the violence, however muted, of this crisis and to invest it with catastrophic meaning is evident in Elam's broader claim: "At the heart of romantic poetry there is a linkage between guilt, mortality, nature and secrecy" (503).

of the verbal echoes as echoes—somatic, agentless repetitions—rather than conscious allusions on the speaker's part. Nothing more specific than the cadence of the line breaks—"hangs / Upon"; "stood / Mute"—reproduces the previous paragraph's sense of quieted uncertainty, of something or someone's fate coming to rest while still hanging in the balance. In *Poems* of 1815 as well as in the 1850 *Prelude* an exclamation mark follows the final "in which he lies"—a seemingly unmotivated marker of pathos that it is tempting to attribute to a hidden cause, a secret, unnameable guilt. The adult speaker is not discharging an elegiac duty to a close family member, but loitering before a stranger's grave that becomes akin to his own precisely because it is as a stranger that he will know his own death.[49] No one may have been more familiar than Wordsworth with the strange effects wrought by such uncompelled prolonged meditation: hang long enough over the other's grave and it inevitably yields insight into the murderousness of one's own self (this is how Dickinson's "Like Eyes that Looked on Wastes" might gloss the poem).[50]

Yet Wordsworth's own practices of indifferent revision also suggest that

49. Rather than psychological "appropriation," however, the trope of "nearness" describes the slide by which a particular content-determined experience shifts, not to another "what" or substantive totality but rather to a general, unspecifiable sense of "thatness." Making groundedness continuous with abstraction, Dorothy Wordsworth's journal entries sometimes also credit this sense that the transferability of attachments, far from loosening the psyche's hold, might bind one all the more closely to this world and to the mere fact of its having been; in the following entry, for example, the disappearance of a capacity for distinction (between one source of sound and another, as between life and death) accompanies intensified sensory reception, as if listening were only to begin once dead: "There was no one waterfall above another—it was a sound of waters in the air—the voice of the air. William heard me breathing and rustling now and then but we both lay still, and unseen by one another. He thought that it would be as sweet thus to lie so in the grave, to hear the peaceful sounds of earth and just to know that our dear friends were near" (*Journals of Dorothy Wordsworth*, 117). For a more sustained elaboration of these claims with respect to William, see my "'O happy living things!'"

50. Thus, for Hartman, growing into self-consciousness (the adult's fate) is as deadly as being absorbed into nature (the boy's fate): "Growing into consciousness means a simultaneous development into death (i.e., the loss of a previous, joyfully unself-conscious mode of being), and not growing further also means death (animal tranquillity, absorption by nature)" (*Wordsworth's Poetry*, 21).

the exclamation point remains, like the one that concludes "A slumber did my spirit seal" in 1800 (itself replaced with a period in 1815), interchangeable with the period of the other versions. Rather than betraying guilt, the exclamation—together with the editorial indecision as to whether even to mark it—may simply register the speaker's surprise at being given back time, "a full half-hour together" (as if the boy's brief and anonymous life had not warranted as much), in the supplemental space beyond the time of action, duty, obligation; such surprise includes as essential to it the uncertainty as to how and whether to register any. Spent on one or a number of "summer evenings" (as in the 1815 version), the iterative, strangely lengthened yet diminutive, "full," in some versions "long," "half hour" telescopes the twelve short years of the boy's abortive life; that nothing comes of either may well reflect the impasse of the self's interrupted development, as described by Hartman, but this impasse produces no guilty conscience, simply the speaker's surprised recognition that he might as well linger, as move on, before the givenness of experience.

As theorized by Cathy Caruth, the Freudian model of trauma does offer illuminating insights into the "latency" of Wordsworthian experience, particularly that which makes it difficult for any remembering consciousness to "claim." Yet this understanding of deferred, deflected experience often continues to think of psychic formation in terms of a founding, originary violence—an event that, once missed, compels one to return both to repeat and avenge its missing. Romanticists have repeatedly compared this originary unachieved act of violence to Abraham's unconsummated sacrifice of Isaac ever since Hartman first described Wordsworth's renunciation of the imagination's apocalyptic powers as an *akedah*—the Hebrew term for the binding of Isaac, whose sacrifice Abraham is ultimately spared (*Wordsworth's Poetry*, 225). This story of transumed agon and averted violence certainly lends ethical valence to the suspension of poetic or psychological development as a stopping short, a reprieve from the need to carry through and complete the sacrifice of limitless, unspecified potential for actual values. Yet we should not forget that the story does take place in time; it does not preserve a state of original ideality or innocence, but burdens its principal characters with the white memory of an all but consummated sacrifice. As Zornberg reminds us, "The burden of the 'all but' . . . cannot be neutralized, though the sacrifice is not literally consummated" (128).[51] As I argued in the first chapter, as long as positivism measures "action" by an event's immediately apparent consequences, it cannot recognize this burden, nor can it weigh the shadows by which reprieve from loss may be darkened as "all but" equivalent to actual loss. The virtue of the method of "denied positivism" (according to which every blank may be supposed to hide an erased plenitude and vice versa) adopted by Romantic new historicism is that it would seem to be better able to take into account the lasting scars inflicted by such "merely" hypothetical violence as Abraham's, and indeed both Liu and Levinson also invoke the *akedah* in their readings of Wordsworth.[52] The difficulty here, as with the psychoanalytic theorization of trauma as an event, the missing of which is fundamental to its occurrence, is that the possibility of accepting as real the escape from violence, like that of God's accepting as sufficient Abraham's "not having withheld" his son, disappears somewhere between the impatient critique of the Romantic poet for "getting away apparently unharmed," without paying the price of historical suffering, and the patient unraveling of this elided agon as a merely illusory

51. Zornberg comments on the various midrashic stories that act as placeholders for the residual aftereffects to the seemingly victimless episode on Mount Moriah: in one, Sarah is said to have died on hearing the false report of Isaac's death at Abraham's hands; in another she dies of the true report of what Abraham was prepared to do (123–27). The underestimation of the difficulty of recovering from such a trial was also Silentio's complaint with Christendom in *Fear and Trembling*.

52. In her comments on Wordsworth's reworking of the *akedah* story in "Michael," Levinson contrasts the Jewish emphasis on the sufficiency of Abraham's virtual sacrifice as something fully effective in God's eyes to *count* as the basis for a renewed covenant, with the Christian emphasis on God's last-minute salvific substitution of a ram for Isaac as prefiguring the comparable substitution of Christ for humankind; she argues that Wordsworth ultimately opts for this latter trope of substitution in sacrificing historical specificity to abstract spiritual value (*Wordsworth's Great Period Poems*, 71, 79). The contrast provides a salient reminder of the ways in which the virtual sufficiency of Abraham's binding of Isaac (which is emphatically not a deferral of the violence of choice, as if Abraham had deferred or been spared making up his mind) may in fact be obscured by the seemingly comparable valuation of "inward" states over external acts in the Pauline figure of a "circumcision of the heart" (Romans 2:29). See also Liu, *Wordsworth: The Sense of History*, 530.

escape—a wounding the realization of which has merely been deferred, not avoided.[53]

This fixation on some originally missed event, like the desire to locate historical experience in the making of a critical difference, whether to be traced back in time to the occasion of its erasure or forward to its belated, spectral manifestations, threatens to betray the mood of quiet reception achieved in Wordsworth's poems, when one missing simply repeats another. As readers from Hartman to Rajan to Fry have emphasized, "A slumber did my spirit seal" presents another instance of this double elision of event, first of any event of loss, then of any crying out to mark that loss. Psychoanalysis encourages us to explain the second movement of effacement by which the suspended speaker renews his silence as a defense against the unspeakable, a way of burying, and thus avoiding, a knowledge he does not want to face. But by reopposing crisis and containment, articulation and repression, this explanation subscribes to the very dualism put to rest by the sequence of Wordsworthian thought as it consigns unheeded time to timeless obscurity. This consignment across stanzas records a recessive progress, from unknowingness to the admission of unknowability; the unaccented movement is neither monological nor agonistic but the occasion of a weightless gain:

> A slumber did my spirit seal,
>   I had no human fears:
> She seem'd a thing that could not feel
>   The touch of earthly years.
>
> No motion has she now, no force;

53. Thus on the one hand, as in Rajan's critique of the monological lyric, Romantic lyricism is faulted as a *denial of agon* by which historical difference is kept from even taking place; on the other hand, as in Liu's reading of Wordsworth, the very *agon* (and agony) *of denial* constitutes the poet's conflicted relationship to history; in the one case there is too much reprieve from violence, in the other no reprieve at all; but neither model accepts as a *completed* temporal sequence the binding and release of Isaac. My argument here owes much to Kevis Goodman's remarks on the tenacity of a certain conception of historical experience as the making of an apocalyptic, catastrophic—if not visibly violent—difference, a conception often underwriting the historicist critique of Romanticism's denial of history. See Goodman, "Making Time for History"; reprinted and revised in Elam and Ferguson, *The Wordsworthian Enlightenment*, 158–71.

She neither hears nor sees;
Roll'd round in earth's diurnal course
With rocks and stones and trees!

Having taken no account of her (of that part of her that was mortal), a lover consigns his love to oblivion. Elemental blindness follows on love's unthinkingness, repeats but neither punishes nor redeems it. The extensive criticism surrounding the poem attests to repeated attempts to rationalize this sequence—whether as the ironic confirmation of a mistaken premise (Hartman), or objective materialization of a secret death wish (feminist/psychoanalytic), or even simply as the agentless punishment of an inadvertent crime—yet the open space between the two stanzas preserves the casualness of the connection; death's doubling of the speaker's state of mind remains, mercifully, unmotivated, accidental, gratuitous.[54] The speaker pauses and picks up again in the present, making us feel that everything but also very little has happened in the interim.

Indeed, the poem arrests because it figures narrative development or the fruition of passing time as the succession of one kind of nonpurposiveness ("having no human fears") on another ("earth's diurnal course"). Its agonless sequence, "I had no thought; I cannot think it now," asks that we rethink causality or narrative reason—what it means for "time 1" to occasion "time 2"—in terms radically opposed to the logic of telos and intentionality, as an unmotivated succession from a weightless misprision that took no thought of the future and had no purchase on the world, to the differently weightless rolling of "rocks and stones and trees." The poem thus substitutes an undemanding relation to time for the catastrophic model of experience that would measure the reception of knowledge by its breaking into a sealed consciousness; this openness to the simple transition from taking someone (or something about oneself) for granted to not having at all invites reading the poem as the record of a nonconsummation. Yet the poem speaks from experience: it does not say that nothing

54. Whereas de Man in "The Rhetoric of Temporality" reads the poem's diachronic pattern as a defensive strategy by which the speaker is able to recognize and distance himself from his initial error, Hartman insists that the passage from the first to the second stanza does not constitute a progress from illusion to disillusion. See de Man, *Blindness and Insight*; and Hartman, *The Unremarkable Wordsworth*, 27. For the feminist argument that Wordsworth defends against Lucy's autonomy or separateness from him by burying her into the landscape, see, e.g., Homans, *Women Writers and Poetic Identity*, 22–23.

happens, but accepts the inconsequence with which love, and then its loss, happens.

Here as in Wordsworth's other meditative lyrics, we find no break, then, between having a thought and quieting it, between a recognition and its renewed forgetting. Or we may note the lapse, but we are not asked to stop over it, or we realize that pausing is the same as passing gently by. A "gentle shock of mild surprise" collapses into one the eruption of a difference in consciousness and its gentling or quieting to a point below consciousness. "Three years she grew in sun and shower" thus passes from Nature's promise of enchantment to the mutely disenchanted legacy of "this heath, this calm and quiet scene," as if in confirmation of that promise whose intentionality steps aside the logic of fulfillment and disappointment. Nature's forward-looking expansiveness adds up to as little as the compression of "A slumber," precisely because Nature does not hierarchize ends. The loose anaphora of "And hers shall be . . . / And hers the silence and the calm / Of mute insensate things. . . . And beauty born of murmuring sound / Shall pass into her face" expresses instead an edenic freedom from the necessity to choose or sacrifice x in return for y, a freedom that carries over into the final equivalence of Lucy's death and life.

iii. *"a leisure of the future": Dickinson and the reprieve from narrative*

> There is a finished feeling
> Experienced at Graves -
> A leisure of the Future -
> A Wilderness of Size.
>
> By Death's bold Exhibition
> Preciser what we are
> And the Eternal function
> Enabled to infer.

With these lines Dickinson declares an end to waiting and finds at the graveside's terminus a deliverance from narrative expectations and an occasion for open-ended vacation. We see better at graves, the poem is saying; its second stanza rehearses a familiar sermon on how death puts our worldly quests in perspective, and the startling phrase "A leisure of the Future" becomes intelligible as a rewriting of Matthew's "Take therefore no thought for the morrow." But just as we forget in "consider[ing] the lilies of the field" to read through to the promise of final redemption, the first stanza comes to rest in its "finished feeling." The clearing of psychic space without subsequent filling reads as the record of a satisfaction, as the two appositives, "A leisure of the Future -/A Wilderness of Size," grow out of without modifying the simple declarative. "Ended ere it begun," like so many of Dickinson's poetic assertions, the sentence continues in the absence of any reason for continuing, and in its supplemental syntax we hear the poet taking the time, now that time is free, for gnomic experimentation.

Dickinson thus transforms the mind's bewilderment at the question of where to turn next, in the absence of anything to come, into a "Wilderness of Size," locating in death's dimensionlessness a surprising trope for imaginative possibility. In its reverberations with release from obligation, recreation, license, opportunity, "a leisure of the Future" both recalls and reinterprets the rich and long-standing tradition of pastoral *otium*, in which indolence alternates with ascesis, and trust in providence can remain so unquestioning of the future as barely to distinguish itself from imaginative blindness—the state of having "no human fears" described in Wordsworth's "A slumber did my spirit seal."[55] Rather than occasioning visionary transcendence, such "leisure of the future" makes hope redundant and collapses the opening up of prospects into its opposite, the inability to do more than stay close to the earth and the little it has yielded.[56]

55. Indeed, as Leslie Brisman has argued with reference to Milton's sonnets, Christian versions of pastoral often combine a rhetoric of providential delivery and promised afterlife with a surprisingly earthbound heedlessness of the morrow. Brisman cites the wonderfully subdued invitation of Milton's Sonnet 20 to "Help wast a sullen day; what may be won/From the hard season gaining," and comments: "Matthew's injunction 'Take therefore no thought for the morrow' makes the *carpe diem* tone not something to be overcome but part of the religious *ascesis* toward *carpe Deum*. . . . The moment and eternity are aligned against the worldly workings of time, so that the invitation to waste a sullen day stands against the feverish pursuit of goods enjoyed only in time" (Brisman, *Milton's Poetry of Choice and Its Romantic Heirs*, 41).

56. Susan Stewart suggests to me that Dickinson's use of the word *finished* may have been informed by the sewing term "finished seam," a suggestion that goes far in illuminating the particular convergence between the pastoral ethos Brisman describes and the combination of domestic occupation, immobility, and detachment from the world peculiar to women of Dickinson's class—a convergence also informing "The Missing All."

Barring hypotaxis and announcing a space in which appositive equivalence is the only mode of relation, the poem's opening on a "finished feeling" describes the developmental impasse that critics almost invariably remark in Dickinson's poetry.[57] This release from the coercion of plot's unmet ends and abandonment of linear referential time for a space immune to progress have repeatedly been read within the terms of a heroic plot—as a critical break, a radical and final departure from the temporal world in which end-determined action still matters. Even David Porter, for example, who otherwise emphasizes Dickinson's capacity for "isolated alteration" "checked by no conceptual concern"—"saying what a thing is as against nothing but what it was a moment before" (*Dickinson*, 272)—nevertheless burdens this capacity with heroic weight by making Dickinson an early voice for modernism's ability to do without coherent structures of meaning.

The catastrophic strain in many of Dickinson's poems, the finality with which the poetic voice can abandon an outer world judged unredeemed and unyielding of its secrets, in many ways encourages this tendency to dramatize developmental lapse as cataclysmic despair.[58] Taking

57. Thus David Porter names the "aftermath" as Dickinson's "crucial experience" (see Porter, "The Crucial Experience in Emily Dickinson's Poetry"). Sharon Cameron in her introduction to *Lyric Time* cites the complaints of earlier critics at the poems' "resistance to the rigors and exactions of sequence and progression" (14), their inability to sustain their beginnings, order connections, and build to effect. Cameron herself compares Dickinson's indifference to sequential development to a Jakobsonian "contiguity disorder" and attributes the "omission of relational words" and elision of referential time frames to the poet's desperate attempt to wrest the lyric moment from the passage of time (32). In contrast with these formalist explanations for the pattern of something "barely announced before its potential unfolding is engulfed," Shira Wolosky argues that Dickinson both registers her culture's "growing doubt concerning traditional metaphysical sanctions for causality, teleology, and axiology" and posits an "alternative teleology" in the face of the collapse of these structures of belief (*Emily Dickinson*, xix, 31).

58. See, for example, Joanne Feit Diehl's argument contrasting Dickinson's explicitly antagonistic relation to a nature of whose potential responsiveness she despairs to Wordsworth's more hopeful if deceptively unassuming "wise passiveness" (Diehl, *Dickinson and the Romantic Imagination*, 42). To the extent that many of her poems do present the self's development as a dramatic foreclosure and violent forfeit of claims to natural or human sympathy, Dickinson marks the limits of the casual relation to loss I am attempting to theorize here.

Dickinson's suspension of time to be representative of the lyric as a genre, in *Lyric Time* Sharon Cameron thus finds despair underlying the lyric's "stunning articulation of the isolated moment"—"despair of the possibility of complete stories, of stories whose conclusions are known, and consequently . . . despair of complete knowledge."[59] I want to suggest instead that Dickinson's "leisure of the Future" does not so much express despair at the failure to seize the end of the story and achieve "complete knowledge" as set aside illusions about the difference "complete knowledge" can make.

These poems elaborate instead an essentially recessive mode of experience, one that we can also distinguish from the orthodox trajectories of feminine and Christian ambition premised as these are on a temporary rather than permanent deferral of gain. "The difference between Despair," for example, dramatizes its own cancellation of drama. Reducing to tautology the movement from "before" to "after," it annuls the possibility of a morally educative *peripeteia* and makes a "wreck" of the Enlightenment faith that narrative experience will produce a socially engaged moral consciousness (aware of both itself and its place in the world)—the hope animating the novel's more expansive development:

> The difference between Despair
> And Fear - is like the One
> Between the instant of a Wreck -
> And when the Wreck has been -
>
> The Mind is smooth - no Motion -
> Contented as the eye
> Opon the Forehead of a Bust -
> That knows - it cannot see -

Inverting, as Cameron points out, the expected temporal sequence from "Fear" to "Despair" (*Lyric Time*, 15), the lines' syntax renders the subject's immobility before an event that she can do nothing to stop and whose own aftermath is immobility beyond all waiting. Dickinson here reverses the familiar gender bias aligning men with experience and women with the preservation of an ideal blankness or purity of mind. Positioned so as to carry the full weight of her irony, "Contented" may well allude to

59. Cameron, *Lyric Time*, 71. In interpreting the lyric's suspension of telos as an embattled struggle to deny mortal time, Cameron invests the lyric with a heroic purpose that its own recessive movement can belie.

the conservative spirit of nineteenth-century conduct books that taught women to keep their places rather than venture out into the world.[60] But such contentment is far from the result of a protective deflection of narrative's violent intrusions. Rather the full frontal force with which violence has been met, not avoided, is apparent in the syntactical breakdown—"The Mind is smooth - no Motion -"—that testifies to the purging of desire's forward-looking intentionality.

The poem is thus not about the blankness of feminine education per se; instead, it reads as a terrible joke on the bildungsroman hero who strives toward self-knowledge as the point at which he can take possession of his worldly due.[61] In just two stanzas, it bears witness to a stunning expropriation of experience: the "wreck" or production in the hiatus between stanzas of a mute psychological insight that no subject can claim—the eye

60. A feminist line emerges here according to which, to the extent that nothing happens in the poem, it locates violence not in the positive act of a predatory sexuality but in the unseen stifling of feminine ambition and desire. The acceptance of limitation and renunciation of development in many other Dickinson poems is more complicated, however, than "The difference between Despair"'s closing bitterness implies. A brief glance at the divergent critical perspectives on Dickinson's engagement with the various and often contradictory virtues associated with femininity—modesty, reticence, childlike unknowingness, self-denial, and renunciation—quickly testifies to the complexity of this engagement; the most common critical temptation, however, has been to read this engagement with loss against itself, as a veiled strategy for empowerment—a parodic and self-conscious reappropriation of otherwise disempowering qualities. For arguments explaining Dickinson's patterns of self-denial in terms of empirical constraints on nineteenth-century American women, in particular, their sense of self and freedom of expression, see, for example, Gilbert and Gubar, *The Madwoman in the Attic*, 581–650; and Dobson, *Dickinson and the Strategies of Reticence*. For readings that, by contrast, insist on Dickinson's commitment to renunciation or negation as an essential rather than contingent mode of being (to the extent that that distinction makes any sense), see Wilbur, "Sumptuous Destitution"; Pollak, "Thirst and Starvation in Emily Dickinson's Poetry"; Eberwein, *Dickinson*; and Doriani, *Emily Dickinson*. These latter works tend to read Dickinson's articulation of experiences of privation through the lens of the Calvinist asceticism of her cultural milieu rather than that of gender.

61. According to Lukács, however, the hero of the novel never reaches this point but only accedes to a self-knowledge that comes always too late and cannot reconcile him to the world.

only "knows - it cannot see." However critical, the "difference between despair and fear," between anticipated dispossession and its memoryless aftermath, remains empirically unverifiable, for the event of loss deprives the subject of the capacity to address the world by it.[62]

In both its diction and form the poem rewrites Wordsworth's "A slumber did my spirit seal," which also meditates on the relation between (absent) "fear" and "despair," between a temporary state of taking no thought of what is to come—"having no human fears"—and a permanent absence of future potential.[63] Both poems capture the seamlessness of the mind's internal revolutions and point to the imperceptibility of a grief so intractable it passes for impassiveness. Yet Dickinson's poem may ultimately be more representative of the recent critical tendency to read Wordsworth's poem as the record of traumatic shock that leaves the subject in a catatonic state unable to make sense of temporal experience. For "The difference between Despair" tautologically collapses what in "A slumber" remains an indefinite pause—the stretch of white space between the two

62. An exquisite instance of the expedience of figurative language—born not in experiential plenitude but in sensory and cognitive deprivation as the subject, deprived of a familiar frame of reference, gropingly recalls or dreams this image out of her dark in which there is no "eye" in the first place to see—

Contented as the eye
Opon the Forehead of a Bust -
That knows - it cannot see -

also strikes a blow at those too easy Platonic or Christian recuperations of the recognition of blindness as not the last but the first and necessary step toward "real" illumination. Dickinson's syntax is ambiguous, and her use of the phrase "Looked opon" in "Like Eyes that looked on wastes" to name the projective, potentially violent, and appropriative dimensions of the seemingly "innocent" act of vision leaves room for a secondary reading according to which the "eye" would feed upon the sightless forehead of a bust in an arrogantly "contented" relishing of its safety from reciprocal scrutiny. In either case Dickinson's spelling of *upon* as "Opon" suggests the open-endedness of this objectless stare, without telos, without development, even as the capital *O*, taken as its graphic representation, ironically gives readers an eye to see.

63. The connections between "The difference," "There's a certain Slant of light," and "A slumber" were first suggested to me by John Shoptaw in his seminar on Dickinson and Whitman, of which I was a lucky auditor, at Princeton University in 1992. Shoptaw has since developed his reading of this grouping in "Listening to Dickinson."

stanzas—and ironizes as the aftermath to an unnameable violence that mood of "contentment" in which a speaker chooses to walk away from rather than take up the fruits of experience.

As a record of the catastrophic disappearance of precisely the ability to witness the making of temporal difference, "The difference between Despair" presents a paradox familiar to accounts of the crisis of human subjectivity under modernity. Thus, in the essay "On Some Motifs in Baudelaire," Benjamin famously describes the conditions of modern life that have left humans "increasingly unable to assimilate the data of the world around [them] by way of experience," and develops, after Freud, a theory of modern shock-consciousness as the very antithesis to a vessel for the reception and transmission of experience—a "screen against stimuli" whose function is to prevent "impressions from entering experience [*Erfahrung*]" by confining them to the sphere of the instant at which they are simultaneously lived and neutralized.[64] "Smooth" as a result of, as much as despite and prior to, the "wreck" it has suffered without assimilating, the poem's "Mind" has lost even the power of "recollection" that, in Valéry's words as cited by Benjamin, "aims at giving us the time for organizing the reception of stimuli which we initially lacked" (*Illuminations*, 161–62). Whether robbed of anything to "show" for the experience by its very traversal, or speaking—impossibly—from the position of the one whose vision has made her forget what it is to see, the Dickinsonian subject thus often seems to offer uncannily prescient glosses on the most tragic elaborations of modernity as a crisis in receivable and transmittable experience. (Cameron's *Lyric Time* remains here unsurpassed as a reading of the large number of Dickinson poems that, like "The difference" or "After great Pain" and "I felt a funeral," meditate on the loss of loss [its symptoms, causes, sources] and present the paradox of a recovery, fading, or transition to an asymptomatic phase indistinguishable from the continuation and indeed eternalizing of suffering.) Yet, as I've been arguing throughout this chapter, critiques of the impoverishment and evacuation of experience under modernity need to be distinguished from a recuperative moralism

64. Benjamin, *Illuminations*, 158, 163. For a suggestive comparison of Dickinson and Baudelaire in light of Benjamin's essay see Arac, *Critical Genealogies*, 194–214. Arac addresses the apparent incongruity of the comparison by inviting us to reread Dickinson's supposed isolation in Amherst as itself defined and enabled by the very conditions of contact-in-abstraction (via newspapers, railroads, etc.) that Benjamin ascribes to modernity.

to which they might seem tacitly to subscribe but that in fact belongs to capitalism's own economic rationalism, according to which nothing is allowed to go to waste and irony blights episodes that do not amount to anything, much less to a coherent life-story.[65] Dickinson's poetry also offers instances of a nonironic experience of superficiality, temporally expressed as the uninflected passage from possession to destitution or, more precisely, from as yet unmet possibility to its simple disappearance. I want to turn next to poems that, unlike "The difference between Despair," do not equate the abandonment of narrative's investments in the future with a definitive "Wreck" but, on the contrary, experience a "leisure of the future" in the release from the coercion of plot's unmet ends.

"We do not play on Graves -/ Because there is'nt Room -/ Besides - it is'nt even - it slants," Dickinson explains in a poem that offers to maintain an ordinary, casual, even superficial relation to loss. A masterpiece of affective dissociation, the poem plays on a child's failure to take death seriously, a failure of consideration that might be condemned as blind self-absorption but is, in fact, closer to the refusal of the girl in Wordsworth's "We Are Seven" to distinguish death as a momentous event radically discontinuous with life. Readers tend to agree that Dickinson's sympathies belong with the child who continues to play even in her explanation of why she does not "play on Graves"—whose reasons for refraining from using the graveyard as her playground are incidental to the significance of the "grave" and miss the gravity of death entirely:[66]

65. I don't wish to be taken as imputing this moralism to Benjamin, who, on the contrary, remains committed to the possibilities opened up by the absentminded attention of the "distracted masses." Moreover, as Martin Jay makes wonderfully clear in comments distinguishing Benjamin's various claims about experience and modernity from Lukács's more Hegelian account in *The Theory of the Novel*, what Benjamin mourns in the loss of the art of storytelling and indicts in modern life is not the loss of narrative telos—not the individual's failure to integrate his experiences into a meaningful Hegelian whole—but the diminishment of transmissible experience, experience whose transmissibility is determined, not by the bearer's personal relationship to it, but by its capacity for memorization. See Jay, *Songs of Experience*, 334–35. The formulations of post-Benjaminian critics of modernity don't always respect the distinction; see, for example, Agamben's claim that "just as modern man has been deprived of his biography, his experience has likewise been expropriated" (Agamben, *Infancy and History*, 3).

66. See, e.g., Juhasz, *Comic Power in Emily Dickinson*, 38–39.

We do not play on Graves -
Because there is'nt Room -
Besides - it is'nt even - it slants
And People come -

And put a Flower on it -
And hang their faces so -
We're fearing that their Hearts will drop -
And crush our pretty play -

And so we move as far
As Enemies - away -
Just looking round to see how far
It is - Occasionally -

If we assume that the poem moves from a child, who finds her play dis-
turbed by intrusive mourners, to an equally self-interested adult, who
from time to time takes stock of how much of life is left to her, then the
poem would appear to satirize the imaginative habits by which the living
come to ignore the fact of death and keep their own mortality at bay.
Indeed, while the third stanza's "And so" marks a temporal break with
the preceding stanzas, the poem's best readers have emphasized that this
is not the record of a moral progress. Yet rather than ask for less evasive
acknowledgment, Dickinson accords "Occasionally" the weight of a full
stop, as if content to win the dead an audience only slightly less per-
functory than their permanent consignment to obscurity. The temporal
equivalent of the perturbation in the ground, "Occasionally" looks back
to the "slant" of the first stanza and attenuates the polarization supposed
by "Enemies": we do not, it seems, move so far away as to disown all relation to alterity, but continue obliquely a mode of address that neither
engages nor abandons but admits of no final partings.

This sense of "occasionally" as a temporal expression of levity and freedom from obligation appears in another poem that also records a meeting
in passing; in this case, however, Dickinson puts herself in the position
of the dead or abandoned object who must make light of the difference
between being taken up and set down free of regret:

So the Eyes accost - and sunder
In an Audience -
Stamped - occasionally* - forever -
So may** Countenance

Entertain - without addressing
Countenance of One
In a Neighboring Horizon -
Gone - as soon as known -

*in instances   **can -

Here, as often in Dickinson, the dashes serve as connectives in the absence of connection and, lengthening the pauses, create the strange continuity of the act of turning toward the other then away again. In line 3 they invite us to assign equal weight to "occasionally" and "forever" so that, in effect, if not grammatically, "occasionally" qualifies "forever"—renders it casual, by no means singular or definitive but a matter of repeated occasions, as the variant "in instances" also indicates. The line diminishes eternity's imperative as a requirement for value, as if the recorder of such an experience were saying with remarkable equanimity, "sometimes the Audience marks one for life, but it hardly matters if it doesn't, for when it does it counts just as little."

Dickinson's lines from "A Prison gets to be a friend"—

The slow exchange of Hope -
For something passiver - Content
Too steep for looking up -

—suggest an alternative to the heroic agon described by Cameron and to the "despair" she posits as the price of renouncing narrative's forward-looking intentionality. This understated change is, in many ways, all that the lyric of inconsequence records by way of exchange or transaction. Dickinson does not provide a clear antithesis to hope, only "something" a shade different; the dash and line break after "Hope" are all that mark the barely noticeable change: the growing downward of "something passiver" out of hope's own passiveness. This transitive process remains difficult to record as such because what is relinquished is itself a way of structuring time, of standing in relation to its promise. The giving up of hope's unrealized claims changes nothing, only whether the present is colored by lack.

iv. "without ceremony": the inconsequential address

Hardy's remarkably muted addresses to his dead wife, Emma, in *Po-ems of 1912–13* perhaps most explicitly illustrate what this relinquishment enables: namely, a moral freedom to assume truths (about oneself, about others, their separateness, their proximity) that nothing—no conclusive circumstantial evidence and no as yet absent authority—will ever compel one to assume. Thus the inconsequent death of his already estranged wife leaves the speaker of "The Walk" *free* to mark the event or not, for empirically, and perhaps even affectively, her passing changes very little for him—only makes permanent and absolute what had seemed a temporary solitude:

> You did not walk with me
> Of late to the hill-top tree
>   By the gated ways,
>   As in earlier days;
>   You were weak and lame,
>   So you never came,
> And I went alone, and I did not mind,
> Not thinking of you as left behind.
>
> I walked up there to-day
> Just in the former way;
>   Surveyed around
>   The familiar ground
>   By myself again:
>   What difference, then?
> Only that underlying sense
> Of the look of a room on returning thence.

This is one of the simplest instances of a poem that uses its two-stanza form to subvert its own promise to take account of time, setting out to demarcate a "then" and a "now" only to find that it has almost no difference to report.[67] The poem may be best read removed from its elegiac

67. Here again Mahar's "Hardy's Poetry of Renunciation" provides illuminating insights into the ways that Hardy's poetry "releases" temporal difference from the obligation to produce significant narrative difference, by making use of rhyme, meter, and the open space between stanzas, rather than the speaker's calculating consciousness, to carry the burden of making connections between earlier and later moments.

context, for only then does one stop with its speaker over the mystery, the real question, of that which separates the indefinite "Of late"—the habitual, always potentially reversible "never"—from the singular "to-day." Typical of Hardy's arcane yet colloquial diction, the phrase "Surveyed around / The familiar ground" resonates with Dickinson's "leisure of the future" in suggesting a mindless, all but objectless, quest: "around" diffuses the intention of "surveyed" and captures the bafflement of one who seeks in vain for evidence of the qualitative difference between his companion's earlier unfelt, untried nearness and her now permanent absence. The difference does not lie in the experiential content of the walk, only in the dim sense of being awaited, or not, on his return—a sense that would have required no direct verbal message on Emma's part, "the look of a room" being enough to tell him of her presence in the house, but not whether she was awaiting his return or would have accompanied him if asked.

The impersonal abstraction of "that underlying sense / Of the look of a room" thus corresponds to the tacitness of their former companionship, premised as it was on not doubting one another's presence and on accepting the excuses, however impoverished when spelled out—"You were weak and lame"—for their mutual estrangement. Here as elsewhere in the sequence, Hardy returns to the moral complexity of the act of leaving another alone; his language reflects the permissiveness that comes with long use and attachment and raises the real question of what is involved when two people cease to speak to one another—a falling off into indifference or a trusting acceptance of one another's unstated nearness? In this case, the nursery-rhyme simplicity of the trochaic lines, "You were weak and lame / So you never came," conveys the words' innocuous inaudibility—a soundlessness that partially neutralizes the ugliness of their meaning, for just as they cannot hurt her now, in life they went mercifully unspoken between them; or more ambiguously, the sense might be: "I could say such things because, then as now, nothing could touch you." His explanation for why he "did not mind" is similarly ambiguous: "Not thinking of you" or "Not thinking of you as left behind"—the carelessness by which he forgot her passes seamlessly into an equally heedless mode of inclusion that counted her presence as a matter of course.

Unlike the Wordsworthian lover, the husband of many years of shared separateness proffers no confident exclamation, "The difference—to me!" Yet it is precisely within the intersubjective terms of Hardy's failed marriage poems that Wordsworth's gesture of falling silent on such a thought might be read as more than a declaration of psychic capital within, a deference to the other's freedom to follow suit (or not) in crediting that difference. Critical attention has often centered on the ironic tensions between Hardy's volubility on the occasion of Emma's death and the silence with which they met each other in life, but while critics have usually disputed the aesthetic and moral worth of Hardy's efforts to compensate for this silence through poetry, they have not questioned the supposed wrongness of the original silence.[68] A starker yet milder—less therapeutic—reading is possible, however, according to which the poems show the mourner coming to terms with the possibility that the deceased may have chosen not to speak in life and that, even given a chance, she would not have completed the picture for him.[69]

"The Going," the sequence's opening poem, begins by asking not "why did you go?" but "why did you let me miss your going?":

Why did you give no hint that night
That quickly after the morrow's dawn,
And calmly, as if indifferent quite,
You would close your term here, up and be gone
    Where I could not follow
    With wing of swallow
To gain one glimpse of you ever anon!

    Never to bid good-bye,
    Or lip me the softest call,
Or utter a wish for a word, while I
Saw morning harden upon the wall,
    Unmoved, unknowing
    That your great going
Had place that moment, and altered all.

68. See, for example, Peter Sacks's claim, "By silence, they had repressed and hence made unnegotiable the path, so to speak, of their estrangement" (Sacks, *The English Elegy*, 253).

69. Here and in what follows, I do not wish to be taken as making claims about Thomas and Emma Hardy's actual life stories; for heuristic purposes I am limiting myself to the fictional marriage plot to which *Poems of 1912–13* as a lyric sequence dimly refer and about which these poems invite us to surmise, rather than engaging with biographical materials such as the ghostwritten Hardy biography.

Much has already been said about the complex defensiveness registered by these rhetorical accusations: the speaker may be defending against the larger loss of Emma's death by focusing first on the presumably lesser loss—a loss specific *to him*—of participation in the event through preparedness and foresight. Or he may be willfully exaggerating the degree to which she stopped addressing him in her need, in order to hide from the knowledge of his own emotional neglect of a suffering that was staring him in the face. But however defensive, these accusations cover, I think, a genuine pathos at the loss and cheat (in this case unassignable), not of something actually possessed but of the mere possibility of conversation and companionship. What hardens on the wall with morning is the transition from something inoperative—a latent and long-dormant relation—to one permanently dead and beyond rescue; syntactically, "I," "morning," and "wall" are all aligned by the delayed epithets "unmoved, unknowing," in implicit contrast with night as the space of latent possibility. Characteristically, Hardy reverses what we might expect as the usual order (and shock) of enlightenment—he awoke to find her dead; here morning hardens and no enlightenment takes place. On the contrary, the hard morning light, like the despair and disillusion by which the couple may have given up on one another long ago, turns out to be the real illusion: a hardness and deadness incapable of imagining or anticipating the loss it nonetheless prefigured.

In the poems that follow, Hardy's speaker will fill out this long-unused space of imaginative possibility with the murmuring of what might have been said, yet in such a way as to suggest how little any one such address, if actually vocalized, might have done to restore communication, except insofar as the kept silence was already proximate to, never far from, latent speaking. The closing stanzas of "Your Last Drive," for example, put to rest the fiction of the difference that "knowledge of complete stories" might make. Like Dickinson's "There is a finished feeling," they belong to a space evacuated of hope and the urgency of its as-yet-unfulfilled promise; their speaker has arrived at the end of the line of plot, but not in the sense of having reached the climactic moment of final reckonings, only in that of being released from the fiction of ultimate judgments:

'You may miss me then. But I shall not know
How many times you visit me there,
Or what your thoughts are, or if you go

There never at all. And I shall not care.
Should you censure me I shall take no heed,
And even your praises no more shall need.'

True: never you'll know. And you will not mind.
But shall I then slight you because of such?
Dear ghost, in the past did you ever find
The thought, 'What profit,' move me much?
Yet abides the fact, indeed, the same, —
You are past love, praise, indifference, blame.

The stanza beginning "You may miss me then" is all surmise, both in the sense that Hardy here supplies the words that Emma might have addressed him but did not speak aloud, and in the sense that her imagined voice wanders lightly over the possible courses that his mourning might take. The caesura at "then" marks the endpoint past which her words become as wind, merely supplemental, and the mildly anaphoric cadence of the rest of the stanza levels the difference between pauses and full stops, suggesting that the voice is as likely to stop as to go on and thus expressing the equivalence of the choices described. Hardy here supplies the ethical corollary to the "leisure of the Future" that Dickinson finds in death's power to make redundant the attainment of final goals: an equally ambiguous release from contractual, in this case marital, obligations. Readers have heard in the rhetorical question, "Did you ever find / The thought 'What profit' move me much?" a defensive denial on Hardy's part of the guilt of producing so wonderfully useless an aesthetic wealth out of his wife's now immutable silence.[70] But the poem's success depends on how well the surmise of her unuttered words retains the sense of her silence: not only did he not heed "the writing upon [her] face," but she did noth-

70. Thus Jahan Ramazani reads the poem in terms of Hardy's "indirect ruminations on the economic problem of mourning—the production of poems from her loss. . . . His inability to read her face becomes in turn the condition of his writing on her face now, when he retrospectively inscribes it with his reverie of her unuttered words" (Ramazani, *Poetry of Mourning*, 53). Ramazani is referring to the previous stanza's image of unread writing:

I drove not with you. . . . Yet had I sat
At your side that eve I should not have seen
That the countenance I was glancing at
Had a last-time look in the flickering sheen,
Nor have read the writing upon your face,
'I go hence soon to my resting-place;

ing to make him see it. The poem thus shifts the locus of action from a productive economy of her experiential loss for his rhetorical gain to the nontransitive syntax of the simple gesture of unheroically assuming the weightless burden of a mutual estrangement, an open secret between them that neither ever compelled the other to acknowledge.

Hardy's marriage seems to have owed its failure, then, to what might also have made its success: a reticence in forcing the other's acknowledgment, if such was not already forthcoming. He and Emma appear to have left too much to chance in relying on one another's potential responsiveness and to have taken the risk of leaving one another free to imagine their desires for one another rather than asking anything of each other outright. It is not my intention here to offer a comprehensive reading of the sequence nor to rehearse the critical debate over the tone—bitter or restrained, angry or remorseful, accusatory or self-punishing—of Hardy's addresses to his dead wife.[71] As a group, the poems are interesting less as exorcisms of the mourner's anger—at the deceased for having died, at himself for having let her—than as meditations on the way in which the other's perceived autonomy both provokes this anger and renders it inadmissible, futile, vain. As in Wordsworth's "Lucy" cycle, the shock of the loved one's unexpected death reverberates with the sudden awareness of the extent to which she was separate even in life; her disappearance in death imitates her capacity to wander off, to be "up and be gone" in life. For the husband who remains, the temptation is always, as in "Without Ceremony," to mistake this vagrancy as directed toward him and to "infer" from her unannounced departures a willful and arbitrary frustration of his possessive desires.[72] In this sense, the sequence's only chastening, therapeutic work consists of purging the speaker of the desire to master

71. Cf., for example, Ramazani's insistence on the poems' latent "guilt, aggression, narcissism and hostility" (*Poetry of Mourning*, 48); and Irving Howe's defense of their "defenseless sincerity" (Howe, *Thomas Hardy*, 186). Howe portrays the Hardy of *Poems of 1912-13* as a figure whose moral exemplarity lies precisely in his desistance from the "impulse to moralize": someone who, "free of that version of pride which consists in relentless self-accusation," "learns not to tamper with his grief and not even to seek forgiveness in his own eyes" (185); such reticence with respect to moral self-accounting finds an unexpected echo in the moral permissiveness that defines, I argue in the final chapter, Austen's attitude toward Fanny—an accepting attitude we cannot even call "forgiving" as long as "forgiving" implies something to forgive.

72. In that poem the speaker shrugs off the slight only by uneasily invoking the misogynist stereotype of irrational and infantile feminine whim.

the loved one—the desire that prompted him in life either to reduce her to the idealized, voiceless phantom of his earlier love or to demonize her for an independence of mind on which he had not counted.[73]

Of the three sets of poems studied in this chapter, Hardy's sequence lends itself most easily to psychological readings, inviting as it does the construction and elaboration of the courtship and marriage plots in the "time lost" of the time before Emma's death. Yet a poem such as "I Found Her Out There" exemplifies the baldness or quiet directness with which Hardy converts possible self-recriminations into simple, constative statements, and forgoes the development of these speech acts, which, as acknowledgments of guilt or better yet recognitions of fantasies of guilt, might in a psychotherapeutic framework signal the beginning of the process called "working through." It is this formal "quiet," as much as their shared thematic content, that makes so persuasive David Bromwich's comparison of the poem to Wordsworth's "A slumber did my spirit seal."[74] For, with the parallel reports opening the first two stanzas, "I found her out there" and "I brought her here," the poem works out (rather than through) the mute—unforgiving but also unpunishing—analogies be-

73. For a more developed account of the ways in which Hardy's poetic persona undermines his own elegiac idealizations by including within the poems ventriloquized instances of Emma's "recalcitrance" and "less-than-obliging memory" (180), see Clifton Spargo's fine pages on the sequence in *The Ethics of Mourning* (177–208). Wonderfully attuned to Hardy's capacity to "caricature the self-importance" (195) of the mourner's accusations, whether self- or other-directed, Spargo's reading provides a salutary corrective to the critical picture I painted above, by putting into dialogue the liberal rationalist investment in mutuality as the measure of healthy relationships (according to which Hardy failed Emma by not addressing her in time and repressing the fact of her being a speaking subject like himself), and the Levinasian critique of precisely such mutuality as a violent denial of the other's alterity. Spargo patiently traces in the poems the dialectical reversals whereby an "ethics of reciprocity" premised on mutual recognition is "eclipsed by a starker ethics of difference, wherein the measure of anyone's authenticity resides in her capacity to oppose the self's pleasures" (181); ironically, this second ethics is no less premised on recognition but only by way of its initial and, according to Ricœur's skeptical reading of Levinas, perhaps permanent failure. Spargo's book appeared when I was in the final stages of editing this manuscript, and I can only acknowledge the consonance between our approaches here.

74. See Bromwich, *Disowned by Poetry*, 131.

tween the lover's possession of his loved one—a possession that was precisely the means of his laying her to rest, missing or stifling her autonomy—and the grave's equally unconsummated possession of the dead:

> I found her out there
> On a slope few see,
> That falls westwardly
> To the salt-edged air,
> Where the ocean breaks
> On the purple strand,
> And the hurricane shakes
> The solid land.
>
> I brought her here,
> And have laid her to rest
> In a noiseless nest
> No sea beats near.
> She will never be stirred
> In her loamy cell
> By the waves long heard
> And loved so well.
>
> So she does not sleep
> By those haunted heights
> The Atlantic smites
> And the blind gales sweep,
> Whence she often would gaze
> At Dundagel's famed head,
> While the dipping blaze
> Dyed her face fire-red;
>
> And would sigh at the tale
> Of sunk Lyonnesse,
> As a wind-tugged tress
> Flapped her cheek like a flail;
> Or listen at whiles
> With a thought-bound brow
> To the murmuring miles
> She is far from now.
>
> Yet her shade, maybe,
> Will creep underground
> Till it catch the sound

Of that western sea
As it swells and sobs
Where she once domiciled,
And joy in its throbs
With the heart of a child.

The poem's conceit makes the "solid land" represent both the safety of marriage and the finality of burial, and then has the deadness and confinement of the one and the latency and endurance of the other become images for one another. According to the implicit cross-analogies between the ocean, the grave, and the speaker's (still beating? or long since stopped?) heart, everything the speaker asserts of the woman's distance or nearness to the western sea, he may also silently be saying of her distance or proximity to him (sometimes in reverse, sometimes not). So the first line of the second stanza, "I brought her here," derives its power from the reader taking "here" to refer to my "heart" as well as to the grave; the simple line shocks in part because it makes "this is how I loved" and "this is how she died" almost indistinguishable. While the flatly constative mood may seem to give way in the third and fourth stanzas to the memory images whose conjuration leads into the fanciful future-tense surmise of the last, even these images, dreamlike in their simultaneous concreteness and abstraction from intersubjective, plot-thick contexts, appear to remember the loved one precisely in her passive exposure to the elements—"the dipping blaze / Dyed her face fire-red"; "a wind-tugged tress / Flapped her cheek like a flail"—the same exposure that defines the dead woman in "Rain on a Grave." The distribution of the same terms—exposure, shut-out-ness—across a supposed binary (life/death) makes it harder to read the speaker's tonal blankness as a sign of his own affective alienation as if he had simply displaced onto the sea's sobs, swells, and throbs the rockings of his grief or motions of his love. Rather, precisely the sparseness of personal commentary by which the poem keeps open the relation among its terms means that it does not recant on the joy of satisfied recovery animating its first line, "I found her out there." The second stanza's "I brought her here" parallels this first line grammatically, but also shortens its metrical breath, as if Hardy were restoring a delicate sense of the arbitrariness of temporal sequence, or giving back to it a rhythm closer to breathing, rather than commenting on the relation between human promises and their fulfillments or betrayals. The first stanza's already happily completed story gives no hint of the necessity of "what came next," so that the two lines, side by side, make for a narrative sequence of one "whole" followed by another reminiscent of "And Enoch walked with God: and he was not."

The masterful abandonment of mastery, the rehearsal and ritualization of loss as a voluntary act of sacrifice—these constitute some of the more paradoxical features of elegy, as Peter Sacks has shown in his important study of the genre. Sacks's argument builds on the Freudian understanding of the work of mourning as a dialectical process of self-mutilation and self-reinforcement, a process by which the mourner repeats the loss of the object from within in order to reestablish control over the self if not the object. According to this view, the formation of the psychoanalytic subject parallels the work of mourning in that both are complete once the subject-mourner no longer perceives the other's absence as a threat to his own autonomy.[75] But Hardy's poems emphasize the paradoxically reductive, even depersonalizing, character of this formative process, as their speaker learns not to see himself accused, deprived, or even addressed by the other's disappearance. This trajectory of negation is evident, for example, in "The Voice," a poem that, as Sacks's own reading highlights, moves from the passionate address, "Woman much missed" to the flat constative of "The woman calling." By the poem's end the speaker no longer even receives this "calling" as a call that might have anything to do with him, but registers its anonymous and unaddressed iterative, along with the other barely differentiated facts of the weather, and his own Abraham-and Michael-like objectless going onward:

75. See Sacks's introduction for a discussion of this parallel. Because Sacks's starting point is the traditional elegy, whose climactic structure and formal resolution tend to impose a definitive, dramatic form on the Freudian narrative of development, his readings tend to emphasize the successful completion of this process over the dispersed character of both psychological experience and modern elegiac sequences. In his schema, for example, the circumscription of direct vision that recurs in traditional elegies signals the end of the elegiac process: the mourner's renunciation of immediate experience for indirect testimony of the deceased is a sign of his imminent recovery. Hardy's sequence, however, puts this trajectory into question (as do in fact numerous elegies), insofar as the impossibility of direct exchange and immediate experience precedes Emma's death and defines the couple's relation from the start: each receives the other's testimony only on condition of not being able to return it.

> Thus I; faltering forward,
> Leaves around me falling,
> Wind oozing thin through the thorn from norward,
> And the woman calling.

The disappearance of even the fiction of responsive connection indicated by the impersonal "the woman," whose call now "companions" him without the power of personal address, its significance diminished and dissipated to little more than a birdcall among the wind and leaves, coincides with the speaker's assumption of guiltless fault (a "fall" implied by the false etymological pun the ear can't help but hear on "fault" and "faltering") and his sinking into a state as gravitationally weightless, as insubstantial and void of questing energies, as hers: on the one hand, these characters and figures bear no relation to one another—the verb tenses suggest there can be no completed action between them; on the other, they share the same suspense within the dreamlike, motionlessly moving tense of the present progressive—as much memory image as descriptive of present separation.[76]

If mourning is crucially repetitive—a process of letting go of someone already gone and never fully possessed—Hardy's poems heighten the paradox, first by placing this withdrawal long before the loved one's death so that the mourner appears to have lost something he never had, then by emptying possession itself of palpable consequence so that even the "having" was as nothing. Thus, as readers have often noted, the iconic images of the young Emma that flare up in the early poems of the sequence have little consolatory power, for they hint at the phantasmatic effects of his earlier passion: he saw her then as he sees her now—as a ghost—and missed her then in love as he misses her now in his grief:[77]

76. This transition from apostrophe to constative is enacted metrically, as Susan Stewart has brilliantly shown, in the fading in this last stanza of the poem's dancelike triple-time dactylic meter, strongly felt in the initial "Woman much missed, how you call to me, call to me," which here subsides into the trochaic "Leaves around me falling," except for a last echo of the "dactylic associated with Emma" (Stewart, *Poetry and the Fate of the Senses*, 135) in "Wind oozing thin through the thorn from norward." According to the dactylic meter's own falling effects, I would add, the "call to me" is already receding from the "Woman much missed" as it is sounded, an effect of lapse heightened in the third line where the "all" of "all to me" is a diminishment of "call."

77. Sacks thus dismisses these objectifying images as representative of the

You were she who abode
By those red-veined rocks far West,
You were the swan-necked one who rode
Along the beetling Beeny Crest,
   And, reining nigh me,
   Would muse and eye me,
While Life unrolled us its very best.   ("The Going")

"Would muse and eye me" prefigures the phantom's silent stare, suggesting that the young couple was no more in the habit of direct communication than later. Yet "At Castle Boterel" moves beyond the irony that the mourner never "had" the lost object to begin with, to the more affirmative claim that the most consummate having looks by its transience like a missing:

What we did as we climbed, and what we talked of
   Matters not much, nor to what it led, —
Something that life will not be balked of
   Without rude reason till hope is dead,
     And feeling fled.

It filled but a minute. But was there ever
   A time of such quality, since or before,
In that hill's story?

The exchange, which was hardly one, "filled but a minute," precisely because it relied on being made continuous with an indeterminate span of undifferentiated hours, just as the couple did nothing to safeguard their happiness but entrusted it to the abstract and unstated promise (written nowhere if not on the landscape) of a long life of shared, sedimentary habit.

The demands of his argument about elegy as a genre may encourage Sacks to insist too programmatically on mourning as an ultimately constructive process (as the Freud of "Mourning and Melancholia" did when

---

idyllic romance that the mature mourner must learn to renounce in order to complete his work of mourning. Sacks's reading implies that the speaker ultimately shares the reader's wariness of the images' tendency to "transfigure" Emma into a disembodied muse. Ramazani, on the other hand, less generously claims that Hardy fixates on these "narcissistic fantasies" so as to "supplant the guilt-ridden present with an idealized past" (*Poetry of Mourning*, 49).

assuming the normativity of the mourner over the melancholic). For the speaker of Hardy's sequence, however, the turning point comes, if at all, not with "the invention of a durable figure" of identity signaling the recuperation and reinvestment of libidinal energies, but with the acceptance of the same divestment of person and latency of all but extinguished passion in which his grief begins. It is not that he ceases to impute thoughts, desires, and words to the woman who can now never speak her own mind; rather he does so reminding the reader that all he can do is interpolate in the absence of any direct access to her. This capacity to supply for oneself the other's imagined voice becomes oddly linked to and nearly indistinguishable from what might seem to be its opposite: a renunciation, not only of any claims to knowledge about that other, but also of any demands on her for authoritative judgment about oneself.

Thus we might compare "The Walk"'s confession of coldness, "I did not mind," to its revision that is hardly a revision in the closing lines of "After a Journey": "Trust me, I mind not." The mindlessness by which in the earlier poem the speaker went without his estranged wife, indifferently taking her absence for companionship, yields here to a different kind of permissiveness or readiness to be led on in an explicitly circumscribed, aubadelike dalliance with false surmise:

> Ignorant of what there is flitting here to see,
>   The waked birds preen and the seals flop lazily;
> Soon you will have, Dear, to vanish from me,
>   For the stars close their shutters and the dawn whitens hazily.
> Trust me, I mind not, though Life lours,
>   The bringing me here; nay bring me here again!
>   I am just the same as when
> Our days were a joy, and our paths through flowers.

The initially objectless phrase, "Trust me, I mind not," derives its rich tonal ambiguity from the context of the pair's apparent estrangement in life: the memory of his former neglect accounts for the hint that her ghost would need such assurance before proceeding to court him a second time. At the same time, the phrase, however encouraging, implies his continued passivity in this ghostly courtship; his willingness to be so led, as if he lacked any direction of his own, resonates with, and indeed barely distinguishes itself from (a) the implied inertia of their relations late in life and

(b) his numbness at the first shock of her death, when he seemed "but a dead man held on end / To sink down soon" ("The Going").

Yet it is perhaps finally to the fact of *her* death that Hardy's speaker remains true by responding with such tender indifference to her fictive invitations; the sense of so qualified an affirmative is, "I don't mind what you do since what you can is so little." Now that it can neither help nor be helped, his assent to whatever he might imagine her to be asking of him is free. It is not just that, as a kind of renewal of lapsed marriage vows, the declaration of desire costs him next to nothing since he has just acknowledged and accepted the transience of her power over him in death as in life. Knowing that he will probably not repeat the pilgrimage to her former haunts, he invites the second time—"nay bring me here again!"—and gives himself up to her memory just when he knows it is about to disappear. The echo of the aubade's trope of dawn whitening, usually the signal urging the lover to make haste and quit the bed so he can safely return the following night, sounds all the more emptily now that life's rudeness ("Life lours") cannot touch the dead, rage how it will. And yet by their very vanity, his words become as light as the image of contented inaction, or happy *otium* of the seals' lazy flopping, and recapture something of the freedom from care—the lightness and indifference to the future—"Ignorant of what there is flitting here to see"—that one can imagine would have defined the couple's first declarations of love.

The figure of the graveside loiterer, or of the mourner whose only aim is essentially unproductive—the letting go of something already gone— provides a rich conceptual image, then, for the redundance and inconsequence of action recorded in these poems. In Hardy's elegies, the speaker's sense of his absent companion being not only incapable of answer but immune either to the healing or wounding power of his words constantly circumscribes his address, emptying it of ordinary claims to significance. In his unwillingness either to move forward from or concretize his loss, this poetic persona would seem to correspond to the paradigm for a loss without an object, the very experience of which has been missed, adumbrated in Freud's "Mourning and Melancholia." Yet inasmuch as Freud's "melancholic" does not so much withdraw from as internalize a libidinal economy of loss and compensation, Freud's paradigm remains inadequate to registering to what an extent these lyric speakers sidestep the calculat-

ing function of psychic economy by the peculiarly undemanding tenacity
with which they remark a loss (or gain) they could as easily commit to
oblivion.[78]

The figure of the indifferent mourner or bearer of weightless loss differs
from Freud's melancholic not simply in the sense that he abstains by his
expressive reserve from excessive shows of "self-reviling," but in the sense
that he does not punish himself, as the melancholic does, for a lack perceived in the other and now displaced onto the self. Later in the chapter I
will have occasion to identify more explicitly the ethical character of this
refusal to assume the burden of the other's lack (as one's own) through
the Cavellian dialectic of acknowledgment and avoidance. At this point,
however, it may be helpful to allow Dickinson, rather than psychoanalysis
or ethics, to spell out the drama of (mis)recognition between "self" and
"other" repeatedly alluded to in Hardy's sequence. I want to close this section with a brief look at "Like Eyes that looked on Wastes," a poem that
thoroughly exorcises the melancholic's rage and the related temptation to
respond to the other's perception of lack in oneself as to an accusation:

> Like Eyes that looked on Wastes -
> Incredulous of Ought
> But Blank - and steady Wilderness -
> Diversified by Night -
>
> Just Infinites of Nought -
> As far as it could see -
> So looked the face I looked opon -
> So looked itself - on Me -
>
> I offered it no Help -

78. "In mourning it is the world which has become poor and empty; in melancholia it is the ego itself." See Freud, "Mourning and Melancholia," in *The
Standard Edition of the Complete Psychological Works of Sigmund Freud*, 14:243–58.
Julia Kristeva's account of the melancholic subject also offers rich insights into
these characters' absence of a will to progress and failure of development, or
"enchaînement." As I understand her account, however, the melancholic subject's
inability not simply to form new attachments but to stand in relation to any object owes more to a fetishization of an original blankness of relation than to an
Emersonian acceptance of the casualness with which new attachments might or
might not be formed. See her description of the melancholic as "a morose athe-
ist" in Kristeva, *Soleil Noir*, 22.

Because the Cause was Mine -
The Misery a Compact
As hopeless - as divine -

Neither - would be absolved -
Neither would be a Queen
Without the Other - Therefore -
We perish - tho' We reign -

Whereas *Poems of 1912–13* afford only glimpses of the unwritten novel
of the Hardys' noncommunicative marriage, Dickinson's poem distills
in extremis the naked image of a "self" and "other" locked in a mutual
self-reliance that may never distinguish itself satisfactorily from shared
solipsism. Here the impossibility of direct communication is not, as in
elegy, a contingent fact, a function of the loved one's death, but the permanent condition of contact between the two concerned. Yet the poem is
characteristic of the lyric of inconsequence studied in this chapter in that
it rehearses—enacts in time—its own setting aside of drama; the progress of its reading introduces time into its apparently frozen psychic landscape. Following the six-line setup of the first term of the comparison—a
wasteland in which the alternation of night and day constitutes the only
temporal difference—there *is* a dramatic turn, a "gentle shock of mild
surprise," by which the reader realizes along with the speaker that if the
eyes look as if they were looking at nothing, it is because they are looking
at her. Time intrudes on the landscape as the other does on the speaker,
yet she does nothing in light of either peripeteia.

At first take the poem's speaker appears to be both the object and
subject of a tragic skepticism that, "incredulous of Ought / But Blank,"
dismisses the world and, in Cavell's formulation, chooses to deny the
existence of others rather than accept their mortality. Within a simpler
version of this drama of denial, we might infer that the "face" appears
to look on "Infinites of Nought" when looking at the speaker, because it
chooses not to see her and remains willfully blind to her existence.[79] Yet the

79. Thus Cameron, pointing to the transitive use of the verb *look* in "looked
itself on Me," insists on the violence of the other's projection, which not only
ignores the particularity of the speaker's being but imposes its self-image on hers
(*Lyric Time*, 141–42). Cameron's reading is more despairing of the poem than
mine, because it posits at the poem's core a pain so great that the overwhelming
need to externalize it makes the world illegible to oneself except as an empty
self-image.

act of passiveness—"I offered it no Help -/ Because the Cause was Mine
-"—by which the speaker responds to this passing by telling us that the
"Face" has read her only too well. "Because the Cause was Mine" confirms the other's insight into the speaker—"I had no help to offer since I
was [as miserable, as empty, as much of a 'nothing'] as the face had seen
me" (or, alternatively, "since my own gaze was as emptying, as evacuating
of an already occupied space")—even as it asserts the speaker's self-sufficiency—"I offered it no help because I was pulling my own weight."

The unextended offer may look like a lack of generosity, a recalcitrant
and self-protective withholding, yet the poem, I want to suggest, concerns
less the failure to give than the burden of reception; its impasse hangs
on the theological problem of how to accept—how not to dismiss—a
world in which the only Other capable of bestowing recognition is mortal
like oneself.[80] The gesture of forbearance thus establishes a compact "as
hopeless as divine" premised paradoxically on not alleviating the other's
doubt and on not meeting her demand for an absolute confirmation of
value. "Misery" has to be read in light of its proximity to the theological
concept of grace, for the word designates the utter helplessness that not
only necessitates divine mediation but is the condition for the reception
of grace.[81] It is from within this theological understanding of the human
creature's passivity in relation to its own depravity and salvation that the
declaration, "I offered it no Help," implies a mode of faithfulness, even
if it is only a stern and unflinching commitment to a world that God's
absence leaves unredeemed. The speaker's repudiation of this world, as
of the other's offer, is, in this sense, illusory, an effect of the last stanza's

80. This burden of secular acknowledgment—the burden of remembering
one's fellow dead in a world devoid of transcendence—has been considered a
central feature of the modern elegy. Thus Ramazani suggests that Hardy's sense
of responsibility for one whom he cannot count on God to remember accounts
for the "anxious proliferation of more than a hundred elegies for his estranged
wife" (*Poetry of Mourning*, 47). See also Esther Schor's discussion of Enlightenment mourning in terms of the "ethical imperative for the living" to perpetuate
the legacy of the past in the absence of divine memory (Schor, *Bearing the Dead*,
4). A similar argument might be made for the connection between the withdrawal of an omniscient God capable of guaranteeing that one will have been
known by another and the importance of marital communion in a secular age.

81. The Calvinist emphasis on the arbitrariness of grace may inform the poem's punning negations of the language of legal obligation and finite responsibility in "Ought" and "Just."

syntactical delay and ambiguous conditional tense ("Neither - would be absolved - / Neither would be a Queen / Without the Other -"), which make it impossible to witness the act of taking between the two selves. It is not clear whether the speaker is describing an impasse or a consummation, whether "Neither - would be absolved - / Neither would be a Queen" are conditions left unfulfilled by their repudiation of one another, or whether "Without the Other -" names the reciprocity by which each renders judgment of and acquits the other, while leaving intact the sovereignty of their self-images. The concluding "Therefore - / We perish - tho' we Reign -" suggests, in any case, that the relief of absolution has not been, as one might have thought, permanently foresworn but, on the contrary, already received. Grace, the poem suggests, lies in being known by the other without incurring any debt to her. Yet the corollary to such relief for the speaker and face is allowing one another to die rather than make something of their mirrored "Infinites of Nought."

"I offered it no Help -" The declaration might stand as the signature line for the lyric antihero whose type I have been identifying among the heedless lovers, indifferent heirs, idle mourners, and passive companions found in Wordsworth, Dickinson, and Hardy. With Dickinson's speaker, these figures ask us to hear in their words an assertion of moral truthfulness rather than a confession of guilt, expression of regret, or admission of failure. The claim insists on the ethical value of doing nothing—of refusing to correct that perception of blankness in oneself, alleviate the other's loss, or compensate for the waste of either's desire.

v. weightless gain: Dickinson and the passing by of experience

Passing too quickly and imperceptibly from an anticipatory to a retrospective mode of reception, Wordsworth's, Dickinson's, and Hardy's lyric speakers find themselves startled into having to take account of finished experience. This is the perspective of harvested experience, from which one is asked to take stock and declare what it all amounted to, that Emerson articulates in his essay "Experience," an essay in which he repudiates the very idea of educative telos associated with the term *experience*: "Let who will ask, where is the fruit? I find a private fruit sufficient. . . . I should feel it pitiful to demand a result on this town and county, an overt effect on the instant month and year" ("Experience," 233). As Emerson goes on to suggest, the reception of experience diminishes the self's capacity for taking hold of it as a possession, and the sum of experience remains "private" not in the sense of being knowable only to the self in question but, on the contrary, in that of not being assignable to any particular cause: "The effect is deep and secular as the cause. It works on periods in which mortal lifetime is lost. All I know is reception; I am and I have: but I do not get, and when I have fancied I had gotten anything, I found I did not" (233).

In its initial anger at the unreal character of even the most significant events—the "most unhandsome" part of our condition—the essay expresses the familiar suspicion that the most critical drama has been evaded and denied, and displays the habit of taking a final empty-handedness as evidence that something has been withheld. But repeating the revisionary movement we have seen in the poems, the essay ends by accepting as constitutive of experience the very absence of those forceful, tangible encounters it sets out to decry as a deficiency of experience. Read as an extended meditation on Emerson's own failure to mourn the death of his son—a project of mourning finally realized in being abandoned—the essay offers, as if in echo of Wordsworth's "A slumber did my spirit seal," insight into the seemingly tautological structure of experience—from unfelt nearness to unbridgeable distance. Surprised to find himself left intact—as he was before—by the loss of his son, Emerson learns that another's being could prove inessential to his own and receives a blank or negative instruction, negative in the sense that it brings him nothing new and cannot count as a positive acquisition. Like the speaker of the "Lucy" poems, he appears not to have taken account of the loved one's separateness until it was too late; yet, as the essay suggests, there may be no way to *live* that separateness, to assume its weightless burden, except by missing it:

> In the death of my son, now more than two years ago, I seem to have lost a beautiful estate,—no more. I cannot get it nearer to me. If tomorrow I should be informed of the bankruptcy of my principal debtors, the loss of my property would be a great inconvenience to me, perhaps, for many years; but it would leave me as it found me,—neither better nor worse. So is it with this calamity: it does not touch me: some thing which I fancied was a part of me, which could not be torn away without tearing me, nor enlarged without enriching me, falls off from me, and leaves no scar. It was caducous. I grieve that grief can teach me nothing, nor carry me one step into real nature. (218)

"We can find no scar, . . . None may teach it -"—Dickinson will echo, pointing to the same mystery of a virginal, negative education in loss. Yet Dickinson's engagement with the frameworks of both feminine education and theological conversion means that she asks very different questions of experience than the Emersonian harvester—not what does it amount to nor how to achieve it, but how to go on in the face of a gift that goes as mysteriously as it comes. In this section I will focus on poems by Dickinson steeped in the cultural and theological language of sexual modesty and humility, two discourses that from the outset entertain different expectations from experience than the Emersonian desire for marked and tangible—graspable—difference. Within the framework of each, the subject is exposed to a crisis (marriage, sexual consummation, death, conversion, or loss of faith) that it can neither seek nor avert but at most put behind. While the discourse of feminine virtue or sexual modesty is explicitly conservative—idealizing a verbal intercourse that leaves the sexually pure mind unchanged—the concept of theological grace may also, though more paradoxically, empty experience of its consequential value: it, too, constitutes an experience that the believer is expected, in one sense at least, to minimize by continuing to strive to fulfill the law as if he had not already been saved.[82] I return to Dickinson at this point, then, because she works within perspectives from which the Emersonian dissatisfaction with blank instruction—instruction so passively received that it may leave one with nothing to show—has already been put to rest. At the same time, of the three poets discussed in this chapter, she is the most likely to make a tragedy of the loss of faith. The crisis of her faith raises the stakes behind a kind of experience—easily ignored and sooner buried than developed—to which one can, at most, maintain a nonpossessive relation.

The movement of concession within Emerson's essay intimates a relation between renouncing expectations of experience and receiving its har-

---

82. In *The New England Mind* Perry Miller offers some remarkable articulations of what seems to have been the Puritans' double command: act as if you have already received grace (and thereby have the power to satisfy the law) *and* as if you haven't (the law still requires satisfying): "Once more we may marvel at the ingenuity of a contrivance which manages to demand what men cannot give and yet not punish them for failing, which forgives the wrongdoer and yet does not ask the law to go unsatisfied. . . . The essential concept was obligation to the law along with commutation of its sentence" (385, 387).

vest that many of Dickinson's poems also assume. If experience, in particular the recognition of others, entails a moral obligation, these poems suggest that this is an obligation to do nothing rather than something in light of what occurs, to bracket rather than pursue particular encounters or meetings with an Other. This antinovelistic conception of experience as asking to be set aside rather than taken up allows us to reread the recession of contact in a poem such as "There's a certain Slant of light" as the very mode of its reception:

> There's a certain Slant of light,
> Winter Afternoons -
> That oppresses, like the Heft
> Of Cathedral Tunes -
>
> Heavenly Hurt, it gives us -
> We can find no scar,
> But internal difference -
> Where the Meanings, are -
>
> None may teach it - Any -
> 'Tis the Seal Despair -
> An imperial affliction
> Sent us of the Air -
>
> When it comes, the Landscape listens -
> Shadows - hold their breath -
> When it goes, 'tis like the Distance
> On the look of Death -

Reminiscent of hymn meter, the alternation of longer and shorter lines establishes the rhythmic inseparability of advance and recession, so that the imposition of the burden of mortality and the lightening of this burden constitute one and the same event.[83] If anything is carried in the

83. At 7-5-7-5 (6-5-7-5 in the third) syllables, the first three quatrains fall one syllable short of the 8-6-8-6 syllable pattern of hymn meter, and one might say that Dickinson further diminishes the "heft" of the "hymn" tune by distributing the odd lines' expected four song beats across unstressed speech parts, if not eliding one beat altogether. According to Shoptaw's sensitive analysis of Dickinson's musical experimentation, the dashes may work as musical rests or graphic markers for the unheard fourth beat; by rendering the length of the lines ambiguous they also take off, diffuse the weight received. See, as well, Shoptaw's account of the final quatrain's expansion and resolution into "regular" common meter.

poem, it is the conceit of burdensome light—never explained but displaced from one metaphor to another—by which Dickinson renders the gravity of grace and reminds us of the "heave" in "Heavenly." The sense of the human work of breathing, of bearing up the body, thus imperceptibly inflects the first two stanzas—from the "Heft" that must be carried across the line break, to the alliterative line "Heavenly Hurt, it gives us -" whose inverted syntax quite literally places the object to be borne before the receiving "us."

As a negative scene of instruction, the poem appears on one level to describe the same movement as "The Difference between Despair"—a shock that intrudes irrevocably on the speaker's psyche to take away the capacity to differentiate between inner and outer, "before" and "after." Alluding, as Cameron notes, to the Book of Revelation (*Lyric Time*, 101), the words "Seal Despair" indicate an apocalyptic, definitive experience—an intimation of death or divine sentencing—that marks the subject for life. "Despair" is a "Seal" that implies psychic death—the loss of the capacity to receive anything from time, to wait on its still unfulfilled promise.

Yet just as the poem's iterative present tense belies the definitiveness of this change and makes a habitual experience of what should be a singular, epiphanic conversion, the poem's language—"Heavenly Hurt, it gives us," "sent us of the air," "When it comes"—testifies to a continued capacity for temporal reception. "Winter Afternoons," taking up an entire line, both lengthens and pillows the "Slant of light"; the internal rhymes and repeated consonants fill out the luxury of that bare and undifferentiated plural—"Winter Afternoons"—in which one can take one's time now that the time for change is past and the urgency of harvesting gone.

The poem in this sense describes an experience that, like the Boy of Winander's, *makes a gift* of the very loss of the ability to take. Thus the abstraction that, beginning with the indefinite declarative, "There's a," makes it difficult to say who is the subject of this experience—it happens to everything and no one—is itself an effect of the "Slant"'s queer and indirect mode of contact. The ostensive gesture that in Wordsworth still invited narrative expectations—the epitaphic interjection "There was a Boy"—is here transposed to the present tense of a certain meteorological condition. By thus making our daily vulnerability to the weather a figure for subjection to an absolute principle of alterity (God's or death's)—Dickinson rewrites for the living the familiar elegiac topos of the simultaneous exposure and invulnerability of the dead to all kinds of weather.

The "we" speaks from no definite point of reference because, like the shadows that must hold their breath, it has no immunity from a contact it can neither avoid nor seek.

Slant, of course, recalls that other "slant" of the grave, the slope or inclination that in "We do not play on Graves" all but elides the presence of buried dead underfoot. The poem's paradoxical association of an abstracted, deathlike passivity with the capacity still to receive anything from the hour or weather (*temps* in both senses it has in French), resonates with numerous other poems in which Dickinson reinvents the elegiac trope of contrasting seasonal change above ground to the stoniness of the grave. A poem such as "Safe in their Alabaster Chambers," for example, repeats the leveling movement of Wordsworth's "A slumber did my spirit seal" in the sense that it recasts what should be an ironic contrast—the insentient beneath the feet of the sentient—as a successive nearness or temporal doubling:

> Safe in their Alabaster Chambers,
> Untouched by morning -
> And untouched by noon -
> Lie the meek members of the Resurrection -
> Rafter of satin - and Roof of stone -
>
> Grand go the Years - in the Crescent - above them -
> Worlds scoop their Arcs -
> And Firmaments - row -
> Diadems - drop - and Doges - surrender -
> Soundless as dots - on a Disc of Snow -[84]

As with "A slumber did my spirit seal," the act of reading the poem puts into time a spatial juxtaposition that implies neither identity nor antithesis but the proximity of incommensurables: in Wordsworth's poem, love's indifference to the "touch of earthly years" is simply succeeded by the state of being wholly given over to immense temporal change—"rolled around in earth's diurnal course." In Dickinson's case, the poem's theological underpinnings already render dialectical the simple ironic contrast between the living and the dead: those sealed in impregnable "Alabaster" "lie" awaiting resurrection and only appear to be beyond all change, while nothing will come of the sweeping pageantry above. The antinomy was

84. This is R. W. Franklin's C version, based on a penciled note sent to Susan Dickinson in 1861 (see Dickinson, *The Poems of Emily Dickinson*, 161).

clearer in the poem's first version, which did use the two-stanza form to set the unsuspected faith below against the heedlessness of creatures of the air:

> Light laughs the breeze
> In the Castle above them -
> Babbles the Bee in a stolid Ear,
> Pipe the sweet Birds in ignorant cadence -
> Ah, what sagacity perished here! [85]

Having apparently already objected to this first version, Susan Gilbert Dickinson wrote in response to Dickinson's second attempt at the second stanza: "It just occurs to me that the first verse is complete in itself it needs no other, and can't be coupled—Strange things always go alone—as there is only one Gabriel and one Sun" (*The Poems of Emily Dickinson*, 161). For Susan to describe the poem's first stanza in terms of self-sufficiency is extraordinarily overdetermined given the paradox on which it hinges: reliance on an as yet unfulfilled divine promise is finally indistinguishable from self-containment.[86]

85. Franklin's B version, transcribed about late 1859 (see Dickinson, *The Poems of Emily Dickinson*, 160).

86. Skeptical readers might object that, in fact, Dickinson renders thoroughly untenable the Christian fiction of resurrection: too much pressure lies on the opening word "Safe" for any but an ironic reading of such sequestering, and the closeness with which "Roof of stone" follows so precisely on "Rafter of satin" leaves no room for transcendence. Yet one might argue instead that the poem captures the extent to which this faith is always already untenable—impossible to put forward: the changeless state rendered by a meter that returns to fall so evenly and indifferently on either of the two syllables of "Untouched" presents the paradox of an openness toward a time-as-yet-to-come, a hope so "meek" and so sure of itself it cannot confess itself as such, and so looks like the "seal Despair." In *Poetry and the Fate of the Senses*, Susan Stewart suggests that Dickinson appears to have made two lines of what a hymn quatrain would have had as its second—even—rhyme line—"Untouched by morning and untouched by noon" (121). Such a line would have less ambiguously placed both its song and speech beats on the "touched" of "untouched"; by instead distributing the same semantic material in the course of two self-quieting lines within a poem otherwise dominated by opening downbeats, Dickinson not only lengthens the time in which nothing happens but makes audible the indifference of stress on this word, whatever its place in the line—a word itself about the nonreception of light as something tactile.

Susan Gilbert's dismissal of Dickinson's repeated experimentations with the second stanza may thus gloss the poem's own paradoxical annulment of fictions of aftering and afterlife, but the criticism misses the way in which the 1861 doubling only heightens the insularity of each stanza. Indeed, here the supplemental character of the second stanza, which can neither complete nor repeal the first, may account for the superb release of movement in "Grand go the years -." Here the dancelike, nearly dactylic meter now expresses the daring, confidence, and *élan* of the epic and worldly, as Dickinson opens up the same form (a hymn quatrain, whose second line has been unfolded into two), occupied in the first instance, in the stanza that "lies" above, by a single subject and verb—the dead lying below—to six different cosmic actions—"Grand go the years - . . . / Worlds scoop their Arcs - / And Firmaments - row -," etc. There is a bold indifference to telos in this queenly sweep and excursive going out; in this sense the two stanzas do not make a pious contrast between the vanity of heroic enterprises and the patient wisdom of those who now remain indifferent to worldly goods. Instead, the telescoping of celestial revolutions recasts the naive pastoral otium of the 1859 variant as the playground of centuries, where the expanse of power is indistinguishable from its squandering. The metonymic abbreviation "Diadems drop" is all we see of the fall of monarchs: heads roll with the lightness of a change of fashion. This swiftness, coupled with the sure-footed meting out of single stressed beats per action, expresses the arrogant nonchalance of one who experiences the course of centuries as "nothing."

But the poem's close does more than bring us back to the perspective of the dead for whom all change in fortune is also as nothing: for in the meting out of syllables whose alliteration enacts the iterative repetitiveness described—"Soundless as dots - on a Disc of snow -"—eternity comes down to a single moment in time. In contrast to the earlier compression of epic action, the last line lengthens the momentary in the simple filling out of an adjectival phrase, and its metric "fall" gives us back the evanescence of real time. The untenable image of the "Disc of snow" reduces the earlier astronomical images of stars and planets to something that can hold no weight and certainly cannot last, and thus makes the reduction of epic telos—its coming down to nothing—inseparable from a return to the temporal and earthly.[87] However "strangely abstracted" and lost to

87. The *OED* gives for *disc* the "(apparently flat) surface or face of a planet as it appears to the eye."

the senses, the image evokes the empirical memory of the almost audible hush that snow spreads.[88] In this sense—like those moments in Milton that it remotely recalls, and in which pastoral metaphors interrupt and suspend the epic's development, reducing its scale to earthly time—the poem's close amounts to a claim for this world, however circumscribed.[89]

As I have been arguing, then, the second stanza's redoubling of the first neither revokes nor confirms the spell under which the dead lie, but puts into time death's annulment of time. However paradoxically, given the poem's focus on what it means to be sealed off from change, the poem ends up being about reception—about receiving something from time, even if it is only a supplementary impoverishment: in the place of the promised resurrection, the poem returns (and returns us) to the temporal world of the senses by emptying it out a second time.

Read together as meditations on the problem of following, or supplying the sequel to, something that expects no *suite* (continuation or consequence), poems such as "Safe in their Alabaster Chambers" and "A slumber did my spirit seal" help explain the setting aside of experience in "There's a certain Slant of light." Here, too, it is not the dead alone who lose the power to develop their experience in the process of receiving it. For the "Slant of light" intrudes not only to mark the subject for life but also to defer and displace that difference onto a permanently indefinite plane. I return to this poem to conclude the exposition of this lyric subgenre, because the poem's second stanza can be taken both to recapitulate and displace the founding of Romantic lyricism in the recognition of "a difference to me." Dickinson recasts this crisis of modern subjectivity in terms of the predicament of the Protestant soul who cannot tell her election by outward signs:

Heavenly Hurt, it gives us -
We can find no scar,

88. David Porter borrows the oxymoronic formulation "strangely abstracted images" from Archibald MacLeish to name the obliteration of sensory experience in Dickinson's poems. Wonderfully attentive to the poem's movement of deprivation in its passage from polysyllabic to monosyllabic words, Porter finds in this reduction a definitive abandonment of the world of the senses, where I am suggesting we can hear a return to time (see Porter, *Dickinson*).

89. I am thinking of those passages from *Paradise Lost* discussed by Hartman in which Milton suddenly telescopes the poem's epic scale and brings the fallen angels down to earth (see Hartman, "Milton's Counterplot").

But internal difference -
Where the Meanings, are -

Yet even as it rehearses this founding moment, the poem puts to rest the fiction of heroic and expansive selfhood that Peter Brooks associates with the "desire for plot" of the nineteenth-century novel, by decreeing the impossibility of acting appropriatively toward such insight. "None may teach it - Any -": either the content of this experience cannot be taught—passed down to others; or "it" has nothing to learn from you, from anyone or anything—"Despair" is sealed to further instruction. In either case the gnomic utterance declares an end to the acquisition and transmission of inheritance.[90]

The poem suggests instead that assuming the burden of such a dispensation means doing nothing—just as one does nothing to receive it. This Protestant emphasis on the passivity of the subject's relation to grace or election informs the last stanza, where the difficult image of "the Distance/ On the Look of Death" expresses the mystery of a grace whose coming near one cannot claim as a directed address and which thus remains as alien as death:

When it comes, the Landscape listens -
Shadows - hold their breath -
When it goes, 'tis like the Distance
On the look of Death -

The state of suspense and attentiveness is simply followed by the "Distance" of having been put beyond expectation, as if the listening itself were to displace the awaited message and the surrender of attention were what counted, not whether there was anything to be received; the world stops breathing, then picks up again immeasurably altered. As readers have repeatedly noted, Dickinson gives no content to the "it" but describes only its effects on the receiving subject, as if in deference

90. Thus one gloss for the line might be the Puritan dismissal of "education" as worthless when it comes to faith; here is Thomas Hooker, as if anticipating the "I can't tell you how I know" of aesthetic taste and irony, as quoted by Perry Miller: "faith is not a thing 'which our nature can attaine to with outward helpes. . . . Neither education, nor examples of others, nor our own resolutions, can settle our hearts upon God, till we find an inward power and authority causing divine truths to shine into our hearts" (Miller, *The New England Mind*, 28).

to the theological prohibition on naming God.[91] This chaste indirection renders the landscape's attentiveness and openness to experience indistinguishable from a refusal to look up, a being prepared to miss. In this sense, the stanza reads as a revision of the passage from Exodus, discussed in my first chapter, where Moses, rather than being allowed to see God face to face, is hidden in the cleft of a rock as God passes by; there, as here, a passing light and its eclipse are only "felt" as a tactile and aural experience. And just as Moses must intuit God's presence from his own momentary blindness as God's hands cover his eyes in passing, here the only face we are given is nature's. The same faith that will not allow the speaker to claim any relation to transcendence but that of distance and deferral keeps her in touch paradoxically with the natural world.

In "Listening to Dickinson" John Shoptaw has traced the poem's dormant religious metaphors of conversion and election as divine ravishment and (dis)possession back to their sources in several hymns by Isaac Watts. Shoptaw emphasizes, as most readers do, the bleakness of the "seal Despair" by which the speaker remains inviolate and yet not inviolate enough: on the one hand, spared/denied the face-to-face contact of the kind a Moses-like Watts seeks in terms analogous to erotic consummation ("How long wilt thou conceal thy face . . . / My God how long delay?"); on the other hand, marked internally—precisely in having been spared, not chosen, not taken up—by the "slant" light, whose "hurt" is to fail to "scar" and that "oppresses" with the weightless "heft" of indirect address or nonaddress. Read this way, the poem performs the by now familiar inversion of the deferral of violence into the violence of deferral, according to which a potential crisis event is all the more traumatizing for being missed and survived without apparent injury. Identifying the "heft of Cathedral tunes" with the curse of *near* intelligibility by which Christendom continues to make demands on Dickinson's antinomian ears, such a reading also makes the poem exemplify the crisis of an incompletely secularized modernity, not unlike the condition that Scholem ascribes to German Jews at the turn of the twentieth century, in which the commands of revealed

91. So Derrida describes the premise of negative theology: "[la négativité serait] une preuve de Dieu *par ses effets*, plus précisément une preuve . . . par des effets sans cause, par le *sans cause*" (*Psyché*, 538). For a discussion of the decentering, Derridean effects of Dickinson's "nonspecific or indefinitely recurring 'it,'" see Cristanne Miller, *Emily Dickinson: A Poet's Grammar*, 97–102.

religion still press on the ears of secular Jews but fail to address them meaningfully. (Thus Cameron classifies the poem among those whose landscapes bear "more meanings than a given speaker can interpret" [*Lyric Time*, 5].) Yet as I have been arguing, comparison with the passage from Exodus allows an alternative reading, according to which the deflection of address and eclipse of epiphanic light (an eclipse indistinguishable from, because continuous with, its diffusion and dissipation) might be constitutive of a differently *completed* revelatory experience and not simply a sign of its blockage—a reading minimally indicated by the poem's own evocation in the vernacular not of a singular crisis event but of a repeated, weatherlike occurrence seemingly sustained a number of times by human and nonhuman experiential subjects, across a rhythm of the heightening and receding of expectations. Whether it designates the gaze of nonrecognition with which the dying look on death, however close its approach, or on the world they once took for near, or whether it evokes an allegorical figure distantly reminiscent of the grim leveler, whose absent gaze would not, even when "marking" you, "mean" you—indeed would be devoid of anything to which you might answer—the remarkably compressed figure "the Distance / On the Look of Death -" (the only face revealed in place of God's) suggests that we understand as part of this recession, the receding of "enigmatic" messages, whether of redemption or damnation, judgment or accusation. In this sense, Dickinson's poem might be read not as the expression of what Scholem called the "nothingness of revelation," whereby "revelation appears to be without meaning, in which it still asserts itself, in which it has validity but no significance" (cited in Santner, *On Creaturely Life*, 39), but rather as the notation of a kind of "antireligious," undemanding "revelation," free of accusative address, and permitting a different kind of attention to the natural world, which one might now call "received" for having been put back or let down into it.[92]

92. I gingerly borrow the phrase "anti-religious revelation" from Santner's reading of Rosenzweig, since Rosenzweig's use of it, as rendered by Santner in *The Psychotheology of Everyday Life*, exposes its fundamental continuities with the "anti-religion" at the core of the Pauline and Protestant trope par excellence: that of the falling away of those reified "idols" or "totems" standing in the way of the subject's proper responsiveness to God: "In a diary entry from 1922 . . . Rosenzweig . . . characterizes revelation as a kind of 'anti-religion' aimed at loosening the grip of the 'religionitis' that ensues when fantasmatic formations or 'totems' of any kind begin to block our often anguished exposure to/answerability within

Another way of expressing the mood of this groundedness, or commitment to the given world, is through the claim of one who, turning up empty-handed, asserts, "Nothing has been delayed, deferred, or sacrificed. I have experienced all." Or "this little can be everything, for me. If reception consists of no more than the act of waiting, and at a certain point, giving up the wait, then the actual fruits of time cannot measure the fullness of a life." This sentiment informs the lightness with which the protagonists of the lyric of inconsequence that I have been identifying in Wordsworth, Dickinson, and Hardy pass over the crisis of modern subjectivity and set aside the legacy of "the difference within." Exemplifying a nonappropriative mode of keeping time, these indifferent heirs do not suffer a loss in committing their gain to inconsequence. "We have had our answer, and it came to naught," they seem to say. "We are chastened of any illusions, not of the possibility of certainty but of the difference that it can make"; "we have had to supply—improvise—our own instruction in the absence of teachers and are by the same logic compelled to divest that experience of any authoritative power over others"; and at the same time, "to the extent that we could not but give the answer we did (we could not have withheld it), this affirmative act does not come from us at all; it is not ours to claim or pass on."

I close this section by looking briefly at one last summation of missed experience. The poem appears at first to be a declaration of having had nothing from life—an explanation of empty-handedness at the hour of reckoning. The female speaker has been kept from exploring the world by questing and confined, instead, to domestic chores—sewing and other sedentary work—that keep her head down. Yet the poem turns the prejudice against the claustrophobic shelter of feminine experience on its head, as its speaker achieves a tone of celestial largesse similar to that struck in the "Grand go the years" stanza of "Safe in their Alabaster Chambers," a

---

the midst of life" (123n53). Rather than calling for more "answerability," in its final recessiveness, Dickinson's poem appears to traverse the fantasy of interpreting phenomena "sent us of the air" as super-egoic demands. In "The Angle of a Landscape -" Dickinson more playfully describes the bounty of weather- and season-supplied phenomena soliciting but also declining her interpretation—offerings seemingly received on condition of accepting the unconcern with which they occasionally "accost" and leave her, in contrast with the steeple's "finger" that never "stirs" but always points in the accusative.

tone that, in its grand indifference to the world, is finally indistinguishable from the modesty of the meek:

> The missing all - prevented me
> From missing minor things -
> If nothing larger than a world's
> Departure from a Hinge,
> Or Sun's extinction - be observed -
> 'Twas not so large that I
> Could lift my Forehead from my work
> For Curiosity -

The speaker's wit lies in letting us know how much she can tell of earthly
loss without looking up from her domestic work—she keeps time with
it, as one might tell the hour by the shadows on the wall. Indeed this
tonal playfulness makes it difficult to take her impassive detachment as
evidence of a traumatic loss so great that the destruction of worlds is
as nothing in comparison.[93] For the queenly lightness with which she
brushes off catastrophe—"If nothing larger than . . . "—corresponds to
the uneventful, inconsequential way in which a "world" may depart "from
a Hinge" (apocalyptic eclipse or quotidian sunset?), and reminds us of
the Emersonian pun on the "casual" in "casualty": "We thrive by casual-
ties. . . . Our chief experiences have been casual" ("Experience," 226).[94]
Far from a refusal to assume the burden of loss, her deficiency of grav-

93. See, for example, J. V. Cunningham's claim that "Only loss of salvation
justifies such hyperbole" (quoted in Cameron, *Lyric Time*, 171). This is another
version of the argument that insists on reading apparent numbness to the world
as the symptom of a secret and catastrophic loss or trauma. Cameron herself
takes some distance from this reading by distinguishing the poem from others
in which Dickinson records "a forfeit so monumental as to render any later
particularity trivial," and by claiming that the speaker's forfeit here instead puts
her in touch with a loss "that is at last recognized as the true face of the natural world, what Dickinson had elsewhere called 'the Distance / On the look of
Death—'" (ibid.). Yet this claim continues to attribute to the speaker's judgment of the world the definitiveness of despair, something that the poem, I am
suggesting, belies.

94. Here again I am indebted to Susan Stewart, who suggests to me that the
poem may be making equivalent the blindness incurred from looking at the sun
during an eclipse and that which follows from doing "close work" in crepuscular
light—a strain that may well have contributed to Dickinson's eye problems.

ity remains faithful to the weightlessness that makes the existent all but already gone. "From a hinge" renders the sense that things have as little hold on life as she does—are as likely, in Wordsworthian language, "to go silently out of mind" as "to be violently destroyed."

A richly ironic representation of feminine modesty, the poem thus vocalizes the perspective of the unassuming observer with a terseness worthy of Austen's Fanny Price. As we will see in the next chapter, Austen's portrayal, like Dickinson's, leaves room to acknowledge the cold and unforgiving aspects of Fanny's prudence. Neither Austen nor Dickinson makes it easy to distinguish the repudiation of spectacle from the selfish ruthlessness of one who, finding herself excluded, commits it all to perdition. But Dickinson's poem is finally a joke on the ethos of having nothing to spare and on the Puritan condemnation of idleness evoked in the last line: "For Curiosity." The ease with which this grammatically unnecessary modifier is carelessly, freely thrown out belies its denotative sense. The effect is like that of the word "Occasionally," with which Dickinson ends the poem "We do not play on Graves," and by it the speaker expresses with quiet mockery the mildly ironic, detached love of her inattentive attention—a disavowal that embraces far more than it abandons.

vi. passing judgment: passivity and the ethics of acknowledgment

> By homely gift and hindered words
> The human heart is told
> Of nothing -
> "Nothing" is the force
> That renovates the World -
>
> —Emily Dickinson
>
> A poem begins and ends in silence. Why not call it nothing then?
> —Allen Grossman, *The Sighted Singer*

Dickinson's, Hardy's, and Wordsworth's poems thus present in the place of dramatic exchange an internal transformation in character that often includes a diminishment of the capacity to register change as such. Their speakers' indifference to narrative economy corresponds to a paratactic relation between "before" and "after" that looks like an absence of prog-

ress; as I have argued, however, this open-endedness of relation is itself
the effect of experience. In marking how close loving another person may
come to missing him altogether, their poems yield insight into the passiveness of moral knowing, a passiveness that has nothing to do with being determined from without by external causes, with having no control
or responsibility, but with the little one has to do, the little one's loving
amounts to. The story that I have sought to tell through my readings of
these poems is thus that of a possible resolution to the crisis of modern
skepticism over the existence and knowability of others, in particular of
an Other capable of verifying one's own existence. Cavell has described
this crisis as a tragedy of avoidance, whereby the skeptic "attempts to convert" into "an intellectual lack" the "metaphysical finitude" that the other
sees in him and represents for him. The skeptic denies the other's knowledge, rather than allow the other to know him, to find him mortal and
separate, which is all the other can do.[95] The problem is a function of the
impossible roles that the "process of secularization"—Cavell calls it "romanticism"—puts humans in the position of playing for one another. For
inasmuch as this process accepts Protestantism's antinomian emphasis on
inner faith over obedience to external laws, it is now up to me to summon
myself before God and determine what is asked of me, shoring up what I
can from my own now boundless experience: "From now on one manages
one's relation to God alone, in particular one bears the brunt alone of being known to God" (Cavell, *The Claim of Reason*, 470). But just as no one
now calls forth my gift, there is no one to acknowledge it but another like
myself, separate and mortal: with the disappearance of the Godhead, "the
other now bears the weight of God, shows me that I am not alone in the
universe" (470). In two new respects, Cavell's language suggests, humans
are asked to assume burdens once carried by God or representatives of
God. These two new roles—my allowing myself to be known and your
playing God to know me, the putting forward and the acknowledging
of the private riches each has within, even the invention of something to
be known and someone to know it—are rife with heroic possibility. Yet

95. Cavell's account presupposes throughout the reversibility of what he calls
skepticism's "active and passive forms"—the denial that I can know another being and the denial that I can be known by another. My argument here draws
heavily on the concluding section to *The Claim of Reason*, "Between Acknowledgment and Avoidance," in particular Cavell's reading of Othello's denial of the
mortal desire Desdemona has discovered in him (329–476).

Cavell goes on to describe the disastrous consequences of "the wish for absolute activeness and absolute passiveness; which is to say, for absolute recognition of and by another" (470), and everything in his argument points to the need to abjure such heroism. The "humanization" of acknowledgment—our assumption of the power to confirm one another's self-images—"places infinite demands upon finite resources" (470), and assuming its burden means, in large measure, renouncing these demands. Unlike divine absolution, in other words, human acknowledgment, even of another's (or one's own) capacity to sustain "infinite interest," must acknowledge its own finitude—it includes and inevitably yields to a sense of the little such acknowledgment can do for another.

Cavell's account of skepticism as a tragic avoidance of the other and the other's insight commands attention here, because it implies an ethics of acknowledgment that would seem to indict the missings recorded in these poems as moral rather than cognitive failures; it articulates the position against which Wordsworth's, Dickinson's, and Hardy's speakers must defend their ellipses, omissions, indirections, continued lightness of address, and capacity for inattention. Cavell wants to insist on the "activeness" of acknowledgment as an ethical choice, a step one must want to take, not something one can assume comes with knowledge: "Acknowledgment 'goes beyond' knowledge, not in the order, or as a feat, of cognition, but in the call upon me to express the knowledge at its core, to recognize what I know, to do something in the light of it, apart from which this knowledge remains without expression, hence perhaps without possession" (428). Again this concept of acknowledgment as a burden for which one is solely responsible presupposes the secular, perhaps paradigmatically Romantic, sense of being alone in the world, the bearer of experiences that without one's broadcast will remain unknown; inevitably Cavell's own terms for it often betray a heroic defensiveness against such emptiness. Hence the forced energy of the sequence, "claim it, stake it, enact it," in his paraphrase of Emerson's stance in "Self-Reliance"—"I'm a being who to exist must say I exist or must acknowledge my existence—claim it, stake it, enact it" (*In Quest of the Ordinary*, 109). In it we hear the rush to lay claim and assign an owner to uncounted time typical of the anxiety over waste in a secular age. The call on individuals to establish rather than merely assume their claims to truth and power can render limitless their sense of responsibility for missed potential.

If acknowledgment is indeed a question of thus claiming, staking, and

enacting otherwise unmet insight, then there is no question that Wordsworth's, Dickinson's, and Hardy's reluctant mourners and undemanding
lovers fail their object by their reticence of notice. But much of Cavell's
argument, in fact, militates against this heroic understanding of acknowledgment by limiting its status as an "event" to a slight adjustment in "attitude," a change in one's way of seeing others whose expression in a direct,
definitive statement may never take place:

> If my attitude towards him expresses my knowledge that he has a soul, my
> attitude may nevertheless not be very definitely expressed, nor very readily. It
> may take ages; it may be expressed now in the way I live. . . . The word "at-
> titude" can be misleading here. It is not, in the matters at hand, a disposition
> I can adopt at will. It will be helpful to take the English word in its physical
> sense, as an inflection of myself toward others, an orientation which affects
> everything and which I may or may not be interested in discovering about
> myself. (*The Claim of Reason*, 360)

The resolution to the impasse produced by the questions, "Does the other
have a soul?" or "Am I one of the elect?" (questions that romanticism
might translate as "Am I knowable to another? to myself?"), does not lie,
then, in the arrival of fresh and conclusive evidence (no evidence could
be reason enough to give an affirmative), but in a simple readjustment
of perspective whereby the questioner does not so much renounce the
possibility of certainty as he does fantasies about the eventfulness of its
achievement. He stops constructing interiority (whether the other's or his
own) as a mystery to be penetrated, a secret that someone is in on, if he
isn't, and instead accepts it as an open secret of which no one is the master
and that he might have chosen to see or not *at any time*.

   Throughout *The Claim of Reason* Cavell thus uses Wittgenstein's refuta-
tion of the "fantasy of a private language," of the idea that the self's relation to itself is one of privileged knowledge, not to dispute skepticism's
"disappointment" with the outward criteria supposed to establish inner
processes but to offset certain exaggerated responses to that disappointment, in particular a certain Romantic misprision of interiority as a do-
main over which the self has sole jurisdiction. Wittgenstein, according to
Cavell, does not so much deny privacy as he does the need to predicate
inwardness on the capacity for secrecy; he wants to spare the self the heroic position of having either to keep itself inviolate, inscrutable to the
eyes of others, or to make itself completely known to another:

[Wittgenstein] seems to trivialize my (inner) life.—In a way this is true. I think one moral of the *Investigations* as a whole can be drawn as follows: The fact, and the state, of your (inner) life cannot take its importance from anything special in it. However far you have gone with it, you will find that what is common is there before you are. The state of your life may be, and may be all that is, worth your infinite interest. But then that can only exist along with a complete disinterest toward it. The soul is impersonal. (361)[96]

When Cavell does enact "acknowledgment," it is as a strangely unsorrowful disappointment and admission of limits, as in this remarkably deflationary passage: my recognition of a "soul" or capacity to sustain "infinite interest," whether within myself or others, coincides with my renouncing certain fantasies of immortality and accepting not only that soul's ordinariness but my divestment from its "infinite interest."

In this sense, Cavell seems to rejoin Simone Weil in defining generosity between humans as inherently deflective—a question not of meeting one another's unreal demands but of forgiving both those demands and our inability to meet them:

Les hommes nous doivent ce que nous imaginons qu'ils nous donneront. Leur remettre cette dette.

96. In subsequent passages Cavell reiterates this counterintuitive claim according to which one's sense of self is predicated on one's learning to accept a nonpossessive and nonprivileged relation to one's experiences:

In *The Senses of Walden* I have argued for an understanding of the having of a self as an acceptance of the idea of being by oneself, and an understanding of being oneself in terms of being beside oneself. . . . It proposes an understanding of self-possession as a certain achievement of aloneness. . . . The achievement requires learning to deal in certain secrets. Not, however private, or rather personal ones, as if someone might in principle keep them (as if for himself or herself); but, like the secrets of philosophy always open ones, ones always already known before I present myself to them. (*The Claim of Reason*, 367)

Cavell's use of the notion of philosophy's open secret to denote a lack of privileged relation to mystery, to that which eludes demonstration and philosophical argument, is congenial to my own. The "open secret" *demystifies without explaining* the humanly unintelligible. The "openness" denotes not the subject's achievement of perfect lucidity but rather the absence of shelter: he or she cannot take refuge in the fiction of a mystery that once penetrated will reveal what to do or who the subject is.

Accepter qu'ils soient autre que les créatures de notre imagination, c'est imiter le renoncement de Dieu.

Moi aussi, je suis autre que ce que je m'imagine être. Le savoir, c'est le pardon.

[Men owe us what we imagine they will give us. Forgive them this debt.

To accept that they are different than the creatures of our imagination is to imitate the renunciation of God.

I too am other than what I imagine myself to be. To know this is forgiveness.][97]

In the contours of Weil's thought, we can follow the same expansive, contractive movement of the drama of secularization described above—the discovery of boundless promise and its voluntary setting aside. The initial claim that "others owe us what we imagine they will give us" surprises by its affirmative boldness; with it Weil turns the social contract's rational economy of mutual obligations on its head. We do not ask in return for services rendered but rather invent the other's gift in advance of any cause or signal to do so; the asking does not wait for reason, and is by itself enough to constitute the claim. Yet here having conferred full declarative power unto the usually passive recipient, Weil abjures its use. Precisely because nothing now limits what we can ask of each other but the capaciousness of our own imaginations, all we can do is "forgive" such imagined debts. For the French verb *remettre* [return, put back]—here trans-

---

97. Weil, *La pesanteur et la grâce*, 17; Weil, *Gravity and Grace*, 9. The aphorism, from "Vide et Compensation," opens with a woman making an unsolicited appeal that she then retracts by supplying her own answer to it: "A beloved being who disappoints me. I have written to him. It is impossible that he should not reply by saying what I have said to myself in his name." The reversal of passive and active roles here in the blurring of petitioner and judge, debtor and creditor, upsets not only the conventional divisions of labor within the Christian hierarchy but also traditional gender expectations. A woman's word goes ahead of and makes redundant anything her lover might say on his behalf. In this respect it would be interesting to consider Weil's emphatic self-effacement as a self-willed rewriting of, rather than regressive return to, the conventions of feminine passivity. By their very assertiveness and forwardness, her gestures of abnegation mark a serious break from both the impassive silence of the "Lady" of courtly love, who always returns the same unforgiving verdict, and the pleading silence of the conduct-book heroine, who waits to be spoken for and asked in marriage.

lated as "forgive"—Dickinson would have given us "remit"; both suggest that the only gift that can, in fact, take place is our returning to others something they never had.[98]

Generosity between humans appears, in this view, to become peculiarly intransitive, a mere deflection or cessation whose occurrence we can hardly register. One aim of this chapter's poetic readings has been to reawaken the sense that the simple gesture of desisting is, in fact, transitive, a going out and conferral of a weightless burden from one to another, through a careful examination of the peculiar use of time made in short Romantic and post-Romantic poems. Indeed the examples of Cavell and Weil already point to the role of the mere passage of time in distilling an "event" of acknowledgment or forgiveness, although nothing, no singular epiphanic event, in time causes one to make up one's mind to it. They tell a story of the reprieve from counting, from both its anticipatory and critical energies, that we find repeated in Wordsworth's, Dickinson's, and Hardy's poems of averted experience. In a pattern that emerges as paradigmatic of scenes of secularized judgment, the supplicant who begins by awaiting an answer to validate his existence, finishes by allowing this demand simply to recede. Weil and Cavell each suggest why this recession should come not merely in the place of, but in the name of, fulfillment. They can help explain the patterns of apparent temporal lapse—of demands made then ceded—that we find in the literary examples discussed above and begin to tell us why these patterns elicit not disappointment but a sense of completion in the initial setting by and soon permanent forgetting of the absent "gift" of judgment.

98. I am indebted to David Bromwich for reminding me of Dickinson's "Remit as yet no grace" from "Further in the Summer than the Birds." "Remit" is also the word Wordsworth uses to describe the recession of the Boy of Winander's anxious listening; see *Poetical Works* 2:440.

§ 4 Fanny's "Labour of Privacy" and the Accommodation of Virtue in Austen's *Mansfield Park*

I was quiet, but I was not blind.
—Jane Austen, *Mansfield Park*

For we must remember that it is the nature of Vice to force itself upon notice, both in the act and by its consequences. . . . But, on the contrary, the virtues, especially those of humble life, are retired; and many of the highest must be sought for or they will be overlooked. . . . How few know anything of the trials to which Men in a lowly condition are subject, or of the steady and triumphant manner in which those trials are often sustained, but they themselves? The afflictions which Peasants and rural Artizans have to struggle with are for the most part secret; the tears which they wipe away, and the sighs which they stifle,—this is all a labour of privacy. In fact their victories are to themselves known only imperfectly: for it is inseparable from virtue, in the pure sense of the word, to be unconscious of the might of her own prowess.
—William Wordsworth, "Essay on Epitaphs"[1]

Circumstance, as usual, did it all. How many of us can say of our intimate *alter ego*, leaving alone friends of the outer circle, that he is the man we should have finally chosen, as embodying the net result after adding up all the points in human nature that we love, and principles we hold, and subtracting all that we hate? The man is really somebody we got to know by mere physical juxtaposition long maintained, and was taken into our confidence, and even heart, as a makeshift.
—Thomas Hardy, *A Pair of Blue Eyes*

1. William Wordsworth, *Selected Prose*, 339.

i. *Fanny's diminished prospects*

> She dwelt among th' untrodden ways
>   Beside the springs of Dove,
> A Maid whom there were none to praise
>   And very few to love:
>
> A Violet by a mossy Stone
>   Half-hidden from the Eye!
> —Fair as a star when only one
>   Is shining in the sky!
>
> She liv'd unknown, and few could know
>   When Lucy ceas'd to be;
> But she is in her Grave, and oh!
>   The difference to me.
>
> —William Wordsworth

In its odd mixture of pathos and banality, Wordsworth's song expresses a feeling central to most Empsonian versions of pastoral: "the feeling that life is essentially inadequate to the human spirit, and yet that a good life must avoid saying so. . . . In pastoral you take a limited life and pretend it is the full and normal one, and a suggestion that one must do this with all life, because the normal is itself limited, is easily put into the trick though not necessary to its power" (Empson, *Some Versions of Pastoral*, 114–15). Mourning a private and irreparable loss, Wordsworth's speaker is also claiming that he has been satisfied, not in the ways of other men but with the little life has offered him. If he has loved Lucy by default because, to put it bluntly, no one else was around, his own images suggest that he would not have asked for more. (Shining only in the absence of other brighter luminaries, violet and star suffice precisely because they clear a space without filling it.) Part of his happiness has been the sense of making do, of accommodating himself to life by virtue of his being able to supply the rest, of his being, in short, adequate to its inadequacy.

Yet the poem invites parody, for even as it sets itself apart from the ways of the world, its powers of accommodation testify to a complacency that, like Austen's Fanny Price, disinclines readers toward sympathy. Not caring to defend his choice of one "whom there were none to praise / And very few to love," the speaker hardly seeks the public approbation denied his unknown love object. For "the difference [is] to [him]," and the poet's trick is to make his feeling seem disproportionate even to the poem by which he conveys it. The poem is thus necessarily disappointing—a poor translation of unknown because unknowable ways of being; its only success lies in suggesting something necessary about that disappointment, that failure to make so much pathos available to others.

Capturing the difficulty of all pastoral celebrations of the lowly and undistinguished, Wordsworth's recuperative gesture leaves itself open to being misunderstood because so hyperbolic and understated an exclamation as "the difference to me" can make itself heard only at a whisper: Wordsworth wants to reclaim a private experience as something worth attending to, yet he does not want to sing that privacy to the world. Success for such poetry depends on making one's silences carry distinct weight, on having their gravity outlast more public and showy forms of expression as in the last lines of the "Intimations Ode": "To me the meanest flower that blows can give / Thoughts that do often lie too deep for tears." If such thoughts can recompense Wordsworth for the curtailment and foreshortening of vision narrated in the Ode, it is perhaps only because their quietness is appropriately elegiac, still aware of "spaces and powers denied."

"A torn awareness of spaces and powers denied" is Nina Auerbach's description of a perspective Jane Austen shares with her Romantic contemporaries, and it informs our own uneasy ambivalence about *Mansfield Park*, a novel that so successfully takes "a limited life and pretends it is the full and normal one."[2] Fanny, who makes no other pretense, is, it seems, too much at ease in this fiction. Or so she has become by the novel's last

---

2. For Auerbach, this "awareness of inexorable denial" creates a "continual tension between the security of a restricted world and its unrelenting imprisonment [that] brings Austen into a special sort of agreement with her Romantic contemporaries" (Auerbach, *Romantic Imprisonment*, 4–5). In this chapter, I will follow Auerbach's lead in formulating the question of "Romanticism" for Austen as the question of accommodating romance to realism, or of the terms (satisfying or unsatisfying) on which human desires and potentialities may be realized in this world. In *The Country and the City* Raymond Williams associates Romanticism with the tendency to hypostatize the political criticism of specific, historically grounded systems of exclusion and oppression into a wholesale dismissal of the world as unfit for the development of human potential. Examining the worldly powers of accommodation of Austen's "most Romantic heroine" (Auerbach, *Romantic Imprisonment*, 28) allows us to test whether this "separation of virtue from any practically available world" is indeed "a feature . . . of Romanticism" (Williams, *The Country and the City*, 65).

paragraph, which presents a prospect of happiness emptied of any awareness of the powers and spaces denied it:

> On that event they removed to Mansfield, and the parsonage there, which under each of its two former owners, Fanny had never been able to approach but with some painful sensation of restraint or alarm, soon grew as dear to her heart, and as thoroughly perfect in her eyes, as every thing else, within the view and patronage of Mansfield Park, had long been. (321)

Yet whatever Fanny's final satisfaction with such enclosure, there is a sideways glance to the world at large here, which, were it her own, would betray a cynicism in her prudence. For the commas around "within the view and patronage of Mansfield Park" suggest that such restriction demands work and cannot be taken for granted; the qualifying clause hints that "everything else" might and should have meant something more. The narrator, if not Fanny, leaves room for the memory—and denial—of other more desirable possibilities; the ironic tensions between the narrative voice and the heroine's silence invite us to remember what it costs to other perspectives to arrive at so self-sufficient a prospect as Mansfield's.

Austen's wit is to make us feel the dissatisfaction that Fanny herself fails in the end to show. The narrator is so unabashed and pointed and determined in her insistence on Fanny's happiness that we find ourselves, like Fanny, resisting and mistrusting its being thrust on us:

> My Fanny indeed at this very time, I have the satisfaction of knowing, must have been happy in spite of every thing. She must have been a happy creature in spite of all that she felt or thought she felt, for the distress of those around her. She had sources of delight that must force their way. She was returned to Mansfield Park, she was useful, she was beloved. (312)

"Happy in spite . . . happy creature in spite"—the repeated words suggest a pun on Austen's part, as if she were anticipating the work of critics who will identify Fanny as a killjoy who nests in the spoils of other people's lives. Putting the sentence in the first person—"I was happy in spite of . . . those around me"—yields a disenchanted prose translation of Wordsworth's poem, and the difference makes the position untenable. In this sense Fanny herself can hardly claim her reward; were she to assert for herself what the narrative "I" has "the satisfaction of knowing," she could never counter the charge that her happiness was merely a poor substitute for the "real thing"—the liveliness of the Crawfords, London, and the future; for she is "useful and beloved" only once there is no one left to love.[3] Instead, only the quickening rhythm of "She was returned to Mansfield Park, she was useful, she was beloved" expresses Fanny's relief that she doesn't have to justify herself anymore—she's found her place. Indeed, the emphatically passive construction "was returned to" indicates that she has been relieved of having to act for herself in her own right, and this release from legal personhood yields the return to a different kind of personal freedom. The surprising yoking of usually antithetical concepts—use and love, domesticity and desirability—in that exhilarating parataxis—"she was useful, she was beloved"—exceeds, I think, the flatly disenchanting irony that she is only loved according to her usefulness. For the sentence has the momentum of coming home, of coming down to earth to the groundedness and concreteness of certain absolutes, however disenchanted.

The tonal ambiguity of Austen's own attitude toward Fanny—gently sardonic in its maternal possessiveness—thus foregrounds the question, "How do we reward the good without making hypocrites of them, if being good means showing oneself ready to go without reward?" Indeed, the phrase "sources of delight that must force their way" ironizes the "fiction" of modesty, according to which a girl must not ask for what she wishes but accept wish-fulfillment only when reality makes it impossible to reject.[4] *Mansfield Park* reserves the conventional happy ending for the only character in the novel who does not act, or whose only action is negative—an ambiguous refusal to play the part expected of her, first in the

3. For the ways in which Fanny depends on the unhappiness of those around her for her own happiness, see Auerbach's chapter "Jane Austen's Dangerous Charm: Feeling as One Ought About Fanny Price," in *Romantic Imprisonment*, 22–37. As Austen's repeated "must have been" indicates, such happiness in any case never takes experiential form but remains pure surmise even for the narrative "I"—a sufficient certainty realized in the absence of lived reality, based on nothing actual, only on Austenian knowledge of the general laws of human psychology.

4. The skeptical crisis produced by the perverse workings of the logic of modesty is well known: because the modest woman is not supposed to declare her own desire, her "no" is never taken to mean "no," and what may be her free consent remains indistinguishable from unwilling submission. Ruth Bernard Yeazell gives a particularly full account of the discrepancies that modesty produces between Fanny's experience of herself and her appearance to others; see Yeazell, *Fictions of Modesty*, 143–68.

private theatricals and then in the conventional marriage plot represented by Henry's proposal. As critics have noted, there are at least three ways to understand her famous one-line declaration "No, indeed I cannot act": (1) she does not plot to ensure her claim on the world but, in Tony Tanner's words, "triumphs by doing nothing," like the "lilies of the field" that "toil not, neither do they spin" (Matthew 6:28), exhibiting a paradoxically self-sufficient reliance on providential grace;[5] (2) she cannot perform—cannot appear as someone she is not or cannot make a spectacle of herself—an inability contradicted by her attention-getting theatrical statement of this powerlessness;[6] and (3) (collapsing 1 and 2) she cannot "act" in her own name but is happy to read, to live imaginatively through others' lines.[7] This lack of any clear correspondence between Fanny's contribution to

5. See Tony Tanner's introduction to the 1966 Penguin edition of the novel (8). Also relevant is Claudia Brodsky's discussion of Fanny's willingness, "by the natural attrition of inaction, to lose whatever part of the world she has been given" as expressive of the novel's alignment of virtue with narrative rather than with plot; see Brodsky, *The Imposition of Form*, 153.

6. The question of whether Fanny does or does not "act," in the related senses of theatrical self-exhibition and compliance to conventional rules, has been the subject of extensive critical debate. Brodsky, Litvak, Marshall, and Yeazell, for example, have all noted the contextual ironies undermining the content of the declaration—"No, indeed, I cannot act" (102)—by which Fanny finds herself at the center of everyone's attention. See, in particular, Brodsky, *The Imposition of Form*, 150–51; and Yeazell, *Fictions of Modesty*, 151–52; as well as Marshall, "True Acting and the Language of Real Feeling." Since Fanny's antitheatrical position, when identified as the novel's own, has traditionally been defended as a commitment to the authentic, grounded self, the "protheatrical" counterattack has often taken the form of exhibiting the scripted, conventional, and, by implication, "false" character of Fanny's own conduct and self-expression or of showing the extent to which the conservative social authority, whose moral judgment she invokes to legitimate her refusal, itself secretly depends on "covert" forms of theatricality. See, e.g., Litvak, "Theatricality in Mansfield Park"; and Galperin, "Austen's Future Shock." For Galperin, the art of "performing one's inability to act" does not uniquely characterize Fanny, but, on the contrary, belongs to the generalized social demand that one exhibit a consistent personal identity. There is a further irony here, however, according to which the persuasiveness of such critiques sometimes relies on the degree to which we already agree with the "antitheatrical position" in valuing an "authentic," self-cognizant relationship to inauthenticity.

7. The ironic constraints of feminine virtue make it impossible for a young

the novel's "action" and the end with which she is rewarded thus collapses a number of contradictions attending success for feminine virtue (or any virtue such as modesty or fidelity or openness of mind that could be said to consist of doing nothing). For on the one hand, her refusal to participate in the world of fictive making seems to align her with those who only "stand and wait."[8] On the other hand, as little more than a house servant, she cannot afford to do anything but. Expressed in her characteristic "I was quiet, but I was not blind" (246), Fanny's reserve, her refusal to exploit her own powers and do and say all she can, makes her, on one level, eminently exploitable; as Claudia Johnson has shown, for much of the novel her modesty appears to make her the compliant, serviceable object of others' desires.[9] She thus presents the uneasy predicament of one who, never thought of except by default, is thereby granted a certain liberty and inwardness that we usually associate with privileged rather than exploited characters.[10] Her unwillingness to bring the workings of her own mind and heart to light and to bear on others also finally leaves her in the unique position of seeing the novel's dénouement reflect, without distortion, her innermost wishes.

Essential to this position—a position that to assert too loudly is to lose—is Austen's third-person narration, which relieves Fanny from first-person assertions and sometimes lends to her states of mind (hardly feelings but self-contained perceptions) a quiet transparency by which they border on the objective and seem hardly hers to have to claim. As I sug-

---

woman to "act in her own name" in the sense of "in her own right," for her "name" is her reputation, and she must not appear to be acting on behalf of it, working to save it, but must let it speak for itself; it is not hers either to claim or sell. These ironies might account, in part, for Fanny's imaginative investments in the emotions of others, evident in her avid reading of Mary and Edmund's lines—investments that invite comparison with the Keatsian chameleon "Poetical Character," who is always "in for[ming]—and filling some other body" (John Keats to Richard Woodhouse, Oct. 27, 1818, in *Letters of John Keats*, 157).

8. "They also serve who only stand and wait" (from Milton, "Sonnet 19" [Milton's own meditation on the parable of the talents]).

9. See "*Mansfield Park*: Confusions of Guilt and Revolutions of Mind," in Johnson, *Jane Austen*.

10. For this see Lynch, *The Economy of Character*. Also relevant here is Adela Pinch's analysis of a similar dialectic of self-absorption and vulnerability to noise in *Persuasion*; see "Lost in a Book: Jane Austen's *Persuasion*," in Pinch, *Strange Fits of Passion*.

gest in this book's first chapter, free indirect style and third-person narration in general have special pertinence to the problem of thoughts and wishes that cannot withstand the work of articulation, because they leave in question the protagonist's relationship to the thought and speech acts attributed to her and assume no necessary connection between stated and lived experience. Free indirect style is a famously elusive mode, and I am thinking here less of what might be deemed its more obvious instances—free-floating questions, interjections, and self-interruptions readily attributable to the character's wondering consciousness even when not distinctly marked off from the site of narrative enunciation—than of reflective judgments that barely pause to distinguish themselves from the "unconcerned" progress of narrative report.[11] The following passage, for example, grants Fanny a measure of self-consciousness and wit about herself to the precise degree that it maintains the ambiguity as to who is doing the sentencing—Austen or Fanny:

> Fanny, not able to refrain entirely from observing them [Mary and Edmund], had seen enough to be tolerably satisfied. It was barbarous to be happy when Edmund was suffering. Yet some happiness must and would arise, from the very conviction, that he did suffer. (191)

The quick headiness with which the passage disposes of judgment to get on with the happiness suggests that at the end of her first ball even Fanny's thoughts may be dancing. The last two sentences form a kind of chiasm, as the first—an extravagant expression of moral blameworthiness at a temporal coincidence worthier of regret than blame—turns

11. Ironically, the moments when the narrative breaks out into what clearly seems to be Fanny's subjective experience—as in the questions and exclamations puncturing the narration of her discovery of Maria's elopement with Henry ("A woman married only six months ago, a man professing himself devoted, even engaged, to another—that other her near relation—the whole family, both families connected as they were by tie upon tie, all friends, all intimate together—it was too horrible a confusion of guilt, too gross a complication of evil, for human nature, not in a state of utter barbarism, to be capable of! . . . What would be the consequence? Whom would it not injure? Whose views might it not affect?" [299–300])—are often also those in which Fanny seems most to be parroting conduct-book ideology and responding unreflectively, in this instance, not as herself "the near relation" whom Henry has jilted for Maria but as an anonymous scandalized newspaper reader.

without pause, and *without regret,* to a stronger assertion of an invidious causal connection between *x*'s happiness and *y*'s suffering, yet this time free of moral condemnation as such. The passage points to the difficulty of treating free indirect style as the result of a delegation of the work of articulation from a primary to a secondary enunciator, or as the effect of a division of labor between the naive "having" of an experience and its ironic reporting.[12] For the impersonal, agentless, and semipassive construction—"it was barbarous"—and the use, specific to written language, of the auxiliary verbs *must* and *would* to refer not to an imperative or hypothetical condition but to an indefinite happening in time, are not simply markers of narrative detachment from the character's subjective experience; they are also readable as the signs of the latter's own tendency toward queenly, self-absolving, analytic cool. By invoking a sphere of habitual, ordinary, repeated experience, they work to naturalize, render "instinctive" and thereby "guiltless," the very "barbarity" with which the ego derives satisfaction from another's hurt. The sentences do nothing to flatter human nature, except to invoke it as such. If Fanny were to say to some confidante, "It's barbarous [of me] to be happy when Edmund is suffering," she might just as easily be taken as wittily urbane in yoking moral hyperbole to the obviously unperturbed, deflationary "it is" (as if this were not something I was doing but a condition that I could not help), as naive in the sentimental overestimation of her guilt. As it is, the passage offers a glimpse of nonpunitive self-knowledge, according to which Fanny's one claim to virtue would reside not in her moral purity but, on the contrary, in her acceptance, without too much or too loud a protest, of a happiness tainted at its source.[13]

12. For this question see Claude Perruchot's important reflections in "Le style indirect libre et la question du sujet dans *Madame Bovary*."

13. I am indebted here to D. A. Miller's reading of Mary Crawford's "She knew it was her way" (35) as an exception to the usual way of understanding "indirect discourse" in terms of a split between a knowing (because detached) narrator and characters whose "intimate relation to the events" recounted denies them this knowingness (Miller, *Narrative and Its Discontents,* 29–30). Miller's reading instead emphasizes the role characters play in their own deferral of self-identification, as if holding off from self were also a way of enacting selfhood. In the passage in question, the deflection or passing off of judgment and the invocation of habit as a sphere at once inaccessible to self-accounting and fundamental to selfhood belong as much to the character Mary Crawford as to a supposedly free-floating narrator.

Austen's style in this sense lightens the weight of Fanny's moral presence and of the ponderous moralizing messages that might be extrapolated from her story. The rare eruption of the narrative voice in the paragraph cited above—"My Fanny, indeed at this time, I have the satisfaction of knowing, must have been happy" (perhaps the novel's only boast of complete satisfaction in knowledge)—is an exception that proves the rule, for with the nonchalance of an aside, the narrator sweeps away as nothing Fanny's own resistance to her happy end—"in spite of all she felt or thought she felt"—and so casts doubt if not on the authenticity and weight of Fanny's inner life then on her mastery of it.[14] "Thought she felt" gives Fanny away as a conduct-book heroine who only feels for the sufferings of others according to what the rules of the book tell her to feel. Yet the parenthesis expresses humorous affection for a creature who cannot tell the difference even within herself between a genuine and an imagined feeling, at least not as well as her creator. The relaxed tone implies that, whatever the falseness of Fanny's excessively conscientious feelings, Austen is not going to disown her heroine for a hypocrisy she does not even recognize: she, unlike many critics to follow, takes Fanny's inconsistencies in stride.[15]

ii. what a "little spirit of secrecy, and independence, and nonsense" can do

It is not easy to say which has bewildered critics more: Fanny's refusal to do anything to help herself—her dependence on the doings of those around her—or the surprise of her coming into her own despite her-

14. Because the narration's wit belongs, to my ears at least, to the figure of voice that we have come to call "Austen," I am permitting myself, in this case, to collapse authorial identity and narrative voice. Readers such as Galperin, who construe Fanny's "miserable narrator" (*The Historical Austen*, 176) as her uncritical echo and mouthpiece, are compelled to insist on this narrator's difference from Austen, while seemingly ignoring the many instances in which the narrative voice deflates, if it does not puncture, Fanny's claims to moral outrage.

15. We can contrast this leniency to Wollstonecraft's angry criticism of conduct books for promoting not simply self-subservience in women but, worse, moral cynicism. For this and a reading of Fanny's complex and, in part, ironic relationship to the conduct-book heroine see Kirkham, *Jane Austen, Feminism, and Fiction*, 101–6.

self and the corresponding asymmetry that the novel asks us to accept between a passive agent and her active effects. For in her unwillingness to put herself forward and to turn her knowledge to good—what Mrs. Norris calls her "little spirit of secrecy, and independence, and nonsense" (219)—Fanny appears to renege on the Enlightenment promise of "improvement," if by such we understand the hope that what one learns one will pass on to others and that the cultivation of the life of the mind will result in an increase in communicable experience. More than forty years ago, Lionel Trilling noted the awkwardness, indeed rudeness, of Fanny's commitment to personal integrity over the demands of the world, by which he understood both the demands of modern readers for a spirited and active heroine capable of fashioning her own fate, and the claims of Fanny's own body—the capacity for pleasure and sensual experience without which no "modern" self is complete.[16] One sign of the prevalence of this "modern" association of fulfilled desire and activity is the extent to which readers coming after Trilling have tended to continue to understand Fanny's immobility and deficiency of social presence as prudential, disciplinary, and defensive rather than as permissive of a differently lived relation to desire and plot. Even Leo Bersani, whose account of Fanny as a center of "observant stillness" implicitly aligns her with a different mode of being than that of character—namely, Austen's own quietly judging, nonparticipatory narrative presence—identifies this stillness as the "deceptively mild" weapon of an established social order threatened by the menace not simply of class mobility but of "psychological indefiniteness" and ontological instability. Only with Henry James's later novels does the feminine "stillness," the patience and ontological "invalidity," the poor purchase on the world of a Milly Theale begin to signify for Bersani that

16. Trilling's comments on the novel's withdrawal "from the dangers of openness and chance" rarely go unmentioned in discussions of *Mansfield Park* (see Trilling, *The Opposing Self*, 185). His declaration that "Fanny is one of the poor in spirit" has often been mistaken for an identification of Fanny's nonassertiveness with unworldly, Christian selflessness, when, in fact, he interprets this "cautiousness and constraint" as a strategy for survival on behalf of the self (187, 184–85). If his argument "idealizes" Fanny, it is inasmuch as his association of her with the "stoic doctrine of apatheia, the principled refusal to experience more emotion than is forced upon one, the rejection of sensibility as a danger to the integrity of the self" (197), underestimates the degree to which Fanny remains not only overly sensitive to the insensitivity of others but unpleasantly susceptible to feeling for them and in their place.

which, far from containing desire, sets it adrift—an other "otherworldli-
ness" drawing James's male protagonists not back "into an ideal social and
novelistic order, . . . but into a community of passion for which there is
no place in the real world, and for which there is no language in realistic
fiction."[17] Questioning Trilling's impulse to "universalize" Fanny as "one
of the poor in spirit" (Johnson, *Jane Austen*, 95), feminist criticism for its
part has exposed the gender politics underlying the cultivation of these
so-called unworldly virtues—modesty, meekness, self-denial—and has
made it impossible to ignore their very worldly effects in facilitating the
easy reign of paternalistic power.[18]

Critics from Trilling to Bersani and Johnson have thus routinely associated *Mansfield Park* with a conservative, anti-Jacobin ideology of retrenchment, even if, as in Johnson's case, it has been to argue that the
novel unmasks rather than endorses the protective fictions proffered by
Burkean domesticity.[19] Since Fanny appears to champion both "the estab-

17. Bersani, *A Future for Astyanax*, 77, 81. In fact, Bersani presents *Mansfield
Park* as a kind of transitional text: arguing that the Crawfords are as conform-
ist—as effective in upholding the reigning social order—as Edmund and Fanny,
he ends his analysis by suggesting Fanny's fixity may no longer be required or
justifiable as a guarantor of the proper functioning of social order; thus "deprived of any real context," her uncompromising—and now pointless—absten-
tion would anticipate the Jamesian "leap out of self, society, and the novel itself"
(80, 81). At the same time, he argues, Fanny continues to "collaborate" with the
novel's "significant form, in which an episode is always a revealing episode, a
contribution to the single meaningful structure of the entire work" (81).

18. Besides Johnson's, other studies that have highlighted the ideological
framework and effects of Fanny's "antivital" passivity include Kirkham, *Jane Austen, Feminism, and Fiction*; Litvak, "Theatricality in *Mansfield Park*"; and Maaja
A. Stewart, *Domestic Realities and Imperial Fictions*.

19. For *Mansfield Park*'s relation to the earlier anti-Jacobin novels of the turn
of the century as well as to the Jacobin premises of Kotzebue's *Lovers' Vows*, see
also Butler, *Jane Austen and the War of Ideas*, 242–44. As Butler's comparison of
the novel to the evangelical revival of the early nineteenth century suggests, the
complexity of *Mansfield Park*'s political allegiances lies in its two-pronged critique of a corrupt aristocracy (the dissipated Bertrams) and a transformative modernity (the mobile Crawfords). As in the case of evangelicalism's championing
of the "humbler classes," Fanny's Cinderella-like ascendancy buries a potentially
"socially radical" critique of class structure within the conservative nostalgia for
an older, more secure establishment. In *Romantic Austen* Clara Tuite addresses

lished norms of state and family" and the uncharted course of individual reason and personal taste, the question of the novel's conservatism is as vexed as that of the "conservatism" of that other kind of retrenchment— the withdrawal from the claims of community so often associated with Romantic solitude. In this chapter I approach the vexed question of Austen's relationship to her Romantic contemporaries by focusing on their shared ambivalence toward the Enlightenment's revolutionary promise to liberate the human spirit from the "trodden ways" of past authority, to unleash the individual's energies, and to substitute transparent, articulate relations between equals for unspoken, mystified relationships of inequality. Rather than reify Romanticism as a coherent ideological position abstracted from its various contradictory articulations, my argument refers to certain Romantic topoi themselves in tension with Romantic hopes for transcendence and liberation, in particular: the reinterpretation of pastoral retreat as the renunciation of public estimation in favor of pleasures of one's own making, and the modulation of pastoral's turn toward the weak and dispossessed, the unnoticed and overlooked, into a preoccupation with the dangers and privileges of having nothing of one's own. The tensions between Fanny's longing for creaturely comfort and her anxious guarding of what she takes from others correspond, I will argue, to similar tensions between the unknowability of Wordsworthian pathos and its expression through the language of "dearness"—the "mean" or commonly known, familiar, and habitual.[20]

---

this ambivalence by arguing that the novel follows a Burkean strategy of appropriating, "incorporating," and neutralizing antiaristocratic topoi such as sentimentality, the "love of nature," and the critique of artifice; according to Tuite, Fanny's installment represents "a bloodless Protestant coup" (127) along the lines of Burke's vindication of the "bloodless" revolution of 1688 in the *Reflections on the Revolution in France* (see Tuite, *Romantic Austen*, 98–155).

20. The question of whether Austen qualifies as a Romantic, which first received broad critical attention in *Wordsworth Circle* 7 (1976), has often been framed in terms of conflicting views of the thrust—isolating or liberating, revolutionary or reactive—of the Romantic revaluation of the imagination; answers also often depend on how one aligns the terms *Austen, conservatism,* and *Romanticism.* Jay Clayton, for example, assents perhaps too readily to the dichotomy between the solipsism of Romantic visionary experience and the demands of community in order to argue that Austen "is not a romantic" (*Romantic Vision and the Novel,* 60). Arguing, on the contrary, that Austen's texts participate in

In *Mansfield Park* two different discourses provide the terms for this preoccupation with neglected talents and undervalued, underrepresented experiences: (1) the older pastoral tradition of relocating the good life away from the public center of exchange and (2) the conventions of feminine modesty. Both discourses are susceptible to the charge of putting the best face on an ugly world and of encouraging accommodation rather than resistance to oppression by hiding or mystifying power—burying its coercive and constructive effects in the inarticulate conventions and habits of life that constitute Burkean "nature." Thus for Johnson, the "system of female manners," according to which women are expected to choose only what they cannot in any case refuse, reduces choice to a matter of mere form, since coercion couched as persuasion effectively demands and gets the same submission as the violent enforcement of patriarchal authority would. Johnson's criticism uses explicitly anti-Burkean language to dismiss the trappings of power by which its coercive effects come to be experienced as natural: "The system of female manners is supposed to eliminate the need for the nakedness of coercion, and the embarrassment this entails, by rendering women so quiescent and tractable that they sweetly serve in the designs of fathers or guardians without wishing to resist and without noting that they have no choice" (*Jane Austen*, 103). Her wariness of the false consciousness nourished by women's seemingly willing submissiveness—"the 'pretense' of choice . . . enables people to compel others without having to regard themselves as bullies" (102)—recalls

---

Romanticism's "naturalization" of the "country" and the complex social relations defining rural ways of life, Tuite leaves unchallenged the supposedly unambiguous "conservatism" of Wordsworthian lyricism (100). At the same time, in claiming that with Austen the novel begins "to discipline its own disciplining strategies" (83)—to exercise a discipline so "discreet" it might not be felt as such—she also echoes Karl Kroeber, who, less suspicious of the isolating and pernicious effects of the "naturalizing" imagination, first located Austen's romanticism in the imaginative exercises by which her characters make themselves known to one another while maintaining "decorous appearances" and "without the aid of gross and violent stimulants" ("Jane Austen, Romantic," 293). For similar arguments see also Juliet McMaster's "Surface and Subsurface," repr. in McMaster, *Jane Austen the Novelist*, 133–49; and Susan Morgan, *In the Meantime*. In *Jane Austen and the Romantic Poets* William Deresiewicz takes a different approach by setting aside the question of what Romanticism is, to read Austen's novels in relation to certain Romantic writers—Wordsworth, Coleridge, Scott, and Byron.

Wollstonecraft's earlier denunciation of the hypocrisy attending feminine virtue, when modesty, far from expressing a freedom from worldly interests, has become no more than strategy—a means of survival for the weak and dependent. Anticipating Johnson, Wollstonecraft exposes the meaninglessness of praising gentleness in those who cannot do otherwise:

> Gentleness of manners, forbearance, and long-suffering, are such amiable Godlike qualities . . . but what a different aspect [gentleness] assumes when it is the submissive demeanour of dependence, the support of weakness that loves, because it wants protection; and is forbearing, because it must silently endure injuries; smiling under the lash of which it dare not snarl. Abject as this picture appears, it is the portrait of an accomplished woman, according to the received opinion of female excellence, separated by specious reason from human excellence.[21]

As we know from "antipastoral" or realist attacks on pastoral, the same bad faith threatens pastoral's quietist and sentimentalizing tendency to celebrate the absence of worldly ambition in people whose class position in any case denies them access to worldly power.[22]

Unerringly pragmatic in their suspicion of the forms by which the exercise of power mutes and conceals itself, these critiques of feminine manners and pastoral conventions throw into doubt both modesty's and

21. Wollstonecraft, *A Vindication of the Rights of Woman*, 33.

22. We might compare, for example, Gray's lines on the blessedly, coolly self-sufficient villagers—

> Far from the madding crowd's ignoble strife,
> Their sober wishes never learn'd to stray;
> Along the cool sequester'd vale of life
> They kept the noiseless tenor of their way.

—to Crabbe's resounding call for a truthful depiction of rural poverty "in verse":

> No longer truth, though shown in verse, disdain
> But own the Village Life a life of pain. ("The Village" [1783])

Yet, as Stuart Curran has argued, Crabbe's satiric exposition of the miserable conditions of the rural poor, while dismissive of the sentimental piety that would rationalize misery as necessary to virtue, promotes a sentimental vision of its own—that of an "enlightened aristocracy" offering relief to the degenerate poor (see Curran, *Poetic Form and British Romanticism*, 101). Fanny appears to share her author's taste for the poet: Edmund points to a copy of Crabbe's *Tales* in her room.

pastoral's renunciation of ambition. From their perspective Fanny's affirmative passivity—her reticence to seek what she happily takes when offered—must look like bad faith. "Pray, is she out, or is she not?" asks a confused Miss Crawford (36), meaning, "Has she made her formal entry into society? Is she on the marriage market? Can she be addressed, spoken to, made love to?" For Mary Crawford, perplexed by Fanny's shadowy public presence, the answer should be clear because these questions are interchangeable: to have desires is to want to speak them. But for Fanny no such connection can be assumed. Indeed, as other readers have suggested, the novel itself is more willing to credit the intrinsic pleasure of not having to assert oneself, independently of whether or not this reserve conforms to others' expectations. Thus the idea that remaining faithful to one's desires may consist not of voicing but of quieting them, and that their prudent censorship is by no means tantamount to their repression, is at the heart of the objection to the private theatricals at Mansfield Park.[23] The theatricals threaten not to provoke desire in the would-be actors but to betray, in Yeazell's words, the "discipline that otherwise keeps certain 'real' desires prudently unspoken" (150).[24] In this chapter I examine Fanny's powers of reserve and their alignment with diminished prospects through the frameworks of (1) the passive Romantic self whose

23. Critics of *Mansfield Park* tend to concur that the novel complicates the Platonic objection to acting by locating the theatricals' moral threat not in the fact that the characters are playing who they are not, but that they are playing themselves—acting out their own desires. Thus Yeazell cites and agrees with Butler's claim that "the impropriety [of the theatricals] lies in the fact that [the characters] are not acting, but are finding an indirect means to gratify desires which are illicit and should have been contained" (Butler, *Jane Austen and the War of Ideas*, 233; cited in Yeazell, *Fictions of Modesty*, 278n). As Yeazell suggests, the integrity threatened by self-dramatization involves more than choosing to speak only in one's own name—knowing how to leave this name unspoken.

24. Yeazell's subtle reading of Fanny's dilemma over whether to hold out in her refusal to act wonderfully captures modesty's double meaning as, on the one hand, "complaisance" or compliance to the demands of others (a quintessentially hypocritical virtue) and, on the other, fidelity to one's own unseen self. Yeazell's argument persuasively suggests that through Fanny, Austen rescues the second meaning from the first and, by insisting on the insightfulness of Fanny's perspective, defends the existence of a "modest consciousness" against the idea that a modest woman either does not know herself and is unconscious of desire, or is conscious of it but acts in bad faith to conceal that desire.

interiorization of pastoral wastes is in contradiction with Romanticism's own more visionary energies and whose claims for self-sufficiency are interestingly complicated by Fanny's example, and (2) the feminine virtue of modesty, understood not as sexual ignorance nor as compliance to male authority, but as a kind of truthfulness to desires one would not want to assert otherwise—thoughts that one prefers to leave unspoken, otherwise unclaimed or "in the closet."[25]

iii. practicing inconspicuous consumption

Improvement, in its early sense of "the turning of a thing to profit or good account" (*OED*), is, as I have said, that which the Princess of Clèves and the other figures of empty-handedness examined in this study decline to make on their experience of the world, others, or themselves.[26] The

25. Although in some ways quite obviously anachronistic, the trope of the closet describes both Fanny's predilection for remaining unobserved and the systematic blindnesses or inattention of which she is frequently, but importantly not always, the object. In the introduction to *The Epistemology of the Closet* Sedgwick reminds us that the closet is as much the effect of long-practiced and all but effortlessly exerted ways of "not knowing" and refusals of recognition on the part of heteronormative culture as of concerted effort at concealment on the subject's part. Thus a minimum of expectations on the part of those around her, rather than anything she does, guarantees Fanny's safety from public notice. The contradictions attending any "epistemology" or concerted study "of the closet"—of experiences that remain unacknowledged even when known—capture the difficulty described by Yeazell of sustaining (let alone persuading others to believe in) a modest consciousness. It is also this predilection for a secrecy she has neither to defend nor pursue that makes possible a queer reading of Fanny—much more so than her apparent fascination for Mary; as Sedgwick's exemplary "Jane Austen and the Masturbating Girl" shows, the queering of Austen has less to do with identifying vectors of same-sex desire than with tracing forms of onanistic self-absorption—pleasures that, in the case of Marianne Dashwood's, are themselves complicated by their availability for public consumption by other characters. See Sedgwick, *Tendencies*, 109–29.

26. My argument in this section of the chapter draws extensively from Williams's nuanced discussion in *The Country and the City* of *improvement*'s ambiguities. In the care with which it avoids telling a linear story either of unambiguous progress or corruption, Williams's account of the transformation of eighteenth-century rural England is richly suggestive of closer readings of Austen, which he himself does not pursue. See, e.g., Edward Said's "Jane Austen and Empire" (itself originally published in a festschrift for Williams).

capacity for narrative waste—the readiness to let event x lapse before it can lead to subsequent event y—has its ethical analogue, I have argued, in the suspension of the impulse to take revenge on the other's difference or separateness from oneself. In such a mood, one accepts the fading by which the fulfillment of potential may remain indistinguishable from its lapse, as no more of a deprivation than the other's autonomy. We have seen this ethos expressed in various attitudes: in the princess's reticence toward bringing about a success she would happily receive at the hands of fate, in Wordsworth's fidelity to experiences whose value diminishes as soon as he has to assert them. But the question of the limits and, indeed, the desirability of social "improvement" is more acutely relevant to *Mansfield Park*, a novel that differs from the previous works in focusing on the "improvement" of one who begins with nothing to lose, no talent to waste, and who cannot unambiguously claim her independence from others. Indeed, Austen constantly qualifies the separateness by which Fanny quietly knows herself better than others do—what in another character and in another work might be unequivocally admired as a bold integrity and nobility of spirit—with the darker and less flattering senses of both "she has nothing to hide" and "she hides nothing." In a brilliant chapter-end toward the beginning of the novel, for example, Sir Thomas takes leave of his niece with the parting suggestion that she has nothing to show for her six years spent at Mansfield:

> But he had ended his speech in a way to sink her in sad mortification, by adding, "If William does come to Mansfield, I hope you may be able to convince him that the many years which have passed since you parted, have not been spent on your side entirely without improvement—though I fear he must find his sister at sixteen in some respects too much like his sister at ten." She cried bitterly over this reflection when her uncle was gone; and her cousins, on seeing her with red eyes, set her down as a hypocrite. (25)

Where her uncle sees too little, her cousins see too much, as have critics who associate Fanny with Christian selflessness. Her eyes are red from wounded vanity rather than from feigned sorrow at Sir Thomas's departure, but the irony here as throughout the novel is that she can as little hide this wound as get it acknowledged; lacking the means to cover herself, she is also spared the kind of attention from others that would require concealment. Indeed, just as Sir Thomas's words cut her more deeply than he cares to know, the drama of those around her, in particular Edmund and Mary's protracted courtship, affects her more keenly than anyone suspects. Yet while her cousins and the Crawfords must resort to subterfuge to veil their self-interest under cover of good intentions, Fanny—initially credited with nothing of her own and in the uncomfortable position of having to "prove" her worth—is relieved of the need to hide her psychic investments from others. The precarious position by which she remains uncertain of any claim to Mansfield Park as of any hold on the imagination of its inhabitants allows her to keep her love for Edmund a secret and, by extension, keep him to herself.[27]

By contrast the open secret as it works in Lafayette's novel leaves the princess and her interlocutors free to pick up on or ignore one another's meanings. Both novels afford little reason to be optimistic about men's capacity to know women—a capacity premised ironically on both the suspension of inquisitiveness and the deferral of judgment, the readiness neither to demand instruction by direct, empirical means nor to presume to know by conventional wisdom. Yet the princess can at least entertain the hope that Nemours and the prince will exercise their imaginative freedom and credit her with a truth that she cannot demonstrate. One cannot in this sense imagine her exclaiming as Fanny does with the terrible secret conviction of a Shakespearean soliloquy, "Edmund, you do not know *me*" (288). As Susan Winnett has suggested with respect to other novels of manners, one reason for this difference may lie in the novels' different historical contexts: the characters in Lafayette's novel belong to a world whose precarious exclusion of the *tiers état* guarantees the maturity or interpretive autonomy of its members. These trust one another to know and abide by an unwritten, unspoken code of "manners"; troubles

27. Only once, when pressing her for a reason for her refusing Henry, does Sir Thomas come close to extracting the truth from her, but he chooses to interpret her ambiguous blushing and inarticulacy as he wishes: "He paused and eyed her fixedly. He saw her lips formed into a *no*, though the sound was inarticulate, but her face was like scarlet. That, however, in so modest a girl might be very compatible with innocence; and chusing at least to appear satisfied, he quickly added, 'No, no, I know *that* is quite out of the question—quite impossible. Well, there is nothing more to be said'" (214–15). While the lips' *O* fully exposes both the hollowness of Fanny's negation and the "nought" of feminine desire, she is shielded, ironically, by the merely formal nature of Sir Thomas's interrogation. In questioning her he not only assumes a preemptory right to knowledge but arrogates the privilege of interpreting her signs as he chooses and in such a way as to close the question.

arise for the princess precisely because she remains just as uninterested in having to spell out the reasons for her behavior, even when it becomes exceptional. She thus brings into play in an *unprecedented* fashion the imaginative freedom of her interlocutors, but the court remains closed to this transformative possibility.[28]

The decentering of authority in Austen's world opens it, on the other hand, to the kind of change of which Fanny's "improvement" is just one manifestation.[29] *Mansfield Park* suggests in particular that the codification of gender differences in the eighteenth century has produced such narrow expectations of feminine behavior that it is foolish for any woman to rely, as Fanny wants to do at the novel's beginning, on male characters to know and speak her meaning for her. In this sense Fanny's silent recognition of Edmund's failure to know or imagine her as she is represents the highest point in her maturation—her emancipation from a no longer tenable faith in "manners" and the powers of discretion on which they were premised. *Mansfield Park* might thus represent Austen's most bleakly progressive rather than conservative novel: that Fanny still consents to marry one whose imagination has already once failed her only darkens the story of her progress.[30]

28. See Winnett, *Terrible Sociability*, 15–36. Winnett's claim that "a pre-revolutionary mondanité can both pretend and afford to ignore the tiers état" (25), together with her insistence that the world of "mondanité" is immune to the "calamities it generates" (24), can illuminate the contrast between Lafayette's and Austen's novels. In the latter the tiers état intrudes in the form of Fanny herself, and while she appears relatively immune to the "calamities generated" by her plot, the world of *Mansfield Park* does not "emerge unchanged" (17). For a more developed account of Fanny's inoculative effects, see again Tuite, *Romantic Austen*, 98–155.

29. For the argument, pace Trilling and others, that the characters of *Mansfield Park* are open to progressive social change and do undergo moral transformation, see Katie Trumpener's consideration of *Mansfield Park* as an "abolition novel" that "labors to link the causes of gradual abolition and moderate feminism and to disengage both causes from a Jacobinism that has, among its other misdeeds, betrayed abolitionist and feminist interests" (Trumpener, *Bardic Nationalism*, 181).

30. That *Mansfield Park* is both more pessimist and more radical in its feminism than *Pride and Prejudice* can be seen by comparing Fanny's anagnorisis to the scene discussed by Kroeber in which Elizabeth recognizes in Darcy's portrait "a smile over the face as she remembered to have sometimes seen when he looked at her" (cited in Kroeber, "Jane Austen, Romantic," 294).

The object of everyone's neglect, Fanny stands to benefit the most from "improvement"'s recuperative energies even as she appears to embrace the contrary ethos of stasis and immobility. Her double rescue—first at the hands of Mrs. Norris and Sir Thomas from her impoverished family, then at the hands of the narrative from the neglect of these very patrons—recalls the more specific, agricultural sense of "improvement"—"the turning of land to better account, the reclamation of waste, or unoccupied land by enclosing and bringing it into cultivation" (*OED*)—a sense, of course, particularly relevant to the most visible and dramatic manifestation of the progress of agrarian capitalism during the eighteenth century—the movement of enclosure that continued through the century's close. Resistance to "improvement" in this sense amounted not to an indifference to "profitable use" but to a protest at the privatization of "use" and a plea for open lands, wastes and commons that had allowed at least some of the propertyless classes to maintain in Raymond Williams's words "a marginal independence" (*The Country and the City*, 101).[31]

It is, however, "improvement" in the last sense given by Williams that applies most directly to the talk in the novel of remodeling the Rushworth estate and, I will argue, to Fanny's peculiar case: the reinvestment (rather than redistribution) of the new wealth generated by the land's increased productivity into social refinement and cultural capital.[32] Referring also to the less tangible conversion of economic value into moral worth, improvement in this sense, Williams argues, is primarily defensive and reactive inasmuch as it serves to obfuscate the labor necessary to the first kind of improvement: expenditures for aesthetic changes to country estates such as Sotherton, like those incurred in the discharge of charity toward impoverished cousins, channel, conceal, and contain economic progress,

31. Even here, however, opposition to "improvement" might present cases of a hoarding rather than redistribution of wealth, for the term also once referred to the cultivation of land for public revenues rather than for the owner's "own profit." The defense of "wastes" against enclosure and the construal of their openness as a public and shared inheritance present, in this sense, similar contradictions to those that inhere in a character at once so exposed and shielded as Fanny Price.

32. "There is improvement of soil, stock, yields, in a working agriculture. And there is the improvement of houses, parks, artificial landscapes, which absorbed so much of the actually increasing wealth" (Williams, *The Country and the City*, 115–16).

strengthening preexisting class divisions as much as facilitating upward social mobility. The tensions that Williams implies between these two kinds of improvement—productive and consumptive—inform, I want to suggest, the ambiguous and difficult interplay between Fanny's material improvement (the process by which she comes both to exploit and to be exploited by the status quo) and her spiritual recessiveness (the habits by which she cultivates, only to keep to herself, her powers of judgment). The very precariousness of Fanny's source of value accounts for her alliance with the status quo: the best hope for the interloper who begins by not being missed, hardly thought of except when wanted, is to continue not to be noticed, but to become so much a part of the regular course of things that she cannot be dispensed with. The ambiguities latent in any desire to be so naturalized (a desire that underscores the very distance from "nature" and the "norm" it would deny) can explain why Fanny resists being thought of in her own right or desired for her own sake, as the goal or end of Crawford's erotic plot, preferring instead to be valued not for herself but for her association with a fixed and regulated way of life.[33] She identifies with that which no one wants or seeks to acquire anymore but is held dear simply for its having been. Making do with less in *Mansfield Park* thus emerges as a form of worldly pragmatism, a strategy of survival for the arriviste from whom too little is expected rather than too much.

As Williams's *The Country and the City* richly demonstrates, the anti-improvement ideology, of which Fanny is a curious specimen, inevitably invokes an older pastoral world innocent of "modern" acquisitive drives and free of the need for work, coercion, and change. Thus Cowper's proverbial "God made the country and man made the town," puts contentment, stasis, and givenness on the side of divinely ordered nature, and malleability, exploitativeness, and instability on that of the human.[34] Yet as Williams also argues, improvement itself, as a process that is always concealing itself as such, is forever undoing this opposition between the

33. Here Alistair Duckworth's discussion of Austen's engagement with Burke's rhetorical distinction between "improvement" (an organic, gradual, and self-moderating form of change) and "innovation" (a destructive principle with no regard for the value of the past) remains as salient as ever (see Duckworth, *The Improvement of the Estate*, 38–54).

34. The line is from the poet and poem Fanny knows from memory: Cowper's *The Task*, "Book I. The Sofa," line 749 (see Cowper, *Poetical Works*, 145).

God-given and the man-made, the timeless and the new. In the same way, I want to suggest, by taking a creature whose "favourite indulgence" is that of "being suffered to sit silent and unattended to" (153), and showing her to be neither as isolated nor as selfless nor as independent as we might think, Austen gives the lie to the separation of virtue from worldliness. For while *Mansfield Park* may have little faith in the capacity of social relations to do justice to private experience, it has even less faith in the possibility of developing human potential except through social cultivation.

Cowper's lines express the suspicion of acquired rather than naturally bestowed value and of material rather than intrinsic worth that one might think was *Mansfield Park*'s. Following the usual identification of high birth, natural endowment, and moral independence, we might be expected to put the poverty of Fanny's character, her constriction and want of positive social presence, down to her poor beginnings, but ironically by the end her lack is all that makes her fit to live at Mansfield Park. If Mary Crawford and the Bertram sisters, and not Fanny, are "richly endowed by nature," they are therefore merely susceptible to corruption, while Fanny's impoverishment, as Auerbach claims, gives her all the potency of the malleable and makes her sister Susan Price "a girl so capable of being made, every thing good" (284; Auerbach, *Romantic Imprisonment*, 37). Such a crossover is possible because, as Williams points out, the analogy between economic and moral improvement is always a loose one, the terms always being critical of as well as dependent on one another:

> Cultivation has the same ambiguity as improvement: there is increased growth, and this is converted into rents; and then the rents are converted into what is seen as a cultivated society. . . . Jane Austen could achieve her remarkable unity of tone—that lightly distanced management of event and description and character which need not become either open manipulation or direct participation—because of an effective underlying and yet unseen formula: improvement is or ought to be improvement. The working improvement, which is not seen at all, is the means to social improvement, which is then so isolated that it is seen very clearly indeed. (*The Country and the City*, 114)

When Austen gently and ambivalently calls Fanny her own, we sense something that is neither "open manipulation" nor "direct participation." Fanny's flatness—her lack not only of any ability but of any desire to please—makes her both socially inadequate and dependent on others, even as her isolation from them forces Austen to have to reclaim her as "My Fanny."[35]

Austen's calling her so is a sign of both her thorough domestication and continued separateness from those around her. For until the novel's close, "some painful sensation of restraint or alarm" everywhere pervades Fanny's interactions with others; her constant "shrinking," "blushing," and "excessive agitation" betray the presence of coercion and resistance to it in a world that claims to offer only comfort. Inseparable from the larger, less visible processes of cultivation and domestication, the successful calming of such sensations, more than any inner moral strength or wisdom, is the basis of Fanny's final "happiness":

> It is true, that Edmund was very far from happy himself. He was suffering from disappointment and regret, grieving over what was, and wishing for what could never be. She knew it was so, and was sorry; but it was with a sorrow so founded on satisfaction, so *tending to ease*, and so much *in harmony* with every dearest sensation, that there are few who might not have been glad to exchange their greatest gaiety for it. (313; emphasis added)

For a creature most responsive to "the effect of education," most ready to be made, maturity means at best a state at which everything "tends to ease."

By insisting on her malleability, Auerbach associates Fanny's monstrous constructive powers with the creative Promethean energies by which Romanticism is said both to pervert and complete the Enlightenment's

---

35. Here it would be worth pursuing the parallels between "the ignominy of a subject's *hopelessly insufficient social realization*" produced by the "failed, or refused, but in any case shameful relation to the conjugal imperative" that D. A. Miller has identified as the "secret" at "the close heart of Austen Style" (Miller, *Jane Austen, or the Secret of Style*, 28; Miller's italics) and Fanny's own comparable "ignominy," or lack of representative social purchase. Although Miller upholds the contrast between Fanny's fumbling social presence and Austen's masterful style, and identifies Fanny as the very type of female person who, always already castrated of style, is marriageable from the start and thus ironically spared the plot of Emma's or Elizabeth's castration (68), his argument is also suggestive of the ways in which Fanny's social deficiency or underrepresentation acts as both double and cover for Austen's own unrepresentability as "a successfully unmarried woman" (28). Such a relation would go a long way toward explaining Austen's maternal possessiveness.

project of improving humankind and remaking the world according to the new vision of a perfectible human nature. Yet Fanny's disinclination toward doing anything more than assimilating to the status quo is nowhere more evident than in her quick repudiation of the chance to remake Crawford in her image. When Edmund ludicrously proposes that "[Crawford] will make you happy, Fanny, I know he will make you happy; but you will make him every thing" (238), Fanny reacts in horror as if at the sense of Crawford's limitless potential for change; she cannot stomach the utter malleability that "makes him everything to everyone" and by which he is as likely to become her husband as Maria's faithless lover: "'I would not engage in such a charge,' cried Fanny in a shrinking accent— 'in such an office of high responsibility!'" Fanny's excessive modesty may border on the farcical, but however mockingly, Austen seems to support her heroine's "realism"—the prudence by which she turns her back on the potential for "everything" and commits instead to the already existent, the probable and very nearly established.

A lot of what falls under Empson's term *pastoral* depends on this kind of realism for its persuasive power and repeatedly forfeits the chance to use its critique of acquisition to bring into being a world free of exploitation. The same poem that proclaims "God made the country and man made the town," for example, contains enough to put to rest its own fiction of the "country" as a world apart, free of the violence of acquisition and innocent of the ruthless processes by which men extract wealth from one another. As the reader soon discovers, the country is to be celebrated not as a second paradise—a separate space untouched by the ways of men and open to limitless change—but as a place where the long entrenchment of social habits has put virtue within "easy reach":

> Blest he, though undistinguished from the crowd
> By wealth or dignity, who dwells secure,
> Where man, by nature fierce, has laid aside
> His fierceness, having learnt, though slow to learn,
> The manners and the arts of civil life.
> His wants, indeed, are many; but supply
> Is obvious, plac'd within the easy reach
> Of temp'rate wishes and industrious hands.
> Here virtue thrives as in her proper soil;
> Not rude and surly, and beset with thorns,
> And terrible to sight, as when she springs

(If e'er she spring spontaneous) in remote
And barb'rous climes, where violence prevails,
And strength is lord of all; but gentle, kind,
By culture tam'd, by liberty refresh'd,
And all her fruits by radiant truth matur'd.
(Cowper, "The Sofa," 592–607)

Only the long processes of cultivation that in due time have produced "temperate wishes" and "industrious hands" distinguish Cowper's England from the "barbarous climes" where "violence prevails / And strength is lord of all." Critical only of unregulated and naked exploitation, rather than exploitation per se, the lines relinquish pastoral utopianism even as they do another kind of idealism—what we might call its Romantic equivalent: the idea that the self dwells among the "untrodden ways" because it draws its moral and imaginative resources from within itself. Cowper's conception of man as a poor and humble animal that only cultivation can empower expresses, on the contrary, very limited faith in what a person can achieve on her own. But the suggestion that to "cultivate" virtue is to feminize and domesticate it—to limit rather than widen human possibilities—remains complacently disenchanted, and the question of whether or not we admire Cowper's stoic realism is also the question of whether we do Fanny's virtue.

Indeed similar ambiguities surround the affirmative passivity by which Fanny enjoys only a happiness put in "easy reach" and is spared putting her virtue to the test. The degree to which this virtue conforms to her own idiosyncrasies, as well as to her weak position with respect to others, renders it difficult to champion Fanny's example, although we may smile at her good luck. Examples of Fanny's refusal to enlighten those around her include the reserve that for much of the novel puts her in the ambiguous position of befriending a woman she neither respects nor trusts, her silence on Henry and Maria's flirtation, and her refusal to advise Crawford to do on her account what she would happily have him do for himself—act justly toward his tenants. She doesn't try to open Edmund's eyes to Mary's "bad" character (until he has seen for himself, and then he sees worse than she ever did), in part because she doesn't trust her opinion—she has her own reasons for disliking her rival—and in part because he hears only what he wishes to hear from her. When asked by Sir Thomas to justify her refusal of Henry's proposal, she cannot bring herself to compromise her cousins by revealing Henry's empty flirtation with them: "She longed to add, 'but of his principles I have [reason to think ill];' but her heart sunk under the appalling prospect of discussion, explanation, and probably nonconviction" (215). As Austen's gently mocking hyperbole "appalling prospect" suggests, her heroine is discouraged from the effort as much by fear for her own comfort as by the selfless desire to protect her cousins' reputation. Here, as throughout, the novel's wit lies in presenting a heroine who never acts on principle alone but whose rational and disinterested judgments repeatedly dovetail with her secret desires and personal debilities. Austen's "realism"—humanist in its readiness to accommodate human limitations—consists of so qualifying the heroism of a self-effacing virtue with conditions that make it easy to practice that Fanny's example is finally less admirable than merely excusable, humanly forgivable.[36] In this sense, the novel completes the turn away from an emulative ethics already implied at the end of Lafayette's novel by the irony of its last, "throwaway" line—"et sa vie, qui fut assez courte, laissa des exemples de vertu inimitables." Fanny's "examples" are, like the princess's, antiexamples, antithetical to the very project of representative instruction, not because they are "inimitable" in the sense of unsurpassable, impossible to live up to, but only inasmuch as they are "unremarkable," indistinguishable from the ordinary round of acts performed by habit and for the sake of creaturely comforts.

Turning now to a closer reading of Fanny as she moves through the novel, I want to examine that which remains peculiarly uncompromising in Fanny's accommodating presence. I will look, in particular, at her capacity to enjoy for their own sake experiences that are thrust her way and that she is not in any case, according to her understated, all but excluded position, allowed to refuse. Although Austen may highlight the fragility of Fanny's "modest consciousness," she does not disown its claim to such solitary pleasures, taken without explanation and without justification.

36. Other readers to note the alliance between Fanny's self-interest and her virtue include Morgan and D. A. Miller. See the latter's discussion in *Narrative and Its Discontents* (55) of the ways in which Fanny's moral judgments repeatedly provide cover for—permit while neutralizing—more richly motivated emotional responses. Other critics, from Alasdair MacIntyre to, most recently, Anne Crippen Ruderman, have also discussed Austen's nuanced and critical engagement with the Hobbesian assumptions of her day, including the supposed incompatibility of virtue and self-interest. See MacIntyre, *After Virtue*, 210–26; and Ruderman, *The Pleasures of Virtue*.

Instead, the novel invites us to test the persuasiveness of Fanny's insistence—however delicately asserted—that what she values, she values not as a matter of expedience but for its own sake and according to her own taste, even when circumstances (including the desires, expectations, and actions of others) appear to rob her of any choice in the matter.

The ambiguous privileges of Fanny's undervalued and all but forgotten spectatorial position are brought out vividly in the episode at Sotherton, where she is left seated "looking over a ha-ha" (68) while the others come and go, busily chasing one another around the park. Dating from the period of enclosures and described by Walpole as a device freeing the garden from "its prim regularity, that it might assort with the wilder country without," the ha-ha shares in Fanny's in-betweeness.[37] There she is left listening and found "still thinking" in the next chapter, the chapter break working as a kind of brilliant line break to give the sense of time passing and little else happening but Fanny's reabsorption in her own thoughts:

> She watched them till they had turned the corner, and listened till all sound of them had ceased.
>
> [Chapter Break]
>
> A quarter of an hour, twenty minutes, passed away, and Fanny was still thinking of Edmund, Miss Crawford, and herself, without interruption from any one. (69)

But such solitary absorption is very quickly shown to be, like the ha-ha itself, deceptive or deceived. Fanny's corner cannot long remain a solitary seat for quiet thoughts; by the end of the afternoon it has become the one piece of ground everyone has covered, has indeed served as a little theater on which they have each in turn made their appearance and exit. The

---

37. Ann Bermingham cites Walpole in *Landscape and Ideology*, 12. Her account links the economic expansion represented by enclosure to a kind of pastoral retrenchment by which it became neither possible nor necessary to leave the park: "As enclosure proceeded, leaving the 'country without' increasingly less wild, professional gardeners refined the planning of prospects to avoid the raw-looking new enclosures. Brown's and Repton's gardens excluded such unpleasant objects from view while allowing real views of the countryside only if they were pleasing and of a piece with the garden" (14). Repton is, of course, the improver so admired by Mr. Rushworth.

entire charged episode has the feel of an outdoor masque with everyone more or less in on its pointed meanings.[38]

Yet the very predictability of the others' movements (and meanings) seriously undermines any claim to their being, unlike Fanny, really at liberty to wander or change their course. As we later discover, "By their own accounts they had been all walking after each other, and the junction which had taken place at last seemed, to Fanny's observation, to have been as much too late for re-establishing harmony, as it confessedly had been for determining on any alteration" (74). Earlier on, Mary insists, too loudly and obviously, on the serpentine character of their course and on the distance they have come since leaving the house. Ready as always to play the game for all it's worth by pumping ordinary conversation for pointed meanings, she tells Edmund: "'Oh! you do not consider how much we have wound about. We have taken such a very serpentine course; and the wood itself must be half a mile long in a straight line, for we have never seen the end of it yet, since we left the first great path'" (68).[39] Edmund's flat, literal-minded response, his refusal even to meet Mary halfway in her willingness to be more lost than she really is, only makes her flirtation all the more transparent as it forces her to admit to her largely figurative manner of speech:

> "But if you remember, before we left that first great path, we saw directly to the end of it. We looked down the whole vista, and saw it closed by iron gates, and it could not have been more than a furlong in length."

> "Oh! I know nothing of your furlongs, but I am sure it is a very long wood; and that we have been winding in and out ever since we came into it; and therefore when I say that we have walked a mile in it, I must speak within compass." (68)

The darker hollowness of such overreaching claims, the fact that there is no getting lost in this wood in any liberating sense, literal or figurative,

38. See Jay Clayton's comparison of Fanny's structural position—"a still center at the heart of the action"—to the classical trope of a locus amoenus (Clayton, *Romantic Vision and the Novel*, 65).

39. Numerous readers have remarked on Mary's "strained" or failed invocation of Romance topoi, in particular the Spenserian Wandering Wood of "Forest of Dalliance" (see, e.g., Edwards, "The Difficult Beauty of Mansfield Park," 53). Reading and exploiting the landscape to her advantage, Mary might also be read as a potential feminist, but her exploitativeness wins her no greater reward than Edmund's woodenness.

is not really felt until we hear them against the quiet but brilliant under-statement made on Fanny's part: "She seemed to have the little wood all to herself" (71). The statement captures the quietness of Fanny's thoughts about herself and is indirect because she cannot reflect on herself without betraying the awkwardness and delicacy of her position. She cannot as-sert her sense of solitude because it is a sense of false solitude—it includes the knowledge that the others are in the wood somewhere, only not with her. This is the force of the word *seemed*—the only clue to an otherwise wonderfully mastered jealousy. Unable to communicate what she is not powerless to know, Fanny in every sense belongs to and is mistress of the "little wood," even as it continues to contain the others. The wood is "little" in the sense of being manageable on a human scale, as well as in the sense of being capable of only very limited expansion; a measure of its having been humanized, domesticated, and peopled with others, its very littleness at the same time affords Fanny the illusion of having it all to herself.

The same muted irony and bemused, all but jealous, wonder inform the single, passing comment, "She found herself more successful in send-ing away, than in retaining a companion" (73). In merely keeping her solitary seat, Fanny finds herself involuntarily, if gently, enforcing a regu-lar and regulating social pattern. The reduction of the others' movements to this working, recognizable pattern is, in effect, the work of her own reduced perspective, however isolated this may be.[40] Through this per-spective Fanny can present herself as not only free from the others' expan-sive, imaginative impulses but as somehow truer to the wood's (and the world's) very limited (and so real) potential. Quietly availing herself of the already existent, Fanny inhabits a domesticated wilderness chiefly attrac-tive for its "realism"—its oddly moral power to be satisfied with less.

iv. virtue and the felicitous circumstance

Although Austen's use of the word *dear* underscores the word's capacity to make one wince under the very banality of the affection it has come to express—"The room was most dear to her" (106); "Dear Fanny! now I shall be comfortable" (304); "as dear to her heart" (321)—she nevertheless

40. Thus Auerbach can speak of the "compelling blighting power of Fanny's spectatorship at Sotherton," of her "solitary animosities against the intricacies of the normal" (*Romantic Imprisonment*, 24), as if Fanny were herself responsible for such simplification.

refuses to despise as mean that which is called "dear" because it ministers to material comforts. Fanny's consolations, unlike Wordsworth's, derive not from within herself, or from daily intercourse with Nature, but from a flatly unimaginative memory of specific actions committed by others on her behalf. Thus even as she exposes the excessiveness of her heroine's gratitude for what is after all next to nothing—kindnesses that cost their owners very little—Austen insists on the limited but very tangible grounds for Fanny's satisfaction:

> So thought Fanny in good truth and sober sadness, as she sat musing over that too great indulgence and luxury of a fire up stairs—wondering at the past and present, wondering at what was yet to come, and in a nervous agitation which made nothing clear to her but the persuasion of her being never under any circumstances able to love Mr. Crawford, and the felicity of having a fire to sit over and think of it. (223)

The sentence wickedly and delightfully accords the same weight to "the persuasion" of never being able to love *X* and the "felicity of having a fire to sit over and think of it": on the one hand, the absolute purity of the modest heroine who, knowing her own mind, insists on the freedom of her desire and refuses "under any circumstances" to prostitute herself before the world, on the other hand, the circumstantial happiness of being unexpectedly provided with the comfort of a fire—not an extraordinary blessing but something that should have been part of the normal course of things if Sir Thomas had only assured himself earlier of Fanny's comfort. Austen's quietly satirical tone denies the incompatibility of imaginative freedom and worldly accommodation and the need to sacrifice the one to the other.

Yet if we cannot dismiss Fanny as a selfless and unworldly exemplum of modesty who keeps herself "a gem of purest ray serene," we can wonder at her remorselessness in accepting social conventions as all one needs to know and live by. "Fix, commit, condemn yourself" (288)—she is devastatingly complete and summary in her prescriptive vision of Edmund's marriage to Mary, and she would more sincerely but no less harshly condemn Crawford to marriage so as to be forever free from his direct, personal advances: "Quite unlike his usual self, he scarcely said anything. He was evidently oppressed, and Fanny must grieve for him, though hoping she might never see him again till he were the husband of some other woman" (248). For such a shy and reticent creature whose manner is "incurably gentle" (222), she is herself bitingly dismissive and unabashedly inflexible in her limited conception of the possible forms of interaction between men and women.

Fanny's inability or refusal to deal with others directly makes her curiously dependent on everyday "comforts" and conventions. So based on material, contingent circumstances, such safety or protection remains precariously thin and leaves her acutely vulnerable to Crawford's pressing advances as open violations of her bodily privacy: "In vain was her 'Pray, Sir, don't—pray, Mr. Crawford,' repeated twice over; and in vain did she try to move away—In the same low eager voice, and the same close neighbourhood, he went on, re-urging the same questions as before. She grew more agitated and displeased" (232). The disproportion between the intensity of Fanny's discomfort at Crawford's closeness and the indifferent or innocent means by which she gets out of that "close neighbourhood" makes it difficult to know how seriously we are meant to take her sense of danger:

> Fanny could hardly have kept her seat any longer, or have refrained from at least trying to get away in spite of all the too public opposition she foresaw to it, had it not been for the sound of approaching relief, the very sound which she had been long watching for, and long thinking strangely delayed.
>
> The solemn procession, headed by Baddely, of tea-board, urn, and cake-bearers, made its appearance, and delivered her from a grievous imprisonment of body and mind. Mr. Crawford was obliged to move. She was at liberty, she was busy, she was protected. (233–34)

The sense in this comic and welcome relief is that such protection—such business—is enough for now (and for as long as need be) to guarantee her liberty. The simple relation of fact—"Mr. Crawford was obliged to move"—expresses a pragmatic readiness to take the effect without worrying the cause (Fanny neither wants to nor needs to know more), while the quick succession of the three short anaphoric clauses leaves no time to question the implied identification of usually opposed terms—liberty, work, and protection.[41] The arrival of the tea things may warm our hearts

41. In one brief staccato-like sentence, Austen dispenses with what Geoffrey Hill calls the "matter of how to relate *otium* to *negotium*." By redefining in terms of the servant's relation to her masters what is usually presented as a problem of the poet's relation to his patrons and readers, Austen can locate "liberty"

to the extent that we enjoy "coming down" from Crawford's high-flown rhetoric of love to the more familiar and mundane, but, as in the moment when Fanny muses over the "felicity" of having a fire, this homecoming involves an implicit switch from the high moral sense of "liberty," as of freedom and integrity of body and mind, back to what is for Williams the earlier, economic sense of "improvement." Thus Austen can say in one breath: "She was at liberty, she was busy, she was protected," the shortness and succinctness of these phrases, their interchangeability and equality of meaning, making it impossible to separate Fanny's impoverished sense of inner self from her adequacy to Mansfield Park.

Lacking the means with which to "express herself" from within, Fanny reinforces and takes sustenance from preexisting social models. Yet her dependence on social conventions in no way contradicts her feelings of social alienation; something deeply radical and all her own remains in her resistance to being directly addressed in public, in her extreme agitation and displeasure at Mr. Crawford's "close neighbourhood." Behind this resistance to public attention is an unwillingness to assume the burden of making her own thoughts, desires, and pleasures known and accountable to public judgment. At worst, this amounts to a hermetic and solipsistic retreat from the claims of community. At best, Fanny's predilection for remaining in public without being seen makes her a representative of the liberal fantasy of a public space hospitable to the unstated preferences of its members and defined not by formal contract, but by the implicit willingness of each to credit the others' powers of judgment and discretion over their own desires and pleasures, however publicly occasioned.

Looking once more at Fanny as she does not like to be looked at, we can see her quietly insisting on an unremarkable or invisible contentment, on the right to an unshared and uncommunicated enjoyment of public things. Auerbach may be right in suggesting that in replacing "common and convivial feasting with a solitary and subtler hunger that possesses its object," Fanny becomes an image of the solitary and anonymous modern reader (*Romantic Imprisonment*, 28). But Austen's wit in *Mansfield Park* is always to stage these readings in public, as in the extraordinary

---

in "the middle ground of circumstance, the field of brokerage, negotiation and compromise" (Hill, *The Enemy's Country*, 4, 11). The sentence's quickening pace suggests volumes about the servant's indifferent contempt for the master's unwanted attentions and the relief found in a type of work that does not call her person into account.

scene where she has Edmund watch Fanny, thinking herself unwatched, really for once forget herself in becoming interested in Crawford's reading aloud:

> Edmund watched the progress of her attention, and was amused and grati-fied by seeing how she gradually slackened in the needle-work, which, at the beginning, seemed to occupy her totally; how it fell from her hand while she sat motionless over it—and at last, how the eyes which had appeared so studiously to avoid him throughout the day, were turned and fixed on Craw-ford, fixed on him for minutes, fixed on him in short till the attraction drew Crawford's upon her, and the book was closed, and the charm was broken. Then, she was shrinking again into herself, and blushing and working as hard as ever. (229)

If there is a lost potential to be recuperated from *Mansfield Park*, as Gray's flower "born to blush unseen, / And waste its sweetness on the desert air," it may be in those few lost minutes of irrecoverable, utterly private "charm" Fanny in effect steals from Crawford. Forcing her to put down her work, this momentary surrender of freely given attention leaves her socially and economically useless. While the length and tempo of the first sentence reproduce the "progress" of Fanny's "gradual slackening," the passage, narrated from Edmund's limited and misinterpreting point of view, describes only the precise effects of Henry's reading on her con-centration, so that we ourselves remain excluded from the action (both the content of the speeches of *Henry VIII* from which Henry is read-ing and Fanny's experience of them), knowing it only negatively, by the slowing down of time and work. This elision of the actual and positive content of experience mediates between, on the one hand, the scene in the garden at Coulommiers where the Princess of Clèves, thinking herself unwatched, gives herself up to the onanistic labor of winding ribbons around Nemours' cane, and, on the other, Dickinson's "The Missing All," in which the speaker contents herself with a negative experience of the world measured by her fixed and downward attention on her work.

Significantly, the charm breaks when Crawford, returning Fanny her gaze, threatens to exact payment for and demand a return on her en-joyment; like Nemours and the prince's spy, both he and Edmund ex-pect to harness this free energy to the progress of the conventional erotic plot. Fanny's retreat into her habitual "shrinking" and "blushing" and "working" as soon as Crawford's eyes "fix" on hers corresponds to the requirements of female modesty, but this retreat also foils the attempt to exploit (to make something of) her freely given attention. She insists, however wordlessly and fleetingly, that certain pleasures and emotions need never be reintegrated into conventional social intercourse, because they derive not from reciprocal relations between fellow humans, still less from the endbound courtship of men and women, but from asymmetrical exchanges between actors and listeners, performers and readers. Here again the novel asks us to reconsider its heroine's far-from-straightforward condemnation of the imaginative license represented by the ill-fated theatricals. For whereas her cousins exploit their theatrical roles as a covert means to realize their own desires, Fanny wants to enjoy "good reading" without being bound to emulate it in life.[42] Claiming moral maturity, she

42. See Brodsky's claim that "only Fanny steers clear of acting on the 'grounds' of 'pleasure,' but solely by remaining clear of the narrative's own action" (*The Imposition of Form*, 162). Taken out of context, Brodsky's wording points to an ambiguity perhaps fundamental to the trope, traced throughout this book, of experiences received and enjoyed on condition of their not being acted on. At a first level, the phrase says that only Fanny does not pursue pleasure but acts on other grounds; whether this means commending her for regulating her action according to higher principles (virtue, duty, etc.) or querying her as a hypocritical killjoy who has only a secret relation to pleasure, the assumption is that the proper or expected relation to pleasure is its pursuit: by not acting on its grounds, not seeking to have more of it, she is depriving herself of pleasure, not allowing herself a straight relation to it. But the phrase might also be glossed as "only Fanny does not instrumentalize her pleasure," in which case only she maintains the "right" relation to pleasure, since pleasure does not in the first place want to be acted on—does not need for its enjoyment to become the grounds of an end-oriented plot. In this sense she would obliquely rejoin flirts such as Henry, who enjoys the theatricals not for the ends to which they might lead but, as Miller points out, precisely for the little deferrals and postponements of the settlement of narrative closure—"Always some little objection, some little doubt, some little anxiety to be got over. I never was happier" (154). In *Narrative and Its Discontents*, Miller argues that Austen's novel, like Fanny herself, follows the structure of Freudian negation in bringing forward "a fascinated delight with unsettled states of deferral and ambiguity" on condition that such delight is ultimately "repudiated" (63–66). Within this paradigm, "experiences received only as long as declined" reads as a kind of compromise formation, as in "you can have them only under cover and as long as they don't ultimately disturb the established course of things." Yet the relation between inconsequence and pleasure can also present itself as causal rather than merely conditional, as in "experiences

asks, like the princess, to be entrusted with feelings on which she has no intention of acting. This insistence on the separation of taste from life, as of pleasure from plot, may sound incongruent in a character who otherwise makes only lifelong commitments, but it belongs to the same appeal to the value of personal liberty that Austen puts, however paradoxically, in the mouth of the one least assured of, and indeed the least interested in achieving, economic self-sufficiency. If Fanny prefers to take without asking rather than call attention to her unmet demands, it is not, as Mrs. Norris claims, from a "little spirit of secrecy, and independence, and nonsense" (219), but from an appreciation of the value of discretion—the felicity of trusting others with enough insight to be spared the work of having either to hide from or "represent" oneself to them.

Thus in the same way Fanny does not wait to have secured a position of autonomy to claim the prerogative of her judgment in her immediate and avowedly prejudicial refusal of Henry Crawford. Surprising in one with so weak a sense of (and, indeed, basis for) entitlement, the commitment to the form that actions take in her own mind, whatever the expedience of circumstances, informs her most resounding speech on behalf of women's freedom of choice: "How then was I to be—to be in love with him the moment he said he was with me? How was I to have an attachment at his service, as soon as it was asked for?" (240). In this sense Edmund and his uncle are right in thinking that Crawford need only bide his time, but not because her negative is merely formal and hides an affirmative that is ready and waiting for him. Rather time alone can provide the terms on which she might reconcile herself to marrying Crawford. This same commitment to the prerogative of her own judgment—even if it is one subject to temporal revision—lies at the heart of her silence regarding her reasons for not marrying Crawford. She astounds Sir Thomas by refusing even to explain a choice so apparently irrational and careless of the welfare of her impoverished brothers and sisters: "She had hoped that to a man like her uncle, so discerning, so honourable, so good, the simple acknowledgment of settled *dislike* on her side, would have been sufficient. To her

---

enjoyed only because and in the course of being left unpursued." Accepting as inevitable the "moral casuistry" (Miller, *Narrative and Its Discontents*, 55) that allows one to accept, when "free," pleasures for which one would refuse to incur moral damage, Austen, Miller's analysis suggests, flirts with the flirts, and perhaps never more so than when relying on contingency and circumstance, rather than a principled aestheticism, to guarantee pleasure its heady emptiness.

infinite grief she found it was not" (215). She would like to be taken at her word, but this is just what she doesn't have to give. Whatever her delusions regarding Sir Thomas's powers of discernment, however, feminist reason thoroughly vindicates Fanny here, since we know that she has legitimate cause to doubt Crawford's seriousness and every reason not to tell Sir Thomas of a previous sentimental engagement that she thoroughly intends to give up. The thought that the "acknowledgment of settled *dislike*" ought to be "sufficient," although indistinguishable for Sir Thomas from sheer willfulness, represents an essential if easily missed implication of Wollstonecraft's argument for treating women as rational creatures. Crediting women with reason means precisely that one will not ask them for reasons but trust their independent powers of judgment. A woman's choices, if reasonable, we can almost hear Fanny thinking, do not require the defense even of reason and should be accepted without the exhausting work of "discussion, explanation, and probable nonconviction" (215).

v. conclusion: waiting on "what time will do"

The insistence on a more than ironic—a necessary and causal—link between the enjoyment of a fulfilled inner life and the readiness to forgo such fulfillment if it does not readily offer itself belongs, as we have seen, to the ethos of passivity that Empson associates with pastoral's tone of contented resignation: "It is only in degree that any improvement of society could prevent wastage of human powers; the waste even in a fortunate life, the isolation even of a life rich in intimacy, cannot but be felt deeply. . . . Anything of value must accept this because it must not prostitute itself; its strength is to be prepared to waste itself, if it does not get its opportunity" (Empson, *Some Versions of Pastoral*, 5). In an earlier chapter, I cited this passage with respect to the aristocratic ethos of grace as form adumbrated by Lafayette's *La Princesse de Clèves*, one of whose ironies is to expose the costliness of such economy, as the prudent censoring of all but costless desire quickly yields to its opposite, the readiness to lay oneself to waste. Indeed, the passivity with which Fanny receives a happy end that she has done nothing to bring about deserves comparison to the self-possession with which Lafayette's heroine walks away from an end (consummation of her love in marriage) that she has herself made possible. Fanny has done nothing except nothing itself, for which she earns the wrath of Mrs. Norris, who "could have charged [her] as the daemon of the piece. Had Fanny accepted Mr. Crawford, this could not have happened" (304).[43] By refusing Crawford without convincing anyone of the definitiveness of this refusal, Fanny puts everyone, characters and readers alike, in the position of waiting, in Mme de Clèves' words, to "see what time will do" ("Attendez ce que le temps pourra faire" [*La Princesse de Clèves*, 175]). In both heroines, we find what I have argued is ultimately only an apparently contradictory rigidity and pliability arising from a double valuation of time—an attachment to prior relations on no more solid a basis than their priority, and a susceptibility to a revision of judgment or change of heart on no more arguable a basis than the passing of time; both heroines wish to honor temporal difference in two seemingly opposed but ultimately inseparable senses—first, in remaining open to the difference the "mere" passage of time *may* make and, second, in giving weight (undue weight in the opinion of those around them) to the temporal form or order that events have taken in their minds—a tendency that leaves them moored on the rocks of what time has done for them. Thus the formal decorum or tact that keeps the princess from ignoring the sequence of events by which she has come to be in a position to take her lover for a second husband, goes hand in hand with the ambiguity of her final gesture of dismissal—half-weary, half-relenting—by which she qualifies her refusal of Nemours as provisional and potentially revisable,

43. The precise chronology of events put into place by Austen appears to corroborate Mrs. Norris here: had Fanny accepted Crawford's proposal to take her from Portsmouth back to Mansfield—a proposal she was inclined to accept for the sake of her own comfort, whatever her distaste for the company—he could not have prolonged his renewed flirtation with Maria to the point of its disastrous consequences; in retrospect, Fanny's decision not to decide for herself the terminus of her stay in Portsmouth but to wait for her uncle's summons seals the fate of all: "Happily, however, she was not left to weigh and decide between opposite inclinations and doubtful notions of right; there was no occasion to determine, whether she ought to keep Edmund and Mary asunder or not. She had a rule to apply to, which settled every thing. Her awe of her uncle, and her dread of taking a liberty with him, made it instantly plain to her, what she had to do. She must absolutely decline the proposal. If he wanted, he would send for her" (296). With an economy of means reminiscent of Lafayette, Austen's narrative makes ironically efficient the submissive deferral to a patriarchal authority that has already repeatedly proved wanting: given his habitual negligence, Sir Thomas might well have kept Fanny waiting forever but for the sequence of events her waiting puts into motion.

according to "what time will do." "How wonderful, how very wonderful the operations of time, and the changes of the human mind!" Fanny expostulates apropos a hedgerow that over time has come to be used as an ornamental walk, as if inviting us to muse on the way she, too, has unobtrusively made herself valuable as a convenience and ornament to those who may soon be "almost forgetting what it [she] was before" (143). Not surprisingly, this reflection on the mind's readiness to be "almost forgetting" is what prompts Fanny's famous tribute to the faculty of memory; her sensitivity to the passing of time includes both her appreciation of that peculiarly unexpected type of "improvement" wrought by time alone and her disinclination to give up a prior attachment that is itself already a "second" love—the effect of a transplantation—and it is with no small irony that Austen uses one of so "retentive" a memory to create suspense over the novel's final issue and to keep in play a sense of the arbitrariness with which one ending is finally chosen over another.[44] Readers anxious that Henry win his suit might as well despair as hope from the fact that she has already transferred her affections once from Portsmouth to Mansfield, and from William to Edmund: because she has once, she might again; because she already has, she can't a second time.[45]

44. Among the responses of Austen's contemporaries to the novel, the following can be taken as exemplary of the experience of a sustained uncertainty as to final issue: Mr. J. Plumptre.—"I never read a novel which interested me so very much throughout. . . . The plot is so well contrived that I had not an idea till the end which of the two wd marry Fanny, H.C. or Edmd" (cited in *Mansfield Park* [1998], 377). One instance of the ways in which Austen teases readers eager to have Fanny "really" improve by changing her mind about Henry is the chapter-end following Henry's visit to Portsmouth, when the pair's springtime walk together within view of the sea appears to open the novel unto previously unperceived horizons, and we assume Henry is appearing to Fanny in a new light; indeed he is—this is how Austen closes the chapter: "Not considering in how different a circle she had been just seeing him, nor how much might be owing to contrast, she was quite persuaded of his being astonishingly more gentle, and regardful of others, than formerly. And if in little things, must it not be so in great? So anxious for her health and comfort, so very feeling as he now expressed himself, and really seemed, might not it be fairly supposed, that he would not much longer persevere in a suit [pursuit] so distressing to her?" (281).

45. Deresiewicz problematically assumes no one reads from Fanny's perspective, not even preadolescent girl readers, whereas my guess is that the trick to coming to accept the novel's end is always to have done so—from the age of ten onward.

The two possibilities correspond to what one might call lyric and novelistic economies of time—the one open and abundant, the other closed and scarce. Deresiewicz's intriguing claim that Austen puts the general reader who has hoped to have Fanny marry Henry, and Mary Edmund, in the position of having to read the novel twice so as to learn, Edmund-like, to "get used to" the deflection of his hopes, opens up the question of whether Austen's chosen form, the novel, is in fact capable of accommodating the recessive "plot" of accommodation—of getting used to x through habit—if what novels do best is to plunge readers (no matter how often they reread) into the single, unfolding series of the characters' immediate and vividly present "now"s. Whether or not one wishes to demystify it as ideology, "naturalization"—the double recession of desire into time and time into desire by which a particular arrangement might come to feel simultaneously natural and chosen—remains particularly elusive to novelistic representation. Instead, in an extraordinary passage detailing Fanny's marking time without object in her father's house in Portsmouth before the newspaper announcement of Julia's elopement comes to her and to the plot's rescue, Austen comes close to representing naturalization's obverse: the permanent alienness of time when, the movement of plot normally impelling narrative forward temporarily suspended, time neither fades into habitual routine nor moves toward teleological fulfillment:

> She was deep in other musing. The remembrance of her first evening in that room, of her father and his newspaper came across her. No candle was *now* wanted. The sun was yet an hour and half above the horizon. She felt that she had, indeed, been three months there; and the sun's rays falling strongly into the parlour, instead of cheering, made her still more melancholy; for sun shine appeared to her a totally different thing in a town and in the country. Here, its power was only a glare, a stifling, sickly glare, serving but to bring forward stains and dirt that might otherwise have slept. There was neither health nor gaiety in sun-shine in a town. She sat in a blaze of oppressive heat, in a cloud of moving dust; and her eyes could only wander from the walls marked by her father's head, to the table cut and knotched by her brothers, where stood the tea-board never thoroughly cleaned, the cups and saucers wiped in streaks, the milk a mixture of motes floating in thin blue, and the bread and butter growing every minute more greasy than even Rebecca's hands had first produced it. (298)[46]

46. For a discussion of this passage in terms of Fanny's revulsion for "dirt" see Yeazell, *Fictions of Modesty*, 160.

The passage does not so much indicate the limits of Fanny's adaptability or capacities for sentimental reattachment as move toward Flaubertian ennui her habitual meditative "stuckness"—her close relationship to place that makes her, in Bersani's phrase, a "center of observant stillness" (*A Future for Asyntax*, 77), a kind of muted genius loci wherever she goes. Such a move permits, in the absence of plot- or character-determined action, a different kind of excitement: the prose's momentarily vivid attention to a materiality to which the presence of figurative consciousness contributes little but the dim perception of time passing.

"The irreversibility of time constitutes an objective moral criterion," writes Adorno, in an aphorism entitled "Morality and Temporal Sequence" of *Minima Moralia*, well aware of the scandal such a concession to so arbitrary a determinant as temporal order poses to rational assumptions about justice, freedom, and moral worth (78). According to Adorno, literature has neglected, on account of its obviousness, the phenomenon of prior engagement or *Besetztseins* (literally the state of being occupied, already taken), as when "a loved person refuses herself" for no better reason than that "a relation already exists that excludes another."[47] Yet *Mansfield Park* would seem to treat exactly of such a theme, at least to the extent that the frustration it routinely elicits from readers derives in large measure from the way it allows "abstract temporal sequence" to play "the part one would like to ascribe to the hierarchy of feelings" and gives priority to the "accidental element" in erotic object choices over the "claims of freedom."[48] Thus Fanny persists in preferring to someone who might love her "for her own sake," whatever this might mean, her former "champion," who for most of the novel only values her company metonymically or associatively—as someone with whom he can talk about another woman. The preference belongs to her more general habit—evident in her taking possession of the schoolroom whose "furniture she would not have changed for the handsomest"—of valuing objects as "hand-me-downs," not according to their intrinsic or original worth, but metonymically, according to their susceptibility of temporal

47. Adorno, *Minima Moralia*, 86.

48. This is one way in which we might understand Austen's famous claim that the subject of *Mansfield Park* is "ordination"—as a kind of shorthand for the problematic of choosing what is already the case, in this case: choosing a profession decreed not by merit or desire but by the fortuitousness of temporal order and the [ill] luck of being born second or third rather than first.

"endearment," and of cherishing past experiences associatively, not for the happiness they may once have yielded on the instant, but for the oddly vague definiteness with which they have laid a claim to being, earning by virtue of their "recurrence" and proximity to other moments a minimal edge over the merely hypothetical, abstract, or speculative:[49]

> She could scarcely see an object in that room which had not an interest-ing remembrance connected with it.—Every thing was a friend, or bore her thoughts to a friend; and though there had been sometimes much of suffering to her—though her motives had been often misunderstood, her feelings dis-regarded, and her comprehension under-valued; though she had known the pains of tyranny, of ridicule, and neglect, yet almost every recurrence of ei-ther had led to something consolatory: her aunt Bertram had spoken for her, or Miss Lee had been encouraging, or what was yet more frequent or more dear—Edmund had been her champion and her friend;—he had supported her cause, or explained her meaning, he had told her not to cry, or had given her some proof of affection which made her tears delightful—and the whole was now so blended together, so harmonized by distance, that every former affliction had its charm. The room was most dear to her. . . . (106)

Whether or not directly referring to this passage, readers have usually un-derstood as a doubly compensatory strategy of accommodation—as a plot

49. One might also argue that faded and worn, such furnishings as "the faded footstool of Julia's work, too ill done for the drawing room" (106), have lost their material edge and are valued precisely as remnants of a material existence that has become easy to ignore as such; this ambiguity—the uncertainty of whether long use, proximity, and companionship give things more or less of a purchase on "being"—informs various readings of Fanny's guardianship of wastes: thus Emily Hipchen, in her essay "Accounting for Fanny," reads Fanny's sentimental attachment to "trash" as a form of miserliness, at once divorced from any ob-jective grounds and excessively materialistic, while in Deresiewicz's account the objects themselves are far less important than the workings of Fanny's Words-worthian memory, which does not so much retain accurate impressions as "sub-stitute" for them a self-deceptive harmony (*Jane Austen and the Romantic Poets*, 59–60). As I discussed in greater detail in an earlier version of this chapter (see François, "Open Secrets"), and as Deresiewicz has more recently argued, it is not by accident that the East room contains a transparency of Tintern Abbey, for the sentimental bonds with which Fanny covers up and eases her sense of having been "misunderstood," "disregarded," and "under-valued" recall Wordsworth's similarly conciliatory efforts in the poem.

by which she gives to herself what the world denies her—Fanny's tendency first to identify with and attach herself to experiences others would normally wish to forget as quickly as possible, and then to remember such lessons according to the transformative workings of her memory, rather than according to their original unpleasantness. Thus criticism, as if mimicking the associative slippage from affliction to charm Austen describes above, slides easily from the notion that Fanny masochistically clings to the memory of past slights and injuries to the claim that she remembers only in bad faith, substituting imaginary value for real privation. Yet that the self may come to value things, persons, and experiences simply for having known them on a daily basis and as part of a quotidian order— to value them indeed because it has become possible to take them for granted—represents, according to a line of skeptical empiricist thought running from Hume to Burke and Wordsworth, an ordinary and nonpathological human experience—one hinted at in the cumulative tempo of the accretive clauses in the passage above, where "frequency" and "dearness" emerge as exchangeable rather than, as one might assume, exclusive terms.[50] In this sense, the salience of comparing Austen and Wordsworth lies for me less in the revisionist fantasies of accommodation that Fanny seems to have learned from the Wordsworth of "Tintern Abbey," than in the question that seems to have fascinated both writers regarding the contingency of our moral attachments to the world: that of how repetition can work as both the complement and antidote to realization, as

50. Although Austen could not have read them, relevant here would be Wordsworth's lines, from Book I of the 1850 *Prelude*, describing the process by which scenes of "vulgar joy" became "By the impressive discipline of fear, / By pleasure and repeated happiness, / So frequently repeated, and by force / Of obscure feelings representative / Of things forgotten," "*Habitually dear;* and . . . by invisible links / Were fastened to the affections" (*The Fourteen-Book Prelude*, 1.581, 603–12; emphasis added).

By having Fanny put her commemorative imagination to such a bland, singularly unimaginative use, restricting its exercise to the simultaneous retention and effacement of what has been, Austen makes her a peculiar caricature of the double default on history as revolutionary promise and history as representative record, of which Wordsworth is often accused. For a discussion of the Burkean aspects of Wordsworth's attachment to past and habitual experiences see David Bromwich, *A Choice of Inheritance*, 43–78. For the question of Wordsworth's ambivalence toward the gently binding power of "habit," see also my "To Hold in Common and Know by Heart."

familiarization can to abstraction, such that processes of diminishment, fading, distancing, and recession seem both to strengthen and weaken the hold persons and phenomena have on one. Elsewhere I have suggested that what marginal claim already existing beings might have over abstract forms of potential life derives less from their anteriority considered likewise in the abstract, as from their simply taking and having taken time—their not being exhausted in the single present instant—something of which their historicity is a sign.[51] With the passage of enough time, Fanny's marginal proprietary claims to "what nobody else want[s]"—the East room, Edmund's mare, Edmund himself, eventually even Mansfield Park—become "generally admitted," as things are simply given up and over to her "use," long before being formally relinquished by their legal owners.[52] Rather than read this transvaluation as signaling the "originality" or perverseness of her psychology of desire, as in "she can appreciate x if no one else can," we might understand this gradual reoccupation and taking possession of "what nobody else wants [anymore]" as realigning "dearness" or affective value not with desire, understood as expectancy on what is yet to come, but with commonness as a love for the existent poor of every claim to value except that of having been and capacity to be again, deprived even of the tantalizing promise of an unknown quantity, except that of what time might do if it had not already done.

According to the dialectical movement of Adorno's aphorism, that which begins as a principled refusal of change—a deference to the right of

51. See François, "'O happy living things!'"; as a polemic against the "improvement" on time, and on having to wait for it, promised by today's genetically modified crops, the essay represents this book's and, in particular, this chapter's "natural" conclusion.

52. "The room had then become useless, and for some time was quite deserted, except by Fanny . . . but gradually, as her value for the comforts of it increased, she had added to her possessions, and spent more of her time there; and having nothing to oppose her, had so naturally and so artlessly worked herself into it, that it was now generally admitted to be her's. . . . Mrs. Norris having stipulated for there never being a fire in it on Fanny's account, was tolerably resigned to her having the use of what nobody else wanted" (105–6). The practice of usufruct persists to the end, for, as Clara Tuite has recently reminded us, Fanny does not in fact actually "inherit Mansfield Park" but only enjoys its vicinity (with the distant possibility of eventual legal inheritance should Tom's moral recovery prove short-lived). See Tuite, *Romantic Austen*, 129–30.

priority that a shared past life may have over a newcomer's suit—ends by legitimating the principle of exchange because the love that clings to its object as a possession, only experiencing it in relation to its possible non-being, thereby already anticipates its loss, and hence eventual substitution and exchangeability with another. I can hardly do justice here to the many tricks *Mansfield Park* plays on this little plot simply by virtue of Austen's making the "newcomer" also the one who practices substitution longest; the irony, however, is not limited to the "cynicism" with which, for Deresiewicz, the novel's end has Edmund "learn to prefer soft light eyes to sparkling dark ones" (319) and exchange Mary for Fanny, in the course of three short paragraphs, whose own brevity and seeming impatience with narrative unfolding belie the "variable" length of time needed for the "cure of unconquerable passions, and the transfer of unchanging attachments."[53] Rather, by keeping before us the oddness and precariousness of

53. On this reading, as if echoing the "piece of wisdom" Adorno ends by attributing to "the exclusive right of priority"—"after all, they are only people, which one it is does not really matter" (*Minima Moralia*, 79–80)—the novel's plot rewards precisely those most capable of trade and thoroughly endorses the ideology of commerce and commodification that naive readers are cynically invited to confine to London. The irony, however, cuts both ways, as Austen reduces the alternatives not to a choice between the agreement to "love whom we have because we can't have whom we love" (Deresiewicz, *Jane Austen and the Romantic Poets*, 78) and the ideal of "unconquerable passions and unchanging attachments"—but to a choice between slower and faster economies of exchange—between the temporal "progress" to which, as Mary tells her, Fanny has been "brought up," and the instantaneous, ready-made miracle for which Mary values money (or so she claims, perhaps satirically) as sparing her all trace of the changes undergone. The love that would resist the process Deresiewicz calls "substitution" and enshrine its object as immune to transfer and revision ends up denying the very historicity that makes it singular, a point the following exchange from Hardy's *A Pair of Blue Eyes* seems to make, as if in answer to Adorno's claim that literature has neglected the theme of prepossession. Upset by her second lover's disappointment on discovering that he is not her first, the heroine responds by reminding him that he should love her for who she is, not for what she has done; ironically she thereby ends up enumerating precisely those blazonlike, timeless "objective" qualities such as "soft light eyes" or "sparkling dark ones" that might most make her a "characterless" and exchangeable "toy"; as nameable qualities that he has predicated of her and that she now repeats back to him, none would be sufficient as causes of love, if by such we

a conservatism whose preference for the "prior" is eminently provisional and revisable as such—on the one hand, merely formal rather than content-driven and, on the other, essentially impure, based on a specificity and determinateness themselves derived from a long process of mixing and shading—Austen's novel restores an ambiguity elided or collapsed in Adorno's thought—the sense of the time it takes for anything to become "quite definite" such that "it cannot be repeated, which is why it tolerates what is different" (*Minima Moralia*, 79).

A meditation on the difficulty of experiencing temporal succession except as a jealousy of the next moment to come and a fear of losing the possessed present to nonexistence, Adorno's thought itself follows a certain irreversible sequence as it moves in the course of the aphorism from observing the apparently innocuous, inoffensive phenomenon of prepossession (troubling only by its very indifference to "objective" worth and freedom of choice) to recognizing in the "exclusiveness (*Ausschließlichkeit*, literally, lock-out, 87) implicit in time," the same logic that leads to the exclusionary practices of big business, and to the fear of the newcomer motivating the "little boy's aversion for his younger brother," xenophobic immigration laws, and finally the "Fascist eradication of the racial minority" (79). Readers familiar with recent political readings of *Mansfield Park* will recognize that the novel plays out its plot of retrenchment on

———

understand attention not to the "what" of personal identity but the "thatness" of a person's existence. Punning on "character," in the older sense of circumstance-defined "ethos," Hardy seems to agree with Elfride on the unfairness of Knight's making his love depend on her "freshness" but not for the reasons she assumes; rather Knight's demand for exclusive possession, like Elfride's own underestimation of the difference made by historical "accident," represents a fantastic denial of time, a wish to live among memoryless ideals with infinite shelf-lives and no expiration dates, rather than within novelistic time, as characters who are no more than their histories:

Elfride sobbed bitterly. "Am I such a—mere characterless toy—as to have no attraction in me, apart from—freshness? Haven't I brains? You said—I was clever and ingenious in my thoughts, and—isn't that anything? Have I not some beauty? I think I have a little—and I know I have—yes, I do! You have praised my voice, and my manner, and my accomplishments. Yet all these together are so much rubbish because I—accidentally saw a man before you!"

"O come, Elfride. 'Accidentally saw a man' is very cool. You loved him, remember." (Hardy, *A Pair of Blue Eyes*, 312)

a similar ideological terrain marked by the waning of the laws of primogeniture and the conflict between a nascent "domestic" nationalism (with its protofeminist concern for the fate of its "domestic slaves," women) and colonial imperialism.[54] Kept alive by its faraway and invisible Antiguan plantation, *Mansfield Park* exemplifies the uneasy relation of material circumstances to moral claims, which for Williams corresponds to the split between "working" and "social improvement," between the generation of wealth and the achievement of culture. As critics have noted, the title *Mansfield Park* may allude to the Mansfield Judgment of 1772, which declared slavery on British soil illegal by following the defense counsel's argument that "England was too pure an air for slaves to breathe in . . . and I hope my lord the air does not blow worse since—I hope they will never breathe here; for this is my assertion, the moment they put their feet on English ground, that moment they are free."[55]

54. As I have been arguing, along with Tuite and others, Fanny's ambiguous status as adoptee and resident alien also decenters this plot; the tears she sheds for Mansfield Park while exiled to her "native" home in Portsmouth are hardly more "honest" than those that Cowper imagines Omai shedding when returned from England to his native island: only metaphorically and by affiliation, those of a "patriot's for his country."

55. From Thomas Clarkson's 1808 *The Abolition of the African Slave Trade* (quoted in Kirkham, *Jane Austen, Feminism, and Fiction*, 118). For a more expanded reading of the novel's relation to the Mansfield Judgment, see Kirkham's suggestion that Austen, following a trope common to early English feminists, conservative and radical alike, is implicitly comparing Fanny's "moral status" (as a woman locked in and made a part of the Mansfield property) to that of the Antiguan slaves (*Jane Austen, Feminism, and Fiction*, 117–19). For other discussions of Mansfield Park's dependence on the unseen slave labor of its Caribbean plantation, see Said, "Jane Austen and Empire"; Ferguson, "*Mansfield Park*: Slavery, Colonialism, and Gender"; Fraiman, "Jane Austen and Edward Said"; Trumpener, *Bardic Nationalism*; Mee, "Austen's Treacherous Ivory"; and Tuite, *Romantic Austen*. The consensus among recent post-Said readers such as Mee and Tuite seems to be that Austen is neither the complacent apologist of "distant"—and because distant, ignored and ignorable—brutality whom Said targets in his reading, nor the unambiguous critic of slavery whom liberal readers sometimes wishfully portray when responding to Said's attack: what muted critique of imperialist practices may be legible in *Mansfield Park* has much more to do with the status of English women than with African slaves, and the very mutedness or indirection of this critique speaks to the double contradictory interpellation

Strangely protective of England rather than of the victims of slavery, the notion that England is "too pure an air for slaves to breathe in" implies that one has only to appeal to England's conscience and the nation will act to declare slavery not only illegal but, within its boundaries, at least, void and unrecognizable, less from any disinterested objection to the injustice of the practice than from that commitment to a pure sense of self we call integrity. The Mansfield Judgment's purist and isolationist language encapsulates the paradox described by Williams whereby an "everyday uncompromising morality which is in the end separable from its social basis" emerges from the process of economic improvement.[56] England can afford the privilege of sacrificing economic advantage to self-image and of being judged on moral rather than expedient grounds because it has attained economic "maturity," but only thanks to the incoming revenues of its colonial exploits abroad. A parody of the Romantic insistence on an irrecoverably singular "difference to me," Mansfield's purist talk at the same time exposes the very limited political consequence of that difference.

Remaining "free of slaves," even as it lives off of the distant slave plantations, England in this sense mirrors Fanny's changeless, motionless relation to the changing world. Yet Fanny's indirect and passive reliance on

---

of women of Austen's class as the mothers of sons of the nation, and as women who should know their place, i.e., know not to know too much about political affairs. While readings addressing this issue usually center on the moment when Fanny reportedly asks Sir Thomas about the slave trade and produces a "dead silence" (136) or gape in discourse—a theatrical coup d'état as fraught with ironies as her "I cannot act"—they do not always take into account the fact that the ambiguities as to how Fanny meant or even worded her question (critically, flatteringly, innocently, etc.) are inseparable from Austen's decision not to represent the scene: readers do not "witness" it in "real time" but only learn of it retrospectively through a reported conversation between Edmund and Fanny.

56. While he does not refer to the Mansfield Judgment itself, in "Jane Austen and Empire" Said makes explicit the imperialist logic of the separation described by Williams, a logic according to which the upholding of a "local" moral standard not only happens to coincide with its "abrogation abroad" but in fact depends on this abrogation (81). We find here at a different scale the same shading and hardening of a contingent into a causal relation, as when Austen invites us to perceive Fanny's happiness as not only coinciding with the dissatisfaction of those around her but deriving from it.

temporal accident and on the contingency of others' desires, actions, and conduct also complicates the idea that virtue should owe nothing or as little as possible to circumstances and that the business of satisfying material wants compromises, if it does not permanently delay, the emergence of a capacity to act freely and hence morally. The ironies of Fanny's hidden centrality to everyone else have repeatedly been noted, but Austen, I have been arguing, is not simply demystifying the Romantic self's claim to autonomy; by making an adopted interloper the chief proponent of the Burkean plot of retrenchment, she may well be registering, as Clara Tuite and others have argued, the oblique and uneasy relation of women of her class to the patrimony they were called on to protect without owning. But Austen's relation to Fanny's example also contests the excessively puritanical insistence on separating personal happiness from necessity and virtue from the aid of external, contingent circumstances, and helps restore the sense of the discontinuity between the various scales on which to weigh "the priority of the fortuitous" (*Minima Moralia*, 78) that the inexorable march of Adorno's thought might seem to collapse.[57]

In a letter to her sister, Austen once claimed, "I do not think it worth while to wait for enjoyment until there is some real opportunity for it."[58] The sentiment appears to contradict the cold purity of those Empsonian figures who, believing that a recognition for which they have had to work is not worth the price of its achievement, resign themselves to waste "if they do not get their opportunity." But Austen's thought is an indictment less of passivity than of the absolutist spirit that holds out for "real opportunity." In *Mansfield Park* this spirit of discontent drives Mary Crawford to resist Edmund's ordination and to forfeit a success that she might have counted on, for a loss in part of her own making. She, not Fanny Price, lacks the easy willingness to take what comes that constitutes in Empson's terms a "queer sort of realism" or embrace of this world as it is given. The pragmatic spirit of Austen's letter in this sense renews the pastoral project of taking "a limited life and pretending it is the full and normal one" and resonates with the claim by which Empson himself qualifies his earlier in-

57. Adorno himself does not end on this note but dialectically returns to the minor key of the example of love, an example his language absolves from the violence of exclusion by figuring it as something feminine and virginal: a vulnerability to otherness that is its own "protection," "the specific lacks the aspiration to totality" (*Minima Moralia*, 79).

58. Quoted in Tave, *Some Words of Jane Austen*, 1.

sistence on the inevitable "isolation even in a life rich in intimacy": "success does not come from mere virtue, and without some external success a virtue is not real even to itself" (*Some Versions of Pastoral*, 114).

Throughout this book, I have examined figures who abdicate the powers of plot and, rather than lay claim to their inheritance from time, affirm only its weightless gain. I have sought to break the illusion that their affirmative passivity corresponds to an ascetic, self-denying, world-hating repudiation of temporal experience. What they receive from time, they receive noninstrumentally, not because they are good ethical subjects but because such experience barely registers even when accurately perceived. If the "literature of uncounted experience," as I have been defining it, does indeed correspond to an ethos of "non-ado"—of casual losses and as easily missed gains—resistant to modernity's call to materialize and make good on given potential, such an ethos does not cast the noninstrumental as a heavy ethical burden; the heroines of these novels, the speakers of these poems, do nothing so heroic as *renounce* ambitions of self-expression; they simply set aside the fantasy of the all-responsible subject.[59] Sitting uneasily between the sense of passivity as submissive acquiescence and that of passivity as privileged leisure, Austen's Fanny presents perhaps an especially uncomfortable note on which to end a book that has thus sought to contest the dominant influences of utilitarianism, expressive individualism, and therapeutic imperatives to improvements. For hers is a disquieting example of how quickly the alternative to this productivist ideology may reify into its bad image—that of the quietist acceptance of the status quo. Yet I take this as a partially satisfying stopping point, precisely because it's only between these two "worldly" senses of passivity—between the leisure of taking no thought and the habit of quietly making do (rather than in relation to the ethical revaluation of passivity as an ideal of responsibility without will, which one finds, for example, in the work of Levinas)—that nonappropriation can emerge, as it does for Austen's Fanny as for Lafayette's princess, not as that which is difficult to do—as entailing sacrifice to self—but as the path of least resistance.

59. They enjoy the "gift of content" (in the sense of contentment, not contents) denied Eustacia Vye of Hardy's *The Return of the Native* (284). Hardy's phrase captures the paradox that precisely the "power" (hardly recognizable as a power) of contentment, of finding the given sufficient, remains, like grace, unearnable, gratuitous. I am grateful to Ann Banfield for suggesting this reference to me.

Austen's commitment to this world expresses itself perhaps most vividly in the project of accommodating virtue to circumstances that either work to prevent its full expression or, on the contrary, render its exercise so easy as to qualify its due. As the only character of those studied to achieve happiness in the conventional marriage plot, Fanny lends the greatest support to Empson's plea for the necessity of "some external success," even as she testifies to the continued fragility of the links between fortune and virtue, fortuitous gain and blind self-sufficiency.

Selected Bibliography

Abrams, M. H. "English Romanticism: The Spirit of the Age." In *Romanticism and Consciousness*, ed. Harold Bloom, 90–118. New York: Norton, 1970.

———. *Natural Supernaturalism*. New York: Norton, 1971.

Adorno, Theodor. *Minima Moralia: Reflexionen aus dem beschädigten Leben*. Frankfurt am Main: Suhrkamp Verlag, 1951.

———. *Minima Moralia*. Trans. E. F. N. Jephcott. London: Verso, 1974.

———. *Notes to Literature*. Ed. Rolf Tiedemann. Trans. Shierry Weber Nicholsen. 2 vols. New York: Columbia University Press, 1992.

———. "Resignation." Trans. Wes Blomster. *Telos* 35 (spring 1978): 165–68.

Agamben, Giorgio. *Homo Sacer: Sovereign Power and Bare Life*. Trans. Daniel Heller-Roazen. Stanford, CA: Stanford University Press, 1998.

———. *Infancy and History: The Destruction of Experience*. Trans. Liz Heron. New York: Verso, 1993.

———. *The Man Without Content*. Trans. Georgia Albert. Stanford, CA: Stanford University Press, 1999.

———. *The Open: Man and Animal*. Trans. Kevin Attell. Stanford, CA: Stanford University Press, 2002.

———. *Potentialities*. Trans. David Heller-Rosen. Stanford, CA: Stanford University Press, 1999.

———. *The Time That Remains: A Commentary on the Letter to the Romans*. Trans. Patricia Dailey. Stanford, CA: Stanford University Press, 2005.

Alliston, April. *Virtue's Faults: Correspondences in Eighteenth-Century British and French Women's Fiction*. Stanford, CA: Stanford University Press, 1996.

Alter, Robert. *The Five Books of Moses: A Translation with Commentary*. New York: W. W. Norton & Co., 2004.

Althusser, Louis. *Essays on Ideology*. London: Verso, 1971.

American Heritage Dictionary. 3rd ed. New York: Houghton Mifflin, 1993.

Arac, Jonathan. *Critical Genealogies.* New York: Columbia University Press, 1987.

Auerbach, Erich. *Mimesis: The Representation of Reality in Western Literature.* New York: Doubleday Anchor Books, 1957.

Auerbach, Nina. *Romantic Imprisonment: Women and Other Glorified Outcasts.* New York: Columbia University Press, 1986.

Austen, Jane. *Mansfield Park.* Ed. Claudia Johnson. New York: Norton, 1998.

———. *Mansfield Park.* Ed. Tony Tanner. New York: Penguin Books, 1966.

———. *Persuasion.* Ed. Patricia Meyer Spacks. New York: Norton, 1995.

Austin, J. L. *How to Do Things with Words.* Cambridge, MA: Harvard University Press, 1962.

Bacon, Francis. *Miscellaneous Tracts upon Human Philosophy.* Vol. 1 of *The Works of Francis Bacon.* Ed. Basil Montagu. London: W. Pickering, 1825.

Baier, Annette. *Moral Prejudices: Essays on Ethics.* Cambridge, MA: Harvard University Press, 1994.

Banfield, Ann. *Unspeakable Sentences: Narration and Representation in the Language of Fiction.* Boston: Routledge and Kegan Paul, 1982.

Barthes, Roland. *Le degré zéro de l'écriture.* Paris: Éditions du Seuil, 1953.

———. *Fragments d'un discours amoureux.* Paris: Éditions du Seuil, 1977.

———. *Le neutre: Notes de cours au Collège de France (1977–1978).* Paris: Éditions du Seuil, 2002.

———. *S/Z.* Trans. Richard Howard. New York: Hill and Wang, 1974.

———. *Writing Degree Zero.* Trans. Annette Lavers and Colin Smith. New York: Farrar, Straus and Giroux, 1968.

Bataille, Georges. "The Notion of Expenditure." In *Visions of Excess.* Ed. and trans. Allan Stoekl, 116–29. Minneapolis: University of Minnesota Press, 1985.

Beasley, Faith. *Revising Memory: Women's Fictions and Memoirs in Seventeenth-Century France.* New Brunswick, NJ: Rutgers University Press, 1990.

Benjamin, Walter. *The Correspondence of Walter Benjamin and Gershom Scholem, 1932–1940.* Ed. Gershom Scholem. Trans. Gary Smith and Andre Lefevre. New York: Schocken, 1989.

———. *Illuminations.* Trans. Harry Zohn. New York: Harcourt, Brace and World, 1968.

Benveniste, Emile. *Problems in General Linguistics.* Trans. Mary Elizabeth Meek. Coral Gables, FL: University of Miami Press, 1971.

Bermingham, Ann. *Landscape and Ideology: The English Rustic Tradition, 1740–1860.* Berkeley: University of California Press, 1986.

Bersani, Leo. *A Future for Astyanax: Character and Desire in Literature.* Boston: Little, Brown, 1969.

———. *Homos.* Cambridge, MA: Harvard University Press, 1995.

Bersani, Leo, and Ulysse Dutoit. *Arts of Impoverishment: Beckett, Rothko, Resnais.* Cambridge, MA: Harvard University Press, 1993.

———. *Caravaggio's Secrets.* Cambridge, MA: MIT Press, 1998.

Bewell, Alan. *Wordsworth and the Enlightenment.* New Haven, CT: Yale University Press, 1989.

Blanchot, Maurice. *L'Entretien infini.* Paris: Éditions Gallimard, 1969.

———. *The Infinite Conversation.* Trans. Susan Hanson. Minneapolis: University of Minnesota Press, 1993.

Blumenberg, Hans. "'Imitation of Nature': Toward a Prehistory of the Idea of the Creative Being." Trans. Anna Wertz. *Qui Parle* 12, no. 1 (spring–summer 2001): 17–54.

Brisman, Leslie. *Milton's Poetry of Choice and Its Romantic Heirs.* Ithaca, NY: Cornell University Press, 1973.

———. "On the Divine Presence in Exodus." In *Exodus: Modern Critical Interpretations,* ed. Harold Bloom, 105–22. New Haven, CT: Chelsea House, 1987.

Brodsky, Claudia. "Contextual Criticism, or 'History' v. Literature." *Narrative* 1 (1993): 93–104.

———. *The Imposition of Form: Studies in Narrative and Knowledge.* Princeton, NJ: Princeton University Press, 1987.

———. "'The Impression of Movement': Jean Racine, Architecte." *Yale French Studies* 76 (1989): 162–81.

Bromwich, David. *A Choice of Inheritance: Self and Community from Edmund Burke to Robert Frost.* Cambridge, MA: Harvard University Press, 1989.

———. *Disowned by Poetry: Wordsworth's Poetry of the 1790s.* Chicago: University of Chicago Press, 1998.

Brooks, Peter. *Reading for the Plot: Design and Intention in Narrative.* Cambridge, MA: Harvard University Press, 1984.

Butler, Judith. *Excitable Speech: A Politics of the Performative.* New York: Routledge, 1997.

———. *Giving an Account of Oneself.* New York: Fordham University Press, 2005.

Butler, Marilyn. *Jane Austen and the War of Ideas.* Oxford: Clarendon Press, 1975.

Cameron, Sharon. *Choosing Not Choosing: Dickinson Fascicles.* Chicago: University of Chicago Press, 1992.

———. *Lyric Time: Dickinson and the Limits of Genre.* Baltimore: Johns Hopkins University Press, 1979.

Carlyle, Thomas. *A Carlyle Reader.* New York: Cambridge University Press, 1984.

Caruth, Cathy. *Unclaimed Experience: Trauma, Narrative, and History.* Baltimore: Johns Hopkins University Press, 1996.

Cavell, Stanley. *The Claim of Reason.* New York: Oxford University Press, 1979.

———. *Conditions Handsome and Unhandsome: The Constitution of Emersonian Perfectionism.* Chicago: University of Chicago Press, 1990.

———. *Disowning Knowledge in Six Plays of Shakespeare.* Cambridge, UK: Cambridge University Press, 1987.

———. *In Quest of the Ordinary: Lines of Skepticism and Romanticism.* Chicago: University of Chicago Press, 1988.

———. *Must We Mean What We Say?* New York: Cambridge University Press, 1976.

Chase, Cynthia, ed. *Romanticism.* Harlow, Essex: Longman, 1994.

Christensen, Jerome. *Romanticism and the End of History.* Baltimore: Johns Hopkins University Press, 2000.

Clayton, Jay. *Romantic Vision and the Novel.* New York: Cambridge University Press, 1987.

Cohn, Dorrit. *Transparent Minds: Narrative Modes for Presenting Consciousness in Fiction.* Princeton, NJ: Princeton University Press, 1978.

Cowper, William. *Poetical Works.* Ed. H. S. Milford. New York: Oxford University Press, 1963.

Curran, Stuart. *Poetic Form and British Romanticism.* New York: Oxford University Press, 1986.

Dean, Jodi. *Publicity's Secret: How Technoculture Capitalizes on Democracy.* Ithaca, NY: Cornell University Press, 2002.

DeJean, Joan. "Lafayette's Ellipses: The Privileges of Anonymity." In *The Princesse of Clèves,* trans. John D. Lyons, 240–68. New York: Norton, 1994. First published in *PMLA* 99, no. 5 (Oct. 1984): 884–902.

Deleuze, Gilles. *Bergsonism.* Trans. Hugh Tomlinson and Barbara Habberiam. New York: Zone Books, 1988.

De Man, Paul. *Aesthetic Ideology.* Minneapolis: University of Minnesota Press, 1996.

———. *Blindness and Insight.* Minneapolis: University of Minnesota Press, 1983.

———. "Time and History in Wordsworth." *Diacritics* 17, no. 4 (winter 1987): 4–17.

De Quincey, Thomas. *Recollections of the Lake Poets.* New York: Penguin, 1970.

Deresiewicz, William. *Jane Austen and the Romantic Poets.* New York: Columbia University Press, 2004.

Derrida, Jacques. *Donner la mort.* Paris: Galilée, 1999.

———. *Donner le temps: 1. La fausse monnaie.* Paris: Galilée, 1991.

———. *The Gift of Death*. Trans. David Wills. Chicago: University of Chicago Press, 1995.

———. *Marges de la philosophie*. Paris: Éditions de Minuit, 1972.

———. *Margins of Philosophy*. Trans. Alan Bass. Chicago: University of Chicago Press, 1982.

———. *Psyché: Inventions de l'autre*. Paris: Galilée, 1987.

Dickinson, Emily. *The Letters of Emily Dickinson*. Ed. Thomas H. Johnson. Cambridge, MA: Belknap Press of Harvard University Press, 1958.

———. *The Poems of Emily Dickinson: Variorum Edition*. Ed. R. W. Franklin. Cambridge, MA: Harvard University Press, 1998.

Diehl, Joanne Feit. *Dickinson and the Romantic Imagination*. Princeton, NJ: Prince-ton University Press, 1981.

Dobson, Jane. *Dickinson and the Strategies of Reticence*. Bloomington: Indiana University Press, 1989.

Doriani, Beth Maclay. *Emily Dickinson: Daughter of Prophecy*. Amherst: University of Massachusetts Press, 1996.

Duckworth, Alistair. *The Improvement of the Estate*. Baltimore: Johns Hopkins University Press, 1971.

Eagleton, Terry. *The Ideology of the Aesthetic*. Cambridge, MA: Basil Blackwell, 1990.

Eberwein, Jane Donahue. *Dickinson: Strategies of Limitation*. Amherst: University of Massachusetts Press, 1985.

Elam, Helen Regueiro, and Frances Ferguson, eds. *The Wordsworthian Enlightenment: Romantic Poetry and the Ecology of Reading*. Baltimore: Johns Hopkins University Press, 2005.

Emerson, Ralph Waldo. "Experience." In *Ralph Waldo Emerson* (Oxford Authors). Ed. Richard Poirier. New York: Oxford University Press, 1990.

Empson, William. *Some Versions of Pastoral*. London: Hogarth, 1974.

Fabre, Jean. *L'art de l'analyse dans "La Princesse de Clèves."* Strasbourg: Presses Universitaires de Strasbourg, 1945.

Ferenczi, Sándor. *Further Contributions to the Theory and Technique of Psycho-Analysis*. Trans. Jane Isabel Suttie and others. New York: Brunner/Mazel, 1980.

Ferguson, Frances. "Jane Austen, *Emma*, and the Impact of Form." *Modern Language Quarterly* 61, no. 1 (March 2000): 160–80.

———. "Rape and the Rise of the Novel." *Representations* 20 (fall 1987): 88–112.

———. "Sade and the Pornographic Legacy." *Representations* 36 (fall 1991): 1–21.

———. *Wordsworth: Language as Counter-Spirit*. New Haven, CT: Yale University Press, 1977.

Ferguson, Moira. "*Mansfield Park*: Slavery, Colonialism, and Gender." *Oxford Literary Review* 13, nos. 1–2 (1991): 118–39.

Finch, Casey, and Peter Bowen. "'The Tittle-Tattle of Highbury': Gossip and Free Indirect Style in *Emma*." *Representations* 31 (summer 1990): 1–18.

Foreman, Dave. *Confessions of an Eco-Warrior*. New York: Harmony Books, 1991.

Fraiman, Susan. "Jane Austen and Edward Said: Gender, Culture, and Imperialism." *Critical Inquiry* 21, no. 4 (1995): 805–21.

François, Anne-Lise. "'O happy living things!': Frankenfoods and the Bounds of Wordsworthian Natural Piety." *Diacritics* 33, no. 2 (2005): 42–70.

———. "Open Secrets: The Literature of Uncounted Experience." PhD diss., Princeton University, 1999.

———. "To Hold in Common and Know by Heart: The Prevalence of Gentle Forces in Romantic Empiricism and Romantic Experience." *Yale Journal of Criticism* 7, no. 1 (1994): 139–62.

Freud, Sigmund. *Moses and Monotheism*. Trans. James Strachey. London: Hogarth, 1964.

———. *The Standard Edition of the Complete Psychological Works of Sigmund Freud*. Trans. under the general editorship of James Strachey. 24 vols. London: Hogarth, 1953–74.

Fried, Michael. *Absorption and Theatricality: Painting and Beholder in the Age of Diderot*. Berkeley: University of California Press, 1980.

Fry, Paul. *A Defense of Poetry: Reflections on the Occasion of Writing*. Stanford, CA: Stanford University Press, 1995.

———. "Green to the Very Door? The Natural Wordsworth." *Studies in Romanticism* 35 (winter 1996): 535–51.

Gallagher, Catherine, and Stephen Greenblatt. *Practicing New Historicism*. Chicago: University of Chicago Press, 2000.

Galperin, William. *The Historical Austen*. Philadelphia: University of Pennsylvania Press, 2003.

Genette, Gérard. *Figures II*. Paris: Éditions du Seuil, 1969.

Gilbert, Sandra, and Susan Gubar. *The Madwoman in the Attic: The Woman Writer and the Nineteenth-Century Literary Imagination*. New Haven, CT: Yale University Press, 1979.

Goethe, Johann Wolfgang. *Sprüche in Prosa: Sämtliche Werke*. 1.13 Frankfurt am Main: Deutscher Klassiker Verlag, 1993.

———. *Wilhelm Meister's Apprenticeship*. Trans. Eric A. Blackall. Princeton, NJ: Princeton University Press, 1995.

Goldmann, Lucien. *Le dieu caché*. Paris: Éditions Gallimard, 1959.

Goodman, Kevis. *Georgic Modernity and British Romanticism: Poetry and the Mediation of History*. New York: Cambridge University Press, 2004.

———. "Making Time for History: New Historicism and the Apocalyptic Fallacy." *Studies in Romanticism* 35 (winter 1996): 563–77.

Gray, Thomas. *The Complete Poems of Thomas Gray: English, Latin and Greek.* Ed. H. W. Starr and J. R. Hendrickson. Oxford: Clarendon Press, 1966.

Greenberg, Mitchell. *Subjectivity and Subjugation in Seventeenth-Century Drama and Prose: The Family Romance of French Classicism.* New York: Cambridge University Press, 1992.

Greene, Roland. *Post-Petrarchism: Origins and Innovations of the Western Lyric Sequence.* Princeton, NJ: Princeton University Press, 1991.

Guillory, John. "Canon." In *Critical Terms for Literary Study*, ed. Frank Lentricchia and Thomas McLaughlin, 233–49. Chicago: University of Chicago Press, 1995.

Habermas, Jürgen. *The Philosophical Discourse of Modernity.* Trans. Frederick Lawrence. Cambridge, MA: MIT Press, 1990.

Hamburger, Käte. *The Logic of Literature.* Trans. Marilynn J. Rose. Bloomington: Indiana University Press, 1973.

Hardt, Michael, and Antonio Negri. *Empire.* Cambridge, MA: Harvard University Press, 2000.

Hardy, Thomas. *A Pair of Blue Eyes.* New York: Oxford University Press, 1985.

———. *The Return of the Native.* New York: Oxford University Press, 1990.

———. *The Variorum Edition of the Complete Poems of Thomas Hardy.* Ed. James Gibson. New York: Macmillan, 1979.

Hartman, Geoffrey. *The Fate of Reading and Other Essays.* Chicago: University of Chicago Press, 1985.

———. "Milton's Counterplot." In *Milton: A Collection of Critical Essays*, ed. Louis Martz, 100–108. Englewood Cliffs, NJ: Prentice-Hall, 1966.

———. *The Unremarkable Wordsworth.* Minneapolis: University of Minnesota Press, 1987.

———. *Wordsworth's Poetry, 1787–1814.* New Haven, CT: Yale University Press, 1964.

Hegel, G. W. F. *Phenomenology of Spirit.* Trans. A. V. Miller. New York: Oxford University Press, 1979.

Hill, Geoffrey. *The Enemy's Country: Words, Contexture, and Other Circumstances of Language.* Stanford, CA: Stanford University Press, 1991.

———. *The Lords of Limit: Essays on Literature and Ideas.* New York: Oxford University Press, 1984.

Hipchen, Emily. "Accounting for Fanny: Reading Inventory Texts in *Mansfield Park* and *The Loiterer*." *Eighteenth-Century Novel* 2 (2002): 305–24.

Homans, Margaret. *Women Writers and Poetic Identity.* Princeton, NJ: Princeton University Press, 1980.

Horkheimer, Max, and Theodor Adorno. *Dialectic of Enlightenment*. Trans. Edmund Jephcott. Stanford, CA: Stanford University Press, 2002.

Howe, Irving. *Thomas Hardy*. New York: Macmillan, 1967.

Jackson, Virginia. *Dickinson's Misery: A Theory of Lyric Reading*. Princeton, NJ: Princeton University Press, 2005.

Jay, Martin. "The Limits of Limit-Experience: Bataille and Foucault." In *Cultural Semantics: Keywords of Our Time*, 62–78. Amherst: University of Massachusetts Press, 1998.

————. *Songs of Experience: Modern American and European Variations on a Universal Theme*. Berkeley: University of California Press, 2005.

Johnson, Claudia. *Jane Austen: Women, Politics, and the Novel*. Chicago: University of Chicago Press, 1988.

Juhasz, Suzanne. *Comic Power in Emily Dickinson*. Austin: University of Texas Press, 1993.

Kamuf, Peggy. *Fictions of Feminine Desire: Disclosures of Heloise*. Lincoln: University of Nebraska Press, 1982.

Kant, Immanuel. *The Critique of Judgement*. Trans. James Creed Meredith. New York: Oxford University Press, 1952.

————. *The Critique of Practical Reason*. Trans. Mary Gregor. Cambridge, UK: Cambridge University Press, 1997.

————. *Grounding for the Metaphysics of Morals*. In *Ethical Philosophy*. Trans. James W. Ellington. Indianapolis, IN: Hackett Publishing, 1983.

————. *The Philosophy of Kant: Immanuel Kant's Moral and Political Writings*. Ed. Carl J. Friedrich. New York: Modern Library, 1949.

Kateb, George. "Technology and Philosophy." *Social Research* 64, no. 3 (fall 1997): 1225–46.

Kaufman, Robert. "Legislators of the Post-Everything World: Shelley's *Defence* of Adorno." *ELH* 63, no. 3 (fall 1996): 707–33.

————. "Negatively Capable: Keats, Vendler, Adorno, and the Theory of the Avant-Garde." *Critical Inquiry* 27, no. 2 (2001): 354–84.

————. "Red Kant." *Critical Inquiry* 26, no. 4 (2000): 682–724.

Keats, John. *Letters of John Keats*. Ed. Robert Gittings. New York: Oxford University Press, 1987.

Kermode, Frank. *The Genesis of Secrecy: On the Interpretation of Narrative*. Cambridge, MA: Harvard University Press, 1979.

Kierkegaard, Søren. *The Concept of Irony*. Trans. Howard V. Hong and Edna H. Hong. Princeton, NJ: Princeton University Press, 1989.

————. *Fear and Trembling*. Trans. Howard V. Hong and Edna H. Hong. Princeton, NJ: Princeton University Press, 1983.

————. *Works of Love*. Trans. Howard V. Hong and Edna H. Hong. Princeton, NJ: Princeton University Press, 1995.

Kirkham, Margaret. *Jane Austen, Feminism, and Fiction*. New York: Methuen, 1986.

Kristeva, Julia. *Soleil noir: Dépression et mélancolie*. Paris: Gallimard, 1987.

Kroeber, Karl. "Jane Austen, Romantic." *Wordsworth Circle* 7 (1976): 291–96.

Lacan, Jacques. *Écrits*. Paris: Éditions du Seuil, 1966.

————. *Écrits: The First Complete Edition in English*. Trans. Bruce Fink, in collaboration with Héloïse Fink and Russell Grigg. New York: Norton, 2006.

————. *Encore: Le Séminaire Livre XX*. Paris: Éditions du Seuil, 1975.

————. *Feminine Sexuality*. Ed. Juliet Mitchell and Jacqueline Rose. New York: Norton, 1985.

LaCapra, Dominick. *History in Transit: Experience, Identity, Critical Theory*. Ithaca, NY: Cornell University Press, 2004.

Lafayette, Marie-Madeleine Pioche de la Vergne de. *Correspondance*. Ed. A. Beaunier. Paris: Gallimard, 1942.

————. *La Princesse de Clèves*. Paris: Garnier Flammarion, 1966.

————. *La Princesse de Clèves*. Trans. Robin Buss. New York: Penguin, 1992.

————. *The Princess of Clèves*. Trans. John D. Lyons. New York: Norton, 1994.

————. *The Princess of Clèves*. Trans. Nancy Mitford. New York: New Directions, 1988.

Laplanche, Jean. *Essays on Otherness*. Trans. John Fletcher. New York: Routledge, 1999.

————. *New Foundations for Psychoanalysis*. Trans. David Macey. Oxford: Basil Blackwell, 1989.

Latour, Bruno. *Politiques de la nature: Comment faire entrer les sciences en démocratie*. Paris: Éditions de la Découverte, 1999.

Levinas, Emmanuel. *Collected Philosophical Papers*. Trans. Alphonso Lingis. Boston: Martinus Nijohh, 1987.

————. *En Découvrant l'existence avec Husserl et Heidegger suivie d'essais nouveaux*. Paris: Librairie Philosophique J. Vrin, 2001.

————. *The Levinas Reader*. Ed. Seán Hand. Cambridge, MA: Blackwell, 1989.

Levinson, Marjorie. "Object-Loss and Object-Bondage: Economies of Representation in Hardy's Poetry." *ELH* 73, no. 2 (summer 2006): 549–80.

————. "Romantic Criticism: The State of the Art." In *At the Limits of Romanticism: Essays in Cultural, Feminist, and Materialist Criticism*, ed. Mary A. Favret and Nicola J. Watson, 269–81. Bloomington: Indiana University Press, 1994.

————. *Wordsworth's Great Period Poems: Four Essays*. New York: Cambridge University Press, 1986.

Litvak, Joseph. "Theatricality in *Mansfield Park*." *ELH* 53, no. 2 (summer 1986): 331–55.

Liu, Alan. "New Historicism and the Work of Mourning." *Studies in Romanticism* 35 (winter 1996): 552–62.

———. *Wordsworth: The Sense of History*. Stanford, CA: Stanford University Press, 1989.

Lukács, György. *The Theory of the Novel*. Trans. Anna Bostock. Cambridge, MA: MIT Press, 1994.

Lynch, Deidre. *The Economy of Character: Novels, Market Culture, and the Business of Inner Meaning*. Chicago: University of Chicago Press, 1998.

MacIntyre, Alasdair. *After Virtue: A Study in Moral Theory*. Notre Dame, IN: University of Notre Dame Press, 1980.

Mahar, Margaret. "Hardy's Poetry of Renunciation." *ELH* 45, no. 2 (summer 1978): 303–24.

Marshall, David. "True Acting and the Language of Real Feeling: *Mansfield Park*." *Yale Journal of Criticism* 3, no. 1 (1989): 87–106.

McGann, Jerome. *The Romantic Ideology*. Chicago: University of Chicago Press, 1985.

McKeon, Michael. *The Origins of the English Novel, 1600–1740*. Baltimore: Johns Hopkins University Press, 1987.

———, ed. *Theory of the Novel: A Historical Approach*. Baltimore: Johns Hopkins University Press, 2000.

McMaster, Juliet. *Jane Austen the Novelist: Essays Past and Present*. New York: St. Martin's, 1996.

Mee, Jon. "Austen's Treacherous Ivory: Female Patriotism, Domestic Ideology, and Empire." In *The Postcolonial Jane Austen*, ed. You-me Park and Rajeswari Sunder Rajan, 74–92. New York: Routledge, 2000.

Metzger, Lore. *One Foot in Eden: Modes of Pastoral in Romantic Poetry*. Chapel Hill, NC: University of North Carolina Press, 1986.

Mill, John Stuart. "What Is Poetry?" In *Essays on Poetry*. Ed. F. Parvin Sharpless. Columbia, SC: University of South Carolina Press, 1976.

Miller, Cristanne. *Emily Dickinson: A Poet's Grammar*. Cambridge, MA: Harvard University Press, 1987.

Miller, D. A. "Foutre! Bougre! Écriture!" *Yale Journal of Criticism* 14, no. 2 (fall 2001): 503–11.

———. *Jane Austen, or the Secret of Style*. Princeton, NJ: Princeton University Press, 2003.

———. *Narrative and Its Discontents*. Princeton, NJ: Princeton University Press, 1981.

———. *The Novel and the Police*. Berkeley: University of California Press, 1988.

Miller, Perry. *The New England Mind: The Seventeenth Century*. Boston: Beacon Press, 1961.

Milton, John. *Complete Poems and Major Prose*. New York: Odyssey Press, 1957.

Morgan, Susan. *In the Meantime: Character and Perception in Jane Austen's Fiction*. Chicago: University of Chicago Press, 1980.

Murdoch, Iris. *The Sovereignty of Good*. New York: Ark Paperbacks, 1970.

Nietzsche, Friedrich. *On the Genealogy of Morals*. Trans. Walter Kaufmann. New York: Random House, 1969.

Nussbaum, Martha. "Tragedy and Justice: Bernard Williams Remembered." *Boston Review* 28, no. 5 (Oct.–Nov. 2003): 35–39.

Oxford English Dictionary. 2nd ed. Prepared by J. A. Simpson and E. S. C. Weiner. New York: Oxford University Press, 1989.

Pascal, Blaise. *Œuvres complètes*. Ed. Jacques Chevalier. Paris: Éditions Gallimard, 1954.

———. *Œuvres complètes*. Vol. 1. Ed. Jean Mesnard. Paris: Desclée de Brouwer, 1964.

Perruchot, Claude. "Le style indirect libre et la question du sujet dans *Madame Bovary*." In *La production du sens chez Flaubert: Colloque de Cerisy*, ed. Claudine Gothot-Mersch, 253–74. Paris: Union Générale d'Éditions, 1975.

Pinch, Adela. *Strange Fits of Passion: Epistemologies of Emotion from Hume to Austen*. Stanford, CA: Stanford University Press, 1996.

Pocock, J. G. A. *Virtue, Commerce, and History: Essays on Political Thought and History, Chiefly in the Eighteenth Century*. New York: Cambridge University Press, 1985.

Pollak, Vivian. "Thirst and Starvation in Emily Dickinson's Poetry." In *Emily Dickinson: A Collection of Critical Essays*, ed. Judith Farr, 62–75. Upper Saddle River, NJ: Prentice-Hall, 1996.

Porter, David. "The Crucial Experience in Emily Dickinson's Poetry." *ESQ: A Journal of the American Renaissance* 20, no. 4 (1974): 280–90.

———. *Dickinson: The Modern Idiom*. Cambridge, MA: Harvard University Press, 1981.

Quinney, Laura. *The Poetics of Disappointment: Wordsworth to Ashbery*. Charlottesville: University Press of Virginia, 1999.

Rajan, Tilottama. "Romanticism and the Death of Lyric Consciousness." In *Lyric Poetry: Beyond New Criticism*, ed. Chaviva Hosek and Patricia Parker, 194–205. Ithaca, NY: Cornell University Press, 1985.

Ramazani, Jahan. *Poetry of Mourning: The Modern Elegy from Hardy to Heaney*. Chicago: University of Chicago Press, 1994.

Rancière, Jacques. *The Politics of Aesthetics*. Trans. Gabriel Rockhill. New York: Continuum, 2004.

Redfield, Marc. *Phantom Formations: Aesthetic Ideology and the* Bildungsroman. Ithaca, NY: Cornell University Press, 1996.

Rey-Flaud, Henri. *La névrose courtoise*. Paris: Navarin Éditeur, 1983.

Ricœur, Paul. *Temps et récit.* Tome II. Paris: Éditions du Seuil, 1984.

Rosenthal, M. L., and Sally M. Gall. *The Modern Poetic Sequence: The Genius of Modern Poetry.* New York: Oxford University Press, 1983.

Ross, Andrew. *Chicago Gangster Theory of Life: Nature's Debt to Society.* New York: Verso, 1994.

Rousseau, Jean-Jacques. *Discours sur l'origine et les fondements de l'inégalité parmi les hommes.* Paris: Librairie Générale Française, 1996.

Ruderman, Anne Crippen. *The Pleasures of Virtue: Political Thought in the Novels of Jane Austen.* London: Rowman and Littlefield, 1995.

Sacks, Peter. *The English Elegy: Studies in the Genre from Spenser to Yeats.* Baltimore: Johns Hopkins University Press, 1985.

Said, Edward. "Jane Austen and Empire." In *Culture and Imperialism,* 80–96. New York: Vintage Books, 1994.

Santner, Eric. *On Creaturely Life: Rilke, Benjamin, Sebald.* Chicago: University of Chicago Press, 2005.

———. *On the Psychotheology of Everyday Life: Reflections on Freud and Rosenzweig.* Chicago: University of Chicago Press, 2001.

Sarna, Nahum. *The JPS Torah Commentary: Exodus.* Philadelphia: The Jewish Publication Society, 1991.

Schiller, Friedrich. *On the Aesthetic Education of Man: In a Series of Letters.* Trans. Elizabeth M. Wilkinson and L. A. Willoughby. New York: Oxford University Press, 1967.

Schmidt, James, ed. *What Is Enlightenment? Eighteenth-Century Answers and Twentieth-Century Questions.* Berkeley: University of California Press, 1996.

Schor, Esther. *Bearing the Dead: The British Culture of Mourning from the Enlightenment to Victoria.* Princeton, NJ: Princeton University Press, 1994.

Sedgwick, Eve Kosofsky. *Epistemology of the Closet.* Berkeley: University of California Press, 1990.

———. *Tendencies.* Durham, NC: Duke University Press, 1993.

———. *Touching Feeling: Affect, Pedagogy, Performativity.* Durham, NC: Duke University Press, 2003.

Shoptaw, John. "Listening to Dickinson." *Representations* 86, no. 1 (2004): 20–52.

Smock, Ann. *What Is There to Say?* Lincoln: University of Nebraska Press, 2003.

———. "Doors: Simone Weil with Kafka." *MLN* 95 (1980): 850–63.

Spargo, Clifton. *The Ethics of Mourning: Grief and Responsibility in Elegiac Literature.* Baltimore: Johns Hopkins University Press, 2004.

Spiegelman, Willard. *Majestic Indolence: English Romantic Poetry and the Work of Art.* New York: Oxford University Press, 1995.

Stanton, Domna. "The Ideal of 'Repos' in Seventeenth-Century French Literature." *L'Esprit créateur* 15 (spring–summer 1975): 79–104.

Stewart, Maaja A. *Domestic Realities and Imperial Fictions: Jane Austen's Novels in Eighteenth-Century Contexts*. Athens: University of Georgia Press, 1993.

Stewart, Susan. *Poetry and the Fate of the Senses*. Chicago: University of Chicago Press, 2002.

Taussig, Michael. *Defacement: Public Secrecy and the Labor of the Negative*. Stanford, CA: Stanford University Press, 1999.

Tave, Stuart. *Some Words of Jane Austen*. Chicago: University of Chicago Press, 1973.

Trilling, Lionel. *The Opposing Self: Nine Essays in Criticism*. New York: Harcourt Brace Jovanovich, 1979.

Trumpener, Katie. *Bardic Nationalism: The Romantic Novel and the British Empire*. Princeton, NJ: Princeton University Press, 1997.

Tuite, Clara. *Romantic Austen: Sexual Politics and the Literary Canon*. New York: Cambridge University Press, 2002.

Valincour, J.-B. de. *Lettres à Madame la Marquise*** sur le sujet de "La Princesse de Clèves."* Ed. Christine Montalbetti. Paris: Flammarion, 2001.

Vendler, Helen. *The Art of Shakespeare's Sonnets*. Cambridge, MA: Harvard University Press, 1997.

Watt, Ian. *The Rise of the Novel: Studies in Defoe, Richardson, and Fielding*. Berkeley: University of California Press, 1957.

Weber, Max. *The Protestant Ethic and the Spirit of Capitalism*. Trans. Talcott Parsons. New York: Charles Scribner Son, 1958.

Weil, Simone. *Gravity and Grace*. Trans. Emma Craufurd. New York: Routledge, 1995.

———. *La pesanteur et la grâce*. Paris: Librairie Plon, 1988.

———. *Poèmes, suivis de* Venise sauvée. Paris: Éditions Gallimard, 1968.

Welsh, Alexander. *Strong Representations*. Baltimore: Johns Hopkins University Press, 1992.

Wilbur, Richard. "Sumptuous Destitution." In *Emily Dickinson: A Collection of Critical Essays*, ed. Judith Farr, 53–61. Upper Saddle River, NJ: Prentice-Hall, 1996.

Williams, Raymond. *The Country and the City*. New York: Oxford University Press, 1973.

———. *Culture and Society: 1780–1950*. 1958. New York: Columbia University Press, 1983.

Winnett, Susan. *Terrible Sociability: The Text of Manners in Laclos, Goethe, and James*. Stanford, CA: Stanford University Press, 1993.

Wollstonecraft, Mary. *A Vindication of the Rights of Woman*. Ed. Carol H. Poston. New York: Norton, 1988.

Woloch, Alex. *The One vs. the Many: Minor Characters and the Space of the Protagonist in the Novel*. Princeton, NJ: Princeton University Press, 2003.

Wolosky, Shira. *Emily Dickinson: A Voice of War*. New Haven, CT: Yale University Press, 1984.

Wordsworth, Dorothy. *Journals of Dorothy Wordsworth*. New York: Oxford University Press, 1971.

Wordsworth, William. *The Fourteen-Book Prelude*. Ed. W. J. B. Owen. Ithaca, NY: Cornell University Press, 1985.

———. *Lyrical Ballads, and Other Poems, 1797–1800*. Ed. James Butler and Karen Green. Ithaca, NY: Cornell University Press, 1992.

———. *The Poetical Works of William Wordsworth*. Ed. Ernest de Selincourt and Helen Darbishire. 5 vols. New York: Oxford University Press, 1954.

———. *Selected Prose*. Ed. John O. Hayden. New York: Penguin, 1988.

———. *The Thirteen-Book Prelude*. Ed. Mark L. Reed. Ithaca, NY: Cornell University Press, 1991.

Yeazell, Ruth Bernard. *Fictions of Modesty: Women and Courtship in the English Novel*. Chicago: University of Chicago Press, 1991.

Zimmerman, Sarah. *Romanticism, Lyricism, and History*. Albany: State University of New York Press, 1999.

Žižek, Slavoj. *The Fragile Absolute*. New York: Verso, 2000.

———. "Melancholy and the Act." *Critical Inquiry* 26, no. 4 (2000): 637–81.

———. *Metastases of Enjoyment: Six Essays on Women and Causality*. New York: Verso, 1994.

———. *Tarrying with the Negative: Kant, Hegel, and the Critique of Ideology*. Durham, NC: Duke University Press, 1993.

———. *The Ticklish Subject: The Absent Center of Political Ontology*. New York: Verso, 1999.

———. *The Žižek Reader*. Ed. Elizabeth Wright and Edmond Wright. Malden, MA: Blackwell, 1999.

Zornberg, Avivah. *Genesis: The Beginning of Desire*. Philadelphia: Jewish Publication Society, 1995.

Index

Abandonment: as deposit, leaving behind, setting down, 10–11, 45, 46, 56–57n83, 126, 129–131, 153, 158–162, 181, 208; as surrender, yielding, giving up, xx, 9n15, 62, 65n93, 68, 75, 79, 102, 141, 143, 172, 177–78, 189, 198, 205, 211. *See also* Recession

Abrams, M.H., xixn6, xxiii, 64n12

Acknowledgment, 9–10, 30, 50, 62–63n90, 82–83, 101, 103, 136n7, 149, 158, 164n, 178, 194–97, 212–217; as *aveu* (avowal), 13, 68–69, 76, 86, 94–99, 253–54; as concession of limits, readiness not to know, *ignoscere*, 11n, 26, 79, 104n42, 113n50, 116, 131–32, 173, 185, 193, 234, 235

Action (act, acting, productive activity, actualization, plot): definitions of, xv, 3, 29–32, 110–11n, 133, 139n; immaterial forms of: imaginative exercise, interpretive license, 8, 16–18, 22, 28, 34, 43–45, 62–78 passim, 81–82, 86, 94, 108–10, 120–2, 167, 171, 180, 209, 231, 251–53; modernity's call to, xvi–xviii, 3–4, 21–25, 93, 135, 148, 198n, 213, 228, 267–8; phallocentric logic of, 61n87; and potentiality, 3–4, 10, 34–38, 40–45, 70, 77, 80, 91–92, 97n, 99,

102, 104n42, 106, 119, 122, 125n, 144, 159, 168–9, 175, 181–3, 220n, 242, 261; and speech, xxiii, 14, 16, 31–32, 95–96, 98, 156n; as theatrical performance, 222–3, 233. *See also* Acknowledgment, Counting, Enlightenment, Narration, Passivity, Recession

Adorno, Theodor, 22–23n35, 24, 24–25n39, 115n52, 121n, 135n, 137–8, 140–1, 142–3n21, 147n29, 151n36, 258, 261, 262n, 263, 266

Aesthetic education (*bildung*) and ideology, xvii–xx, xxii–xxiv, 134n, 138n, 140–2, 253–4n; *bildungsroman*, 134n; elided instruction, nonexemplarity, as alternatives to, xxiv, 50, 78, 116, 126–8, 136–9, 142–3, 154, 163–4, 168–70, 174–5, 197–201, 206, 244

Agamben, Giorgio, 11n, 24n38, 63, 64–65n93, 97n, 177n65

Alliston, April, 71n, 76–77n, 106n, 107n, 113n50, 116–7n54

Alter, Robert, 47n67, 55

Althusser, Louis, 5n8, 111n47

Arac, Jonathan, 176n

Auerbach, Erich, 19n, 56

Auerbach, Nina, 220, 222n3, 240–1, 247n, 250

MERIDIAN

Crossing Aesthetics

Niklas Luhmann, *Art as a Social System*

Emmanual Levinas, *God, Death, and Time*

Ernst Bloch, *The Spirit of Utopia*

Giorgio Agamben, *Potentialities: Collected Essays in Philosophy*

Ellen S. Burt, *Poetry's Appeal: French Nineteenth-Century Lyric and the Political Space*

Jacques Derrida, *Adieu to Emmanuel Levinas*

Werner Hamacher, *Premises: Essays on Philosophy and Literature from Kant to Celan*

Aris Fioretos, *The Gray Book*

Deborah Esch, *In the Event: Reading Journalism, Reading Theory*

Winfried Menninghaus, *In Praise of Nonsense: Kant and Bluebeard*

Giorgio Agamben, *The Man Without Content*

Giorgio Agamben, *The End of the Poem: Studies in Poetics*

Theodor W. Adorno, *Sound Figures*

Louis Marin, *Sublime Poussin*

Philippe Lacoue-Labarthe, *Poetry as Experience*

Ernst Bloch, *Literary Essays*

Jacques Derrida, *Resistances of Psychoanalysis*

Marc Froment-Meurice, *That Is to Say: Heidegger's Poetics*

Francis Ponge, *Soap*

Philippe Lacoue-Labarthe, *Typography: Mimesis, Philosophy, Politics*

Giorgio Agamben, *Homo Sacer: Sovereign Power and Bare Life*

Emmanuel Levinas, *Of God Who Comes to Mind*

Bernard Stiegler, *Technics and Time, 1: The Fault of Epimetheus*

Werner Hamacher, *pleroma—Reading in Hegel*

Serge Leclaire, *Psychoanalyzing: On the Order of the Unconscious and the Practice of the Letter*

Serge Leclaire, *A Child Is Being Killed: On Primary Narcissism and the Death Drive*

Sigmund Freud, *Writings on Art and Literature*

Cornelius Castoriadis, *World in Fragments: Writings on Politics, Society, Psychoanalysis, and the Imagination*

Thomas Keenan, *Fables of Responsibility: Aberrations and Predicaments in Ethics and Politics*

Emmanuel Levinas, *Proper Names*

Alexander García Düttmann, *At Odds with AIDS: Thinking and Talking About a Virus*

Maurice Blanchot, *Friendship*

Jean-Luc Nancy, *The Muses*

Massimo Cacciari, *Posthumous People: Vienna at the Turning Point*

David E. Wellbery, *The Specular Moment: Goethe's Early Lyric and the Beginnings of Romanticism*

Edmond Jabès, *The Little Book of Unsuspected Subversion*

Hans-Jost Frey, *Studies in Poetic Discourse: Mallarmé, Baudelaire, Rimbaud, Hölderlin*

Pierre Bourdieu, *The Rules of Art: Genesis and Structure of the Literary Field*

Nicolas Abraham, *Rhythms: On the Work, Translation, and Psychoanalysis*

Jacques Derrida, *On the Name*

David Wills, *Prosthesis*

Maurice Blanchot, *The Work of Fire*

Jacques Derrida, *Points . . . : Interviews, 1974–1994*

J. Hillis Miller, *Topographies*

32764344R00194

Made in the USA
Lexington, KY
01 June 2014